Tactical Air P

CW01636093

This book introduces a much-needed theory of tactical air power to explain air power effectiveness in modern warfare with a particular focus on the Vietnam War as the first and largest modern air war. Phil Haun shows how, in the Rolling Thunder, Commando Hunt, and Linebacker air campaigns, air power alone repeatedly failed to achieve US military and political objectives. In contrast, air forces in combined arms operations succeeded more often than not. In addition to predicting how armies will react to a lethal air threat, he identifies operational factors of air superiority, air-to-ground capabilities, and friendly ground force capabilities, along with environmental factors of weather, lighting, geography and terrain, and cover and concealment in order to explain air power effectiveness. The book concludes with an analysis of modern air warfare since Vietnam along with an assessment of tactical air power relevance now and for the future.

Phil Haun is a retired US Air Force Colonel and decorated A-10 pilot. He is a Professor at the US Naval War College and Research Affiliate with the Massachusetts Institute of Technology's Security Studies Program and his previous publications include *A-10s over Kosovo*, *Coercion, Survival, and War*, *Lectures of the Air Corps Tactical School*, and *Air Power and the Age of Primacy*.

Cambridge Military Histories

Edited by

GREGORY A. DADDIS, USS Midway Chair in Modern US Military History and Director of the Center for War and Society, San Diego State University

HEW STRACHAN, Professor of International Relations, University of St Andrews and Emeritus Fellow of All Souls College, Oxford

GEOFFREY WAWRO, Professor of Military History and Director of the Military History Center, University of North Texas

The aim of this series is to publish outstanding works of research on warfare throughout the ages and throughout the world. Books in the series take a broad approach to military history, examining war in all its military, strategic, political and economic aspects. The series complements *Studies in the Social and Cultural History of Modern Warfare* by focusing on the 'hard' military history of armies, tactics, strategy and warfare. Books in the series consist mainly of single author works – academically rigorous and groundbreaking – which are accessible to both academics and the interested general reader.

A full list of titles in the series can be found at:

www.cambridge.org/militaryhistories

Tactical Air Power and the Vietnam War

Explaining Effectiveness in Modern Air Warfare

Phil Haun
US Naval War College

CAMBRIDGE
UNIVERSITY PRESS

CAMBRIDGE
UNIVERSITY PRESS

Shaftesbury Road, Cambridge CB2 8EA, United Kingdom

One Liberty Plaza, 20th Floor, New York, NY 10006, USA

477 Williamstown Road, Port Melbourne, VIC 3207, Australia

314–321, 3rd Floor, Plot 3, Splendor Forum, Jasola District Centre, New Delhi – 110025, India

103 Penang Road, #05–06/07, Visioncrest Commercial, Singapore 238467

Cambridge University Press is part of Cambridge University Press & Assessment, a department of the University of Cambridge.

We share the University's mission to contribute to society through the pursuit of education, learning and research at the highest international levels of excellence.

www.cambridge.org
Information on this title: www.cambridge.org/9781009364171

DOI: 10.1017/9781009364201

© Phil Haun 2024

This publication is in copyright. Subject to statutory exception and to the provisions of relevant collective licensing agreements, no reproduction of any part may take place without the written permission of Cambridge University Press & Assessment.

First published 2024

A catalogue record for this publication is available from the British Library.

Library of Congress Cataloging-in-Publication Data
Names: Haun, Phil M., author.
Title: Tactical air power and the Vietnam War : explaining effectiveness in modern air warfare / Phil Haun.
Description: Cambridge, United Kingdom ; New York : Cambridge University Press, 2023. | Series: CAMH Cambridge military histories
Identifiers: LCCN 2023020486 (print) | LCCN 2023020487 (ebook) | ISBN 9781009364171 (hardback) | ISBN 9781009364195 (paperback) | ISBN 9781009364201 (epub)
Subjects: LCSH: Vietnam War, 1961-1975–Aerial operations, American. | United States. Air Force–Tactical aviation. | Air power–United States. | Air warfare–United States.
Classification: LCC DS558.8 .H389 2023 (print) | LCC DS558.8 (ebook) | DDC 959.704/348–dc23/eng/20230501
LC record available at https://lccn.loc.gov/2023020486
LC ebook record available at https://lccn.loc.gov/2023020487

ISBN 978-1-009-36417-1 Hardback
ISBN 978-1-009-36419-5 Paperback

Cambridge University Press & Assessment has no responsibility for the persistence or accuracy of URLs for external or third-party internet websites referred to in this publication and does not guarantee that any content on such websites is, or will remain, accurate or appropriate.

To the memory of Stephen Chiabotti

Contents

List of Figures — *page* viii
List of Maps — ix
List of Tables — x
Preface — xi
List of Abbreviations — xiv

1 Introduction — 1
2 Tactical Air Power Theory — 13
3 Vietnam and Rolling Thunder: 1965–1966 — 35
4 Khe Sanh and Tet: 1967–1968 — 77
5 Commando Hunt I–III and Cambodia: 1969–1970 — 108
6 Commando Hunt V–VII and Lam Son 719: 1971–1972 — 139
7 Easter Offensive and Linebacker I & II: 1972–1973 — 163
8 Analysis and Conclusion — 202
9 Epilogue — 229

Appendix A Air Power Theory — 251
Appendix B Modern US Air Wars after Vietnam — 270
Index — 287

Figures

2.1	Targeting the military	*page* 29
2.2	When armies are vulnerable to air attack	31
3.1	A-1H Skyraider	39
3.2	F-100 Super Sabre	40
3.3	F-105 Thunderchief	40
3.4	F-4 Phantom II	41
3.5	A-4 Skyhawk	41
3.6	B-52 Stratofortress	44
3.7	B-57 Canberra	49
3.8	SA-2 Guideline	53
3.9	MiG-17 Fresco	62
3.10	MiG-21 Fishbed	62
3.11	F-8 Crusader	63
3.12	O-1 Birddog	71
4.1	A-6 Intruder	85
5.1	O-2 Skymaster	119
5.2	OV-10 Bronco	120
5.3	AC-130 Spectre	123
A.1	Clausewitz's triangle: targeting the population	258
A.2	Targeting the economy	262
A.3	Targeting the leadership	264
A.4	Targeting military lines of communication	267

Maps

3.1 North Vietnam *page* 43
3.2 North Vietnam Route Packages 60
3.3 South Vietnam's four military regions 68
4.1 Quang Tri province 94
4.2 Khe Sanh 97
5.1 Ho Chi Minh Trail 112
6.1 The Easter Offensive 151
7.1 Fall of Quang Tri 170
7.2 Battle of An Loc 173
7.3 Battle of Kontum 179

Tables

1.1 Modern US air campaigns *page* 8
4.1 USAF air operations in South Vietnam: 1965–1967 90
7.1 USAF major strike activity in Linebacker I 190
8.1 Operational factors affecting air operations 208
8.2 Environmental factors affecting air operations 214
8.3 Coding operational–environmental factors and military–political outcomes for modern US air campaigns 219

Preface

The origins of this book date back to the spring of 1999. While flying an A-10 over Kosovo, I was frustrated attempting to locate, identify, and attack Serbian fielded forces.[1] Later, I studied air power theory at the US Air Force School of Advanced Air and Space Power Studies (SAASS) at Maxwell Air Force Base, Alabama. While I read much on strategic bombing, there was little on directly attacking fielded forces, with two exceptions. In *Air Power and Armies*, J. C. Slessor argued against close air support (CAS) apart from in exceptional cases, preferring an indirect approach against an army by bombing production facilities and interdicting war supplies from arriving on the battlefield.[2] In *Bombing to Win*, Robert Pape advocated air power against enemy armies, especially the interdiction of conventional mechanized forces' supply lines. Pape did not, however, provide a theory for tactical air power. He acknowledged that "coercive air strategies based on denying the enemy victory on the battlefield developed without the benefit of an air theorist to organize the ideas into a coherent set of principles, though John C. Slessor, a British airman who wrote in the 1930s, came the closest."[3]

After SAASS, I deployed to Afghanistan and flew in counterinsurgency and counterterrorism operations. Afterward, I completed graduate work at Massachusetts Institute of Technology (MIT) and began teaching military strategy at the US Naval War College and later at Yale University, where I lectured on air power in the Vietnam War. Through research, discussion with colleagues, and reflection, I developed the tactical air power (TAP) theory presented in this book. Critics may claim that as an A-10 pilot, I would naturally argue that the most crucial utilization of air power is directly attacking enemy fielded

[1] Christopher Haave and Phil Haun, eds., *A-10s over Kosovo* (Maxwell AFB: Air University Press, 2003).
[2] J. C. Slessor, *Air Power and Armies* (Oxford: Oxford University Press, 1936).
[3] Robert Pape, *Bombing to Win: Air Power and Coercion in War* (Ithaca, NY: Cornell University Press, 1995), 69.

forces. An author is captive to time and experience. I do not deny a deep emotional attachment to the combat aircraft I flew, which still claims a hold on my personal and professional identity. However, an advantage of being an expert practitioner is that it allows for a deeper understanding of the profession's challenges. From first-hand experience of over 200 combat missions flown over Iraq, Bosnia, Kosovo, and Afghanistan, I have learned what tactical air power can and cannot accomplish. I have also noted how the enemy reacts to the credible threat of air strikes. I developed the theory presented in Chapter 2 and observed the operational and environmental factors considered in Chapter 8 from years of combat and study. Finally, to the disappointment of my A-10 squadron mates, this book does not advocate for the A-10 or CAS. This position may be a surprise, since CAS has proven essential in counterinsurgency operations in Afghanistan and Iraq for two decades. Dispersed occupation forces did not have the organic firepower to suppress insurgent attacks. Friendly ground forces depended on air power to respond quickly. However, in modern conventional warfare, air power has best been employed beyond the frontlines. Instead of CAS, tactical aircraft (tacair) have been most effective in armed recce (reconnaissance). Armed recce, direct attacks against enemy fielded forces flown beyond the range of CAS, has been known by many names and acronyms over time and in different wars, including AFAC, FACA, DAS, Kill-Box CAS, SCAR, Killer Scout, BAI, and battlefield interdiction. Air power has had its greatest impact through armed recce, by deterring enemy armies from concentrating and maneuvering.

I am grateful to the many who have contributed to this book. From MIT's Security Studies Program (SSP), I am forever indebted to the community of dedicated scholars led by such brilliant minds as Barry Posen and Taylor Fravel. They have provided me with an intellectual home. I am further indebted to Owen Cote for the countless dinners where we discussed topics related to this book. Other SSP alumni who have provided inputs include Caitlin Talmadge, Josh Rovner, and Josh Shifrinson. Special thanks go out to two fellow SSP alumni Brendan Green and Jon Lindsay, who provided invaluable inputs to an early draft, along with Heather Venable, Tom Kitsch, and Mike Poznansky. My coauthor, colleague, and friend Colin Jackson has further aided and encouraged me.[4] Our trip to Vietnam, which included visits to An Loc, Hue, Khe Sanh, the demilitarized zone (DMZ), Hanoi, and Dien Bien

[4] The coauthored article provides the basis for Chapter 7. Phil Haun and Colin Jackson, "Breaker of Armies: Air Power in the Easter Offensive and the Myths of Linebacker I and II in the Vietnam War" *International Security* 40:3 (Winter 2015/16): 139–178.

Phu, was crucial to my better appreciation of geography, terrain, and weather in the region. In addition, at the US Naval War College I have been encouraged by Tim Schultz, Mike O'Hara, Milan Vego, Andy Stigler, Sally Paine, and Nick Sarantakes. I also appreciated input from Adrian "Yo" Schuettke, who cotaught with me a course on Modern Air Power Theory. I have been mentored and befriended by Tom Hughes and Rich Mueller from SAASS. On an International Studies Association panel, Monica Duffy Toft provided a timely and much-needed assessment of an early draft of the theory chapter. To Bonnie, my long-time editor-in-chief, thanks for the dedication, honest feedback, and constant reminders to make my prose more readable to a broader audience.

Finally, I want to acknowledge the contributions of a departed mentor, colleague, and friend, Stephen Chiabotti. He encouraged me to take on this ambitious project and contributed to its early theoretical development.

The views expressed by the author do not reflect those of the Department of Defense or its services.

Abbreviations

A2/AD	anti-access/area denial
AAA	anti-aircraft artillery
AAGS	Army Air Ground System
ABCCC	Airborne Command and Control Center
ACTS	Air Corps Tactical School
AFAC	airborne forward air controller
AGOS	air-ground operation system
AIM	Air Intercept Missile
ALO	Air Liaison Officer
ANGLICO	Air Naval Gunfire Liaison Company
Armed Recce	armed reconnaissance
ARVN	Army of the Republic of Vietnam (South Vietnam)
ASOC	Air Support Operation Center
ATO	air tasking order
AWACS	airborne warning and control system
BAI	battlefield air interdiction
BDA	battle damage assessment
BVR	beyond visual range
C2	command and control
CAP	combat air patrol
CAS	close air support
CBU	cluster bomb unit
CIA	Central Intelligence Agency
CINCPAC	Commander-in-Chief of US Pacific Command
COLOSSYS	Coordinated LORAN Sensor Strike System
COSVN	Central Office of South Vietnam (Viet Cong)
DAF	Desert Air Force
DARPA	Defense Advanced Research Projects Agency
DAS	direct or deep air support
DASC	direct air support center
DIA	Defense Intelligence Agency
DMZ	demilitarized zone

ECM	electronic counter measures
FAC	forward air controller
FACA	forward air controller airborne
FASL	forward air support links
FLIR	forward-looking infrared
FLOT	forward line of own troops
FOFA	follow-on forces attack
FSCC	fire support coordination center
FSCL	fire support coordination line
GBAD	ground-based air defense
GCI	ground-controlled interception
GLO	ground liaison officer
GPS	global positioning system
HADPB	high-altitude daylight precision bombing
HUMINT	human intelligence
IADS	integrated air defense system
IAF	Israeli Air Force
ICBM	intercontinental ballistic missiles
ICC	Intelligence Control Center
IED	improvised explosive device
IFF	identification friend or foe
IRST	infrared search and track
ISC	Infiltration Surveillance Center
ISR	intelligence, surveillance, and reconnaissance
JCS	Joint Chiefs of Staff
JSTARS	Joint Surveillance Target Attack Radar System
JTAC	joint tactical air controller
KLA	Kosovo Liberation Army
KTO	Kuwaiti Theater of Operation
LGB	laser-guided bomb
LOC	lines of communication
LOO	lines of operation
LORAN	long-range navigation
LRASM	long-range anti-ship missile
LVC	live, virtual, and constructive
MACV	Military Assistance Command Vietnam
manpads	man-portable air defense system
MTI	moving target indicator
NATO	North Atlantic Treaty Organization
NTC	National Transition Council (Libya)
NVA	North Vietnamese Army
NVG	night vision goggles

OAF	Operation Allied Force
OMG	Operational Maneuver Group
PACAF	Pacific Air Forces
POL	petroleum oil lubricants
POW	prisoner of war
RAF	Royal Air Force (Great Britain)
recce	reconnaissance
ROE	rules of engagement
RP	Route Package or Route Pack
RPA	remotely piloted aircraft
RVNAF	Republic of Vietnam Air Force (South Vietnam)
RVNMF	Republic of Vietnam Military Forces (South Vietnam)
RWR	radar warning receivers
SAASS	School of Advanced Air and Space Power Studies
SAM	surface-to-air missile
SCAR	strike coordination and reconnaissance
tacair	tactical aircraft
SEAD	suppression of enemy air defenses
SLAR	side-looking air-to-ground radar
SLOC	sea lines of communication
tac recce	tactical reconnaissance
TACC	Tactical Air Control Center
TACP	tactical air control party
TACS	tactical air control system
TAP	tactical air power
TIC	troops in contact
TOW	tube-launched, optically tracked, wireless-guided
TTP	tactics, techniques, and procedures
UAG	*Udarnyye Aviatsionnyye Grouppy* (Air Strike Groups)
UKAF	Ukrainian Air Force
USAAF	United States Army Air Forces
USAF	US Air Force
USMC	US Marine Corps
USN	US Navy
VPAF	Vietnam People's Air Force (North Vietnam)
VC	Viet Cong
VCI	Viet Cong infrastructure
VKS	*Vozdushno-kosmicheskiye sily* (Russian Aerospace Force)
VR	visual reconnaissance
VVS	*Voyenno-Vozdushnyye Sily* (Soviet Air Force)
WMD	weapons of mass destruction

1 Introduction

In June 2002, the United States commenced an air campaign to roll back Iraqi air defenses. US air forces responded when radars illuminated their fighters by adjusting the rules of engagement for self-defense, attacking not only those specific sites but the entire Iraqi air defense system.[1] By the time of the ground invasion in March 2003, the United States had long achieved air superiority. In anticipation of facing an air-only campaign, the Iraqi Army dispersed rather than concentrated its forces at strategic choke points. As a result, the ground forces of the US-led coalition met little resistance in what quickly turned into a race to Baghdad. By deterring the enemy army from massing and maneuvering, air power had made its most significant contribution to the war before the first pair of American boots touched Iraqi soil.[2] The invasion would have taken on a different character without air power overhead. Allowed to fight from prepared defenses, the Iraqis could have slowed the invasion and inflicted more casualties, similar to how nineteen years later the Ukrainians stalled the Russian advance on Kyiv.[3]

The invasion of Iraq demonstrates how air power works when directly attacking fielded forces. Under a lethal air threat, enemy armies disperse and hide, which provides friendly ground forces a significant advantage. Coordinated air and ground attacks place an army on the horns of a dilemma. Does it concentrate and maneuver, as the North Vietnamese Army (NVA) did at Khe Sanh and again in the Easter Offensive, only to be decimated by airstrikes? Or does it disperse and hide, as the Iraqi Army did, and be overrun?

Threatened armies usually choose the latter course, with air power deterring them from massing and maneuvering. When most effective, air

[1] Throughout this book US air forces refer to the Air Force, Navy, and Marine fixed-wing aviation.

[2] Benjamin Lambeth, *The Unseen War: Allied Air Power and the Takedown of Saddam Hussein* (Annapolis, MD: Naval Institute Press, 2013), 66–71.

[3] The argument is not that the Iraqis would have stopped the invasion, as the Ukrainians did, but that it could have imposed more costs.

forces do not destroy armies, with Khe Sanh and the Easter Offensive being exceptions, but instead deny the enemy army its preferred strategy of concentrating at the decisive point.[4] Just as the better measure of a police force is not the total arrests made but the number of crimes committed, an air force should be evaluated not by the number of targets destroyed but by how air power affects the enemy's decision-making.[5] Carl Von Clausewitz, in *On War*, understood the significance of enemy actions not taken when he argued that one must account for the consequences of the engagements not waged.[6]

This book introduces a theory of tactical air power (TAP) to explain why, how, and when modern air power works. After World War II, two technologies changed the character of air warfare. First, in the Cold War the proliferation of thermonuclear weapons and the exorbitant costs anticipated from nuclear war deterred the United States and the Soviet Union. Given the risk of escalation, the United States fought wars not against other nuclear-armed nations but against weaker state and non-state actors. Nuclear rivals have competed through their allies and proxies by supplying weapons, training, and diplomatic support, as in Vietnam, Afghanistan, and Ukraine. The asymmetric nature of these wars has, in turn, shaped how US air power has been employed.

The second technology characterizing modern air warfare has been the proliferation of radar- and infra-guided air-to-air and surface-to-air missiles. Since the early 1960s, the lethality of these systems has significantly increased the risks of combat in contested air space. To survive such hostile conditions, US air forces transitioned from bombers to tactical aircraft (tacair) as their primary combat platform. B-52s continued to provide strategic deterrence as part of the US nuclear triad, and later, stealth bombers armed with precision-guided weapons conducted strategic bombing. In addition, conventionally armed bombers have also flown in lower-threat areas, such as over South Vietnam. However, overall tacair has been the workhorse of modern air combat, utilized for air superiority, strategic bombing, air interdiction, and direct attack.

This book examines modern US air warfare, conflicts where non-nuclear nations, protected by integrated air defense systems (IADS), have,

4 Carl Von Clausewitz, *On War* (Princeton, NJ: Princeton University Press, 1976), 195; This also follows Sun Tzu's advice of attacking the enemy's strategy. Sun Tzu *The Art of War* (Oxford: Oxford University Press, 1983), 77.

5 There are other reasons why crime rates may be low that have little to do with the effectiveness of the police force. The problem of showing causation when the only proof is the lack of evidence is like the problem of assessing the effectiveness of deterrence. How does one know that it was the threat of air strikes that deterred enemy action?

6 Clausewitz, *On War*, 181.

to varying degrees, contested air superiority.[7] Omitted from examination are conflicts with states without viable air defenses, including Grenada, Panama, and Afghanistan. Also excluded are counterinsurgency and counterterrorism operations. Over the past two decades, US air forces have targeted non-state actors in the Middle East, Central Asia, and Africa. In these cases, where air supremacy has been assumed, the type of aircraft and tactics utilized have differed markedly from the modern air wars considered in this book. How best to employ air power to counter insurgencies and terrorists remains an important topic, but not one examined in detail here.[8]

Strategic Bombing, Air Interdiction, and Direct Attack

The United States has fought numerous modern air wars over the past six decades, facing North Vietnamese, Iraqi, Bosnian Serb, Serbian, and Libyan air defenses. In several of these conflicts, the United States conducted multiple air campaigns.[9] For instance, the United States initiated the Rolling Thunder air campaign over North Vietnam while simultaneously fighting a joint, combined arms campaign in South Vietnam.

The type of air campaign can be categorized by its theory of victory for how air power achieves military and political objectives. There are three general types of air campaigns: strategic bombing, air interdiction, and direct attack. Strategic bombing aims to obtain political goals by coercing the enemy nation to make concessions. Air forces conduct strategic bombing independent of surface forces, overflying the battlefield to target the enemy's population, economy, or leadership.

Air interdiction, by contrast, indirectly targets the enemy military by cutting off its supply lines and reinforcements. Air interdiction can weaken the enemy as part of a denial strategy to coerce the enemy to make concessions, as the United States failed to do in Rolling Thunder. Also, air interdiction can contribute to a brute-force ground invasion, as

[7] Prior to Desert Storm Iraq procured its KARI (Iraq spelled backwards in French) air defense system from France.

[8] See James Corum and Wray Johnson, *Air Power in Small Wars: Fighting Insurgents and Terrorists* (Lawrence: University Press of Kansas, 2003); Anthony Schinella, *Bombs without Boots: The Limits of Airpower* (Washington, DC: Brookings, 2019); Phil Haun, Colin Jackson, and Tim Schultz, eds., *Air Power in the Age of Primacy: Air Warfare since the Cold War* (Cambridge: Cambridge University Press, 2021).

[9] A campaign is defined as a series of related operations constrained by time and space to achieve military or strategic objectives. Department of Defense, *Dictionary of Military and Associated Terms* (November 2021), 29, www.supremecourt.gov/opinions/URLs_Cited/OT2021/21A477/21A477-1.pdf.

attempted in Desert Storm in 1991. Airstrikes may occur deep in enemy territory, targeting the source of the enemy's military capabilities. During Linebacker I, the United States bombed North Vietnamese railways and harbors to prevent imports from China and the Soviet Union. These air interdiction missions struck large, fixed structures such as bridges, railway stations, and port facilities. Alternatively, air interdiction may attack mobile transports, such as the trucks traversing the Ho Chi Minh Trail through southern Laos.

Direct attack is the third type of air campaign, usually as part of a combined arms operation, as occurred in South Vietnam. The 1999 US-led NATO (North Atlantic Treaty Organization) air war against the Serbian Army in Kosovo was an exception. Serbian soldiers initially responded to direct air attacks by dispersing and hiding. However, without the credible threat of an opposing ground force, the Serbs soon swapped their military vehicles for civilian automobiles. They continued their ethnic cleansing while NATO tacair circled helplessly overhead.[10] As this book will demonstrate, direct air attack missions are more often and more effectively coordinated with friendly armies.

Those familiar with combined arms doctrine for direct attack will first think of close air support (CAS), missions conducted near friendly armies. To avoid fratricide, CAS requires detailed coordination and integration with the ground scheme of maneuver. Joint tactical air controllers (JTACs), embedded in ground units, identify targets and control airstrikes. CAS has been referred to as "flying artillery" since it provides the same essential function as artillery supporting ground units. Dedicated CAS aircraft, such as the A-1 Skyraider over Vietnam and the A-10 Warthog over Iraq and Afghanistan, have long been hailed by soldiers. They are appreciated, in part, because the troops can observe the aircraft working overhead. Emergency CAS is particularly valued for troops in contact (TIC) situations where airstrikes may be critical to the soldiers' survival, as occurred throughout the Battle of Khe Sanh and repeatedly during the Easter Offensive. Especially prized is CAS in counterinsurgencies, where dispersed friendly troops rely on the quick response of air power. While popular with soldiers, CAS is limited in its effectiveness by JTAC and target availability. Also, each mission takes significant time to brief inbound aircraft on the target, threats, and restrictions. CAS is also inefficient since usually fewer missions can be executed than the sorties available. Also, by definition, CAS only occurs

[10] The author flew as an A-10 Airborne Forward Air Controller (AFAC) in Kosovo. See Christopher Haave and Phil Haun, eds., *A-10s over Kosovo* (Maxwell AFB, AL: Air University Press, 2003).

when friendlies are near the enemy. As a result, the tacair allocated for CAS is often diverted to strike behind the front lines.

Tacair has more often directly attacked fielded forces beyond the range of CAS. Various names have been used to describe these deeper strike missions in different wars, including armed recce (reconnaissance), BAI (battlefield air interdiction), Kill Box CAS, Killer-Scout, push-CAS, FACA (forward air controller airborne), AFAC (airborne forward air controller), and SCAR (strike coordination and reconnaissance). Before the Vietnam War, the US Air Force referred to this mission as battlefield interdiction but removed the term from its doctrine during the war.[11] Afterward, it reintroduced the role, renamed battlefield air interdiction, to support the US Army's AirLand Battle doctrine. Air Force commanders then refused to call armed recce sorties BAI during Desert Storm and after the war again struck BAI from its doctrine. Armed recce is a challenging mission that requires sharing targeting prioritization with Army commanders.[12] By contrast, US Marine Corps aviation has retained the armed recce mission, which, along with air interdiction, it refers to as deep air support (DAS).[13] This book uses the term armed recce to refer to these direct attack missions flown above the battlefield but beyond the range of CAS.

Unlike air interdiction, armed recce requires coordination with ground forces for strikes inside the bomb line, now referred to as the fire support coordination line (FSCL). In the Vietnam War, the bomb line was a deconfliction measure to reduce fratricide and indicate where air forces needed to coordinate with the ground forces. In modern air warfare, airstrikes against enemy armies have more often been conducted as armed recce. In practice, there have been fewer opportunities to conduct CAS. Tacair assigned to CAS often do not find their assigned JTACs with available targets and are diverted to armed recce to search for targets of opportunity beyond the battlefront. The paradox with direct attack is that from a theater perspective, air power conducts operations jointly to be the hammer for the army's anvil.[14] At the tactical level, however, aircrew more often conduct armed recce missions independently,

[11] Air Force Manual (AFMAN) 1-7, *Theater Air Forces in Counterair, Interdiction and Close Air Support 1 March 1954* (Washington, DC: Department of the Air Force, 1954); Terrance McCaffrey, *What Happened to Battlefield Air Interdiction?* (Maxwell AFB, AL: Air University Press, 2004), 16.

[12] Phil Haun, "Peacetime Military Innovation through Inter Service Cooperation" *Journal of Strategic Studies* 43:5 (2020), 10.

[13] US Marine Corps, *Aviation Operations* MCWP 3–20 (Washington, DC: Marine Corps Headquarters, 2018), 2-1–2-2.

[14] I credit Robert Pape for this analogy.

beyond the control of ground forces. Air power's primary impact on these missions is to cause the enemy to disperse and hide.

Direct Attack

In modern warfare, US air power is most effective as direct attack, employed as part of a joint combined arms campaign. For most of its history, however, air force leaders have contended that the true value of air power is squandered when used in such a manner. Early air power advocates argued that the invention of the airplane changed the nature of warfare. An air force could be a substitute for armies and navies. Interwar strategic bombing theorists, including Giulio Douhet, Hugh Trenchard, Billy Mitchell, and, at the end of the Cold War, John Warden, called for air forces to be independent, wielding air power decisively by striking the enemy's population, economy, or leadership.[15] Even those who conceded the necessity of defeating the enemy's military contended that air power is best employed indirectly, neutralizing the sources of enemy war production or interdicting its lines of communication (LOC).[16] Unfortunately, strategic bombing and air interdiction rarely succeed.[17] Conventional strategic bombing campaigns usually do not impose sufficient costs to coerce.[18] While theoretically appealing, air interdiction against enemy land LOC usually fails as enemy armies stockpile supplies, repair roads and bridges, and develop alternate routes. Air power advocates developed their theories based on how they wished air power to be

[15] Giulio Douhet, *Command of the Air 1921* (Washington, DC: Air Force History and Museums Program, 1998); Hugh Trenchard, "Memorandum from Royal Air Force Chief of Air Staff Hugh Trenchard to CHIEFS OF STAFF Subcommittee on the War Objective of an Air Force, 2 May 1928" in Phil Haun, ed., *Lectures of the Air Corps Tactical School and American Strategic Bombing in World War II* (Lexington: University Press of Kentucky, 2019), Appendix 1; John Warden, "The Enemy as a System" *Airpower Journal* X:1 (Spring 1995), 40–55; William Mitchell, *Winged Defense: The Development and Possibilities of Modern Air Power Economic and Military* (New York: Putnam, 1925).

[16] J. C. Slessor, *Air Power and Armies* (Oxford: Oxford University Press, 1936); Haun, *Lectures of the Air Corps Tactical School.*

[17] Robert Pape, *Bombing to Win: Air Power and Coercion in War* (Ithaca, NY: Cornell University Press, 1995); Phil Haun, *Coercion, Survival & War: Why Weak States Resist the United States* (Palo Alto, CA: Stanford University Press, 2015).

[18] Kosovo is the exception, where Serbian President Slobodan Milosevic likely conceded because of the war's impact on the weakened Serbian economy. There remains some dispute as to the primary cause for Milosevic's decision to concede Kosovo. For examples see contrary assessments by two RAND reports by Stephen Hosmer, *The Kosovo Conflict: Why Milosevic Decided to Settle When He Did* (Santa Monica, CA: RAND, 2001), and Benjamin Lambeth, *NATO's Air War for Kosovo: Strategic and Operational Assessment* (Santa Monica, CA: RAND, 2001).

employed, often to justify independent service status, rather than on how air power has proven most effective in combat. As an alternative to existing air power theories, which look promising on paper but disappoint in practice, this book presents a theory for why, how, and when tactical air power works in modern air warfare.

Since 1965, the United States has waged twenty-three modern air campaigns in Vietnam, Iraq, Bosnia, Serbia, and Libya (Table 1.1). Even though Air Force leaders preferred strategic bombing and air interdiction, they reluctantly supported combined arms operations when ordered to do so. In nearly half of the cases (eleven of twenty-three), US air forces directly attacked the enemy's fielded forces and achieved their military objectives most of the time (nine of eleven). When militarily successful, they further contributed to obtaining US political objectives over half the time (five of nine). By contrast, in just over a quarter of the cases (six of twenty-three), strategic bombing campaigns succeeded only twice (two of six). The United States also attempted air interdiction six times, with all but one campaign failing. In sum, in modern air warfare, though US air power has not always been effective in achieving military and political objectives, the direct attack of military forces has been the strategy most often implemented and that has most often succeeded.

From Table 1.1, the Vietnam War stands out as the first modern air war. By the early 1960s, the rapid growth in the thermonuclear arsenals of the United States and Soviet Union deterred a nuclear war between the superpowers. The concern over escalation, by Chinese or Soviet intervention, constrained US air strikes and dissuaded the United States from a ground invasion of North Vietnam. The introduction of radar-guided surface-to-air missiles (SAMs) increased the lethality of the North Vietnamese air defense system. Heavy bombers could not freely conduct strategic bombing campaigns as the United States had done in World War II and the Korean War. Vietnam is also the longest modern air war, spanning almost eight years. It was here that most modern air warfare took place (thirteen of twenty-three cases), including multiple strategic bombing, air interdiction, and direct attack campaigns. Air superiority was also contested, with the United States losing over 9,000 fixed and rotary-wing aircraft.[19] During the Vietnam War, the character of modern air power was revealed under the crucible of combat, where

[19] Combat- and non-combat-related losses included 3,744 fixed-wing and 5,607 helicopters. Chris Hobson, *Vietnam Air Losses: Air Force, Navy and Marine Corps Fixed-Wing Aircraft Losses in Southeast Asia 1961–1973* (North Branch, MN: Specialty Press, 2001); Gary Roush, "Helicopter Losses during the Vietnam War" Vietnam Helicopter Pilots Association (December 2018), vhpa.org/heliloss.pdf.

Table 1.1 *Modern US air campaigns*[1]

Year	Air campaign	Opponent	Strategy	Mil/pol outcome
Mar–Jul 1965	Rolling Thunder	North Vietnam	Strategic bombing	Failure/failure
Mar 65–Dec 66	Rolling Thunder	North Vietnam	Interdiction	Failure/failure
Jul 65–Dec 66	Combined Arms	North Vietnam	Direct attack	Success/failure
Jan 67–Mar 68	Rolling Thunder	North Vietnam	Interdiction	Failure/failure
Jan 67–Mar 68	Khe Sanh/Tet	North Vietnam	Direct attack	Success/failure
Apr–Dec 1967	Rolling Thunder	North Vietnam	Strategic bombing	Failure/failure
Nov 68–Jun 70	Commando Hunt I-III	North Vietnam	Interdiction	Success/failure
Apr–Jun 1970	Cambodia	North Vietnam	Direct attack	Success/failure
Nov 70–Mar 72	Commando Hunt V-VII	North Vietnam	Interdiction	Failure/failure
Feb–Mar 1971	Lam Son 719	North Vietnam	Direct attack	Failure/failure
Mar–Sep 1972	Easter Offensive	North Vietnam	Direct attack	Success/success
May–Oct 1972	Linebacker I	North Vietnam	Interdiction	Failure/failure
Dec 1972	Linebacker II	North Vietnam	Strategic bombing	Success/success
Jan–Feb 1991	Instant Thunder	Iraq	Strategic bombing	Failure/failure
Jan–Feb 1991	Desert Storm	Iraq	Interdiction	Failure/failure
Jan–Feb 1991	Desert Storm	Iraq	Direct attack	Success/success
Apr 91–Oct 98	No Fly Zones, WMD	Iraq	Direct attack	Success/failure
Aug 1995	Bosnia	Bosnian Serbs	Direct attack	Success/success
Mar–Jun 1999	Serbia	Serbia	Strategic bombing	Success/success
Mar–Jun 1999	Kosovo	Serbia	Direct attack	Failure/failure
Mar 2003	Operation Iraqi Freedom	Iraq	Strategic bombing	Failure/failure
Mar 2003	Operation Iraqi Freedom	Iraq	Direct attack	Success/success
Mar 2011	Odyssey Dawn	Libya	Direct attack	Success/success
Total Direct attack			**11/23**	**9/11 Mil success** **5/11 Pol success**
Total Strat bombing			**6/23**	**2/6 Pol success**
Total Air interdiction			**6/23**	**1/6 Mil success** **0/6 Pol success**

[1] The thirteen cases of the Vietnam War are examined in detail in Chapters 3–7 while the coding for the remaining ten cases are explained in Appendix B.

aircrew refined the operational concepts for modern air warfare, most of which remain valid today.

Because of the Vietnam War's central role in developing modern US air power, the body of this book (Chapters 3–7) analyzes its thirteen air campaigns. Vietnam can be thought of as a historical laboratory used to test the tactical air power theory introduced in the following chapter. In the process, the effectiveness of strategic bombing, air interdiction, and direct attack are measured, and the various operational and environmental factors that place limitations and constraints on air power are identified. However, chapter-length assessments of all twenty-three US modern air campaigns go beyond this single volume's ambitions. Appendix B summarizes the ten modern air campaigns that followed Vietnam. A more detailed analysis is available in *Air Power in the Age of Primacy: Air Warfare since the Cold War.*[20] An evaluation of modern air warfare in the Vietnam War provides a better understanding of why, how, and when to employ air power today and in the future.

Organization of the Book

The book proceeds as follows: Chapter 2 provides a historical account of the development of tactical air power during the interwar period and World War II in Germany, the Soviet Union, Great Britain, and the United States (readers unfamiliar with air power theory may want to read Appendix A first). Air and ground force coordination has largely been ignored in peacetime, and only in combat has a sense of urgency arisen for developing and refining joint doctrine. Even then, the focus has been on defining air and ground command relationships and improving the coordination between an air force's tactical air control systems (TACS) and the army's air-ground systems (AAGS). These doctrinal efforts increased the efficiency of allocating and controlling air power to support ground operations. However, largely left unspoken and unwritten has been an understanding of why, how, and when tactical air power works. TAP theory answers these questions by asserting that air power's asymmetric advantage is its ability to locate and attack massed and maneuvering armies. With air superiority secured, lethal air-to-ground forces threaten armies, causing them to disperse and hide. The enemy's reaction, in turn, provides friendly ground forces an advantage in conducting both offensive and defensive operations. Unfortunately, a theory

[20] Haun et al., *Air Power in the Age of Primacy.*

explaining the primary impact of air power in modern warfare has been absent until now.[21]

The body of the book evaluates TAP theory during the Vietnam War. Chapter 3 examines the first two years of major US combat operations from 1965 through 1966. Over North Vietnam, the Rolling Thunder air campaign failed to either isolate communist forces in South Vietnam or coerce North Vietnam to withdraw its support of the insurgency. Air power proved more effective in the direct attack of the North Vietnam Army and Viet Cong (NVA/VC) in South Vietnam. The US combined arms campaign thwarted an offensive aimed at dividing South Vietnam. Instead, well-executed allied air-to-ground operations compelled the enemy to disperse and hide.

Chapter 4 evaluates US tactical air power from 1967 to 1968. Over North Vietnam, the Rolling Thunder air interdiction campaign struggled to isolate NVA/VC forces. Simultaneously, a strategic bombing campaign could not coerce Hanoi to withdraw its support of the insurgency. The direct attack of the NVA/VC forces in South Vietnam proved more effective, with the ultimate test occurring near the demilitarized zone (DMZ) at the US Marine base at Khe Sanh. Here, the NVA massed two divisions, hoping to overrun the marines to achieve a decisive victory, as the North Vietnamese had against the French in 1954 at Dien Bien Phu. Instead, the American combined arms campaign defeated the NVA. The massing of ground forces at Khe Sanh differed from the NVA's previous tactics of dispersing and taking sanctuary in Laos and Cambodia. Such defensive measures had previously allowed the NVA/VC to survive but had also delayed plans to launch a general offensive and general uprising. When the NVA/VC finally commenced their offensive in early 1968, they failed militarily at Khe Sanh and, more broadly, in the Tet Offensive. However, more importantly, the North Vietnamese succeeded politically as American support for the war evaporated.

Chapter 5 assesses US air power following the Tet Offensive through the cross-border incursion into Cambodia in 1970. The newly elected US president, Richard Nixon, sought an American withdrawal from South Vietnam. However, he initially expanded the conflict into Cambodia to deny the NVA/VC sanctuary and sever their southern supply lines. Leading up to the invasion, the Commando Hunt air interdiction campaign in southern Laos slowed the movement of supplies. It also imposed substantial costs on North Vietnam to keep the Ho Chi Minh Trail open. Commando Hunt could not halt the NVA troops

[21] Pape, *Bombing to Win*, 69.

from making the journey to South Vietnam on foot, but the direct attack of fielded forces in South Vietnam and Cambodia did continue to keep the NVA/VC dispersed and hidden. Keeping the North Vietnamese on the defensive provided the time and space for South Vietnam's pacification program to take root and for the Vietnamization program to generate conventional capabilities for the Army of the Republic of Vietnam (ARVN) to replace withdrawing American combat troops.

Chapter 6 assesses the impact of US air power as the ARVN shifted its offensive into southern Laos in 1971. After the Cambodian incursion, a Democratic Party-led Congress voted the Cooper–Church amendment into law, forbidding US ground troops beyond South Vietnamese borders. The ARVN objective in Laos was to achieve what US air power alone during Commando Hunt was unable to do: close off the Ho Chi Minh Trail. Instead, the ill-fated Lam Son 719 raid revealed significant shortcomings in allied air–ground coordination. The South Vietnamese, minus their US military advisors and tactical air controllers, could not take advantage of the available air power to prevent the NVA from driving the ARVN from Laos. The NVA's victory encouraged the North Vietnamese to gamble with another general offensive.

Chapter 7 examines air power during the Easter Offensive and the Linebacker I & II air campaigns. When the NVA launched the Nguyen Hue Offensive, referred to in the West as the Easter Offensive, in the spring of 1972, the question remained whether the ARVN could incorporate air–ground coordination lessons from Lam Son 719. The ARVN successfully held on two of three fronts but faltered along the DMZ, where the NVA overran Quang Tri province. Effective US air power and resolute ARVN forces, coordinated by skilled US military advisors and air liaison officers, held off further NVA advances as the ARVN regrouped to launch a counteroffensive to retake Quang Tri. Meanwhile, President Nixon reached détente with China and the Soviet Union such that he felt confident to order an air campaign into North Vietnam without the risk of further escalation. In May, the United States launched Linebacker I to interdict enemy LOC. However, the North had already deployed its forces and stockpiled supplies to overcome any shortfalls. Linebacker I ultimately failed to weaken the NVA as it fought through the summer. Instead, in September the ARVN and US air forces combined arms offensive retook Quang Tri. The decisive defeat of the NVA finally convinced Hanoi to accept a US-offered peace treaty. However, South Vietnamese President Nguyen Thieu, excluded from the secret talks, balked at any deal which allowed NVA troops to remain in the country. After the November 1972 election, President Nixon gave an ultimatum for Thieu to accept the agreement or face the withdrawal of

US aid. To bring the North Vietnamese back to the negotiating table, Nixon ordered Linebacker II, the bombing of Hanoi, which commenced before Christmas. The North Vietnamese, no longer backed by the Soviets or Chinese, agreed to terms once they ran out of surface-to-air missiles. The strategic bombing campaign, which featured B-52 strikes, compelled the North Vietnamese to return to Paris, but only to sign an agreement they had previously accepted in October following their defeat in the Easter Offensive.

Chapter 8 provides a brief history of the development of US air power doctrine after World War II, along with a synopsis of modern air wars since Vietnam. Four operational and five environmental factors that impacted air operations in Vietnam are introduced to help explain when air power is likely to be effective. These nine factors are air superiority, air-to-ground capability, friendly ground force capability, enemy ground force capability, weather, lighting, geography and terrain, civilians, and concealment and cover. A summative assessment follows, which correlates these conditional factors with the military and political outcomes for the twenty-three modern US air campaigns listed in Table 1.1. Finally, nine general observations are provided as to the overall effectiveness of modern air power.

An epilogue explores several topics regarding the future of modern air warfare. The first section offers recommendations for how the United States can better prepare for modern air warfare. The second considers air power in counterinsurgency and counterterrorism operations. The third anticipates the role of air power in extending deterrence to allies. The fourth demonstrates how TAP theory can assess the potential effectiveness of air power by analyzing the Russian Air Force in the Battle of Kyiv. The final section considers additional challenges facing the United States during an emerging era of great power competition.

For those unfamiliar with air power theory, Appendix A presents a brief history of the development of air power. It introduces a typology for four schools of thought on air power, differentiated by targeting priority. A Clausewitzian model of a nation consisting of its people, military, and government is used to explain the differing theories of air power victory.

Finally, Appendix B provides summaries of the ten modern air wars occurring after Vietnam, including the rationale for coding the operational and environmental factors for the air campaigns.[22]

[22] For chapter-length discussions on these cases, see Haun et al., *Air Power in the Age of Primacy*.

2 Tactical Air Power Theory

> *The greatest historical joke on airmen was that they – having struggled for a century to escape the battlefield in their quest for equal status and independence – having fought so many bitter battles to free themselves from the indignity of providing "mere support" to ground forces – it was on the battlefield where air power finally achieved not mere equality, but its claim to ascendancy.*[1]

For over a century, air power advocates have proclaimed that air forces alone could win wars. Their claims, in turn, have supported the creation and sustainment of independent air forces. Unfortunately, these theorists have reflected airmen's hopes more than explained how air power works best in modern warfare. Of the US air campaigns identified in Table 1.1, directly attacking the enemy's fielded forces was the strategy most often adopted. Direct attack also had more success in achieving military and political objectives than strategic bombing or air interdiction. Air power is a complement to, not a substitute for, ground forces. Air forces and armies work best in combined arms operations, where tactical aircraft (tacair) finds and strikes the enemy's fielded forces well behind the front lines. The lethal threat from air power has its most significant impact by inhibiting an enemy army from concentrating at the decisive point.[2]

Paradoxically, to date, an air power theory for why, how, and when air forces are most commonly and effectively employed has been omitted.[3] Under certain conditions, air power can decimate a massed and maneuvering army. In practice, such occasions have been rare, as threatened troops usually disperse and hide. Taking such defensive measures comes

[1] Stephen Budianky, *Air Power: The Men, Machines, and Ideas That Revolutionized War, from Kitty Hawk to Gulf War II* (New York: Viking, 2004), 441.

[2] Carl Von Clausewitz, *On War* (Princeton, NJ: Princeton University Press, 1976), 195.

[3] James Corum and Wray Johnson allude to, but do not develop, such a theory. *Airpower in Small Wars: Fighting Insurgents and Terrorists* (Lawrence: University Press of Kansas, 2003), 7.

at a high price, though, as a scattered force forfeits the initiative or is left vulnerable to an opposing army's attack. The most significant impact of air power on the battlefield is measured not by the damage inflicted but by the degree to which air power deters the enemy from executing its preferred strategy.

This chapter develops a theory of tactical air power (TAP) for the direct attack of fielded forces. The chapter begins in the interwar period with a brief history of the development of the tactical air power doctrine in Germany, the Soviet Union, Great Britain, and the United States. (Those unfamiliar with air power theory may want to first refer to Appendix A.) Before World War II, most airmen believed that, after gaining air superiority, air forces should strategically attack the enemy's war industries and interdict their lines of communication. Without tactical air doctrine, airmen later scrambled during combat to support friendly troops. Left undeveloped was a theory for why and how air power works against fielded forces.[4] When threatened from the air and the ground, an enemy army is placed on the horns of a dilemma. Does it disperse and hide against the air threat, to be left defenseless against the opposing ground force? Or does it instead concentrate and maneuver, only to be vulnerable to airstrikes? TAP theory explains when fielded forces are most susceptible to air attack and the enemy's reaction.

History of Tactical Air Doctrine

Tactical air doctrine development commenced in World War I but matured in World War II, first by the German Luftwaffe and later by the Soviet VVS (*Voyenno-Vozdushnyye Sily*), the British RAF (Royal Air Force), and the US Army Air Force.[5] Initially, the air doctrine of all but the VVS prioritized gaining air superiority, followed by strategic attack and air interdiction against the enemy's war industries and lines of communication (LOC). Air doctrine provided only tertiary consideration of the direct attack on the enemy's fielded forces. The tactical air doctrine that was developed focused on practical measures such as operating a functioning command and control (C2) system. Left unspoken and unwritten were explanations for why and how directly targeting enemy armies from the air could impact whether battles were fought and the outcome of those that were.

4 Robert Pape, *Bombing to Win* (Ithaca, NY: Cornell University Press, 1995), 69.
5 *Voyenno-Vozdushnyye Sily* translates as Military Air Force.

The Luftwaffe

Tactical air forces played a significant role in the German combined arms operations unleashed across Europe at the outset of World War II.[6] Though the 1920 Versailles Treaty had banned military aviation, the Germans secretly maintained an air staff that assessed air power in World War I. They concluded their air force had not been sufficiently aggressive. The priority should have been to gain air superiority by offensive action, engage the enemy's air force, and persistently attack the enemy air force's supporting infrastructure. Air superiority would be hard-won and require a sustained effort.[7] In 1933, the Nazi Party provided ample resources to produce aircraft and recruit personnel. The newly formed Luftwaffe grew exponentially, procuring a fleet of 1,900 airplanes by 1935, when it published its service doctrine, *Conduct of Aerial Warfare*.[8] The 100-page regulation articulated air power's role in the German concept of operational warfare. The Luftwaffe was an independent air force, but its doctrine emphasized joint warfighting. Once it gained air superiority, the Luftwaffe could indirectly pressure the enemy by striking deep or directly supporting the Wehrmacht.[9]

Conduct of Aerial Warfare stressed a flexible approach to targeting, depending on the enemy and the situation. The regulation discussed in detail how to gain air superiority, but afterward limited its consideration of targeting to strategic attack on the enemy's war production or interdiction of the enemy's transportation.[10] Surprisingly, the doctrine did not mention how the Luftwaffe should directly support the Wehrmacht. The Condor Legion revealed a shortfall in tactical air doctrine the following year when it deployed to support Nationalist forces in the

[6] James Corum, *The Luftwaffe: Creating the Operational Air War, 1918–1940* (Lawrence: University Press of Kansas, 1997); Robert Citino, *The German Way of War* (Lawrence: University Press of Kansas, 2005); Williamson Murray, "German Army Doctrine 1918–1939, and the Post-1945 Theory of 'Blitzkrieg Strategy'" in Carol Fink, Isabel Hull, and MacGregor Knox, eds., *German Nationalism and the European Response, 1890–1945* (Norman: University of Oklahoma Press, 1985); Gerhard Gross, *The Myth and Reality of German Warfare: Operational Thinking from Moltke the Elder to Heusinger* (Lawrence: University Press of Kansas, 2016).

[7] James Corum and Richard Muller, *The Luftwaffe's Way of War: German Air Force Doctrine 1911–1945* (Baltimore, MD: Nautical and Aviation Publishing Company of America, 1998), 6–7.

[8] Corum and Muller, *The Luftwaffe's Way of War*, 9.

[9] Corum and Muller, *The Luftwaffe's Way of War*, 118–157.

[10] Strategic targeting also included power production. Corum and Muller, *The Luftwaffe's Way of War*, 133.

Spanish Civil War.[11] In combat, the Condor Legion cobbled together basic procedures for close air support (CAS). Later, the Luftwaffe continued to refine its techniques for supporting mobile ground forces in 1939 and 1940 with back-to-back blitzkrieg offensives against Poland, Denmark, Norway, Belgium, and France.

Conduct of Aerial Warfare presented the rationale for air superiority, strategic bombing, and interdiction but left unanswered why, how, or when its air force should directly attack an enemy's army. However, the Luftwaffe was not alone, as similar experiences befell the Soviets, British, and Americans.

The Soviet Air Force

In 1917, the Bolsheviks claimed the remnants of Russia's Imperial Air Force with its assortment of obsolete aircraft.[12] The Communists were determined to develop an air fleet to support its Red Army.[13] A strong military required an expanded industrial base, and the Soviet Union included aircraft factories in its five-year plans.[14] In 1922, to augment production, the Soviets secretly collaborated with the Germans, exchanging training facilities for technical assistance.[15] By 1928, the Soviet Union had established within the Red Army a professional air force, the VVS, which comprised 10 percent of its military.[16] With Joseph Stalin's continual support, the VVS established itself as a first-rate air power by the early 1930s.[17] The Soviet's penchant for building

[11] Williamson Murray, *The Luftwaffe: 1933–45: Strategy for Defeat* (London: Brassey's, 1996), 15.

[12] David Jones, "The Beginning of Russian Air Power, 1907–1922" in Robin Higham and Jacob Kipp, eds., *Soviet Aviation and Air Power* (Boulder, CO: Westview Press, 1977), 21; Von Hardesty, *Red Phoenix: The Rise of Soviet Air Power: 1941–1945* (Washington, DC: Smithsonian, 1982), 36, 41; Asher Lee, *The Soviet Air Force* (New York: John Day Company, 1962), 23; Kenneth Whiting, *Soviet Air Power* (Boulder, CO: Westview Press, 1986), 5.

[13] Hardesty, *Red Phoenix*, 42; Lee, *The Soviet Air Force*, 27.

[14] Neil Heyman, "NEP and the Industrialization to 1928" in Higham and Kipp, eds., *Soviet Aviation and Air Power*, 42–43; Hardesty, *Red Phoenix*, 43; Lee, *The Soviet Air Force*, 30–34.

[15] Kenneth Whiting, "Soviet Aviation and Air Power under Stalin, 1928–1941" in Higham and Kipp, eds., *Soviet Aviation and Air Power*, 49; Whiting, *Soviet Air Power*, 10; Alexander Boyd, *The Soviet Air Force since 1918* (New York: Stein & Day, 1977), 10, 23.

[16] Heyman, "NEP and the Industrialization to 1928," 48; Hardesty, *Red Phoenix*, 45; Whiting, *Soviet Air Power*, 12.

[17] Higham and Kipp, *Soviet Aviation and Air Power*, 4; Hardesty, *Red Phoenix*, 45; Ray Wagner, ed., and Leland Fetzer, trans., *The Soviet Air Force in World War II: The Official History, Originally Published by the Ministry of Defense of the USSR* (New York: Doubleday, 1973), 8.

enormous structures in part explains the VVS fielding by 1935 the world's largest bomber aircraft. In addition, Soviet fighters proved first-rate, with the Il-15 the standard combat aircraft flown by the Loyalists in the Spanish Civil War.[18]

However, a series of conflicts in the late 1930s revealed shortcomings with the VVS. By 1937, during the Spanish Civil War, the Soviet "volunteer" force was outclassed when the Germans outfitted their Condor Legion with the latest Bf-109 fighters and Ju-87 Stukas.[19] In addition, VVS bombers, which comprised 60 percent of the Soviet fleet, performed poorly in Spain.[20] In 1938, Soviet airmen fared better in confronting the Japanese in Manchuria.[21] However, in late 1939, during the Winter War, the VVS again struggled, meeting fierce resistance from Finnish airmen flying western aircraft.[22] Though the Soviets ultimately compelled Finland to accept a peace agreement, the VVS suffered heavily, including losing half its bombers.[23]

As the VVS grappled with foreign powers, it was simultaneously thwarted domestically by Stalin's purges.[24] The purges decimated the leadership ranks of the Red Army and VVS, leaving the Soviet Union vulnerable to invasion in June 1941.[25] Operation Barbarossa exposed severe weaknesses in Soviet military preparedness, organization, technology, and doctrine.[26] However, the Luftwaffe's extraordinary operational success, destroying three-quarters of the VVS in the first few days, did not translate into a political victory for Hitler.[27] Though the Soviets suffered enormous losses, they endured and regrouped in the east,

[18] Hardesty, *Red Phoenix*, 46; Whiting, "Soviet Aviation and Air Power under Stalin," 51.

[19] R. A. Mason and John Taylor, *Aircraft, Strategy and Operations in the Soviet Air Force* (Coulsdon: Jane's, 1986), 26; Hardesty, *Red Phoenix*, 50; Lee, *The Soviet Air Force*, 36, 42; Whiting, *Soviet Air Power*, 17; James Sterrett, *Soviet Air Force Theory, 1918–1945* (London: Routledge, 2007), 61.

[20] Whiting, *Soviet Air Power*, 15.

[21] Hardesty, *Red Phoenix*, 51; Whiting, "Soviet Aviation and Air Power under Stalin," 59–62; Whiting, *Soviet Air Power*, 18; Boyd, *The Soviet Air Force since 1918*, 86.

[22] Lee, *The Soviet Air Force*, 47; Whiting, *Soviet Air Power*, 20; Sterrett, *Soviet Air Force Theory*, 70.

[23] Hardesty, *Red Phoenix*, 52; Whiting, "Soviet Aviation and Air Power under Stalin," 65.

[24] Hardesty, *Red Phoenix*, 54; Lee, *The Soviet Air Force*, 39.

[25] Mason and Taylor, *Aircraft, Strategy and Operations in the Soviet Air Force*, 26; Whiting, "Soviet Aviation and Air Power under Stalin," 62–63; Boyd, *The Soviet Air Force since 1918*, 81.

[26] Whiting, *Soviet Air Power*, 24–25; Wagner, *The Soviet Air Force in World War II*, 9–10; Boyd, *The Soviet Air Force since 1918*, 50; John Greenwood, "The Great Patriotic War, 1941–1945" in Higham and Kipp, eds., *Soviet Aviation and Air Power*, 77.

[27] Hardesty, *Red Phoenix*, 61; Lee, *The Soviet Air Force*, 53–54; Boyd, *The Soviet Air Force since 1918*, 110–111; Sterrett, *Soviet Air Force Theory*, 86.

trading space for time. A key to Soviet resiliency proved to be the relocation of armament and aircraft factories east of the Urals.[28]

The Red Army and the VVS resisted the German advance where they could, but ultimately the expansive terrain and the brutality of the Russian winter ground the Wehrmacht to a halt short of Moscow in December 1941.[29] The following spring, the VVS's chief, Marshal Alexander Novikov, initiated a series of reforms.[30] Novikov exerted more centralized control and flexibility by reorganizing the VVS into air strike groups (*Udarnyye Aviatsionnyye Grouppy* or UAGs). Instead of being dispersed, the UAGs could now concentrate.[31] He kept an air corps in reserve to commit where and when needed.[32] Novikov also assigned air deputies to frontline army groups to improve the cooperation between air and ground commanders.[33] Improved radio communications further allowed the VVS to conduct coordinated combined arms offensives. Finally, Soviet mass production generated aircraft to compete with the Luftwaffe in both quantity and quality.[34]

In the winter of 1942–43, the VVS grew more aggressive.[35] When dedicated UAGs concentrated attacks at critical points, the VVS gained local air superiority and conducted preparatory strikes to support a combined arms breakthrough.[36] Once the Soviets breached the German lines, the VVS pursued retreating forces to prevent the reestablishment of the German defenses.[37] At the Battle of Stalingrad, the Red Army counterattacked with a pincer movement, which cut off the German 6th Army. The VVS then imposed an air blockade to prevent the Luftwaffe's aerial resupply effort.[38] At subsequent battles in the

[28] Lee, *The Soviet Air Force*, 54. By 1943, these plants were mass producing the next generation of Soviet fighters, attack, and medium bombers required for the deep battle, combined arms operations envisioned by Marshal Mikhail Tukhachevsky. Richard Simpkin, *Deep Battle: The Brainchild of Marshal Tukhachevsky* (London: Brassey's Defence Publishers, 1987); Hardesty, *Red Phoenix*, 58; Lee, *The Soviet Air Force*, 55.

[29] Hardesty, *Red Phoenix*, 74; Lee, *The Soviet Air Force*, 55; Whiting, *Soviet Air Power*, 27.

[30] Hardesty, *Red Phoenix*, 82; Sterrett, *Soviet Air Force Theory*, 100; Greenwood, "The Great Patriotic War," 88–89; Boyd, *The Soviet Air Force since 1918*, 141–145; Wagner, *The Soviet Air Force in World War II*, 89.

[31] Hardesty, *Red Phoenix*, 86. [32] Sterrett, *Soviet Air Force Theory*, 101.

[33] Hardesty, *Red Phoenix*, 87, 118.

[34] This included the latest Yak fighters and the IL-2 *shturmovik* attack aircraft. Hardesty, *Red Phoenix*, 88–89; Lee, *The Soviet Air Force*, 56–57; Whiting, *Soviet Air Power*, 35–36.

[35] Hardesty, *Red Phoenix*, 91.

[36] Mason and Taylor, *Aircraft, Strategy and Operations in the Soviet Air Force*, 62.

[37] Hardesty, *Red Phoenix*, 106–107; Mason and Taylor, *Aircraft, Strategy and Operations in the Soviet Air Force*, 64.

[38] Hardesty, *Red Phoenix*, 118; Lee, *The Soviet Air Force*, 58–59; Boyd, *The Soviet Air Force since 1918*, 160–161; Wagner, *The Soviet Air Force in WWII*, 142–146.

spring and summer of 1943, at Kuban and Kursk, the VVS continued to refine its tactical air doctrine to concentrate air and ground forces in massive, combined arms offensives.[39]

Unlike the Germans, British, and Americans, the Soviets never seriously envisioned the independent employment of their air force. The realities of being a continental power with the threat posed by the German Wehrmacht motivated the Soviets to focus on a tactical air doctrine to support the Red Army. For the British and Americans, however, the advantage of geography and the stopping power of water (or beaches) provided these two maritime powers the luxury of being able to consider independent air operations. The crucible of battle in World War II would force both nations, as it had the Germans and the Soviet Union, to develop and adapt their tactical air doctrine.

The Royal Air Force

Unlike the Luftwaffe and VVS, which both acknowledged the need for joint operations, the RAF viewed air power as a substitute for ground forces and prioritized heavy bombers for strategic attack.[40] The closest the RAF had to a tactical air power theorist was J. C. Slessor. While on the Army Staff College faculty in the interwar period, Slessor lectured on and later published *Air Power and Armies*.[41] Like the Luftwaffe, Slessor articulated a theory of air power for the indirect attack of armies based on deep strikes on munition factories and interdicting enemy lines of communication. Neither approach required detailed coordination with the British Army, leaving the RAF free to develop its strategic bombing force. Not until the defeat of the British Army on the Continent, culminating in the evacuation at Dunkirk in May 1940, followed by a series of sobering battles in North Africa in 1941, did the RAF acknowledge the need for better air–land cooperation.[42]

39 Hardesty, *Red Phoenix*, 121–180; Greenwood, "The Great Patriotic War," 97–104; Boyd, *The Soviet Air Force since 1918*, 176–177; Wagner, *The Soviet Air Force in World War II*, 162–163, 185–186; Sterrett, *Soviet Air Force Theory*, 111–117.

40 Tami Biddle, *Rhetoric and Reality in Air Warfare: The Evolution of British and American Ideas about Strategic Bombing, 1914–1945* (Princeton, NJ: Princeton University Press, 2002), 69–127; Philip Meilinger, "Trenchard, Slessor, and Royal Air Force Doctrine before World War II" in *The Paths of Heaven: The Evolution of Airpower Theory* (Maxwell AFB, AL: Air University Press, 1997), 40–60.

41 J. C. Slessor, *Air Power and Armies* (Oxford: Oxford University Press, 1936); Meilinger, *The Paths of Heaven*, 61; Philip Meilinger, *Airwar: Theory and Practice* (London: Frank Cass, 2003), 64–74.

42 Paul Johnston, "The Question of British Influence on U.S. Tactical Air Power in World War II" *Air Power History* 52:1 (Spring 2005), 19; H. Smyth, "From Coningham to

The Desert Air Force (DAF) commander, Air Marshal Arthur Tedder, tasked Vice Air Marshal Arthur "Mary" Coningham to improve air–land relations.[43] The key to cooperation began with a mutual understanding between army and air force commanders for what each service could contribute, along with a shared vision of how to integrate air and land forces.[44] Coningham relocated his headquarters next to the 8th Army headquarters to enhance cooperation, understanding, and trust. In September 1941, a series of conferences by the DAF and 8th Army resulted in an *Air Support Directive* that provided the foundation for successful British air–land cooperation for the remainder of the war.[45]

Not until a year later, at the Second Battle of El Alamein in September 1942, would the British finally field a mature air–ground system.[46] As with the Luftwaffe, the first objective for the DAF remained gaining air superiority. Air forces could then strike the enemy's lines of communication, as envisioned by Slessor, or provide direct support to ground forces.[47] Air support control measures included centralized command and control of all theater air assets, with the army's air requests prioritized at the joint headquarters. In addition, the new doctrine standardized attack profiles, set requirements for placement of the bomb line, and regulated air/ground communications and signals.[48] The DAF deployed a wireless communication system featuring a "tentacle"-like network with multiple forward air support links (FASL), which connected forward air controllers (FACs) to headquarters via radio. FASLs were assigned to army division headquarters to request air support and provide deconfliction and targeting guidance when aircraft arrived

Project Coningham-Keyes: Did British Forces Relearn Historical Air-Land Cooperation Lessons During Operation 'Telic'" *Defence Studies* (June 12, 2007), 261, 265.

43 Arthur Tedder, *With Prejudice: The World War II Memoirs of Marshal of the Royal Air Force Lord Tedder, Deputy Supreme Commander of the Allied Expeditionary Force* (Boston, MA: Little, Brown & Co.,1966), 162.

44 Smyth, "From Coningham to Project Coningham-Keyes," 265.

45 The directive was later codified in March 1942 as Middle East (army and air) Training Pamphlet No. 3A, *Direct Air Support.* Richard Hallion, *Strike from the Sky: The History of Battlefield Air Attack, 1911–1945* (Washington, DC: Smithsonian, 1989), 4; Smyth, "From Coningham to Project Coningham-Keyes," 267; David Hall, *Learning How to Fight Together: The British Experience with Joint Air–Land Warfare* Research Paper 2009-2 (Maxwell AFB, AL: Air Force Research Institute, March 2009), 17.

46 *The End of the Beginning: Bracknell Paper No. 3 A Symposium on the Land/Air Cooperation in the Mediterranean War 1940–43* (Bracknell: RAF Staff College, 1992), 21.

47 Smyth, "From Coningham to Project Coningham-Keyes," 271.

48 The bomb line was known as the bomb safety line and is now known as the fire support coordination line (FSCL). It was usually a physical feature of geography easily identifiable from the air and ground. It is a deconfliction measure to reduce fratricide and coordinate fire. Smyth, "From Coningham to Project Coningham-Keyes," 267.

overhead.[49] In addition, reconnaissance aircraft began to function as rudimentary airborne FACs, and air liaison officers (ALOs) provided additional advice and support for intermediate-level army commands.[50] The British tactical air doctrine was prescriptive, however, telling airmen and soldiers how to coordinate their forces but not explaining the reasoning for why or how a combined arms approach could be effective.

The RAF developed a purpose-designed air support aircraft, a modified Hawker Hurricane, assigned to directly attack enemy fielded forces.[51] "Hurribomber" pilots developed dive-bombing techniques to increase the accuracy of their 250-pound bombs, a tactic like that employed by the Luftwaffe's Ju 87 Stuka dive bombers.[52] The British pushed westward with a functioning air-support system, reaching Tunisia by February 1943. They were joined in North Africa by the United States. As with the British experience, the Americans would have to learn critical lessons for air–ground cooperation the hard way.

The United States Army Air Forces

Unlike the Luftwaffe and RAF, the American air forces, like the VVS, were not independent. In anticipation of the coming war and the importance air power would play in the conflict, in June 1941 the US Army Air Corps was elevated in status to the US Army Air Forces (USAAF). Still, army generals governed the USAAF. When war came, the US Army quickly updated its doctrine on air–ground cooperation in Field Manual 31-35, *Aviation in Support of Ground Forces*, published in April 1942.[53] On the surface, the regulation looked like the British *Direct Air Support* doctrine with two caveats. First, the air commander advised the ground commander, with no hint of the coequal status enjoyed by the RAF. Second, the regulation allowed air units to be directly assigned to ground units, an option exercised by General Dwight D. Eisenhower, the commanding officer of Operation Torch, the invasion of French North

49 John Terraine, *The Right of the Line: The Role of the RAF in World War II* (Barnsley: Pen & Sword Aviation, 1985), 348; Roderic Owen, *The Desert Air Force* (London: Hutchinson & Co., 1948), 64.

50 Shelford Bidwell and Dominick Graham, *Fire-Power: British Army Weapons and Theories of War 1904–1945* (London: George Allen & Unwin, 1982), 271; Smyth, "From Coningham to Project Coningham-Keyes," 268.

51 Hall, *Learning How to Fight Together*, 16.

52 Smyth, "From Coningham to Project Coningham-Keyes," 269.

53 War Department FM 31-35 *Basic Field Manual Aviation in Support of Ground Forces*, April 9, 1942 (Washington, DC: General Printing Officer, 1942).

Africa.[54] By December 1942, however, RAF Air Marshal Tedder had convinced Eisenhower of the error in dispersing the American air forces and the necessity to reorganize Allied Forces in North Africa, a decision ratified at the Casablanca Conference in January 1943. Unfortunately, Eisenhower was still restructuring his forces when, in February, the defeat of the US Army's II Corps by Rommel's Afrika Corps in western Tunisia revealed the disadvantage of dispersed air forces.[55] The American humiliation at Kasserine Pass highlighted the need for updating US tactical air doctrine. All air forces in theater must be under the command of a single airman, with priority given to first gaining air superiority. With the freedom to operate obtained, air power's inherent flexibility would allow air forces to be allocated where they were most needed. In July 1943, a new US field manual, FM 100-20 *Command and Employment of Air Power*, reflected these fundamental principles for the employment of tactical air forces.[56]

Uppercase letters in the first bullet on the first page of FM 100-20 declared, "LAND POWER AND AIR POWER ARE COEQUAL AND INTERDEPENDENT FORCES; NEITHER IS AN AUXILIARY OF THE OTHER." The second bullet further emphasized that "THE GAINING OF AIR SUPERIORITY IS THE FIRST REQUIREMENT FOR THE SUCCESS OF ANY MAJOR LAND OPERATION."[57] The remainder of the fourteen-page document explained that, because of its inherent flexibility, air forces should be under the control of a theater air commander, subordinate only to the overall joint force commander. Importantly, FM 100-20 also provided targeting priority for tactical air forces.[58] First, the emphasis would be to gain air superiority by destroying hostile air forces and attacking their bases. The second priority would be the interdiction of the enemy's lines of communication to prevent the movement of troops and supplies into and within the theater. The last priority would be CAS, as such efforts were complex, required detailed coordination to avoid fratricide, and targets were dispersed and therefore less lucrative.[59] A combination of factors contributed to CAS's tertiary consideration. It had become

[54] Eduard Mark, *Aerial Interdiction: Air Power and the Land Battle in Three American Wars* (Washington, DC: Center for Air Force History, 1994), 30.

[55] Richard Hallion, *Strike from the Sky: The History of Battlefield Air Attack, 1911–1945* (Washington, DC: Smithsonian, 1989), 171.

[56] *War Department Field Manual FM 100-20: Command and Employment of Air Power* July 21, 1943 (Washington, DC: Government Printing Office, 1943).

[57] *FM 100-20*, 1.

[58] Michael Doubler, *Closing with the Enemy: How GIs Fought the War in Europe, 1944–1945* (Lawrence, KS: University Press of Kansas, 1994), 64.

[59] FM 100-20, 2, 8, 10, 11.

evident that it was too difficult to conduct combined arms operations without air superiority. The USAAF also had not yet developed effective CAS procedures. And finally, airmen anticipated artillery would be more effective, efficient, and available to engage the enemy's fielded forces near the battlefront.

FM 100-20 became the baseline for air–land cooperation between US air forces and armies. Operations in Sicily in 1943 and later the static fighting in Italy through 1944 allowed for further maturation of the US tactical air doctrine. The first element was the genuine cooperation required between air and army commanders and their staffs. Air liaisons assigned at intermediate levels of army command assisted in collaboration and coordination. The second element was a responsive tactical air request network and efficient command-and-control system for tactical airstrikes with standardized preplanned and on-call missions. Improvements included more effective forward air controllers, such as the rover system, first used by the British, which deployed experienced combat pilots alongside soldiers on the front lines with radios to communicate directly with assigned strike aircraft.[60] Enhancements also included airborne forward air controllers (AFAC), where an army advisor flew alongside a pilot in an L-5 observation aircraft.[61] By the time of the invasion of France in June 1944, the United States had in place the template for air–ground coordination that would persist throughout and after the war.[62]

Meanwhile, the US Navy and US Marine Corps (USMC) developed a tactical air control system for amphibious operations in the Pacific. Their approach was like that employed in Europe in that air commanders controlled their air forces and gave air superiority primary consideration. However, the Navy–Marine Corps doctrine viewed CAS and interdiction, called DAS (direct or deep air support) against fixed targets that did not require direct control, as equally important.[63] Emphasis on direct attack was partly due to the Marines not having as much artillery as the

[60] Doubler, *Closing with the Enemy*, 69.
[61] Alan Wilt, "Allied Cooperation in Sicily and Italy 1943–45" in Benjamin Cooling, ed., *Case Studies in the Development of Close Air Support* (Washington, DC: Office of Air Force History, 1990), 208, 209, 213, 217, 226; Doubler, *Closing with the Enemy*, 65.
[62] It would still take the crucible of combat in Europe to perfect the procedures for the implementation of effective direct attack. Doubler, *Closing with the Enemy*, 63–86; Allan Millet, "Korea, 1950–1953" in Cooling, ed., *Case Studies in the Development of Close Air Support*, 347–348; Thomas Hughes, *Overlord: General Pete Quesada and the Triumph of Tactical Air Power in World War II* (New York: Free Press,1995), 128, 129.
[63] Peter Davies, *Marine Corps F-4 Phantom II Units of the Vietnam War* (Long Island City, NY: Osprey, 2012), 26.

Army.[64] The Navy–Marine Corps system focused on speed by delegating responsibility for prioritizing air requests to Marine aviators assigned to tactical air control parties (TACP) in frontline units. These experienced airmen further served as ground FACs. The Navy–Marine Corps maintained their air–ground coordination system after the war, while the Army–Air Force system suffered from neglect.[65]

The US Air Force (USAF) gained its independence in 1947, but its leaders still promised to support the Army as it had in World War II. By September 1950, the Army and Air Force had developed FM 31-35 *Joint Training Directive for Air–Ground Operations.*[66] The instruction recognized three tactical air power missions: air superiority, interdiction, and close air support. Significantly, the doctrine differentiated two types of interdiction missions. Bombers and tactical aircraft would cut off enemy lines of communication by attacking fixed targets, including roads, bridges, railroads, and waterways, or by attacking concentrated troops along with their equipment and supplies.[67] This disruption of the enemy's lines of communication would later become known as air interdiction. In addition, tacair on armed recce (reconnaissance) missions would search for and engage suitable targets in designated areas beyond the bomb line. The direct attack of fielded forces short of the bomb line but beyond the range of CAS was not yet recognized – it would later be called battlefield interdiction. While the Air Force retained this doctrine for air–ground operations, it failed to maintain the requisite personnel, equipment, or training of the air–ground operation system (AGOS) to execute direct attack missions when war came to Korea.[68]

When North Korean troops marched south of the 38th parallel in June 1950, neither the US Army nor the Air Force had prepared for combined arms operations.[69] The Air Force had transitioned to jet aircraft, which flew from bases in Japan. US fighters quickly gained air superiority over the Korean peninsula, but the jets had limited loiter time. USAF tacair pilots struggled to conduct CAS or armed recce due to reduced time on station, increased airspeeds of jet aircraft, and

64 Robert Futrell, *The United States Air Force in Korea* (Washington, DC: Office of Air Force History, 1983), 705.
65 Millet, "Korea, 1950–1953," 352.
66 Terrance McCaffrey, *What Happened to Battlefield Air Interdiction? Army and Air Force Battlefield Doctrine Development from Pre-Desert Storm to 2001* (Maxwell AFB, AL: Air University Press, 2004), 13.
67 McCaffrey, *What Happened to Battlefield Air Interdiction?*, 13.
68 Millet, "Korea, 1950–1953," 349.
69 Millet, "Korea, 1950–1953," 363; Conrad Crane, *American Airpower Strategy in Korea 1950–53* (Lawrence: University Press of Kansas, 2000), 30.

minimal prior air-to-ground training. Tacair compensated by relying on airborne FACs, which controlled 90 percent of all Air Force direct attack missions. Most of these strikes fell well beyond the location of friendly forces and therefore did not require the detailed coordination and deconfliction of CAS. Though recorded as CAS missions at the time, they are better characterized as armed recce.[70]

By contrast, Navy and Marine Corps aviation operated prop-driven aircraft from carriers offshore.[71] These dedicated air assets could quickly respond to requests by ground FACs that controlled close strikes in front of Marine ground forces.[72] The lack of responsiveness of the Army–Air Force air–ground system drew criticism compared to the Navy–Marine Corps. However, reproach did not alter the USAF prioritization of air superiority, strategic bombing, air interdiction, and, only as a last resort, the direct attack of fielded forces.[73]

After the Korean War, USAF air–ground doctrine was revised in 1954 and again in 1957, recognizing that armed recce could also be conducted short of the bomb line but beyond the range of CAS.[74] At the beginning of the Vietnam War, in 1964, *Tactical Air Command Manual* (TACM) 1-1 finally acknowledged in Air Force doctrine that armed recce missions against enemy fielded forces required coordination with ground commanders. TACM 1-1 referred to these armed recce missions as battlefield interdiction. Unfortunately, two years later, in the midst of combined arms operations in South Vietnam, the USAF revised TACM 1-1, removing any reference to battlefield interdiction.[75]

During the Vietnam War, it would be armed recce, missions tasked with locating and attacking fielded forces beyond the frontlines, that would be the primary means by which US air forces directly attacked the North Vietnamese Army and Viet Cong (NVA/VC). CAS occurred less frequently than armed recce, as there were fewer opportunities to attack enemy forces close to friendlies. The lopsided ratio of armed recce to CAS missions is not unique to Vietnam, as this has been the norm for modern air warfare.

Interestingly, the reverse has been the case for counterinsurgency operations, where CAS has proven essential when friendly forces

70 Millet, "Korea, 1950–1953," 364–365; Futrell, *The United States Air Force in Korea*, 705.
71 Davies, *Marine Corps F-4 Phantom II Units of the Vietnam War*, 26.
72 Millet, "Korea, 1950–1953," 367; Crane, *American Airpower Strategy in Korea*, 29.
73 Millet, "Korea, 1950–1953," 397; Futrell, *The United States Air Force in Korea*, 706.
74 AFMAN 1-7 *Theater Air Forces in Counterair, Interdiction and Close Air Support* March 1, 1954 (Washington, DC: Department of the Air Force, 1954); *Tactical Air Command Manual* (TACM) 55-3; McCaffrey, *What Happened to Battlefield Air Interdiction?*, 14.
75 McCaffrey, *What Happened to Battlefield Air Interdiction?*, 15–16.

disperse to occupy territory. Under these conditions, troops often do not have the organic firepower to react to insurgent attacks. Also, during counterinsurgencies, tactical aircrew on armed recce missions have found it challenging to differentiate insurgents from civilians and friendly forces. In counterinsurgent operations ground tactical air controllers are crucial for employing CAS while minimizing collateral damage and the risk of fratricide.[76]

Returning to modern mechanized warfare, it would not be until the late 1970s that cooperation between the US Army and Air Force improved. Their joint effort to bolster conventional deterrence in Europe resulted in the Army's AirLand Battle doctrine and NATO's Follow-On Force Attack. In both doctrines, tacair played a critical role in gaining air superiority and conducting armed recce. The Air Force named the armed recce mission as battlefield air interdiction (BAI). BAI would halt the Soviet Army's Operational Maneuver Groups (OMGs). Held in reserve, the OMGs were designed to exploit breakthroughs in the battle lines.[77]

BAI would remain a USAF tacair mission until 1991 during Desert Storm, when Lieutenant General Chuck Horner, the air commander of the coalition forces in the Middle East, omitted BAI missions from the air tasking order (ATO). By doing so, Horner excluded Army commanders from the target prioritization process by not apportioning CAS sorties until the start of the ground campaign. When the ground war began, Horner did not assign any BAI missions but instead substituted a push CAS system, like the British Cabrank procedures employed in the Mediterranean theater in World War II.[78] Upon check-in with their assigned FACs, if there were no available CAS targets, as was common, tacair would then flow to preplanned interdiction targets or predesignated armed recce areas. Ground commanders had the advantage of having readily available CAS, but without BAI they no longer had a say in the priority of targets for the deeper battle. After Desert Storm, Air Force leaders struck BAI from doctrine just as they had removed battlefield interdiction during the Vietnam War. As a result, Army commanders could no longer interfere with prioritizing targets beyond the front.[79]

76 The author commanded an A-10 squadron in Afghanistan in 2004, which was responsible for providing CAS to support friendly ground forces conducting counterinsurgent operations.

77 Phil Haun, "Peacetime Military Innovation through Inter Service Cooperation" *Journal of Strategic Studies* 43:5 (2020), 10.

78 Wilt, "Allied Cooperation in Sicily and Italy," 209.

79 United States Air Force, *Air Force Doctrine Document* (September 1, 1997).

Today, there remains no doctrinal distinction in USAF doctrine between interdiction missions that directly target fielded forces beyond the forward line of own troops (FLOT) and missions that target the enemy's lines of communication by striking fixed targets, such as roads, bridges, and railways. Armed recce, which has always been the most systematic way tacair has directly targeted fielded forces, is no longer identified as a specified mission in USAF doctrine.[80] The result has been neglect in acquiring aircraft, sensors, and specially designed weapons for armed recce. There has also been inattention to improving tactics, techniques, and procedures (TTP) and insufficient training for this crucial mission.

By contrast, the Marine Corps maintains the armed recce mission. Marine Corps aviation doctrine separates close air support and deep air support.[81] CAS missions "are in close proximity to friendly forces. CAS requires detailed integration of each air mission with the fire and movement of friendly forces." DAS does not require such detailed coordination. DAS is flown on either side of the fire support coordination line (FSCL), formerly the bomb line. DAS further divides air interdiction and armed recce. Air interdiction "destroys, neutralizes, or delays the enemy military potential before it can be brought to bear effectively against friendly forces." While air interdiction is against known targets, armed recce requires aircrew to locate targets of opportunity, attacking enemy materiel, personnel, or facilities in assigned areas on either side of the FSCL.[82]

The tactical air doctrine of the Luftwaffe, VVS, RAF, USAF, and USMC informed airmen, soldiers, sailors, and marines how to organize and employ their air and land forces in combined arms operations. However, the doctrines did not, and still do not, explain how and why air power can be effectively employed against enemy armies. The next section introduces tactical air power theory to provide these explanations. The most common way US air forces fight modern conventional wars is by directly attacking fielded forces by armed recce, not CAS. That the USAF does not recognize armed recce or BAI as a separate mission from air interdiction is indicative of the view long held by advocates of an

[80] United States Air Force, *Counterland Operations* AFDP 3-03 (2020), www.doctrine.af.mil/Portals/61/documents/AFDP_3-03/3-03-AFDP-COUNTERLAND.pdf, 6.

[81] Jack Shulimson and Charles Johnson, *U.S. Marines in Vietnam: The Landing and the Buildup 1965* (Washington, DC: History and Museums Division Headquarters Marine Corps, 1978), 154; US Marine Corps, *Aviation Operations MCWP 3-2* (Washington, DC: HQ USMC, 2000), 1–2.

[82] US Marine Corps, *Aviation Operations MCWP 3-20* (Washington, DC: Marine Corps Headquarters, 2018), 2-1–2-2.

independent air force that air power is better considered as a substitute for land power rather than a complement.[83]

Tactical Air Power (TAP) Theory

When fighting an army, an air force has two options: attack its fielded forces or interdict its lines of communication, operation, and retreat. As demonstrated in the following chapters, direct attack has proven more effective.[84] Yet the few air power theorists who recommend targeting militaries instead advocate an indirect approach.[85] While theoretically appealing, in practice air power alone is usually not effective in interdicting an enemy's lines of communication or disrupting its lines of operation.[86] Figure 2.1 uses the Clausewitzian triangle to model the state as consisting of its population, military, and government (see Appendix A).[87] The arrows in Figure 2.1 illustrate the theory of victory for direct attack where sufficient pressure is placed on the military to change the political calculations of the targeted nation's leaders.

A military's ability to mass and maneuver is essential; it is so fundamental that mass and maneuver are principles of war.[88] Clausewitz maintained that the primary operational objective of an army was to concentrate at the decisive point.[89] However, the challenge facing

[83] Phil Haun, "Foundation Bias: The Impact of the Air Corps Tactical School on United States Air Force Doctrine" *Journal of Military History* 85:2 (2021), 453–474.

[84] From Table 1.1, direct attack campaigns succeeded militarily 73 percent of the time (eight of eleven) and politically 45 percent (five of eleven). In comparison, air interdiction succeeded militarily only 17 percent of the time (one of six) and politically never (none of six), and strategic bombing campaigns succeeded politically 33 percent (two of six).

[85] Slessor, *Airpower and Armies*. Robert Pape also argues that interdiction is contingent on the type of enemy army, with interdiction against conventional mechanized forces being effective. Pape, *Bombing to Win*, 74.

[86] Air interdiction of sea lines of communication may have better results, as the US Navy and Coast Guard achieved off the Vietnamese coast in Operation Market Time. Alex Larzelere, *The Coast Guard at War, Vietnam 1965–1975* (Annapolis, MD: Naval Institute Press, 1997). The enemy develops alternative LOC and works to reopen its primary LOC quickly. In addition, armies can neutralize the impact of attacks on their LOC by stockpiling supplies. Also, when on the offensive an attacker gets to decide when to strike and only does so when its LOC are secured. By contrast, defending armies do not extend their LOC, expend overall less energy than on attack, and consume fewer supplies. Richard Hallion, "Battlefield Air Support: A Retrospective Assessment" *Airpower Journal* (Spring 1990), 11–12; Phil Haun and Colin Jackson, "Breaker of Armies: Air Power in the Easter Offensive and the Myth of Linebacker I and II in the Vietnam War" *International Security* (Winter 2015/16), 139–178.

[87] Clausewitz, *On War*, 89.

[88] US Joint Doctrine Pub 1 (July 12, 2017), I-3, https://irp.fas.org/doddir/dod/jp1.pdf.

[89] Clausewitz, *On War*, 204.

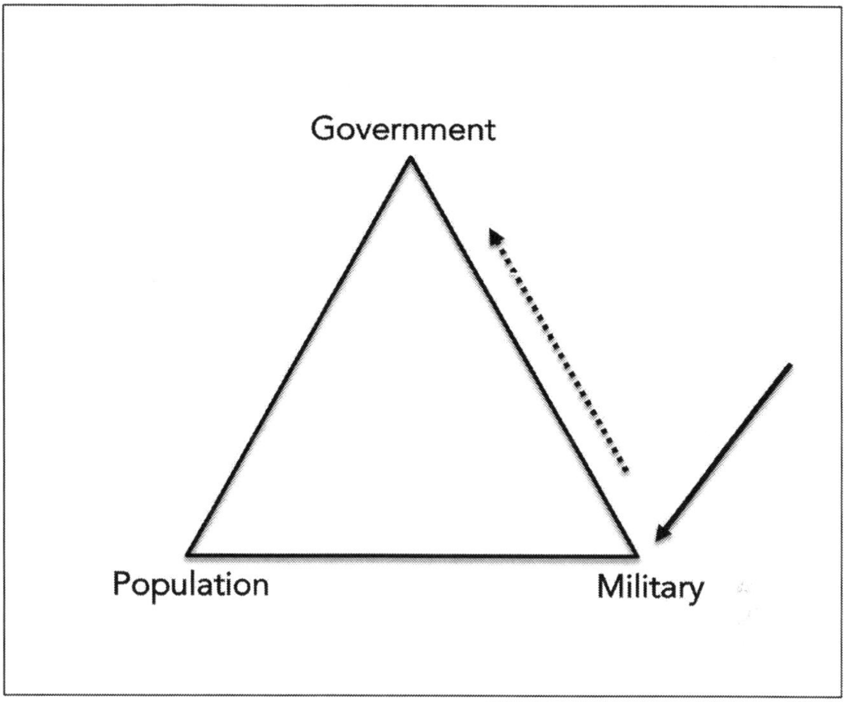

Figure 2.1 Targeting the military

modern ground forces is how to mass, maneuver, and *survive*, given the marked rise in the lethality of weaponry. In *Military Power: Explaining Victory and Defeat in Modern Battle*, Stephen Biddle highlights that "by 1914, firepower had become so lethal that exposed mass movement in the open had become suicidal. Subsequent technological change has only increased the range over which exposure can be fatal."[90] Biddle explains that armies can only reduce their vulnerability by utilizing what he terms the *modern system*. This technique is "a tightly interrelated complex of cover, concealment, dispersion, suppression, small-unit independent maneuver, and combined arms at the tactical level, and depth, reserves, and differential concentration at the operational level."[91]

The risk/reward tradeoff in a contested environment is between survivability and lethality. Concentrating and closing with the enemy

[90] Stephen Biddle, *Military Power: Explaining Victory and Defeat in Modern Battle* (Princeton, NJ: Princeton University Press, 2004), 3.
[91] Biddle, *Military Power*, 3.

improves the ability to locate, identify, and attack, but it may provide an even better opportunity for the defender to do the same. Focusing solely on offensive capability while leaving oneself vulnerable to attack has proven to be a recipe for disaster, as the NVA discovered at Khe Sanh (see Chapter 4). The same can also be true for air forces, as evidenced by the defeat of American bombers at the hands of Luftwaffe fighters in 1943.[92] While Biddle's modern system may be a solution for a mechanized army's survival on the battlefield, for air forces the pressing challenge is to gain and maintain sufficient air superiority to conduct air-to-ground operations with acceptable losses.[93]

With air superiority secured, the lethality of an air force resides in its asymmetric advantage of observing ground forces when they mass or maneuver. Though Clausewitz lived before the invention of the airplane, in *On War* he discussed the benefits of commanding the heights, where a characteristic relevant to air power is having a *wider view*.[94] Observing the battlefield from above reduces the vertical surface obstructions, which restrict the horizontal line of sight for ground forces. From above, air forces can locate and destroy massed armies in the open and on the move.

Even with the advantage of a *wider view*, most tacair operate at high speeds and high altitude, making it difficult to identify small targets, such as a tank in a tree line or well-camouflaged guerrillas. By contrast, a large, mechanized ground unit struggles to conceal its position, leaving it vulnerable to detection from above. Massed units have fewer places to hide and emit more visual, infrared, and electromagnetic cues to be identified and tracked. In addition to being easier to find, massed formations provide an opportunity for multiple airstrikes, increasing the efficiency of a single sortie.

Movement, like mass, also exposes ground forces. The contrast of a vehicle in motion against a static background attracts the eye's attention or that of a radar's moving target indicator.[95] Though dynamic targets have historically been harder to hit than fixed targets, airmen have

[92] Phil Haun, *Lectures of the Air Corps Tactical School and American Strategic Bombing in World War II* (Lexington: University Press of Kentucky, 2019), 204.

[93] Acceptable attrition is determined not by the number of airstrikes required to achieve the military objective but by the losses accrued weighed against the political value of the objective. For non-vital national objectives, the value of the object may be so low that the survivability of aircrew may outweigh the value of any airstrike.

[94] Clausewitz witnessed one of the earliest attempts to employ air forces when, in 1795 as a teen, he saw the French deploy tethered balloons to observe the enemy's positions and movement at the siege of Mainz. Clausewitz, *On War*, 352–354.

[95] Moving target indicators utilize doppler radar to distinguish moving targets from the static background.

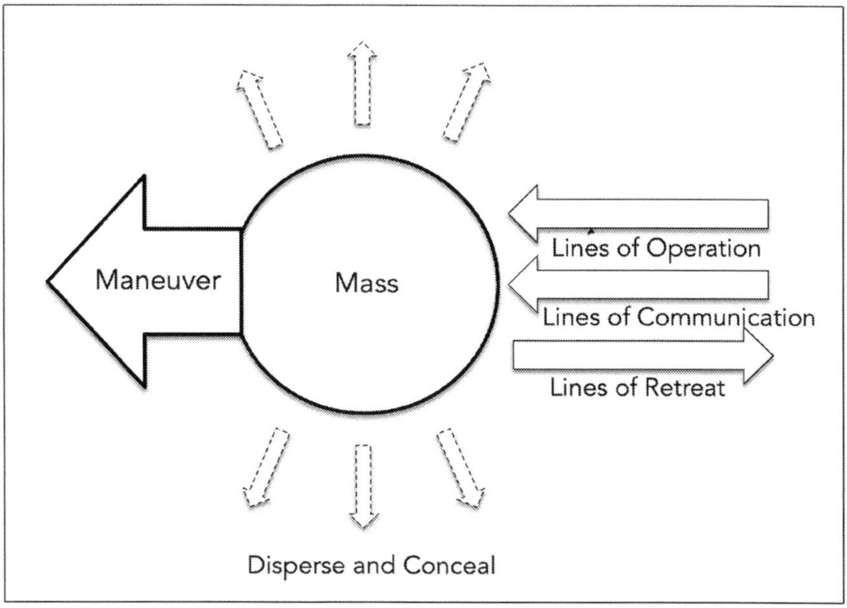

Figure 2.2 When armies are vulnerable to air attack

adapted their tactics and weaponry to be lethal against movers as well.[96] Armies that both mass and maneuver are particularly at risk, as the NVA discovered at the battles of An Loc and Kontum during the Easter Offensive (see Chapter 7).

Figure 2.2 illustrates the conditions when ground forces are most susceptible to air attack and the measures taken to reduce vulnerability. The large circle represents massed forces. Again, massed armies are more likely to be identified from the air, and their concentration increases the lethality of air attacks. The large arrow left of the circle represents concentrated forces on the move. These forces have the double disadvantage of being large and dynamic, making them easier to observe.

The three parallel arrows right of the circle represent an army's lines of operation, lines of communication, and lines of retreat. Lines of operation are how an army gets to the battlefield, the initial deployment of

[96] Tacair utilizes precision-guided weapons to engage moving targets such as the fire-and-forget Maverick air-to-surface missile. Recently A-10 aircraft have employed laser-guided rockets against ISIS. Kris Osborn, "America's A-10 Warthogs Need More Laser-Guided Rockets against ISIS" *The National Interest*, nationalinterest.org/blog/the-buzz/americas-10-warthogs-need-more-laser-guided-rockets-attack-21147.

forces, and subsequent reinforcements. Likewise, the LOC, with the inflow of ammunition and supplies, are vital for continued operations, especially for mechanized units. As such, LOC have long been a target for air interdiction. Finally, an army in retreat is exposed, particularly in a hasty withdrawal. Though these lines of communication, operation, and retreat are, in theory, vulnerable to attack, they have proven less so in practice than when armies mass and maneuver on the battlefield. For example, the North Vietnamese usually kept the Ho Chi Minh Trail sufficiently open to supply operations in South Vietnam. US air forces were even less effective in interdicting the NVA's line of operation as troops continuously marched southward throughout the war (see Chapter 6).

In contrast to the circle and horizontal arrows represented in Figure 2.2, where the larger size denotes when armies are most vulnerable, the smaller dashed arrows radiating from the circle indicate an army's reaction when threatened. When able, troops disperse and conceal their positions to reduce detection and lessen the impact of airstrikes. Air power alone rarely defeats armies because of their ability to scatter and hide. Chapters 4 and 7 examine two rare cases where the NVA chose instead to concentrate and maneuver. As part of combined arms operations, US air power destroyed two North Vietnamese divisions during the Battle of Khe Sanh and again defeated fourteen NVA divisions in the Easter Offensive. In both cases, the North Vietnamese sacrificed their armies in an attempt to achieve broader political goals.

Under the lethal threat from airstrikes, most army commanders will not expose their forces but instead order their troops to disperse and hide. They find concealment under ground cover, dig defensive positions for protection, and move only at night and in bad weather to avoid detection. However, such defensive reactions come at a price. Air power overhead prevents an army from massing to conduct offensive operations and leaves it dispersed and vulnerable to an opposed ground force attack. Though not intuitive, air power's most significant impact against an enemy's fielded forces is usually not measured by the number of soldiers killed or tanks destroyed but by how the threat of airstrikes disrupts the enemy's strategy. An example of air power deterring ground forces from concentrating and maneuvering occurred during the lead-up to the invasion of Iraq in 2003. Anticipating an air-only operation, Iraq dispersed its forces. Such action may have diminished the direct impact of airstrikes, but it left Iraq vulnerable to the subsequent US ground invasion.

Unfortunately, instead of evaluating the effect air power has had on the enemy's overall strategy, military analysts have often focused on measuring the attrition of enemy ground forces.[97] Such an approach – examining the battlefield to determine what weapons destroyed which tanks – may be necessary for the tactical analysis of the lethality of specific munitions. However, it is not a measure of the overall operational effectiveness of air power and misses the broader point. It is usually not how many targets have been destroyed that determines the outcome but how the threat of further attack impacts enemy decision-making and subsequent action or inaction. The dead make no decisions and take no actions on the battlefield. Instead, it is the threat of death that deters and coerces. When effective, air forces strike few targets as the enemy anticipates such losses and reacts by dispersing and concealing to survive. Doing so may decrease the enemy army's vulnerability to air attack but diminishes its ability to execute its preferred strategy and, as previously mentioned, leaves it vulnerable to a ground attack.

As demonstrated in the following chapters, air power's most significant impact is what does not occur on the battlefield – the dogs that do not bark. This includes enemy air strikes that do not happen, enemy reserves that do not make it to the battlefield because they have been harassed and delayed along the way, and enemy forces that disperse instead of massing and maneuvering. The most significant impact of air power in warfare has often been neglected and misunderstood because of its unobserved effects, those actions that do not take place but would have had air power not been present. In addition, there has been little incentive for Army generals to highlight air power's vital role in their battlefield victories. Nor have Air Force generals, predisposed to prefer air power to be employed independently, advocated for what they perceive as a supporting role. There has also been little interest by military analysts or historians to analyze and write about military operations that have not taken place. Clausewitz, however, cautions against such omissions when he warns that the outcomes of possible engagements must be regarded as real because of their consequences.[98]

While explaining how and why air power works against ground forces, TAP theory does not predict that air forces will always be effective. Contextual variables, discussed in detail in Chapter 8, significantly impact the effectiveness of air power in specific conflicts. Operational factors of air superiority, air-to-ground capabilities, friendly and enemy ground force capabilities, along with environmental factors of weather,

97 For an example of an analyst basing air power effectiveness on enemy attrition, see Kenneth Pollack, "Air Power in the Six-Day War" *Journal of Strategic Studies* 28:3 (2005), 471–503.

98 Clausewitz, *On War*, 181.

lighting, geography and terrain, civilians, and cover and concealment work to enhance or limit the ability of air power to deter an army from executing its preferred strategy.

Conclusion

This chapter introduced a theory of tactical air power. As Chapters 3–7 will demonstrate, in the Vietnam War strategic bombing and air interdiction largely failed. Instead, air power proved more effective in directly attacking fielded forces as part of combined arms operations. Air power proved most lethal against ground forces when the enemy massed and maneuvered. As a result, armies usually dispersed and hid when threatened from above. Rather than attrit an enemy force, air power instead deterred armies from concentrating and maneuvering, denying the enemy two principles of war necessary to achieve battlefield victory or avoid defeat.

3 Vietnam and Rolling Thunder: 1965–1966

In early 1965 the United States commenced large-scale conventional air operations in Southeast Asia. The following five chapters assess the military effectiveness of air power against the North Vietnamese from the escalation of the war in 1965 through the conclusion of major air combat with Linebacker II in January 1973. This chapter provides an overview of the lead-up to the deployment of American combat forces in Vietnam, then analyzes both the Rolling Thunder air campaign in North Vietnam and the combined arms operations in South Vietnam from March 1965 through December 1966. Rolling Thunder struggled to interdict the North Vietnamese supply lines during this period. Meanwhile, the US direct air attack campaign in South Vietnam kept the North Vietnamese Army and Viet Cong (NVA/VC) dispersed and in hiding, as anticipated by the Tactical Air Power (TAP) theory introduced in the previous chapter.

The Lead-Up to the US Intervention in Vietnam: 1945–1964

After World War II, the French returned to reclaim their colonies in Indochina only to face the Vietminh. This insurgent group had fought the Japanese and continued their struggle to gain independence from France. Nine years later, in 1954, the Vietminh decisively defeated the French at Dien Bien Phu, leading to the Geneva peace agreement. The agreement divided Southeast Asia into Laos, Cambodia, and Vietnam, with Vietnam further subdivided along the 17th parallel into South and North. In Saigon, President Ngo Dinh Diem, backed by the United States, formed a republic. In Hanoi, Chairman Ho Chi Minh, supported by the Soviet Union and China, established a communist regime. Over time, Ho Chi Minh would gradually cede party control to Le Duan. Le Duan, born in the southern province of Quang Tri, consistently advocated for violent reunification.[1] With the division of Vietnam, 10,000 Vietminh, known as the Viet Cong, remained behind in the South. By 1959, under North Vietnamese supervision, the VC had expanded their influence to threaten President Diem's control over the countryside.[2] To contain the spread of communism, the United States committed thousands of military advisors and millions in aid. By late 1963, however, Diem's strong-armed domestic policies towards land reform and restrictions to religious freedom had alienated the majority of South Vietnamese and President John F. Kennedy's administration. In a US-condoned coup, Diem was murdered in November 1963, three weeks before Kennedy's own assassination.[3]

Saigon struggled through a series of coups and countercoups for the next year and a half while, in Hanoi, Le Duan ordered preparations for an invasion. Le Duan further urged the VC to incite a general uprising.[4] In the absence of a functioning South Vietnamese government, President Lyndon B. Johnson, who had retained Kennedy's top foreign policy advisors, turned his administration's foreign policy attention to pressuring Hanoi to stop supporting the VC.[5] By June 1964, in response to the deteriorating security situation in South Vietnam, the Joint Chiefs of Staff (JCS) at the Pentagon had developed a master list of ninety-four targets to strike in North Vietnam.[6] Though proposed as a strategic bombing campaign, the target list avoided the North Vietnamese population, its agriculturally centered economy, and its leadership. Instead, most targets were military facilities and the transportation infrastructure

[1] Lien-Hang Nguyen, *Hanoi's War* (Chapel Hill: University of North Carolina Press, 2012), 43; Bui Tin, *Following Ho Chi Minh: Memoirs of a North Vietnamese Colonel* (Honolulu: University of Hawaii Press, 1995), 34, 43, 45; Ang Cheng Guan, *The Vietnam War from the Other Side: The Vietnamese Communists' Perspective* (New York: RoutledgeCurzon, 2002), 21, 80.

[2] The Viet Cong were known as the People's Liberation Armed Force (PLAF) by the North Vietnamese. Douglas Pike, *PAVN: People's Liberation Army Vietnam* (Novato, CA: Presidio, 1986), 44; Bui Tin, *Following Ho Chi Minh*, 41; Dale Andrade, "Westmoreland Was Right: Learning the Wrong Lessons from the Vietnam War" *Small Wars and Insurgencies* 19:2 (2008), 152.

[3] For the history of US involvement in Vietnam see Fredrik Logevall, *Embers of War: The Fall of an Empire and the Making of America's Vietnam* (New York: Random House, 2012); Lyndon B. Johnson, *The Vantage Point: Perspectives of the Presidency 1963–1969* (New York: Holt, Rinehart and Winston, 1971), 43; Dean Rusk, *As I Saw It* (New York: Norton, 1990), 439–440; Truong Nhu Tang, *A Vietcong Memoir: An Insider Account of the Vietnam War and Its Aftermath* (New York: Vintage, 1986), 89.

[4] Nguyen, *Hanoi's War*, 49, 63, 65; Johnson, *The Vantage Point*, 64; Andrade, "Westmoreland Was Right," 153.

[5] Johnson, *The Vantage Point*, 19; John Sherwood, *Afterburner: Naval Aviators and the Vietnam War* (New York: New York University Press, 2004), 7.

[6] Earl Tilford, *Crosswinds: The Air Force's Setup in Vietnam* (College Station: Texas A&M University Press, 1993), 66.

that supported the movement of troops and supplies headed south along the Ho Chi Minh Trail.[7]

In early August 1964, the Navy alleged that, on two occasions, torpedo boats had attacked US destroyers operating in international waters off the North Vietnamese coast.[8] In response, Johnson ordered limited airstrikes on North Vietnamese military facilities. Shortly thereafter, Congress overwhelmingly approved the Gulf of Tonkin resolution giving the president broad, open-ended powers to take all necessary measures to protect US forces and allies in Southeast Asia.[9] The US military planned further strikes and deployed additional forces, but Johnson delayed action until after the November elections, which he won handily. After a series of VC attacks, Johnson finally responded, triggered by a raid on a US Army camp near Pleiku, in February 1965.

Large-Scale Combat Operations: March 1965–December 1966

In early 1965, fighting escalated with a series of retaliatory US airstrikes. On February 7, after the VC raid on Pleiku, Johnson approved Air Force, Navy, and RVNAF (Republic of Vietnam Air Force) air strikes, code-named Flaming Dart, which targeted NVA barracks across the demilitarized zone (DMZ) and along the coast.[10] After another VC raid, US and South Vietnamese air forces conducted a similar strike three days later (US air forces hereafter refers to Air Force, Navy, and Marine Corps

[7] Hoang Khoi, *The Ho Chi Minh Trail* (Hanoi: Gioi Publishers, 2008), 49–54; Bui Tin, *Following Ho Chi Minh*, 47.

[8] For a detailed book-length analysis of the Gulf of Tonkin Incident see Edwin Moise, *Tonkin Gulf and the Escalation of the Vietnam War* (Annapolis, MD: Naval Institute Press, 2019); a North Vietnamese attack took place on August 2, but not August 4. McNamara interview "Fog of War" Documentary 2003; Edward Marolda, *Approaching Storm: Conflict in Asia, 1945–1965* (Washington, DC: Naval History and Heritage Command, 2009) 70; Rusk, *As I Saw It*, 444; Guan, *The Vietnam War from the Other Side*, 80; John Prados, *Vietnam: The History of an Unwinnable War, 1954–1975* (Lawrence: University Press of Kansas, 2009), 93–95; "U.S. Involvement in the Vietnam War: The Gulf of Tonkin and Escalation, 1964" *Foreign Relations of the United States*, Milestones: 1961–68, https://history.state.gov/milestones/1961–1968/gulf-of-tonkin; Peter Mersky and Norman Polmar, *The Naval Air War in Vietnam* (Annapolis, MD: Nautical & Aviation Publishing Company of America, 1981), 13–18.

[9] Eighty-Eighth Congress of the United States "Gulf of Tonkin Resolution," August 10, 1964, www.archivesfoundation.org/documents/tonkin-gulf-resolution/; Johnson, *The Vantage Point*, 114–118; Rusk, *As I Saw It*, 445; Robert McNamara, *In Retrospect: The Tragedy and Lessons of Vietnam* (New York: Vintage, 1995), 132–135.

[10] William Westmoreland, *A Soldier Reports* (New York: De Capo, 1976) 115–116; Prados, *Vietnam: The History of an Unwinnable War*, 110–114; Tilford, *Crosswinds*, 68.

fixed-wing aviation).[11] The White House publicly announced these as a "response to provocations ordered and directed by the Hanoi regime," with the actions "carefully limited to military areas … supplying men and arms for attack in South Vietnam." The press release concluded that the United States did not seek to widen the war but that "the key to the situation remain[ed] the cessation of infiltration from North Vietnam and the clear indication by the Hanoi regime that it [was] prepared to cease aggression against its neighbors."[12] Though described as a strategic bombing campaign of gradual escalation, the missions would primarily be air interdiction aimed at isolating the NVA/VC in South Vietnam and coercing Hanoi to withdraw its support from the VC.

For the Flaming Dart raids, the RVNAF and USAF (US Air Force) had available, respectively, propeller-driven A-1H Skyraiders and jet-powered F-100 Super Sabres. These tactical aircraft (tacair) were being used for close air support (CAS) and armed recce (reconnaissance) missions in the lower threat areas of Laos and South Vietnam (see Figures 3.1 and 3.2).

As additional air assets arrived in theater, the USAF began to rely on the higher-performance F-105 Thunderchief and F-4C Phantom II for the higher-threat areas of North Vietnam (see Figures 3.3 and 3.4).[13] The US Navy operated aircraft carriers off the coast as a part of Task Force 77 with a mix of A-1s and A-4 Skyhawks (see Figure 3.5).[14] The

11 Carl Berger, *The United States Air Force in Southeast Asia, 1961–1973* (Washington, DC: Office of Air Force History, 1984), 69; Project CHECO, *Rolling Thunder: March–June 1965* (HQ PACAF: Tactical Evaluation Team, 1966), 6–7; Editorial Note, *Foreign Relations of the United States Volume II, Vietnam, January–June 1965*, https://history.state.gov/historicaldocuments/frus1964-68v02/d106; Rene Francillion, *Tonkin Gulf Yacht Club: US Carrier Operations off Vietnam* (Annapolis, MD: Naval Institute Press, 1988) 32; Mersky and Polmar, *The Naval Air War in Vietnam*, 23, 26.

12 White House Statement issued February 7, 1965 "United States–South Vietnamese Retaliatory Air Attacks against North Viet-Nam 'in Response to Provocations Ordered and Directed by the Hanoi Regime'" Document IX-89, *American Foreign Policy: Current Documents, 1965* (Washington, DC: Department of State, 1968), 828.

13 USAF in Vietnam had forty-eight A-1Es, seventy-two C-123Bs, ten B-57s, three RB-57s, thirty F-100s, six F-102s, twelve RF-101s, twenty-two O-1Fs plus auxiliary. In Thailand eighteen F-105s, fifteen F-100s, four F-102s, ten T-28s, ten RT-28s, and eight search-and-rescue helicopters. Jacob Van Staaveren, *USAF Plans and Operations in Southeast Asia 1965* (Washington, DC: USAF Historical Division Liaison, October 1966), 2.

14 The Navy operated F-8E, F-4B, A-4C, and A-1 aircraft aboard the Hancock, Ranger, and Coral Seas, although the average number of carriers in Task Force 77 would be two. Marolda, *Approaching Storm*, 81; Norman Polmar and Edward Moraldo, *Naval Air War: The Rolling Thunder Campaign* (Washington, DC: Department of the Navy, 2015), 5; Sherwood, *Afterburner*, 8. For an overview of Navy Carrier operations see Francillion, *Tonkin Gulf Yacht Club*; Peter Mersky, *US Navy and Marine Corps A-4 Skyhawk Units of*

Figure 3.1 A-1H Skyraider

Navy also soon flew its higher-performance F-4B Phantom IIs in increasing numbers.[15] The Marine Corps deployed A-4s, F-8E Crusaders, and

the Vietnam War (New York: Osprey, 2007); Richard Burgess and Rosario Rausa, *US Navy A-1 Skyraider Units of the Vietnam War* (New York: Osprey, 2009).

15 Mersky and Polmar, *The Naval Air War in Vietnam*, 65.

Figure 3.2 F-100 Super Sabre

Figure 3.3 F-105 Thunderchief

Figure 3.4 F-4 Phantom II

Figure 3.5 A-4 Skyhawk

F-4Bs to South Vietnam to support marine ground forces.[16] In addition, the RVNAF initially flew in Flaming Dart, but as the air threat increased and the political situation remained unstable, it focused instead on operations in South Vietnam.[17]

Following Flaming Dart, the JCS recommended escalating to an eight-week, later expanded to a twelve-week, air campaign codenamed Rolling Thunder.[18] The plan called for two to four strikes per week against fixed military and transportation targets from the DMZ along the 17th parallel northward to the 19th parallel (see Map 3.1). Strikes later expanded to the 20th parallel just above the city of Thanh Hoa.[19] The approved target list progressively expanded northward, with an incremental increase in the number of authorized strikes. By gradually increasing pressure, the expectation was that the risk of further strikes would compel Hanoi to stop supporting the VC and cease the deployment of NVA infantry units to South Vietnam.[20] The bombing of North Vietnam also was thought to bolster the flagging morale of the South Vietnamese.[21] The JCS further called for additional combat aircraft,

[16] Most Marine missions were flown in support of friendly forces in South Vietnam. Jack Shulimson and Charles Johnson, *U.S. Marines in Vietnam: The Landing and the Buildup 1965* (Washington, DC: History and Museums Division Headquarters Marine Corps, 1978), 149–150, 154; Keith McCutcheon, "Marine Aviation in Vietnam, 1962–1970" in *The Marines in Vietnam 1954–1973: An Anthology and Annotated Bibliography* (Washington, DC: History and Museums Division Headquarters Marine Corps, 1985), 265; Mersky and Polmar, *The Naval Air War in Vietnam*, 86–87.

[17] The RVNAF had ninety-two A-1Hs by 1965. Robert Futrell, *The Advisory Years to 1965* (Washington, DC: Office of Air Force History, 1981), 263.

[18] US Joint Chiefs of Staff, "Memorandum from the Joint Chiefs of Staff to Secretary of Defense McNamara" JCSM 100-65, February 11, 1965, www.history.state.gov/historicaldocuments/frus1964-68v02/d109; Mark Clodfelter, *The Limits of Air Power: The American Bombing of North Vietnam* (New York: Free Press, 1989), 8; Van Staaveren, *USAF Plans and Operations in Southeast Asia 1965*, 25; U. S. Grant Sharp, *Strategy for Defeat: Vietnam in Retrospective* (San Francisco, CA: Presidio Press, 1978), 69; Tilford, *Crosswinds*, 69.

[19] Project CHECO, *Rolling Thunder: March–June 1965*, 13–14; Van Staaveren, *USAF Plans and Operations in Southeast Asia 1965*, 8; William Momyer, *Airpower in Three Wars* (Maxwell AFB, AL: Air University Press, 2003), 21; Westmoreland, *A Soldier Reports*, 118.

[20] "Notes on a Meeting, White House" December 1, 1964, *Foreign Relations of the United States, 1964–1968 Volume I, Vietnam 1964*, www.history.state.gov/historicaldocuments/frus1964-68v01/d432; William Bundy and J. McNaughton, "Courses of Action in Southeast Asia" Paper Prepared for the National Security Council Working Group, November 21, 1964, *Foreign Relations of the United States 1964–1968 Volume I, Vietnam 1964*, https://1997–2001.state.gov/about_state/history/vol_i/393_440.html; CIA, *An Evaluation of Allied (US and GVN) Air Attacks against North Vietnam*, November 8, 1965, 1, 9, www.cia.gov/library/readingroom/document/cia-rdp79t00472a000800020017-1; Clodfelter, *The Limits of Air Power*, 80; Tilford, *Crosswinds*, 70.

[21] Westmoreland, *A Soldier Reports*, 119.

Map 3.1 North Vietnam

including deploying thirty B-52 Stratofortresses to Guam (see Figure 3.6). However, given the air defenses in North Vietnam, the bombers would primarily fly in South Vietnam and later in Laos and Cambodia.[22]

[22] Van Staaveren, *USAF Plans and Operations in Southeast Asia 1965*, 9; B-52s would also conduct air interdiction strikes on the Ho Chi Minh Trail in southern Laos.

Figure 3.6 B-52 Stratofortress

Weather, Geography, Cover, and Civilians

Environmental conditions had a significant impact on US air operations in Southeast Asia.[23] Vietnam is roughly the size of California, and the variation in geography impacted local climate patterns. In North Vietnam, between the 17th and 20th parallels, the weather from February until mid-May was characterized by low cloud cover with solid decks at medium altitude. Weather was usually worse in the morning, with gradual improvement throughout the day.[24] By June, the clouds began to clear, for better flight operations until the rainy monsoon season arrived in August.[25]

[23] Tilford, *Crosswinds*, 75.
[24] Project CHECO, *Impact of Darkness and Weather on Air Operations in SEA* (HQ PACAF: Tactical Evaluation Team, 1969), 6; Townsend Hoopes, *The Limits of Intervention* (New York: McKay, 1969), 77.
[25] Sharp, *Strategy for Defeat*, 66; Project CHECO, *Rolling Thunder: March–June 1965*, 37; Clodfelter, *The Limits of Air Power*, 133.

In addition to clouds, the ground cover of southern North Vietnam provided forests and dense vegetation to disperse men, vehicles, and supplies. Though it did not have the triple-layer jungle canopies of southern Laos and South Vietnam, the foliage was sufficient to conceal troops and trucks from armed recce sorties.

While ground cover degraded the ability of US airmen to locate NVA forces, overall, the geography in southern North Vietnam, from the DMZ northward to the city of Vinh at the 19th parallel, was conducive for air operations. The region is a narrow strip of land 25–40 miles wide. A mountain range runs north–south along the border, with peaks topping 5,000 feet. The Ho Chi Minh Trailhead originated in this area and crossed into Laos at two major mountain passes.[26] In contrast to the western border, the coastal region consists of flat arable terrain. The restricted topography channeled traffic down two north–south highways and a rail line. These terrain features assisted US air-to-ground operations by funneling NVA supply lines along predictable routes.

Southern North Vietnam was thinly populated, with only the two cities of Thanh Hoa and Vinh. Most people lived in small hamlets along the eastern coast or scattered along the north–south highways a few miles inland. Overall, the dispersed population did not limit US air operations south of the 20th parallel.

Rolling Thunder

On February 13, 1965, President Johnson approved Rolling Thunder, "a program of measured and limited air action jointly with the [South Vietnamese] against selected military targets in [North Vietnam]."[27] Following a delay of two weeks, where the South Vietnamese countered yet another coup, Rolling Thunder commenced on March 2 with a strike package of 104 USAF and 28 RVNAF aircraft attacking a small naval base and nearby ammo depot just north of the DMZ.[28] The air raid damaged the targets but lost six aircraft to enemy flak.[29] On March 14,

26 Project CHECO, *Impact of Darkness and Weather on Air Operations in SEA*, 2.

27 *Pentagon Papers* Gravel Edition (1971), Vol. 3, "The Air War in North Vietnam: Rolling Thunder Begins, February–June 1965" (Boston, MA: Beacon Press, 1971).

28 Project CHECO, *Rolling Thunder: March–June 1965*, 16; *Pentagon Papers*, "The Air War in North Vietnam: Rolling Thunder Begins, February–June 1965"; CIA, *An Evaluation of Allied Air Attacks against North Vietnam*, November 8, 1965, 10; Tilford, *Crosswinds*, 69.

29 Project CHECO, *Rolling Thunder: March–June 1965*, 22; Van Staaveren, *USAF Plans and Operations in Southeast Asia 1965*, 13.

twenty-four RVNAF A-1s, supported by USAF fighters, struck an NVA barracks on Tiger Island, twenty miles off the coast, and the following day a combination of 137 USAF and US Navy (USN) aircraft attacked an ammunition depot in southern North Vietnam.[30]

Meanwhile, on March 8, the first US combat ground units arrived with two Marine battalions landing on the beach at Da Nang.[31] On March 15, following a policy review of Southeast Asia, President Johnson authorized more troops and aircraft.[32] While he backed off insisting on combined airstrikes with RVNAF aircraft, Johnson continued to restrict airstrikes in the North to pre-approved targets.[33]

Aircraft losses over North Vietnam prompted the adaptation of US air tactics during late March and early April to include fewer large strike packages. Seven to ten fixed targets were approved weekly, along with daily armed recce sorties assigned to attack vehicles and rolling stock.[34] The effectiveness of the North Vietnamese early warning system forced the United States to shift its targeting priority in late March to strike nine radar sites.[35] By April, the CIA's (Central Intelligence Agency) initial assessment was that Rolling Thunder had so far been ineffective, as the limited number of airstrikes on North Vietnamese military facilities had failed to compel Hanoi to reconsider its policy regarding South Vietnam.[36]

Following another policy review in early April, Johnson approved National Security Action Memo 328, a directive to "continue roughly the present slowly ascending tempo of Rolling Thunder operations."[37]

[30] Project CHECO, *Rolling Thunder: March–June 1965*, 25; Van Staaveren, *USAF Plans and Operations in Southeast Asia 1965*, 13; Sharp, *Strategy for Defeat*, 65.

[31] George Hoffman, *The Path to War: U.S. Marine Corps Operations in Southeast Asia 1961 to 1965* (Quantico, VA: History Division of Marine Corps University, 2014), 93.

[32] Westmoreland, *A Soldier Reports*, 124.

[33] Van Staaveren, *USAF Plans and Operations in Southeast Asia 1965*, 20; *Pentagon Papers*, "The Air War in North Vietnam: Rolling Thunder Begins, February–June 1965"; Sharp, *Strategy for Defeat*, 66.

[34] Project CHECO, *Rolling Thunder: March–June 1965*, 26; Though most airstrikes consisted of fifteen or fewer aircraft, the allies conducted several large raids, such as an eighty-one-aircraft attack on the Phu Van supply depot on March 19 and a thirty-four-aircraft raid on the Vu Con army barracks on March 21. Sharp, *Strategy for Defeat*, 69.

[35] CIA, *An Evaluation of Allied (US and GVN) Air Attacks against North Vietnam*, November 8, 1965, 10. The North Vietnamese radars, however, proved resilient to airstrikes. Project CHECO, *Rolling Thunder: March–June 1965*, 27.

[36] John McCone, "Letter from Director of Central Intelligence McCone to President Johnson," April 2, 1965, https://history.state.gov/historicaldocuments/frus1964-68v02/d234; Sharp, *Strategy for Defeat*, 72.

[37] National Security Action Memorandum No. 328, April 6, 1965, https://fas.org/irp/offdocs/nsam-lbj/nsam-328.htm; *Pentagon Papers*, "The Air War in North Vietnam: Rolling Thunder Begins, February–June 1965"; Sharp, *Strategy for Defeat*, 70.

On April 7, under increasing domestic and international criticism, Johnson announced his willingness for "unconditional discussions" with Hanoi.[38] North Vietnam responded by demanding a complete withdrawal as a precursor to any negotiations.[39] Rolling Thunder shifted from striking military facilities to targeting transportation in early April.[40] Of note on April 3, the USAF conducted two strikes on a key choke point at the heavily defended Thanh Hoa rail and road bridge.[41]

Rolling Thunder attacked transportation targets south of the 20th parallel through April.[42] Most of the assigned fixed targets were bridges, but armed recce missions also continued to be authorized, with sorties flown day and night.[43] At a conference in Honolulu on April 20, Secretary of Defense Robert McNamara voiced skepticism about whether bombing the North would coerce Hanoi to accept an agreement. He instead recommended allied air forces support ground operations in the South.[44] McNamara proposed Rolling Thunder should continue, but with more emphasis on air interdiction.[45] By April 23, improved weather increased sortie rates, and a maximal effort destroyed seven bridges. Overall, the Air Force and Navy committed 44 percent of all sorties flown in Southeast Asia toward Rolling Thunder.[46]

The effectiveness of airstrikes depended on several factors, including the quality and availability of intelligence, surveillance, and reconnaissance (ISR) assets; the air-to-ground sensors onboard strike aircraft; the accuracy of weapons delivery systems; the type, number, and quality of aircraft and munitions; and the experience, training, doctrine, and organization of air forces. In early 1965, American ISR capabilities over North Vietnam were limited to high-altitude U-2 overflights and

[38] Van Staaveren, *USAF Plans and Operations in Southeast Asia 1965*, 28; President Lyndon Johnson, 7 April, "Peace without Conquest," Address at Johns Hopkins University, https://millercenter.org/the-presidency/presidential-speeches/april-7-1965-address-johns-hopkins-university; Sharp, *Strategy for Defeat*, 76; Johnson, *The Vantage Point*, 133.

[39] Pham Von Dong's "April 8, 1965 Four Points Speech," www.cia.gov/library/readingroom/document/cia-rdp80r01720r000500030019-0; Sharp, *Strategy for Defeat*, 76.

[40] Sharp, *Strategy for Defeat*, 67, 77; CIA, *An Evaluation of Allied (US and GVN) Air Attacks against North Vietnam*, November 8, 1965, 10.

[41] CIA, *An Evaluation of Allied (US and GVN) Air Attacks against North Vietnam*, 11.

[42] Tilford, *Crosswinds*, 71. [43] Project CHECO, *Rolling Thunder: March–June 1965*, 36.

[44] Robert McNamara, "Memorandum from Secretary of Defense McNamara to President Johnson," April 21, 1965, https://history.state.gov/historicaldocuments/frus1964-68v02/d265.

[45] Project CHECO, *Rolling Thunder: March–June 1965*, 43; *Pentagon Papers*, "The Air War in North Vietnam: Rolling Thunder Begins, February–June 1965."

[46] Project CHECO, *Rolling Thunder: March–June 1965*, 37.

medium-altitude tactical reconnaissance (tac recce) missions. A combination of cloud cover and altitude restrictions, which kept tac recce flying above the flak and clouds, undermined the usefulness of aerial reconnaissance.[47] These ISR assets utilized day-only cameras to identify large, fixed target arrays such as military barracks and bridges. ISR could not, however, provide timely intelligence of small, mobile targets and air defense systems. The tripling of the number of armed recce sorties flown offers evidence of the lack of tactical intelligence. Armed recce required the tacair crew to locate, identify, strike, and then provide battle damage assessments on mobile targets of opportunity.[48]

The United States and South Vietnam initially relied upon their A-1s, A-4s, and F-100s for airstrikes just north of the DMZ. While these aircraft conducted effective daytime CAS and armed recce throughout South Vietnam, as the Rolling Thunder campaign slowly progressed northward, these lower-performance aircraft proved too vulnerable to anti-aircraft artillery (AAA), surface-to-air missiles (SAMs), and MiGs.

The F-105 Thunderchief took over as the primary USAF striker in Rolling Thunder. Designed during the early Cold War, the tactical nuclear weapons delivery platform was a large and fast jet that could carry a heavy conventional bomb load. But it had limitations for aircrew visibility and maneuverability, and at low altitude the F-105 was vulnerable to small arms and AAA.[49] In the late spring of 1965, the F-4 Phantom II became available to the Air Force, Navy, and Marine Corps in Southeast Asia, proving to be a remarkably versatile air-to-air and strike aircraft. As for US bombers, the high threat level meant that B-52 Superfortresses and B-57 Canberras rarely bombed north of the DMZ (see Figure 3.7).[50]

As for the accuracy of air-to-ground weapons, tacair employed free-fall munitions, including general-purpose bombs, cluster bomb units (CBU), and napalm. These weapons were effective against area targets but required low-altitude release in the heart of the flak envelope.[51] As

47 Project CHECO, *Rolling Thunder: March–June 1965*, 29.

48 In April 1965, armed recce missions equaled the number of airstrikes on fixed targets. By July, armed recce sorties were triple those against fixed targets. CIA, *An Evaluation of Allied Air Attacks against North Vietnam*, January 1–September 30, 1966, table A-10, A-19; John Nichols, *On Yankee Station: The Naval Air War over Vietnam* (Annapolis, MD: Naval Institute Press, 1987), 113.

49 Marshall Michel, *Clashes: Air Combat over North Vietnam 1965–1972* (Annapolis, MD: Naval Institute Press, 1997), 70.

50 Clodfelter, *The Limits of Air Power*, 133; Westmoreland, *A Soldier Reports*, 119.

51 Project CHECO, *Rolling Thunder: March–June 1965*, 21; The only precision-guided weapon available, the AGM-12 Bullpup, had the disadvantage of increasing the risk to the aircrew, as they guided the missile by remaining directly behind the weapons

Figure 3.7 B-57 Canberra

losses mounted, tactics adapted. Initially, large strike packages hit fixed targets, with considerable air assets dedicated to suppressing flak. Airmen soon abandoned flak suppression, however, as most losses occurred on the suppression missions. Further, identifying flak sites proved challenging as the North Vietnamese dispersed and camouflaged their AAA. Over time, strike formations decreased in size, making more tacair available for armed recce.[52]

The limited ISR capabilities and demanding low-altitude weapons release parameters impaired effective air-to-ground operations in Rolling Thunder. So, too, did the decision not to threaten a ground invasion, which would have compelled the North Vietnamese to concentrate their ground forces. As TAP theory anticipates, the lack of a credible ground threat allowed the North Vietnamese to disperse and hide to mitigate the impact of airstrikes. As a result, even with increased air activity, by May 1965 US intelligence assessed Rolling Thunder as having done little to isolate South Vietnam or compel Hanoi to change its

throughout its flight profile. Napalm is an incendiary comprised of a jellied mixture of naphthalene, palmitate, and gasoline.

[52] Project CHECO, *Rolling Thunder: March–June 1965*, 30.

policies. Instead, the Communists stepped up from guerrilla activity to regimental-sized offensives in the Central Highlands and near Saigon.[53] The most impact airstrikes had against the Ho Chi Minh Trail was to cause delays and increase the costs for the North Vietnamese to maintain their primary lines of communication (LOC). The NVA adapted by moving supplies more slowly at night and diverting labor by mobilizing the population to repair bridges and create bypasses.[54]

In response to diplomatic and political pressure, Johnson ordered a bombing pause on May 13 to gauge Hanoi's mood and "to clear a path either toward restoration of peace or toward increased military action, depending on the reaction of the Communists."[55] Hanoi replied by renouncing US actions.[56] Johnson resumed Rolling Thunder five days later, approving strikes on targets south of the 20th parallel. The Air Force and Navy allocated 260 sorties a week against transportation, military facilities, and power plants near Thanh Hoa.[57] In addition, one strike package per week flew north of the 20th parallel targeting military facilities. Out of fear that the war might escalate should casualties include Soviet or Chinese advisors, none of the targets chosen was close to Hanoi or the Chinese border. The first strike north of the 20th parallel occurred on May 22, and the first strike north of Hanoi in late June.[58] A pattern emerged where the military submitted weekly target requests for consideration by Johnson at Tuesday luncheons in the White House Rose Garden.[59]

Meanwhile, the NVA continued to infiltrate infantry units to the south.[60] These lightly armed troops required fewer supplies than the mechanized divisions that would later fight the conventional battles of

53 Westmoreland, *A Soldier Reports*, 137.

54 Merle Pribbenow, trans., *Victory in Vietnam: The Official History of the People's Army of Vietnam, 1954–1975* (Lawrence: University Press of Kansas, 2002), 163; Sharp, *Strategy for Defeat*, 74; Project CHECO, *Rolling Thunder: March–June 1965*, 45.

55 "Telegram from Department of State to the Embassy in Vietnam" *Foreign Relations of the United States, 1964–1968 Volume II, Vietnam, January–June 1965*, https://history.state.gov/historicaldocuments/frus1964-68v02/d288; *Pentagon Papers*, "The Air War in North Vietnam: Rolling Thunder Begins, February–June 1965"; Berger, *The United States Air Force in Southeast Asia*, 79; Sharp, *Strategy for Defeat*, 81; CIA, *An Evaluation of Allied (US and GVN) Air Attacks against North Vietnam*, 12; Westmoreland, *A Soldier Reports*, 120; McNamara, *In Retrospect*, 185; Hoopes, *The Limits of Intervention*, 48.

56 Sharp, *Strategy for Defeat*, 82.

57 Sharp, *Strategy for Defeat*, 95; Project CHECO, *Rolling Thunder: March–June 1965*, 51; CIA, *An Evaluation of Allied (US and GVN) Air Attacks against North Vietnam*, 11.

58 Berger, *The United States Air Force in Southeast Asia*, 70.

59 Project CHECO, *Rolling Thunder: March–June 1965*, 52; Sharp, *Strategy for Defeat*, 86; Rusk, *As I Saw It*, 454, 458.

60 Pribbenow, *Victory in Vietnam*, 164; Vo Nguyen Giap, *Big Victory Great Task* (New York: Praeger, 1968), 6; Guan, *The Vietnam War from the Other Side*, 90–94.

the Easter Offensive.[61] As a result, North Vietnamese logistics units could move sufficient supplies along the Ho Chi Minh Trail, even under the constant threat of airstrikes.[62] The NVA adapted by traveling under cloud cover and at night. As US airmen attacked railways, the North Vietnamese transitioned to using roadways.[63] Hanoi mobilized its urban workforce, sending tens of thousands of laborers to southern North Vietnam and southern Laos to repair damaged roads and bridges and construct bypasses and ferries.[64] In South Vietnam, the NVA/VC employed light infantry and guerrilla tactics, which required limited supplies. They also obtained food from local sources. The minimal supply requirements and the resilience of the NVA logistics system negated the air interdiction effort.[65]

By late spring, the NVA had deployed a regular infantry division to South Vietnam with two more on the way.[66] US Army General William Westmoreland, the Military Assistance Command Vietnam (MACV) commander, responded with B-52 airstrikes and ordered his ground forces to engage NVA/VC positions. In June, Westmoreland requested another forty-four battalions to transition from a defensive enclave to a search-and-destroy strategy.[67] These actions alleviated pressure on an ineffective South Vietnamese government, which had changed leadership five times in the previous eighteen months. Finally, RVNAF General Nguyen Cao Ky, who acceded to the Republic of Vietnam premiership, and ARVN General Nguyen Van Thieu, who assumed the position of Chief of Staff, formed a weak but stable government.

Meanwhile, in the North the approved Rolling Thunder target list for June 1965 included more armed recce and additional strikes against fixed targets north of the 20th parallel. In support of this new air activity, the USAF increased its tacair to 193 aircraft in theater.[68] In mid-July, Johnson began approving strikes on a biweekly basis. The JCS 94-target list had expanded to 249, most being military and transportation

61 Intelligence estimated North Vietnam required only 32,000 metric tons per month to maintain combat operations. Clodfelter, *The Limits of Air Power*, 93, 99; Bui Tin, *Following Ho Chi Minh*, 49.

62 Robert McNamara, "Memorandum from Secretary of Defense McNamara to President Johnson" *Foreign Relations of the United States, 1965–1968 Volume III, Vietnam, June–December 1965*, https://history.state.gov/historicaldocuments/frus1964-68v03/d100.

63 Clodfelter, *The Limits of Air Power*, 132.

64 Pribbenow, *Victory in Vietnam*, 168.

65 Giap, *Big Victory Great Task*, xii, xv.

66 Westmoreland, *A Soldier Reports*, 137; Gregory Daddis, *Westmoreland's War: Reassessing American Strategy in Vietnam* (Oxford: Oxford University Press, 2014), 76.

67 Westmoreland, *A Soldier Reports*, 137, 140.

68 Project CHECO, *Rolling Thunder: March–June 1965*, 73.

facilities. By then, 91 of 117 targets south of the 20th parallel had already been attacked, compared to 18 of 132 north of the line.[69]

Air Superiority over North Vietnam

From February through July 1965, US air power enjoyed air superiority. The most serious threat came from North Vietnamese small arms and an estimated 1,426 AAA pieces deployed, rapidly growing to 2,000 by July.[70] The USAF, USN, and RVNAF suffered a combined sixty-three combat losses over North Vietnam from February through June, of which all but two were the result of ground fire.[71] Combat losses were significantly higher than those endured in South Vietnam and Laos. Even so, the Americans considered the Rolling Thunder attrition rate low enough for sustained operations.[72] In response to the increased American air activity, and with the assistance of the Soviets and Chinese, the North Vietnamese upgraded their integrated air defense system (IADS).[73] By the end of May 1965, US intelligence had identified the construction of three SA-2 surface-to-air missile sites.[74] However, Johnson denied requests to strike the SAM sites and MiG airfields preemptively, given his concern that Soviet casualties might further escalate the war.[75] By July, intelligence had identified five active SA-2 sites (see Figure 3.8).[76] To counter this increased threat, the United States relied more on its higher-performance tactical aircraft, assigning to Rolling Thunder Air Force F-105s, F-4Cs, and Navy and Marine F-4Bs.

69 Berger, *The United States Air Force in Southeast Asia*, 70; Project CHECO, *Rolling Thunder: March–June 1965*, 65–66; CIA, *An Evaluation of Allied (US and GVN) Air Attacks against North Vietnam*, November 8, 1965, 13. Admiral Sharp noted the increase in targets but reported it at 236 by the end of 1965. *Pentagon Papers*, "IV.C.7.(a) Volume I: The Air War in North Vietnam," 16, www.archives.gov/research/pentagon-papers. Johnson had not authorized attacks on either of the two MiG bases at Phuc Yen or Cat Bi or any of the SA-2 batteries. Project CHECO, *Rolling Thunder: March–June 1965*, 66.

70 Project CHECO, *Air Tactics against NVN Air/Ground Defenses* (HQ PACAF: Tactical Evaluation Team, 1967), 2, 61.

71 During the Vietnam War known causes for USAF fixed-wing combat losses was 87 percent from AAA and small arms, the USN rate was 77 percent, and the USMC 97 percent. Nichols, *On Yankee Station*, 53.

72 The USAF had twenty-six combat losses in South Vietnam and Laos, compared to thirty-four in North Vietnam from February to July 1965. Van Staaveren, *USAF Plans and Operations in SEA 1965*, 95.

73 Prados, *Vietnam: The History of an Unwinnable War*, 153.

74 Project CHECO, *Air Tactics against NVN Air/Ground Defenses*, 7–8.

75 Project CHECO, *Rolling Thunder: March–June 1965*, 57.

76 Project CHECO, *Rolling Thunder: March–June 1965*, 61. The first US tacair aircraft lost to the SA-2 was an F-4C downed on July 23. Project CHECO, *Rolling Thunder: March–June 1965*, 65; Berger, *The United States Air Force in Southeast Asia*, 74.

Figure 3.8 SA-2 Guideline

Assessing Rolling Thunder: March–July 1965

During the first five months of Rolling Thunder, the air campaign had primarily targeted the capability of the North Vietnamese to support its operations in South Vietnam.[77] Though described as a strategic bombing campaign of gradual escalation, the early Rolling Thunder operations conducted only a handful of airstrikes against a few electric power plants. Airmen instead flew most missions as armed recce south of the 20th parallel, interdicting the enemy's supply lines as it entered the Ho Chi Minh Trail (discussed in detail in Chapter 5) and targeting the military facilities that supported the North's logistical effort.

In practice, Rolling Thunder incrementally increased the percentage of missions assigned north of the 20th parallel while total ordnance dropped on fixed targets remained constant. What grew was armed recce flown south of the 20th parallel, those attacking mobile military and

[77] Charles Kamps, "The JCS 94-Target List: A Vietnam Myth That Still Distorts Military Thought" *Air and Space Power Journal* 14:1 (Spring 2001), 67–80.

transportation targets of opportunity.[78] In April, armed recce sorties equaled airstrikes against fixed targets, but this ratio rose to three to one by July.[79] Even as Rolling Thunder escalated, additional airstrikes could not isolate South Vietnam as the North Vietnamese absorbed the impact of the air interdiction campaign.[80]

The North Vietnamese responded by dispersing and concealing their military personnel, equipment, and supplies and adapting their transportation system to minimize the impact of airstrikes.[81] Also, without the threat of a ground invasion, the NVA did not have to concentrate its forces to defend its border.

President Johnson decided against sending ground forces into North Vietnam, fearing that the war could escalate, as had happened during the Korean War when MacArthur's march to the Yalu River triggered Chinese intervention.[82] However, the lack of friendly ground forces in North Vietnam denied US air power the ability to operate as part of a combined arms effort as in South Vietnam.[83] Consequently, north of the DMZ, the NVA freely dispersed and concealed its forces. The decision to restrict ground operations to only South Vietnam significantly constrained what the United States could achieve militarily and politically with air power alone.[84] Unwilling to threaten an invasion that would risk North Vietnam's survival, limited airstrikes could not generate sufficient pressure to coerce Hanoi to abandon its nationalistic aspirations of a united Vietnam.

Overall, Rolling Thunder from March through July 1965 could not sufficiently disrupt the flow of men and supplies along the Ho Chi Minh Trail or exert sufficient costs to compel the North Vietnamese to reconsider their policy of unification. A single reason cannot be isolated, as

[78] Tilford, *Crosswinds*, 72.

[79] CIA, *An Evaluation of Allied Air Attacks against North Vietnam*, 2; CIA, "Table A13 Ordnance Delivered by Air on North Vietnam, by Month and by Program March–December 1965 and January–September 1966" *The Effectiveness of the Air Campaign against North Vietnam 1 January–30 September 1966* (Langley, VA: Directorate of Intelligence, December 1966), A-22.

[80] Sharp, *Strategy for Defeat*, 99; CIA, *An Evaluation of Allied Air Attacks against North Vietnam*, 2.

[81] CIA, *An Evaluation of Allied Air Attacks against North Vietnam*, 8.

[82] Rusk, *As I Saw It*, 456. There is evidence North Vietnamese leaders likewise believed an invasion would lead to direct Soviet intervention. Prados, *Vietnam: The History of an Unwinnable War*, 191.

[83] Air Force Manual 1-7, *Theater Air Forces in Counter Air, Interdiction, and Close Air Support*, March 1, 1954.

[84] The author is not arguing that the United States should have invaded North Vietnam, but rather that the restraint shown by not threatening a ground invasion limited the coercive pressure available.

several factors contributed to this outcome. As long as the South Vietnamese government remained unstable and unable to control the countryside, the North Vietnamese deemed their efforts warranted. Second, restrictions enacted by President Johnson to avoid an escalation of the war with China and the Soviet Union, along with concerns over North Vietnamese civilian casualties, constrained US air operations regarding the number of sorties flown and the location and type of targets struck.[85] Finally, the incremental nature in which the Americans gradually executed their escalation strategy, including a five-day bombing pause in May, provided ample opportunity for NVA logistics to absorb the impact of airstrikes.[86]

In addition to the critiques on political constraints and strategic miscalculations, Rolling Thunder proved operationally challenging. Air power alone could not effectively interdict the Ho Chi Minh Trail given the minimum supply requirements of NVA infantry and VC guerrillas. Nor could the restricted nature of the airstrikes impose sufficient costs to compel Hanoi to cease its support of the insurgency in the South.[87] Recognizing the limits of Rolling Thunder, the United States responded by expanding air and ground operations in South Vietnam to directly attack the NVA/VC fielded forces.[88]

Air and Ground Wars in Vietnam: July 1965–December 1966

In the spring of 1965, a series of ARVN setbacks led General Westmoreland to request additional US combat troops. As a result, in mid-July Secretary McNamara embarked on a week-long fact-finding trip to Saigon.[89] Upon returning to Washington, McNamara offered a bleak assessment to Johnson: "the situation in South Vietnam is worse than it was a year ago (when it was worse than a year before that)."[90] McNamara supported Westmoreland's recommendation of increasing troop levels in South Vietnam to take the initiative and turn the tide.

[85] Daddis, *Westmoreland's War*, 68.
[86] Sharp, *Strategy for Defeat*, xxi; Clodfelter, *The Limits of Air Power*, 125, 145; Momyer, *Airpower in Three Wars*, 30.
[87] Robert Pape, *Bombing to Win* (Ithaca, NY: Cornell University Press, 1996), 189–195.
[88] McNamara, *In Retrospect*, 204.
[89] *Stemming the Tide, May 1965 to October 1966: The United States Army in Vietnam* (Washington, DC: Center of Military History United States Army, 2000), 45; McNamara, *In Retrospect*, 201.
[90] Robert McNamara, "Memorandum from Secretary of Defense McNamara to President Johnson" Washington, July 20, 1965, https://history.state.gov/historicaldocuments/frus1964-68v03/d67; McNamara, *In Retrospect*, 203.

However, he rejected the desire by the JCS to escalate Rolling Thunder into a strategic bombing campaign aimed at destroying North Vietnam's industrial capacity. He believed that Hanoi would persevere so long as there was hope of victory in the South, regardless of the costs.[91] Instead, Rolling Thunder would continue as an air interdiction campaign but be expanded northward above the 20th parallel to disrupt the import of supplies and weapons from the Soviet Union and China.[92]

On July 28, President Johnson publicly announced what would be a turning point in the war: a significant increase in troop levels to "raise our fighting strength from 75,000 to 125,000 men almost immediately. Additional forces will be needed later, and they will be sent as requested." Another 95,000 would deploy in 1966. He further acknowledged a doubling "of the monthly draft call from 17,000 over a period of time to 35,000 per month."[93] Combined with the ongoing air operations in South Vietnam, North Vietnam, and Laos, these additional troops would support Westmoreland's conventional search-and-destroy strategy. The following section continues assessing Rolling Thunder before evaluating the joint, combined arms operations in South Vietnam.

Rolling Thunder Air Interdiction: July 1965–December 1966

Until July 1965, Rolling Thunder had primarily targeted the military facilities and transportation networks south of the 20th parallel that supported NVA infiltration efforts across the DMZ and through southern Laos along the Ho Chi Minh Trail. The air campaign now shifted north to include attacks on the rail lines from the Chinese border to Hanoi. However, Johnson refrained from attacking or mining Haiphong Harbor, the primary port of entry for Soviet weapons, supplies, and advisors.[94] Closing Haiphong Harbor at this juncture of the war likely would not have curtailed supplies and troops continuing down the Ho Chi Minh Trail. Still, shutting down the port would have impaired Soviet efforts to import air defense weapons to expand the North Vietnamese IADS.

91 *Pentagon Papers*, "IV.C.7.(a) Volume I: The Air War in North Vietnam," 12, www.archives.gov/research/pentagon-papers; McNamara, *In Retrospect*, 186; Gregory Daddis, *Westmoreland's War*, 65–66.

92 Tilford, *Crosswinds*, 74.

93 Lyndon Johnson, "The President's News Conference of July 28, 1965" *Public Papers of the President 1965*, 795, www.presidency.ucsb.edu/documents/the-presidents-news-conference-1038.

94 Project CHECO, *Rolling Thunder July 1965–December 1966*, 3–4, 14–15, 20–21.

Along with the more publicized increase in ground troops, the United States air effort doubled in Southeast Asia. Rolling Thunder expanded armed recce from 4,000 to 8,000 sorties per month.[95] Armed recce was no longer constrained south of the 20th parallel as Air Force and Navy tacair now roamed freely across North Vietnam to exclude only the restricted areas near the Chinese border, Hanoi, and Haiphong.[96] In addition, armed recce tripled in Laos, while in South Vietnam armed recce and CAS doubled by year's end.[97]

Even with this sharp rise in air operations, by the end of 1965 US intelligence presented a depressing assessment of the interdiction effort.[98] Rolling Thunder had not significantly disrupted the flow of troops and supplies in support of the insurgency in the South.[99] Instead, the North Vietnamese adapted to the bombings by diverting 20 percent of their non-agricultural workforce to disperse supplies and repair damage to transportation networks. Imports from other communist countries offset the negative impact of the bombings on North Vietnam's economy. Further, the NVA's lines of communication proved resilient, bypassing damaged roads and railways and ferrying supplies where bridgeways had been severed.[100] By year's end, North Vietnam had tripled its flow of supplies, able to support a 40 percent increase of NVA troops in South Vietnam, which, along with the VC, could now conduct operations at ten times their previous tempo.[101]

Along with intensified air and ground operations in South Vietnam, in the second half of 1965 McNamara contemplated a lengthy bombing halt in North Vietnam to provide Hanoi six to eight weeks to agree to negotiations. Even though military leaders strongly argued against the

95 CIA, *Effectiveness of the Air Campaign against North Vietnam*, January 1–September 30, 1966, table A9; CIA, *Evaluation of Allied (US and GVN) Air Attacks against North Vietnam*, November 8, 1965, 13, figure 3.

96 Restricted within thirty miles of the CHICOM (Chinese Communist) border and Hanoi and ten miles of Haiphong Harbor. CIA, *Evaluation of Allied (US and GVN) Air Attacks against North Vietnam*, 1. At this point in the war, most Marine Corps tacair were supporting operations in South Vietnam, though occasionally a few missions were allocated for Rolling Thunder.

97 CIA, *Effectiveness of the Air Campaign against North Vietnam*, January 1–September 30, 1966, table A3, A4.

98 In 1965 the Navy and Marine Corps flew 61,000 sorties over North and South Vietnam while the USAF flew 50,000 sorties. Polmar and Moraldo, *Naval Air War*, 35.

99 CIA, *The Role of Air Strikes in Attaining US Objectives in North Vietnam*, February 28, 1966, 6; *Pentagon Papers* IV.C.7.A, 56–57.

100 Joint Chiefs of Staff, "JCS Briefing of the Board of National Estimates of US Plans for Air Attacks in North Vietnam, Laos, and South Vietnam," February 26, 1966.

101 CIA, *The Role of Air Strikes in Attaining US Objectives in North Vietnam*, February 28, 1966, 7–9.

pause, on December 24 President Johnson ordered a halt to Rolling Thunder that would last thirty-seven days.[102]

The bombing pause failed to convince North Vietnam to reconsider its policies. Rolling Thunder recommenced in February 1966, with the passing of each month bringing a further expansion of armed recce sorties flown. Even so, Johnson remained reluctant to authorize additional strikes on the JCS fixed target list. In comparison, in September 1965 and February 1966, the United States conducted 6,500 and 6,800 armed recce missions, respectively. By September 1966, however, that number had nearly tripled. By contrast, strikes against fixed targets, which in 1965 had averaged 1,000 per month, had dropped close to zero in 1966.[103] The shift from attacking fixed targets to armed recce reflected how few fixed targets were available and how effectively the North Vietnamese had been dispersing and concealing their military and transportation facilities. This circumstance led to the call by Admiral Ulysses Sharp, Commander-in-Chief of US Pacific Command (CINCPAC), to "mount an intensified armed reconnaissance program without sortie restriction, to harass, disrupt, and attrit the dispersed and hidden military facilities and activities south of 20 degrees." Sharp's request had merit as it focused efforts on the narrow stretch of southern North Vietnam most susceptible to air interdiction. Evidence of the significant impact of such a concentrated air effort would occur two years later, after the Tet Offensive, when President Johnson restricted airstrikes on North Vietnam to south of the 20th parallel (see Chapter 5).[104]

Admiral Sharp further requested attacking petroleum, oil, and lubrication (POL) facilities, severing rail lines from China, and closing North Vietnamese ports to Soviet ships.[105] Since November 1965, discussions between senior US officials had been ongoing about targeting POL as part of a broader interdiction campaign. By the end of the year, Rolling Thunder had already struck four POL sites, destroying an estimated 17 percent of North Vietnam's bulk storage capacity.[106] During the bombing pause, the JCS continued to push for a more robust air

102 Project CHECO, *The War in Vietnam* (HQ PACAF: Tactical Evaluation Team, 1967), 31–32; *Pentagon Papers* IV.C.7(a), 20–26; Sharp, *Strategy for Defeat*, 105, 111; McNamara, *In Retrospect*, 207–231; Hoopes, *The Limits of Intervention*, 48; Tilford, *Crosswinds*, 77.

103 CIA, *Effectiveness of Air Campaign in North Vietnam*, January 1–September 30, 1966, table A-10, A-18–19.

104 Lewis Sorley, ed., *The Abrams Tapes 1968–1972: Vietnam Chronicles* (Lubbock: Texas Tech University Press, 2004), 648.

105 CIA, *Effectiveness of Air Campaign in North Vietnam*, January 1–September 30, 1966, 32.

106 CIA, *Effectiveness of Air Campaign in North Vietnam*, January 1–September 30, 1966, 53, 66.

campaign to include strikes on POL. However, intelligence agencies noted North Vietnamese efforts to disperse its POL. Though airstrikes would impose some costs, analysts doubted they would significantly impact North Vietnam's transportation system or economy.[107] In March 1966, the JCS finally received backing from the CIA, and McNamara endorsed POL airstrikes in an April memo to the president. Johnson, however, remained reluctant to escalate the air war in the North, a delay that sparked yet another policy review.

Meanwhile, protests against Ky and Thieu's regime erupted in Saigon and Da Nang in April and May. The demonstrations produced international pressure for South Vietnamese elections. In America, Johnson also suffered a marked decline in popular support for the war.[108]

Despite urging from the Pentagon, Johnson remained unwilling to proceed with the POL campaign through May.[109] He finally conceded to targeting seven major POL sites near Hanoi and Haiphong Harbor in late June.[110] Three days of airstrikes damaged 70 percent of North Vietnamese POL storage capacity.[111] However, Hanoi had long anticipated such an attack and had dispersed its POL. In the end, US intelligence assessments confirmed that the strikes had little impact.[112]

The highly publicized POL strikes were a minor blip in the overall Rolling Thunder campaign. In 1966, 98 percent of sorties over North Vietnam were armed recce, of which 70 percent were flown below the 20th parallel.[113] Difficulties in deconflicting Air Force and Navy aircraft multiplied with the rapid rise in daily sorties. This confusion led the Air Force and Navy in early 1966 to divide North Vietnamese airspace into Route Packages, which would also be known as Route Packs (see Map 3.2).[114] To the south, in Route Pack I (RP I) near the demilitarized zone, MACV controlled the

107 *Pentagon Papers*, IV.C.7.a, 75–76. 108 *Pentagon Papers*, IV.C.7.a, 92–93, 116.

109 *Pentagon Papers*, IV.C.7.a, 92–93, 118; Prados, *Vietnam: The History of an Unwinnable War*, 159–162.

110 Tilford, *Crosswinds*, 79; Polmar and Moraldo, *Naval Air War*, 41.

111 *Pentagon Papers*, IV.C.7.a, 92–93, 125–127; Berger, *The United States Air Force in Southeast Asia*, 79; Project CHECO, *War in Vietnam 1966*, 21; Project CHECO, *Rolling Thunder July 1965–December 1966*, 64; Mersky and Polmar, *The Naval Air War in Vietnam*, 77.

112 *Pentagon Papers*, IV.C.7.a, 141–142; John Schlight, *The War in South Vietnam: The Years of the Offensive 1965–1968* (Washington, DC: USAF History and Museums Program, 1999), 49; Tilford, *Crosswinds*, 80; Polmar and Moraldo, *Naval Air War*, 41.

113 CIA, *Effectiveness of Air Campaign in North Vietnam*, January 1–September 30, 1966, 8. In 1966, Johnson approved only twenty-two JCS targets. Clodfelter, *The Limits of Air Power*, 123.

114 Michel, *Clashes*, 38; Schlight, *The War in South Vietnam*, 48; Project CHECO, *War in Vietnam 1966*, 52–53.

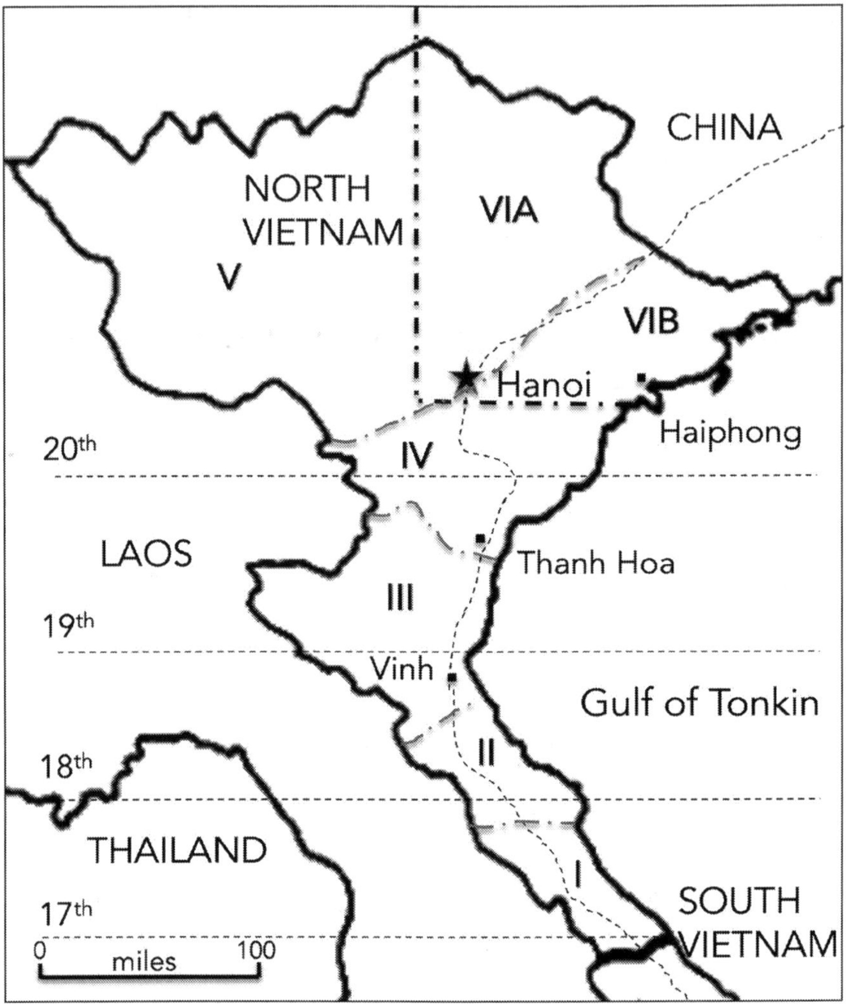

Map 3.2 North Vietnam Route Packages

missions allocated primarily to the USAF, US Marine Corps (USMC), and RVNAF.[115] Along the coast the Navy was assigned RP II, III, IV, and VIB, in reach of short-range tacair launched from carriers off the coast.[116] The

[115] Project CHECO, *Rolling Thunder July 1965–December 1966*, 42; Sharp, *Strategy for Defeat*, 127.

[116] Polmar and Moraldo, *Naval Air War*, 7; Sherwood, *Afterburner*, 10; Francillion, *Tonkin Gulf Yacht Club*, 33. The Navy operated 2–3 carriers at Yankee Station for operations in

USAF, flying from bases in Thailand and South Vietnam, with the benefit of KC-135 air refuelers, were assigned RP V and RP VIA to the west and north of Hanoi.[117] RP VI, split diagonally into RP VIA and RP VIB, had the most lucrative and heavily defended targets around Hanoi and Haiphong. Over time, the Route Packs would symbolize bitter interservice rivalry between the Air Force and Navy, as measured by the monthly competition for sortie and bomb totals, targets attacked, and air-to-air kills.

Intensification of the Struggle for Air Superiority

The North Vietnam People's Air Force (VPAF), initially comprising only seventeen MiG 17 Fresco and thirty-six MiG 15 Fagot fighters (see Figures 3.9 and 3.10), flew defensive CAPs (combat air patrols).[118] The MiGs demonstrated their potential in an April 1965 slashing attack that downed two F-105s.[119] By late summer, the number of MiG 15/17s had risen to sixty-six. The MiGs, operating from two airfields near Hanoi, harassed Rolling Thunder operations throughout 1965. But the MiGs would not become a severe threat until April 1966 with the introduction of the higher-performance MiG-21 Fishbed.[120] The MiG-21, armed with the AA-2 Atoll heat-seeking missile, proved superior to the F-105 and comparable to the F-4 and F-8 fighters (see Figure 3.11).[121]

The North Vietnamese improved their integrated air defense system (IADS), doubling their early warning radars and training ground-controlled interception (GCI) radar personnel to direct MiG interceptors.[122] The proficiency of North Vietnamese GCI operators would steadily improve as they gained experience and adjusted to US tactics. By contrast, the United States had restricted radar coverage over North Vietnam. Off the coast, Navy ship radars were limited in range.[123] In

North Vietnam and one carrier at Dixie Station to operate in South Vietnam. Project CHECO, *War in Vietnam 1966*, 44; Michel, *Clashes*, 27.

117 Project CHECO, *War in Vietnam 1966*, 22.

118 In April 1965 the Soviets agreed to provide MiGs and SAMs, along with pilots and specialists. Guan, *The Vietnam War from the Other Side*, 80; Tilford, *Crosswinds*, 81.

119 Project CHECO, *Air Tactics against NVN Air/Ground Defenses* (HQ PACAF: Tactical Evaluation Team, 1967), 2; Pribbenow, *Victory in Vietnam*, 167; Michel, *Clashes*, 8–10.

120 Polmar and Moraldo, *Naval Air War*, 35.

121 Berger, *The United States Air Force in Southeast Asia*, 74–75; Project CHECO, *Rolling Thunder July 1965–December 1966*, 4; Michel, *Clashes*, 62, 83; Polmar and Moraldo, *Naval Air War*, 14–15. For F-8 operations in Vietnam see Peter Mersky, *F8 Crusader Units of the Vietnam War* (London: Osprey, 1998).

122 Project CHECO, *Air Tactics against NVN Air/Ground Defenses*, 44; Michel, *Clashes*, 44–45.

123 Polmar and Moraldo, *Naval Air War*, 38; Sherwood, *Afterburner*, 82.

Figure 3.9 MiG-17 Fresco

Figure 3.10 MiG-21 Fishbed

addition, the airborne radar aboard USAF EC-121D provided a general threat warning but could not control intercepts.[124]

By 1966, the US fighter inventory consisted of USAF F-105s and F-4Cs and USN and USMC F-8s and F-4Bs.[125] Fighters were initially armed with the AIM-9B (Air Intercept Missile) sidewinder heat-seeking missile, although the Navy later upgraded to the AIM-9C. The AIM-9C

[124] Michel, *Clashes*, 46–51.
[125] On the F-8 see Sherwood, *Afterburner*, 225; Mersky and Polmar, *The Naval Air War in Vietnam*, 71–72.

Figure 3.11 F-8 Crusader

had a more sensitive semi-active radar seeker, which doubled the missile's range.[126] In addition, the F-4, with an air-to-air radar operated by a second aircrew member, was armed with the radar-guided AIM-7 missile. However, all of the era's missiles were notoriously unreliable, and air-to-air ineffectiveness was compounded by the decision not to mount a gun in the early models of the F-4.[127] Despite weapon problems, as the number of sorties assigned north of the 20th parallel increased, so did the frequency of air-to-air encounters. US fighters proved superior in these engagements, downing twenty MiGs while suffering nine losses for a two-to-one kill ratio.[128]

126 Michael Weaver, "An Examination of the F-8 Crusader through Archival Sources" *Journal of Aeronautical History* 2018:2 (2018), 70–71. Instead of upgrading to the AIM-9D, the Air Force developed the AIM-4, a heat-seeking missile with a cooled seeker. The AIM-4 proved to be a failure. Michel, *Clashes*, 111.

127 The F-8 also had an air-to-air radar, but the Navy's single-seat pilots rarely used it. Michel, *Clashes*, 43, 55.

128 Project CHECO, *Air Tactics against NVN Air/Ground Defenses*, 56.

While the United States enjoyed air-to-air superiority, the nature of the surface-to-air threat changed markedly with the arrival of the radar-guided SA-2 Guideline, which drew first blood on July 24, 1965 with the shootdown of a USAF F-4C.[129] As US airstrikes moved progressively north toward Hanoi, the combined threat from SA-2s and MiGs was amplified. No longer could US tacair safely fly at medium altitude. However, President Johnson's fear of escalation precluded strikes on SAM sites and MiG airfields with deployed Soviet personnel.[130] As a result, the North Vietnamese systematically and unimpededly constructed one of the world's most lethal IADS of the era.[131]

Once the SA-2 sites became active, US aircrew were not permitted to fire until fired upon. The restrictive rules of engagement (ROE) further precluded retaliatory attacks immediately after airmen detected a missile launch. The delay in strike approval allowed SA-2 crews to reposition and convert their previous launch sites into flak traps.[132] US intelligence identified fifty-six SAM sites within forty miles of Hanoi by the end of 1965 but with only a handful occupied at any given time.[133] By dispersing and constantly repositioning their SA-2s and utilizing decoys to fill vacant sites, the North Vietnamese negated US efforts to locate and destroy the SAMs.[134]

The SAM threat compelled US airmen to adjust their tactics by flying at low altitude, exposing them to small arms and AAA.[135] Over time, the USAF and USN developed electronic countermeasures to counter the SA-2, including EB-66s and EA-3Bs that could detect and jam its Fansong radar and the fire control radars for larger AAA.[136] In addition, dedicated suppression of enemy air defense (SEAD) missions, known as Iron Hand, were flown by USN A-4s and USAF F-100Fs and later by F-105Fs and F-4s.[137] The USAF-dedicated SEAD aircraft, known as Wild

[129] Momyer, *Airpower in Three Wars*, 23. The Navy's first loss to an SA-2 was an A-4 on the night of August 11–12. Michel, *Clashes*, 32; Tilford, *Crosswinds*, 82.

[130] Momyer, *Airpower in Three Wars*, 133. [131] Momyer, *Airpower in Three Wars*, 133.

[132] Michel, *Clashes*, 32; Sharp, *Strategy for Defeat*, 102–103. SAMs became more active in the late afternoon and evening when there was sufficient time over night for the SAM batteries to reposition to avoid any retaliatory attacks.

[133] Berger, *The United States Air Force in Southeast Asia*, 74. By September 1966, US intelligence located 144 sites for 20–25 SA-2 SAM systems. CIA, *The Effectiveness of the Air Campaign against North Vietnam: 1 January 1965–1 September 1966*, B-22. By the end of 1966, 155 sites had been identified. Tilford, *Crosswinds*, 84. Momyer discusses mobile SAM tactics in 1967 with 200 sites for 20–30 battalions, each with four launchers: *Airpower in Three Wars*, 137, 139.

[134] Michel, *Clashes*, 32. [135] Michel, *Clashes*, 33; Nichols, *On Yankee Station*, 59.

[136] Michel, *Clashes*, 30–31, 44; Berger, *The United States Air Force in Southeast Asia*, 75; Project CHECO, *Rolling Thunder July 1965–December 1966*, 2.

[137] Michel, *Clashes*, 34; Polmar and Moraldo, *Naval Air War*, 33; Sherwood, *Afterburner*, 9; Francillion, *Tonkin Gulf Yacht Club*, 37; Mersky and Polmar, *The Naval Air War in Vietnam*, 35.

Weasels, were modified with directional radar detectors and manned by well-trained electronic warfare officers in the rear cockpit of the two-seat fighters.[138] In early 1966, the Navy's A-4s began carrying the Shrike, an anti-radiation missile that homed in on the Fansong radar emissions.[139] Wild Weasels received the Shrike later that year.[140]

For defensive electronic countermeasures (ECM) against the Fansong radar, the Navy installed the ALQ-51 jammer in its A-4s and A-6s.[141] However, the ALQ-51 proved less effective than the USAF QRC-160 jamming pod, introduced on F-105s in the summer of 1966 (the F-4C would not get the QRC-160 until 1967). The pod jammed both SA-2 and AAA radars, which led to a 50 percent drop in F-105 losses to SAMs. Tactically, the QRC-160 allowed the F-105s to again ingress and egress at medium altitude, thus reducing their exposure to AAA and small-arms fire.[142]

From July through December 1965, the United States suffered 108 combat losses over North Vietnam. Of those, SA-2s downed only eleven aircraft, and in 1966 SA-2s accounted for only 5.6 percent of all aircraft losses over North Vietnam.[143] Even so, the threat posed by SA-2s compelled tacair into the low altitude regime, where the threat of small arms and AAA was ever present.[144] AAA sites continued to grow, from 5,000 to 7,400, throughout 1966.[145] As a result of the increased air threat and US air activity, combat losses over North Vietnam soared from 171 aircraft in 1965 to 318 in 1966.[146] Though most losses were credited to small-arms and AAA fire, an increasing number resulted from SAM and MiG engagements.[147]

138 Jacob Van Staaveren, *Gradual Failure: The Air War over North Vietnam 1965–1966* (Washington: Air Force History Program, 2002), 163–195; Momyer, *Airpower in Three Wars*, 145–148; Michel, *Clashes*, 35.

139 Polmar and Moraldo, *Naval Air War*, 33; Francillion, *Tonkin Gulf Yacht Club*, 38; Nichols, *On Yankee Station*, 60.

140 Michel, *Clashes*, 35–36; Tilford, *Crosswinds*, 83.

141 Francillion, *Tonkin Gulf Yacht Club*, 38; Polmar and Moraldo, *Naval Air War*, 32. By 1969 the Navy had transitioned to the ALQ-94, which provided adequate warning. Nichols, *On Yankee Station*, 93–94.

142 Michel, *Clashes*, 38, 62, 71–72.

143 Project CHECO, *Rolling Thunder July 1965–December 1966*, 23; CIA, *The Effectiveness of the Air Campaign against North Vietnam: 1 January 1965–1 September 1966*, A-15; Berger, *The United States Air Force in Southeast Asia*, 75; Project CHECO, *Rolling Thunder July 1965–December 1966*, 111–112; Francillion, *Tonkin Gulf Yacht Club*, 354.

144 Guan, *The Vietnam War from the Other Side*, 95, 97; Tilford, *Crosswinds*, 83.

145 Project CHECO, *Rolling Thunder July 1965–December 1966*, 122.

146 Tilford, *Crosswinds*, 81.

147 Although total aircraft losses nearly doubled, the average loss rate dropped by half from 0.66 percent to 0.39 percent per attack sortie. *Pentagon Papers*, IV.C.7.a, 177–179.

Despite the growing lethality of the North Vietnamese IADS, US tacair retained sufficient air superiority to conduct air interdiction operations across North Vietnam, even to the north and east of Hanoi. However, air operations in these higher-threat areas required dedicated CAPs and SEAD. Strike aircrew often had to take self-defense measures, which restricted their time and ability to focus on their primary air-to-ground mission of interdicting the NVA's lines of communication.[148]

Assessment of Rolling Thunder: July 1965–December 1966

By the fall of 1966, a pessimistic study by the Jason Group – young, independent scholars from the Institute of Defense Analyses – seeded doubts in Secretary McNamara's mind over the war's progress.[149] Their report prompted a pivotal trip to Saigon in mid-October.[150] Against the recommendation of his military commanders, McNamara then advised capping Rolling Thunder sorties, constructing an anti-infiltration barrier along the DMZ and into southern Laos, and limiting troop levels to 100,000 below the 570,000 total requested by General Westmoreland for the following year.[151]

Two short bombing pauses for the Christmas and New Year holidays brought 1966 to a conclusion. The Johnson administration remained divided between McNamara's desire to restrict Rolling Thunder to air interdiction only and senior military commanders calling for its expansion into a strategic bombing campaign.[152] The year had witnessed a dramatic increase in Rolling Thunder, from 55,000 attack sorties in 1965 to 148,000 in 1966.[153] Further, bomb tonnage had risen from 33,000 to 128,000 tons.[154] Still, even with the intensification of the air interdiction effort, Rolling Thunder had accomplished little more than it had the previous year. North Vietnam remained resolved and only redoubled its effort to infiltrate troops and supplies to the South.[155]

148 Tilford, *Crosswinds*, 84. 149 Tilford, *Crosswinds*, 88.

150 *Pentagon Papers*, IV.C.7.a, 143, 149; Andrew Krepinevich, *The Army and Vietnam* (Baltimore, MD: Johns Hopkins University Press, 1986), 183; Clodfelter, *The Limits of Air Power*, 123.

151 *Pentagon Papers*, IV.C.7.a, 162; Bui Tin, *Following Ho Chi Minh*, 48; Tilford, *Crosswinds*, 89.

152 Sharp, *Strategy for Defeat*, 124. 153 Tilford, *Crosswinds*, 81.

154 While the air interdiction effort increased the number of Rolling Thunder sorties flown, strikes against the JCS master targeting list fell from 158 in 1965 to 27 in 1966. Even though fixed target strikes decreased, there were more attacks north of the 20th parallel, to include Petroleum, Oil, and Lubrication (POL) storage sites.

155 *Pentagon Papers*, IV.C.7.a, 177–179.

Combined Armed Operations in South Vietnam: July 1965–December 1966

While the Air Force and Navy fought the Rolling Thunder air campaign over North Vietnam, by the summer of 1965 the Army and Marine Corps had deployed 60,000 troops to conduct large-scale operations in South Vietnam. By the fall, this number had risen rapidly to 153,000.[156] In September 1965, US and South Vietnamese Marines in the northern-most military region near the DMZ commenced offensive operations, including an amphibious assault along the central coast south of DaNang. The US Army's 1st Infantry Division deployed to engage the VC near Saigon.[157] In the Central Highlands, the NVA's October siege of the special forces camp at Plei Me set conditions for the first major *search-and-destroy* operation to be carried out by the 1st Air Cavalry Division in the Ia Drang Valley.[158] The *search* portion involved taking the initiative to seek out and engage enemy forces. The 1st Army Cavalry relied heavily on its helicopters to provide mobility, command and control, resupply, medical evacuation, and CAS.[159] The *destroy* part of Westmoreland's strategy relied upon firepower from artillery, naval gun-fire near the coast, helicopter gunships, tacair, and bombers.[160] While ground forces depended on fixed-wing air support, these elite ground units, armed with helicopters and artillery, generated their own mobility and firepower.

To coordinate air-to-ground activity, the Army and Air Force had in place by August 1965 a Joint Air–Ground Operation System, which fell under MACV"s command and control organization. MACV divided South Vietnam into four areas of responsibility corresponding to the ARVNs four military regions (see Map 3.3).[161] In addition, the Army's

[156] Van Staaveren, *USAF Plans and Operations in Southeast Asia 1965*, 53.

[157] John Carland, *Stemming the Tide: May 1965 to October 1966 Combat Operations* (Washington, DC: Center of Military History, 2000), 74; Westmoreland, *A Soldier Reports*, 163; Vo Nguyen Giap, *Big Victory Great Task* (New York: Praeger, 1968), 7.

[158] Van Staaveren, *USAF Plans and Operations in Southeast Asia 1965*, 54; Vinh-Loc, *Why Pleime?* (Pleiku: Information Ministry, 1966), 49; Schlight, *The War in South Vietnam*, 100. The 1st Cavalry and 1st Infantry Divisions deployed to Vietnam during this period. Carland, *Stemming the Tide*, 51, 68, 99; Warren Wilkins, *Grab Their Belts to Fight Them: The Viet Cong's Big Unit War against the U.S., 1965–1966* (Annapolis, MD: Naval Institute Press, 2011), 82–95.

[159] Shelby Stanton, *The Rise and Fall of an American Army: U.S. Ground Forces in Vietnam 1965–1973* (San Francisco: Presidio, 1985), 91–92; Daddis, *Westmoreland's War*, 95.

[160] Carland, *Stemming the Tide*, 359–361; Giap, *Big Victory Great Task*, 40; Rusk, *As I Saw It*, 452.

[161] Donald Mrozek, *Air Power and the Ground War in Vietnam: Ideas and Actions* (Maxwell AFB, AL: Air University Press, 1988), 38.

Map 3.3 South Vietnam's four military regions

Air–Ground System (AAGS) consisted of dedicated units, personnel, and communication networks to coordinate CAS and tac recce requests from the USAF's tactical air control system (TACS). The TACS supported the Army's requests by allocating airborne forward air controllers (FACs), tacair, and tactical airlift sorties. Meanwhile, the Marine Corps operated its direct air support center (DASC) to control the air in support of Marine units.

Environmental Factors Affecting Air Operations in South Vietnam

Environmental factors of weather, geography, and terrain significantly impacted air operations throughout Southeast Asia. The weather in South Vietnam differs from that in the North, with the climate dominated by two major weather patterns. From late September to April, the northeast monsoons bring heavy cloud cover along the coast, while hot, dusty, and dry conditions persist in the Central Highlands and Mekong Delta. The pattern reverses with the northwest monsoons from April to September bringing low clouds and rain to the Central Highlands and Mekong Delta.[162] The rainy season in the mountains made it difficult for the North Vietnamese to move men and supplies along the Ho Chi Minh Trail across southern Laos and into central South Vietnam.[163] The NVA thus initially timed their offensives to coincide with the dry season when improved mobility allowed them to maneuver and concentrate against US positions. Clear skies, however, also assisted both rotary- and fixed-wing aviation, which the 1st Air Cavalry Division exploited to good effect in November 1965 by maneuvering ground forces, providing rapid resupply, and applying firepower to stall the NVA's offensive. The NVA soon learned to adjust its actions taking account the climate so as to negate the impact of airstrikes, moving men and supplies during the dry season, and going on the offensive under the cloud cover at the beginning of the rainy season.[164] Overall, poor weather, particularly bad with the onset of the monsoon seasons, significantly hampered air operations throughout the war.

As for the impact of geography in South Vietnam, the strategic location of the mountain ranges was the primary reason the NVA chose to launch its offensive into the Central Highlands. From this high ground, the NVA could control the lines of communication connecting northern and

[162] Stanton, *The Rise and Fall of an American Army*, 92; Carland, *Stemming the Tide*, 277.
[163] Project CHECO, *Rolling Thunder July 1965–December 1966*, 9.
[164] Carland, *Stemming the Tide*, 306.

southern South Vietnam.[165] The rugged terrain also allowed for greater depth and secure lines of communication as the mountain chain straddled the western border with sanctuary areas in Laos and Cambodia.

South Vietnam, Laos, and Cambodia also offered a variety of vegetation, including forests, triple-layered jungles, and high grass plateaus, which provided concealment for NVA/VC units to hide and maneuver. To deny the enemy concealment, USAF special operators began defoliation operations in early 1962, a program expanded in 1965. C-123 and C-130 tactical airlifters sprayed Agent Orange over large swathes of South Vietnam.[166] Defoliation also caused damage to South Vietnamese crops, however, and the VC exploited the economic losses for propaganda purposes.[167] Ground cover in South Vietnam significantly impacted the effectiveness of air-to-ground operations, discussed next, by making it difficult to locate and strike enemy forces from the air.

Direct Air Attack of Fielded Forces: July 1965–December 1966

US air power had supported the South Vietnamese long before the commencement of the large-scale Army and Marine offensives in 1965. Since November 1961, the USAF had contributed to the counterinsurgency in an air operation known as Farmgate. Air Force special operators utilized older cargo aircraft, airborne FACs, and light attack aircraft and bombers to train and fly alongside the South Vietnamese.[168] In January 1962, the USAF deployed a TACS to control aircraft operating throughout South Vietnam. In April 1963, the Americans established a tactical air control squadron to coordinate air requests from ground units and train the RVNAF pilots as FACs.

Additionally, DASCs operated in each of the four military regions with RVNAF and USAF personnel assigned to direct aircraft to CAS missions, controlled by either airborne FACs or ground-based tactical air control parties (TACPs).[169] In August 1964, in the wake of the Gulf of

[165] Hoang Minh Thao, *Military Operations in the Central Highlands* (Hanoi: Gioi Publishers, 2012), 79.

[166] Futrell, *The Advisory Years to 1965*, 26, 112–117, 247; Westmoreland, *A Soldier Reports*, 280.

[167] Futrell, *The Advisory Years to 1965*, 113.

[168] Aircraft included C-123, T-28, L-19 and O-1, A-1D, and B-26. Futrell, *The Advisory Years to 1965*, 81; John Schlight, *A War Too Long: The History of the USAF in Southeast Asia* (Washington, DC: Air Force History and Museum Program, 1996), 6.

[169] Project CHECO, "Support Document *Joint Air Ground Operations System* 3," https://vva.vietnam.ttu.edu/repositories/2/digital_objects/550260.

Figure 3.12 O-1 Birddog

Tonkin incident, USAF combat aircraft began deploying to Southeast Asia in larger numbers, including F-100s and F-105s, the B-57 Canberra medium bomber, and C-130 airlifters.[170] The Navy also beefed up its carrier task force and, later in the year, added higher-performance tacair by deploying F-4 Phantom IIs and A-6 Intruders.[171] The Marine Corps also deployed A-4 and F-4 squadrons to Da Nang to support Marine ground units.[172] In September 1965, to coordinate and control the substantial increase in air support requests, the Air Force, Army, and Marine Corps deployed FACs flying the O-1 Birddog, a prop-driven Cessna 170 (Figure 3.12).[173] From July 1965 to December 1966, the USAF provided over 100,000 tacair strikes and 200,000 airlift missions

[170] Futrell, *The Advisory Years to 1965*, 229–230.

[171] Mersky and Polmar, *The Naval Air War in Vietnam*, 49; Nichols, *On Yankee Station*, 114.

[172] Peter Davies, *US Marine Corps F-4 Phantom II Units of the Vietnam War* (New York: Osprey, 2012), 17.

[173] The Army designated the O-1 as the L-19. Schlight, *The War in South Vietnam*, 75; Davies, *Marine Corps F-4 Phantom II Units of the Vietnam War*, 28.

to support allied ground operations in South Vietnam, more than double the air effort of Rolling Thunder.[174]

Tacair provided a lethal strike capability during the day but struggled at night.[175] As a result, all the military services deployed new platforms and sensors. The Army and Air Force deployed, respectively, OV-1Cs and RB-57s. These ISR aircraft were fitted with infrared sensors for locating enemy positions in the dark.[176] For nighttime CAS, USAF special operators had since 1964 been developing a concept to laterally mount machine guns, and later artillery, onto cargo planes. This technical innovation was a favorite with ground troops, who demanded continuous night air support. The first squadron of AC-47 gunships deployed to Vietnam in late 1965.[177] For the Navy and Marines, the introduction of the A-6A Intruder, with its advanced avionics suite and dedicated second crewmember, provided a much-needed all-weather/night strike capability.[178] Despite these innovations, US air power had limited night capability, a deficiency that would remain a challenge throughout the war.

To improve its night and all-weather strike capability, the United States turned to its strategic bombing force as thirty B-52 Stratofortresses deployed to Guam in February 1965 and began conducting missions in June. By the end of the year, the heavy bombers averaged 300 sorties per month, expanding to 400 by the late summer of 1966.[179] USAF leaders chafed at utilizing their nuclear-capable bombers to attack suspected NVA/VC positions. Instead, they preferred to reserve the B-52s for nuclear deterrence.[180] General Westmoreland, though, loved the B-52's day/night, all-weather dependability, and heavy bomb load.[181] However, the bomber proved too vulnerable and valuable to fly routinely into North Vietnam and was instead assigned to missions in

174 Schlight, *The War in South Vietnam*, 325–326; CIA, *Effectiveness of the Air Campaign against North Vietnam*, January 1–September 30, 1966, table A3, A4, A9; George MacGarrigle, *Taking the Offensive: October 1966 to October 1967* (Washington, DC: Center of Military History US Army, 1998), 46–47.

175 Davies, *US Marine Corps F-4 Phantom II Units of the Vietnam War*, 19.

176 Futrell, *The Advisory Years to 1965*, 244–245.

177 Futrell, *The Advisory Years to 1965*, 241; Westmoreland, *A Soldier Reports*, 279.

178 Polmar and Moraldo, *Naval Air War*, 10.

179 Project CHECO, *Arclight June 1967–December 1968* (HQ PACAF: Tactical Evaluation Team, 1969), xiii; William Head, *War above the Clouds: B-52 Operations during the Second Indochina War and the Effects of the Air War on Theory and Doctrine* (Maxwell AFB, AL: Air University Press, 2002), 19; Schlight, *The War in South Vietnam*, 257.

180 The diversion of B-52s and KC-135s to support the mission impacted their training and readiness to conduct Strategic Air Command's primary mission of nuclear readiness. Head, *War above the Clouds*, 18.

181 Westmoreland, *A Soldier Reports*, 283.

South Vietnam, Laos, and Cambodia.[182] The high-altitude bombers initially used their air-to-ground radar for calculating weapons delivery, but this method proved too inaccurate, particularly for employing near friendly positions. In 1966, the USAF solved the problem by deploying ground-based radar stations to calculate the bomb release point more accurately. This technique enabled B-52s on Arc Light missions to drop their massive bomb loads as close as 1 kilometer from friendly positions.[183] Over eighteen months, B-52s conducted 6,800 sorties, the majority in South Vietnam, with monthly totals rising steadily from 27 in July 1965 to 659 by December 1966.[184] Even with the expansion in B-52 availability, Westmoreland's demand for the Arc Light missions grew insatiably.[185] However, the effectiveness of the B-52 strikes largely depended on the quality of the intelligence, the concentration of enemy troops, and whether the NVA/VC had sufficient warning to take cover.

North Vietnamese Army and Viet Cong: July 1965–December 1966

In October 1965, the North Vietnamese planned an offensive in South Vietnam.[186] With the two infantry divisions that had infiltrated the Central Highlands, they anticipated crossing the plains to Kontum, continuing south to Pleiku, and then driving eastward to the coast to divide South Vietnam in half.[187] Instead, the NVA at Plei Me encountered a forceful US presence that spoiled Hanoi's strategy. The NVA initially stood and fought even as the 1st Air Cavalry Division mounted its counteroffensive. The NVA deployed units without mechanized armor, artillery, or air support. Though their infantry's supply requirements were modest, these NVA units soon suffered from a lack of food and ammunition as their supplies in the rear came under constant air attack.

As predicted by TAP theory, the NVA responded to the US air threat by dispersing its forces and moving its division headquarters and supply depots to sanctuaries across the Laos and Cambodia borders. To avoid

182 Berger, *The United States Air Force in Southeast Asia*, 71.
183 In Vietnam, there were insufficient distinct geographic offset aim points to update the B-52 radar system. Project CHECO, *Arclight June 1967–December 1968*, 52.
184 Schlight, *The War in South Vietnam*, 257.
185 Schlight, *The War in South Vietnam*, 256.
186 James Corum and Wray Johnson, *Airpower in Small Wars: Fighting Insurgents and Terrorists* (Lawrence: University Press of Kansas, 2003), 267.
187 Dang Vu Hiep, *Memory of Tay Nguyen: The Central Highlands* (Hanoi: Gioi Publishers, 2012), 14–15, 28; MacGarrigle, *Taking the Offensive*, 62; Daddis, *Westmoreland's War*, 95.

air and artillery strikes, North Vietnamese also pushed their forward-deployed troops as close as possible to allied soldiers in a tactic known as "grab them by the belt and fight."[188] By the end of 1965, the lesson learned by the NVA was to disperse to avoid airstrikes and large-force engagements and only to engage in small unit skirmishes when at an advantage.[189] The infiltration of additional NVA infantry divisions into South Vietnam would continue throughout 1966. The NVA/VC were no longer on the offensive, but they maintained the tactical advantage by choosing when and where to fight. They relied upon ambush and measured retreats to inflict casualties on US and ARVN troops.[190] Though the overall strength of the Communists continued to grow in the South, because of US air power, they could not mass and maneuver to launch a major offensive.[191]

Assessment of Combined Arms Operations: July 1965–December 1966

The initial US combat operations in South Vietnam in the second half of 1965 staved off the NVA and VC offensives.[192] The combined arms approach performed above expectations for the first major combat operations of the war. Conspicuously absent were the inter-service bickering and finger-pointing that occurred in previous and future wars, a hallmark of a failure in joint cooperation.[193] As TAP theory anticipated, during this period the dual threat of effective air and ground forces kept the enemy army off-balance, unable to employ its preferred strategy of concentrating at the decisive point.

After its initial combat operations in late 1965, for the US Army 1966 would be dedicated to the deployment of additional large units

188 Project CHECO, *The Seige at Plei Me* (HQ PACAF: Tactical Evaluation Team, 1966), 8; Carland, *Stemming the Tide*, 302, 366; Wilkins, *Grab Their Belts to Fight Them*, 38; Daddis, *Westmoreland's War*, 98.

189 Giap, *Big Victory Great Task*, 35; McNamara, *In Retrospect*, 221.

190 Carland, *Stemming the Tide*, 153, 175, 260; McNamara, *In Retrospect*, 212.

191 Pribbenow, *Victory in Vietnam*, 191.

192 Robert McNamara, "Draft Memorandum from Secretary of Defense McNamara to President Johnson," November 3, 1965, *Foreign Relations of the United States, 1964–68 Volume III, Vietnam, June–December 1965*, https://history.state.gov/historicaldocuments/frus1964-68v03/d189; Carland, *Stemming the Tide*, 147; Wilkins, *Grab Their Belts to Fight Them*, 127.

193 Such finger-pointing due to ineffective air-to-ground coordination occurred early in World War II during Operation Torch in the North African campaign and more recent days in Afghanistan after Operation Anaconda. Momyer, *Airpower in Three Wars*, 44; Richard Kugler, Michael Baranick, and Hans Binnendijk *Operation Anaconda: Lessons for Joint Operations* (Washington, DC: National Defense University, 2009), v.

and overcoming the associated command and control and logistics challenges.[194] At a Honolulu conference in early February 1966, President Johnson granted General Westmoreland's request for even more forces, with the number of US troops in South Vietnam growing to 429,000 by the end of the year.[195] The Army's 1st and 25th Infantry Divisions aimed to secure the area north and west of Saigon, while the 1st Air Cavalry continued operations in the Central Highlands.[196] Most of the new Army divisions were in place by early fall, and Westmoreland urged his commanders to expand their activity.[197]

Meanwhile, the Marines in Military Region I near the DMZ maintained a separate TACS, relying mainly on Marine aviation assets, with an air wing of helicopters, A-4s, and F-4s dedicated to each division.[198] In the spring, however, ARVN and US Marine operations in MR I were complicated by domestic unrest. Protests against Ky and Thieu's government and uprisings at Hue and Da Nang even drew support from some ARVN units.[199]

Further to the south, joint Army and Air Force combined arms operations, such as Operation Attleboro in the Iron Triangle just north of Saigon in November, presented the NVA/VC with a dilemma.[200] The NVA/VC could choose to concentrate and fight US ground forces, as they had tried unsuccessfully the previous fall, or disperse and hide from air attack. They could then only operate as small units, and then only when at a tactical advantage. The NVA/VC again chose the latter course and denied General Westmoreland the decisive battle he sought.[201] But in doing so, the North Vietnamese also forsook their strategic objective of dividing South Vietnam.[202]

As US forces took responsibility for direct combat action against the NVA/VC, the South Vietnamese assumed the burden of counterinsurgency

194 Carland, *Stemming the Tide*, 161.

195 Westmoreland, *A Soldier Reports*, 159.

196 Stanton, *The Rise and Fall of an American Army*, 97–116; Carland, *Stemming the Tide*, 166.

197 Carland, *Stemming the Tide*, 249; Daddis, *Westmoreland's War*, 78, 100.

198 Westmoreland, *A Soldier Reports*, 342–344.

199 Andrew Wiest, *Vietnam's Forgotten Army: Heroism and Betrayal in the ARVN* (New York: New York University Press, 2008), 59–63; Stanton, *The Rise and Fall of an American Army*, 117–129.

200 Two-thirds of the 1,600 tacair and 225 B-52 sorties flown in support of Attleboro were armed recce. MacGarrigle, *Taking the Offensive*, 56, and 31–59; Bernard Rogers, *Cedar Falls-Junction City: A Turning Point* (Washington, DC: Department of the Army, 1989), 11; Krepinevich, *The Army and Vietnam*, 191; Wilkins, *Grab Their Belts to Fight Them*, 101.

201 Daddis, *Westmoreland's War*, 94.

202 Carland, *Stemming the Tide*, 356; Wilkins, *Grab Their Belts to Fight Them*, 202, 205.

operations.[203] By the end of 1966, the Johnson administration was sufficiently satisfied with the progress on the ground to order General Westmoreland to dedicate more resources towards pacification.[204]

Conclusion

In North Vietnam, the indirect attack of the NVA/VC through Rolling Thunder's independent air campaign had failed to stem the flow of troops and supplies heading south. By contrast, as predicted by TAP theory, a lethal air threat along with effective air and ground cooperation in South Vietnam compelled the NVA/VC to scatter and hide. Doing so, the NVA/VC survived but the Communists had to abandon their strategic objectives for the time being.

By contrast, without the credible threat of a ground invasion of North Vietnam, Hanoi had the luxury of committing its armies to the South. North Vietnam never had its survival at stake and therefore never seriously considered giving up its nationalistic and territorial objective of uniting Vietnam. The North Vietnamese communist government, dominated by the risk-taking Le Duan, had the support of both the Soviet Union and China.[205] In response to setbacks in the South, Le Duan doubled down with plans for the large-scale infiltration of South Vietnam for a general offensive and general uprising for the following year. The next chapter continues the analysis of US air operations in 1968 as the war escalated with the Battle of Khe Sanh and the Tet Offensive.

[203] Wiest, *Vietnam's Forgotten Army*, 49; Carland, *Stemming the Tide*, 152; Daddis, *Westmoreland's War*, 75, 124.

[204] Westmoreland, *A Soldier Reports*, 210–213; Carland, *Stemming the Tide*, 185, 193, 351; Andrade, "Westmoreland Was Right," 160.

[205] Daddis, *Westmoreland's War*, 73.

4 Khe Sanh and Tet: 1967–1968

This chapter continues from the last one by evaluating the effectiveness of US air power in the Vietnam War from 1967 to 1968. The year 1967 witnessed a significant expansion in both the air war in North Vietnam and the ground war in the South. In late April, the United States expanded Rolling Thunder to include a strategic bombing campaign to impose economic costs on Hanoi. The United States attempted to isolate the North Vietnamese Army and Viet Cong (NVA/VC) and coerce Hanoi to withdraw its support of the insurgency. Air power proved more effective in directly attacking enemy fielded forces in South Vietnam, with the ultimate test occurring in early 1968 along the demilitarized zone (DMZ). At the US Marine base at Khe Sanh, under a lethal air threat, the NVA did not disperse and hide as expected by tactical air power (TAP) theory. Rather, it took the risky step of massing two regular infantry divisions in the hopes of achieving a major military victory. Instead, a combined arms operation featuring air power decisively defeated the NVA. This massing of ground forces differed from the NVA's previous tactics of dispersing and taking sanctuary in Laos and Cambodia. Assuming such defensive measures in the past had preserved its forces, but doing so had also delayed the North Vietnamese from executing their preferred strategy of launching a general offensive and uprising. Though the Communists failed militarily at Khe Sanh and, more generally in the Tet Offensive, they achieved a political victory in the United States.

Military success at Khe Sanh and in the Tet Offensive did not produce the political results desired by President Johnson as the North Vietnamese remained resolute. Instead, after three years of combat, disillusioned by its military and political leaders, and with no end in sight, a frustrated and fractured American public concluded that Vietnam was not worth its blood and treasure. Khe Sanh and the Tet Offensive changed the nature of the war as the United States, instead of seeking victory, now sought a way out of South Vietnam.

This chapter examines the escalation of Rolling Thunder into a strategic bombing campaign in 1967, followed by assessing the effectiveness of air power in the Battle of Khe Sanh and the broader Tet Offensive in 1968.

Strategic Bombing and Rolling Thunder: January–July 1967

In early January 1967, the Commander-in-Chief of the Pacific (CINCPAC), Admiral Ulysses S. Sharp, submitted a request to the Joint Chiefs of Staff (JCS) to increase pressure on the North by attacking previously off-limits military, transportation, and industrial targets around Hanoi and Haiphong.[1] Sharp argued that for interdiction to be effective required targeting North Vietnamese supplies upon arrival from the Soviet Union and China.[2] However, the request was dead on arrival at the Pentagon, as Secretary of Defense Robert McNamara opposed any escalation of Rolling Thunder.[3] From February 2 to 12, US and South Vietnamese forces observed a unilateral ceasefire during the Tet Holidays while the White House made diplomatic overtures. The North Vietnamese took advantage of the bombing pause to conduct a massive resupply effort.[4] Only upon the recommencement of Rolling Thunder did Hanoi respond, rejecting all negotiations until Johnson announced a permanent bombing halt.[5]

After the diplomatic effort failed to generate talks, Washington reconsidered Admiral Sharp's request. In late February 1967, Johnson permitted a limited escalation of the war, approving actions so long as they did not risk counter-escalation by the Soviets.[6] President Johnson's decision meant more latitude to fire artillery across the DMZ and expanded operations into Laos for US ground forces. For naval forces, Johnson permitted mining North Vietnamese rivers and estuaries.[7] The Navy also

[1] *Pentagon Papers*, "IV.C.7.b, Evolution of the Air War in the North: 1965–1968, Volume II," 1, www.archives.gov/research/pentagon-papers; U. S. Grant Sharp, *Strategy for Defeat: Vietnam in Retrospective* (San Francisco, CA: Presidio Press, 1978), 125–126, 280–284.

[2] Sharp, *Strategy for Defeat*, 134.

[3] Robert McNamara, *In Retrospect: The Tragedy and Lessons of Vietnam* (New York: Vintage, 1995), 244–247.

[4] Project CHECO, *War in Vietnam January–June 1967* (HQ PACAF: Tactical Evaluation Team, 1968), 88–89.

[5] *Pentagon Papers*, IV.C.7.b, 4, 7.

[6] The White House was less concerned about escalation with China as it was involved in domestic turmoil, with Mao having launched his Cultural Revolution.

[7] John Sherwood, *Afterburner: Naval Aviators and the Vietnam War* (New York: New York University Press, 2004), 12.

moved warships up the coast to conduct naval gunfire as far north as the 20th parallel. The authorization did not extend to mining deep-water harbors, however, for fear of sinking Soviet ships. Finally, US air forces received approval to strike power plants and industrial sites, though some restrictions remained around Hanoi and Haiphong.[8]

In late March, at a conference in Guam with senior US and South Vietnamese leaders, President Johnson approved strikes near Haiphong and further authorized the deployment of B-52s to Thailand.[9] However, bad weather hampered Rolling Thunder until late April and May, when the skies finally cleared to permit airstrikes that damaged electrical power plants near Hanoi.[10] During these five weeks, twenty fixed targets were struck, compared to twenty-two for all of 1966. By June, airstrikes had reduced North Vietnamese electrical power by 85 percent, interrupted 30 percent of the rail system, and disrupted steel and cement production.[11]

Though the attacks on electrical power and industry had disabled the intended targets, there remained doubts in Washington about the overall effectiveness of a strategic bombing campaign targeting the infrastructure of an underdeveloped country. The Johnson administration split between its military and civilian leaders. Chairman of the JCS General Earle Wheeler, CINCPAC Admiral U. S. Sharp, and MACV General William Westmoreland called for a further expansion of the bombing of Hanoi and the mining of Haiphong Harbor. At the same time, civilian leaders and advisors, including Secretary of Defense Robert McNamara, Assistant Secretary of Defense John McNaughton, National Security Advisor Walt Rostow, and former National Security Advisor McGeorge Bundy, sought a reduction in airstrikes north of the 20th parallel.[12] They had concerns not only about Rolling Thunder's effectiveness but also about how further escalation would impact the American population's willingness to continue the war.[13]

The heated internal debate over the future of Rolling Thunder was temporarily interrupted, however, by the outbreak of the Third Arab–Israeli War in early June. After a mid-July trip to Saigon, McNamara returned to the White House to again urge a de-escalation of Rolling Thunder, a recommendation President Johnson ignored in favor of additional strikes on fixed targets and more armed recce

[8] *Pentagon Papers*, IV.C.7.b, 14; Norman Polmar and Edward Moraldo, *Naval Air War: The Rolling Thunder Campaign* (Washington, DC: Department of the Navy, 2015), 46.
[9] *Pentagon Papers*, IV.C.7.b, 16. [10] *Pentagon Papers*, IV.C.7.b, 17–18, 20.
[11] Project CHECO, *Air War in Vietnam January–June 1967*, 106, 108.
[12] On the debate within the Johnson administration, see *Pentagon Papers*, IV.C.7.b, 29–58.
[13] *Pentagon Papers*, IV.C.7.b, 27.

(reconnaissance) missions. Still, Johnson kept restrictions against attacks on Haiphong Harbor and the MiG airfields with deployed Soviet personnel.[14]

War in the South: January–July 1967

While Rolling Thunder escalated in the North, the US Army and Army of the Republic of Vietnam (ARVN) conducted a series of seek-and-destroy operations to initiate contact with the enemy.[15] In January, the allies commenced a major offensive northwest of Saigon, the largest to date with 30,000 soldiers.[16] Cedar Falls had as its objective the eradication of the VC from its stronghold in the Iron Triangle, an area twenty kilometers from Saigon.[17] Air support included 102 B-52 sorties and 1,100 tactical aircraft (tacair) strikes over the course of three weeks.[18] Allies surprised and overran the enemy's base of operations, gaining a trove of documents and disrupting VC activity in and around Saigon. Rather than standing to fight, the VC avoided contact, denying General Westmoreland a decisive battle. Later the Communists migrated back into the area after the allies departed.[19]

In late February 1967, allied units returned to the region for an even more expansive and extended operation of nearly two months. Operation Junction City aimed to engage enemy units in War Zone C, the area extending from the Iron Triangle north and west of Saigon to the Cambodian border.[20] Over 2,000 airlift missions supported the lengthy

[14] *Pentagon Papers*, IV.C.7.b, 80; William Momyer, *Airpower in Three Wars* (Maxwell AFB, AL: Air University Press, 2003), 29.

[15] Bernard Rogers, *Cedar Falls–Junction City: A Turning Point* (Washington, DC: Department of the Army, 1989), 156; George MacGarrigle, *Combat Operations: Taking the Offensive: October 1966 to October 1967 (United States Army in Vietnam)* (Washington, DC: Center of Military History United States Army, 1998), 45; Vo Nguyen Giap, *Big Victory Great Task* (New York: Praeger, 1968), 10, 11; McNamara, *In Retrospect*, 243; Warren Wilkins, *Grab Their Belts to Fight Them: The Viet Cong's Big Unit War against the U.S., 1965–1966* (Annapolis, MD: Naval Institute Press, 2011), 219.

[16] John Prados, *Vietnam: The History of an Unwinnable War, 1954–1975* (Lawrence: University Press of Kansas, 2009), 176.

[17] For specifics on Cedar Falls, see Rogers, *Cedar Falls–Junction City*, 19–73; Gregory Daddis, *Westmoreland's War: Reassessing American Strategy in Vietnam* (Oxford: Oxford University Press, 2014), 106–107.

[18] John Schlight, *The War in South Vietnam: The Years of the Offensive 1965–1968* (Washington, DC: Office of Air Force History, 1988), 349.

[19] Rogers, *Cedar Falls–Junction City*, 74; *Pentagon Papers*, IV.C.6.b, 34.

[20] Rogers, *Cedar Falls–Junction City*, "Map 5," 16, 83; US Army General Command and Staff College (USAGCSC), *Operation Junction City: Vietnam 1967 Battlebook* (Leavenworth, KS: Air Command and General Staff College, 1983), 12, https://apps.dtic.mil/dtic/tr/fulltext/u2/a139612.pdf. 35,000 troops participated in Junction City. MacGarrigle, *Combat Operations*, 122.

operation, and ground forces relied heavily upon the firepower of 126 B-52 and 5,000 tacair sorties. Airstrikes and artillery inflicted heavy casualties, forcing the VC to move their headquarters and supply depots back across the Cambodian border.[21] Still, Westmoreland had again not gotten the decisive battle he sought. The NVA/VC avoided large-force action while maintaining the tactical initiative by choosing the time and place to engage with smaller units.[22] Once again, after the allies departed the VC crept back in.[23]

Similar Army, Marine Corps, and ARVN operations were conducted across South Vietnam. In late spring, as the rains migrated south, the heavier fighting shifted northward towards the Central Highlands and the DMZ, where NVA units were more active and growing in number.[24]

Division in America: August–December 1967

Intense civilian-military, political, and social division in America marked the second half of 1967. As the bombing of North Vietnam intensified and casualties mounted, the debate within the Johnson administration over the war spilled into the public arena. In August, John Stennis, a hawkish senator from Mississippi, used his platform as chair of the Senate Preparedness Investigating Subcommittee of the Armed Services Committee to conduct nine days of hearings. The testimony in favor of escalation provided by senior military officials undermined the message of restraint by Secretary of Defense Robert McNamara.[25] To coopt the hearings, President Johnson authorized strikes on sixteen targets, including the first attack on the Paul Doumer Bridge. At this chokepoint the rail lines from China and Haiphong Harbor met to cross the mile-and-a-half-wide Red River just north of Hanoi.[26] After the Stennis hearings and throughout September, Johnson again toned down Rolling Thunder to provide yet another opportunity for Hanoi to

[21] MacGarrigle, *Combat Operations*, 117–118, 139; Schlight, *The War in South Vietnam*, 349; Dale Andrade, "Westmoreland Was Right: Learning the Wrong Lessons from the Vietnam War" *Small Wars and Insurgencies* 19:2 (2008), 161.

[22] MacGarrigle *Combat Operations*, 142–143, 175.

[23] USAGCSC, *Junction City Battlebook*, 14, 27, 35–37.

[24] MacGarrigle, *Combat Operations*, 209, 215. For fighting in the Central Highlands, see MacGarrigle, *Combat Operations*, 287–310; Daddis, *Westmoreland's War*, 109.

[25] "Air War against North Vietnam," *Air Force Magazine*, August 31, 1967, www.airforcemag.com/article/0712keeperfile/; Sharp, *Strategy for Defeat*, 190–198; *Pentagon Papers*, IV.C.7.b, 90; McNamara, *In Retrospect*, 284–291.

[26] Graham Cosmas, *The Joint Chiefs of Staff and the War in Vietnam 1960–1968 Part 3* (Washington, DC: Office of History JCS, 2009), 69; *Pentagon Papers*, IV.C.7.b, 91; Sherwood, *Afterburner*, 14.

respond to secret diplomatic overtures.[27] In a late September speech in San Antonio, President Johnson publicly announced his willingness to negotiate, an offer rejected out of hand by Hanoi.[28]

In mid-October 1967, the JCS responded to an inquiry from Johnson on how to increase pressure on North Vietnam. They recommended lifting restrictions against all military targets, mining its deep-water ports, and expanding operations into Laos.[29] As a result, six of seven North Vietnamese airfields were attacked, as were all targets of economic or military value, except for Haiphong Harbor.[30]

At the end of October, at a Tuesday White House luncheon, Secretary McNamara recommended a halt to Rolling Thunder and an attempt to stabilize South Vietnam without increasing troop levels.[31] Later that week, President Johnson met with his "Wise Men," a senior group of advisors, including former Secretary of State Dean Acheson, long-time White House counsel Clark Clifford, and former Ambassador to South Vietnam Henry Cabot Lodge. The Wise Men disagreed with McNamara, advising Johnson to take more decisive action.[32] When Johnson sided with them, McNamara offered his resignation, though he remained Secretary of Defense through February 1968.[33]

President Johnson faced intense political pressure from both hawks and doves. In 1966, Senator J. William Fulbright of Arkansas, chair of the Senate Foreign Relations Committee, opened a series of hearings critical of the Vietnam War. As the war intensified and the Pentagon's appetite for draftees and tax dollars seemed unsatiable, a diverse but passionate anti-war movement emerged. On October 21, 1967, the most dramatic demonstration occurred when 100,000 protestors gathered on the Mall in Washington. Nearly half then crossed the Potomac to march

[27] The mediation was in part conducted by a consultant to the Johnson administration, Harvard University professor Henry Kissinger. Office of the Historian, US State Department, "263 Editorial Note" *Foreign Relations of the United States, 1964–1968, Volume V, Vietnam, 1967*, https://history.state.gov/historicaldocuments/frus1964-68v05/d263.

[28] Lyndon Johnson, "Speech on Vietnam," September 29, 1967, https://millercenter.org/the-presidency/presidential-speeches/september-29-1967-speech-vietnam; *Pentagon Papers*, IV.C.7.b, 102.

[29] Joint Chiefs of Staff, "Increased Pressures on North Vietnam" JCSM-555–67 17 October 1967; *Pentagon Papers*, IV.C.7.b, 108–112.

[30] *Pentagon Papers*, IV.C.7.b, 114.

[31] Robert McNamara, "Memo to the President, 1 November 1967," https://history.state.gov/historicaldocuments/frus1964-68v05/d375.

[32] Jonathon Kirshner, "When the Wise Men Failed" *New York Times*, October 31, 2017, www.nytimes.com/2017/10/31/opinion/lyndon-johnson-vietnam-war.html?_r=0; Dean Rusk, *As I Saw It* (New York: Norton, 1990), 481.

[33] Townsend Hoopes, *The Limits of Intervention* (New York: McKay, 1969), 83–91; Prados, *Vietnam: The History of an Unwinnable War*, 213–216.

on the Pentagon. The Washington protest and other large demonstrations across the country reflected a general war-weariness, as evidenced by Johnson's declining approval ratings for the war, which plummeted to 28 percent by the end of October.[34]

In November, Democratic Senator Eugene McCarthy of Minnesota announced his presidential candidacy on an anti-war platform. In response to the growing criticism, Johnson summoned Westmoreland back to Washington to address publicly the progress made in South Vietnam.[35] By early December, Johnson approved all the targets requested by his military leaders except for airstrikes and mining of Haiphong Harbor.

Rolling Thunder: August–December 1967

While in the United States debate over the Vietnam War grew increasingly contentious, the impact of the strategic bombing on the North Vietnamese economy in 1967 also intensified. Airstrikes damaged Hanoi's industrial base by destroying electric power plants and disrupting trade. Exports were down by a third and the total economic suffering from two and a half years of bombing exceeded $400 million. This figure was substantial for an agrarian society with an annual gross national product of only $500 million.[36] However, offsetting these economic losses was a surge in aid from communist countries valued at $600 million in 1967.[37] In addition to the financial costs was the human suffering: 48,000 civilian and 28,000 military casualties and the dislocation of hundreds of thousands adversely impacted a nation with a population of only 18 million.[38] An additional 93,000 men and women were assigned air defense duties, and half a million full- and part-time workers

[34] William Lunch and Peter Sperlich, "American Public Opinion and the war in Vietnam" *Western Political Quarterly* 31:1 (March 1979), 26; George Herring, America's Longest War: The United States and Vietnam, 1950–1975, 4th Edition (New York: McGraw, 2001), 189–191; Hoopes, *The Limits of Intervention*, 97.

[35] William Westmoreland, *A Soldier Reports* (New York: Da Capo, 1976), 234.

[36] Jean-Pascal Bassino and Pierre van der Eng, "Economic Divergence in East Asia: New Benchmark Estimates of Levels of Wages and GDP, 1913–1970," www.researchgate.net/publication/242771349_Economic_Divergence_in_East_Asia_New_Benchmark_Estimates_of_Levels_of_Wages_and_GDP_1913-1970, 15; Hoopes, *The Limits of Intervention*, 106.

[37] CIA Intelligence Handbook, *The Economy of North Vietnam*, December 1972, 14, www.cia.gov/readingroom/docs/CIA-RDP85T00875R001500200008-2.pdf; Giap, *Big Victory Great Task*, 88.

[38] CIA Intelligence Handbook, *The Economy of North Vietnam*, December 1972, 3; Giap, *Big Victory Great Task*, 78.

were diverted to repair damaged roads and bridges.[39] Although the costs imposed were steep, Rolling Thunder did not coerce Hanoi, as the Communists' nationalist message of unification, along with its strong-armed central government, motivated the population to endure the suffering and continue the struggle.

Even with the emphasis on strategic bombing, most of Rolling Thunder consisted of armed recce missions that did not target economic infrastructure but attempted to prevent the flow of supplies to the South. Despite an increase sortie count, air interdiction continued to be ineffective, as evidenced in the second half of 1967 by the infiltration of additional NVA divisions and logistical support in preparation for the launch of a major offensive.[40] One reason for the ineffectiveness of Rolling Thunder was cloud cover over North Vietnam for much of the year, a limitation US air forces sought to correct with new technologies.

New Technologies in Rolling Thunder: 1967

The weather continued to plague Rolling Thunder. In particular, the monsoon seasons dictated when and where airmen could operate. The desire to keep pressure on the North Vietnamese led to new all-weather and night strike capabilities. F-105s utilized the MSQ-77 ground-based radar to conduct Skyspot airstrikes similar to the B-52 Arc Light missions.[41] However, the extended range of the radar sites, located in South Vietnam and Laos, degraded the accuracy of the F-105s medium-altitude bombing.[42] More precise strikes could be flown at night and in bad weather by the Navy and Marine A-6 Intruders, which performed low-altitude navigation and bomb deliveries with their air-to-ground radars (Figure 4.1).[43] These technologies provided additional round the clock strike capability against fixed but not mobile targets.

39 CIA, "The Effects of Air Strikes in North Vietnam and Laos," June 6, 1968, 8.

40 CIA, "The Effects of Air Strikes in North Vietnam and Laos," June 6, 1968, 2, www.cia.gov/readingroom/document/cia-rdp78t02095r000600110001-1; Giap, *Big Victory Great Task*, 80.

41 Donald Mrozek, *Air Power and the Ground War in Vietnam: Ideas and Actions* (Montgomery, AL: Air University Press, 1988) 141.

42 Project CHECO, *War in Vietnam January–June 1967*, 103–104.

43 Keith McCutcheon, "Marine Aviation in Vietnam, 1962–1970" in *The Marines in Vietnam 1954–1973: An Anthology and Annotated Bibliography* (Washington, DC: History and Museums Division Headquarters Marine Corps, 1985), 280; Project CHECO, *War in Vietnam January–June 1967*, 89. The USAF accelerated the deployment of its new F-111s with similar all-weather capabilities, but combat action was delayed until March 1968 and then interrupted after three mysterious aircraft losses grounded the aircraft. W. Howard Plunkett, "Radar Bombing during Rolling

Figure 4.1 A-6 Intruder

Air Superiority and Rolling Thunder

The battle for air superiority intensified in 1967 with the strategic bombing campaign into the heart of North Vietnam's integrated air defense system (IADS). The North Vietnamese tactics adapted to the US electronic countermeasures, with surface-to-air missile (SAM) operators firing multiple missiles per engagement. From April through June, the United States lost 98 aircraft in Rolling Thunder, the highest loss rate of the war, including 11 tacair downed by a reported 431 SA-2 missile launches.[44] The loss rate around Hanoi in Route Pack VI was heaviest, six times that suffered in the southern Route Packs.[45] The US Air Force (USAF) responded to the SAM threat by relying even more on its

Thunder – Part II: Combat Lancer and Commando Club" *Air Power History* 53:2 (Summer 2006), 4–19.

44 Project CHECO, *Air Tactics against NVN Air/Ground Defenses December 1966–November 1968* (HQ PACAF: Tactical Evaluation Team, 1969), 11.

45 *Pentagon Papers*, IV.C.7.b, 31.

electronic countermeasures, transmitted by the QRC-160 jamming pods onboard F-105s flying in tight formations. These compressed strike packages, in turn, reduced the time required on station for Wild Weasels and EB-66 jammers to suppress enemy air defenses.[46]

As for the air-to-air threat, the North Vietnamese People's Air Force (VPAF) capability had improved measurably the previous year with the arrival of the MiG-21 Fishbed. Its AA-2 Atoll heat-seeking missile downed its first aircraft at the end of 1966.[47] The air-to-air advantage at the beginning of 1967 remained with the Americans, however, as demonstrated on January 2 when the Air Force disguised forty-six F-4C air-to-air fighters in Operation Bolo. The F-4s downed seven of the eleven MiG-21s that flew into the ambush to zero losses.[48] Upon receiving the QRC-160 pods, F-4Cs could again escort F-105s inside the SA-2 threat rings, something they had been prevented from doing since the previous summer.[49] In addition, by mid-May, the F-4Cs assigned for air escort were finally armed with an externally mounted gun pod, giving them a much-needed short-range air-to-air capability.[50]

May and June of 1967 proved to be the most active months for air-to-air engagements to date. Relaxing the restrictions against enemy airfield attacks resulted in thirty to forty MiGs destroyed to accompany the thirty-eight MiGs downed in air-to-air action. The surviving MiGs took sanctuary in China or congregated on two heavily defended and off-limit airfields near Hanoi.[51] The outlook for US tacair over North Vietnam also improved with the arrival of the QRC-248. This highly classified radar system could recognize and interrogate the MiG's identification friend or foe (IFF) transponders required by North Vietnamese ground-controlled interception (GCI) operators to direct intercepts.[52]

The MiG threat had abated, until late August when the North Vietnamese returned to the skies with vigor.[53] A smaller number of MiG-21s, flown by more proficient pilots and directed by experienced

[46] Marshall Michel, *Clashes: Air Combat over North Vietnam 1965–1972* (Annapolis: Naval Institute Press, 1997), 123.
[47] Project CHECO, *Air Tactics against NVN Air/Ground Defenses December 1966–November 1968*, 2.
[48] Michel, *Clashes*, 73–74; Project CHECO, *Air Tactics against NVN Air/Ground Defenses December 1966–November 1968*, 5.
[49] Michel, *Clashes*, 88. [50] Michel, *Clashes*, 101–103.
[51] Project CHECO, *Air Tactics against NVN Air/Ground Defenses December 1966–November 1968*, 11; Michel, *Clashes*, 108, 116.
[52] Michel, *Clashes*, 100. IFF transponders are used on aircraft to provide positive identification to friendly forces. The ability to interrogate enemy aircraft IFF provided a significant advantage in separating friendly from enemy aircraft.
[53] Polmar and Moraldo, *Naval Air War*, 51.

controllers, engaged selectively and aggressively.[54] By the end of 1967, the air-to-air advantage had tilted toward the VPAF.[55] In the first half of 1967, the F-4 to MiG-21 kill ratio was 13 to 0, but in the second half the advantage reversed to 5 to 1 in the MiG-21's favor. Also, the VPAF increased its MiG inventory by a third during the same period.[56]

The high-priority Rolling Thunder missions required the dedication of tacair assets for air-to-air escort and suppression of enemy air defenses (SEAD) duty. Though aircrew developed tactics to degrade the MiG and SAM threat, small arms and anti-aircraft artillery (AAA) continued to be lethal, being responsible for 86 percent of combat losses over North Vietnam.[57] Overall, flying in the North came at a much greater risk than in the South. By the end of 1967, even though assigned fewer missions for Rolling Thunder, the Air Force, Navy, and Marine Corps had lost 950 aircraft over the North while suffering 450 losses in the South.[58]

War in South Vietnam: July–December 1967

As US air forces attempted to disrupt the movement of supplies along the Ho Chi Minh Trail, the number of enemy soldiers infiltrating South Vietnam grew.[59] By early September, on the eve of the South Vietnamese national election, the security of US Marine bases near the DMZ in Military Region I had so deteriorated that Westmoreland ordered additional Army units as reinforcement.[60] Unlike the mobile warfare further south, along the DMZ the Marines fought from static firebases, relying upon support from overlapping artillery fire, airstrikes, and naval gunfire for firebases near the coast.[61] Confronting the Marines were regular NVA divisions now with artillery support, forces better armed than their comrades to the south.

While on the defensive until late 1967, the NVA/VC still attacked when and where they could, inflicting casualties even as they suffered

[54] Michel, *Clashes*, 118, 130. [55] Giap, *Big Victory Great Task*, 44.

[56] Michel, *Clashes*, 140.

[57] CIA Analysis, *Rolling Thunder January 1966–April 1967*, 65, www.cia.gov/readingroom/docs/CIA-RDP78T02095R000300120001-3.pdf. At the beginning of 1967, North Vietnam was defended by an estimated 5,000–7,000 AAA pieces. Project CHECO, *Air Tactics against NVN Air/Ground Defenses December 1966–November 1968*, 1.

[58] Hoopes, *The Limits of Intervention*, 76. By contrast, the US Navy downed thirty-two MiGs and the USAF eighty-one MiGs from 1965 to 1968. Polmar and Moraldo, *Naval Air War*, 58; Sherwood, *Afterburner*, 10.

[59] Joseph Long, *Hill of Angels: U.S. Marines and the Battle for Con Thien 1967 to 1968* (Quantico, VA: History Division Marine Corps University, 2016), 17.

[60] MacGarrigle, *Combat Operations*, 209, 257, 260, 265.

[61] MacGarrigle, *Combat Operations*, 261.

even heavier losses.[62] Until October 1966, the United States had, over the previous six years, lost 5,737 personnel. This death toll more than doubled over the next twelve months, with an additional 8,237 fatalities as the scope of ground combat expanded.[63]

Unable to execute an offensive to divide the South, and having been on the defensive for more than a year and a half, the North Vietnamese realized the need to change their military strategy.[64] In July 1967, the Communist Party leader Le Duan revealed plans to senior political and military leaders to embark upon a general offensive and general uprising. The NVA would draw out US and ARVN forces from South Vietnamese cities and towns while the VC incited a popular revolt.[65] Hanoi's leadership, however, was divided over taking such extreme measures.[66] Le Duan summoned the commander of the NVA in South Vietnam, General Nguyen Chi Thanh, to Hanoi to brief the plan to the Politburo and Military Central Committee.[67] Thanh mysteriously died soon after the meeting, compelling Le Duan to delay the offensive until he could silence senior party dissent, including that from Ho Chi Minh and General Vo Nguyen Giap.[68]

In the latter half of 1967, the NVA infiltrated across the DMZ and the Laotian and Cambodian borders to entice American forces away from population centers.[69] The NVA deployed 278,000 troops to South

62 *Pentagon Papers*, IV.C.6.a, 29. 63 MacGarrigle, *Combat Operations*, 440.

64 Andrade, "Westmoreland Was Right," 162; Wilkins, *Grab Their Belts to Fight Them*, 210–211; James Robbins, *This Time We Win: Revisiting the Tet Offensive* (New York: Encounter, 2010), 65; Daddis, *Westmoreland's War*, 86, 139.

65 Lien-Hang Nguyen, *Hanoi's War* (Chapel Hill: University of North Carolina Press, 2012), 101; Giap, *Big Victory Great Task*, 105; Prados, *Vietnam: The History of an Unwinnable War*, 193.

66 Giap, *Big Victory Great Task*, 55; Robbins, *This Time We Win, 68.*

67 Nguyen, *Hanoi's War*, 99. Westmoreland believed his death to be due to medical complications after being injured by a B-52 strike. Westmoreland, *A Soldier Reports*, 310. Official North Vietnamese military history claims he died of a heart attack. Merle Pribbenow, trans., *Victory in Vietnam: The Official History of the People's Army of Vietnam, 1954–1975* (Lawrence: University Press of Kansas, 2002), 211; Bui Tin, *Following Ho Chi Minh: Memoirs of a North Vietnamese Colonel* (Honolulu, HI: University of Hawaii Press, 1995), 61–62; Ang Cheng Guan, *The Vietnam War from the Other Side: The Vietnamese Communists' Perspective* (New York: RoutledgeCurzon, 2002), 117–118; Robbins, *This Time We Win*, 75; Prados, *Vietnam: The History of an Unwinnable War*, 195.

68 General Giap would be brought back to command Tet after General Thanh's untimely death. Nguyen, *Hanoi's War*, 102, 107; Pribbenow, *Victory in Vietnam*, 214; Edwin Moise, *The Myths of Tet: The Most Misunderstood Event of the Vietnam War* (Lawrence: University Press of Kansas, 2017), 113; Robbins, *This Time We Win*, 74–75.

69 James Willbanks, *The Tet Offensive: A Concise History* (New York: Columbia University Press, 2007), 15; Pribbenow, *Victory in Vietnam*, 212, 216; MacGarrigle, *Combat Operations*, 264. The NVA surged supplies heading south, with US intelligence identifying 480 trucks in September, 1,100 in October, 3,800 in November, and 6,300 in December. Schlight, *The War in South Vietnam*, 276.

Vietnam, up from 204,000 the previous year.[70] Facing the NVA were 350,000 South Vietnamese and 486,000 American forces.[71]

The NVA grew ever more aggressive and, at the end of 1967, in the Central Highlands initiated a large-force battle at Dak To.[72] In December, General Westmoreland returned to the United States with a public message of optimism over the war's progress while privately sounding the alarm that the North Vietnamese were preparing for a major offensive.[73]

Air Power in Combined Arms Operations: 1967

In 1967, while the focus was on Rolling Thunder, the US air forces continued to support ground troops in South Vietnam. Though the number of USAF tacair assigned (approximately 400 aircraft) remained unchanged, the number of airstrikes increased by 40 percent from the previous year.[74] Table 4.1 indicates this growth rate in the Air Force effort from 1965 through 1967.

In early 1967, the Air Force coordinated with the Army on combined arms operations in the Central Highlands and near Saigon. By summer, Marine Corps units in Military Region I met the heaviest pressure as additional NVA divisions infiltrated across the DMZ and through southern Laos. The Marine Corps operated its own fixed- and rotary-wing aircraft under a separate direct air control system.[75] Carriers off the coast at Yankee Station also launched Naval tacair to support the Marines and Army.[76] US airmen paid particular attention to Tally Ho, the area in Route Pack I just north of the DMZ. Facing a surface-to-air threat that prevented O-1 FACs from operating, the Air Force and Marines adopted new tactics. Two-seat versions of their more survivable jets were assigned as fast-FACs.[77] The fast-FACs took

70 Pribbenow, *Victory in Vietnam*, 211.

71 Willbanks, *The Tet Offensive*, 7; Jeffrey J. Clarke, *Advice and Support: The Final Years, 1965–1973* (Washington, DC: Center of Military History USA, 1988), 275.

72 MacGarrigle, *Combat Operations*, 434–435.

73 *Pentagon Papers*, IV.C.7.b, 90; Westmoreland, *A Soldier Reports*, 315–316.

74 Schlight, *The War in South Vietnam*, 159, 186, 187, 257.

75 Jack Shulimson and Charles Johnson, *U.S. Marines in Vietnam: The Landing and the Buildup 1965* (Washington, DC: Department of the Navy History and Museums Division, 1978), 152.

76 Project CHECO, *War in Vietnam 1966* (HQ PACAF: Tactical Evaluation Team, 1967), 44.

77 The Air Force flew the F-100F and the Marine Corps utilized the TF-9 Cougar and TA-4F. Peter Davies, *US Marine Corps F-4 Phantom II Units of the Vietnam War* (New York: Osprey, 2012), 29, 69; McCutcheon, "Marine Aviation in Vietnam, 1962–1970," 272,

Table 4.1 *USAF air operations in South Vietnam: 1965–1967*[1]

Year	Tacair strikes	B-52 strikes	FAC sorties	ISR[2] sorties	Airlift sorties
1965	37,645	1,538	14,124	24,373	61,606
1966	73,911	4,290	27,532	59,396	167,492
1967	122,638	6,610	43,600	94,077	372,722

[1] Schlight, *The War in South Vietnam*, 341–343. By contrast, during Rolling Thunder from 1965 through 1968 the USAF flew a total of 153,784 tacair strikes and the US Navy and Marines 152,399. Polmar and Moraldo, *Naval Air War*, 61.
[2] Intelligence, surveillance, and reconnaissance (ISR) listed here are from dedicated tactical recce sorties.

responsibility for visual reconnaissance (VR) and air strike control duties in these higher-risk areas.[78]

Close air support (CAS) and armed recce were two missions for directly attacking enemy fielded forces. CAS was flown in close proximity to friendlies and relied upon an airborne or ground forward air controller (FAC) for deconfliction, target identification, and strike control. The problem of air-to-ground fratricide was significant in South Vietnam, where battles were nonlinear, and there were few visible means to discern the forward positions of friendly troops. In addition, the enemy's tactic of closely engaging ground forces to avoid US airstrikes made the deconfliction of fire especially challenging. Though the US military developed extensive rules of engagement to reduce the potential for friendly casualties, incidents still occurred, with 24 mishaps in 1967 for the 157,000 total tacair sorties flown.[79]

While CAS required detailed coordination, armed recce did not.[80] Most airstrikes in the Vietnam War are best categorized as armed recce. The Marines also referred to armed recce as direct air support (DAS). By contrast, the USAF called these direct attack missions beyond the bomb

279, 281; Peter Mersky and Norman Polmar, *The Naval Air War in Vietnam* (Annapolis, MD: Nautical & Aviation Publishing Company of America, 1981), 131.

78 Over the summer of 1967, 5,400 tacair and 1,400 FAC and visual recce missions were flown in Tally Ho. Schlight, *The War in South Vietnam*, 262, 266; Don Shepperd, ed., *Misty: First Person Stories of the F-100 Misty Fast FACs in the Vietnam War* (Bloomington, IN: 1st Books Library, 2002), xix–4.

79 Schlight, *The War in South Vietnam*, 258–261.

80 Through 1966, most US strike missions in South Vietnam were battlefield interdiction at a ratio of 3–1 to CAS. In November, however, this ratio reversed, and throughout 1967 CAS exceeded battlefield interdiction by 3–1. Schlight, *The War in South Vietnam*, 342–343.

line battlefield interdiction until 1966, when they removed the term from Air Force doctrine.[81] As anticipated by TAP theory, these deeper strikes compelled the NVA/VC to relocate their headquarters and supply depots to safe areas across the Laotian and Cambodian borders. In addition, the NVA dispersed and concealed their troops in the field to reduce their exposure to airstrikes. Once engaged in battle, the NVA also moved their forces forward into close contact with US and ARVN troops to avoid the brunt of airstrikes.

There were, however, certain disadvantages to armed recce compared to CAS, as airmen were responsible for locating targets. This task was always difficult, given the poor weather, rugged terrain, and abundant ground cover. In addition, it remained challenging to verify battle damage.[82]

As with tacair sorties, B-52 Arc Light missions increased in 1967 once the Thai government permitted the heavy bombers to fly from U Tapao. This move increased the availability of B-52s in theater from 50 aircraft conducting 450 strikes a month in August 1966 to 60 aircraft performing 800 strikes by March 1967. This higher sortie rate remained steady through December, with nearly 10,000 B-52 Arc Light missions flown over South Vietnam, Laos, and the southernmost region of North Vietnam. With the onset of the Tet Offensive in 1968, the B-52 sortie rate further surged to 1,460 in February and 1,850 in March.[83]

Overall, air-to-ground effectiveness was mixed. Interdiction efforts in North Vietnam and southern Laos could not halt the flow of troops and supplies in preparation for the NVA/VC's Tet Offensive. On the other hand, as expected by TAP theory, direct air attacks, primarily by armed recce, compelled the North Vietnamese to remain on the defensive through 1967. The NVA/VC responded to the threat of airstrikes by dispersing into smaller units and, as a result, extending their lines of communication (LOC) as commanders sought the sanctuary of Laos and Cambodia for their headquarters and supply bases. Both the Army, with its "search and destroy" strategy, and the Marine Corps, manning the static defenses along the DMZ, remained dependent upon air power, artillery, and naval gunfire. Even so, these effective joint, combined arms operations did not compel Hanoi to abandon the objective of a unified communist Vietnam. Instead, Le Duan gambled by ordering a major offensive for 1968.

81 Terrance McCaffrey, *What Happened to Battlefield Air Interdiction?* (Maxwell AFB, AL: Air University Press, 2004), 15–16.
82 MacGarrigle, *Combat Operations*, 10, 172.
83 Schlight, *The War in South Vietnam*, 256–257.

The Battle of Khe Sanh and the Tet Offensive: January–March 1968

As fighting erupted across the South, Rolling Thunder airstrikes were limited to the southern North Vietnamese panhandle due partly to the early arrival of the northeast monsoon season, which disrupted airstrikes around Hanoi.[84] At the onset of the Battle of Khe Sanh, the Air Force and Navy diverted their air assets to the South.[85] President Johnson's pronouncement at the end of March of a pause in the bombing against Hanoi ended the strategic bombing campaign, though armed recce interdiction sorties would continue south of the 20th parallel. Rolling Thunder had failed on three counts. The bombing of the North Vietnamese economy had not coerced Hanoi to give up on a unified Vietnam. The interdiction of the NVA's LOC had not stopped the flow of supplies, ammunition, and weapons to the South. Finally, though Rolling Thunder had caused some delays and imposed costs on North Vietnam, it had not prevented the buildup of NVA divisions along the DMZ in preparation for the Battle of Khe Sanh. Nor had US air power stopped the infiltration of additional units into the Central Highlands and further south near Saigon for the broader Tet Offensive.

On January 21, 1968, an obscure Marine outpost along the border of Laos, just south of the DMZ near the village of Khe Sanh, captured the world's attention. Over the next seventy-seven days, the North Vietnamese would launch an attack pitting 20,000 troops against 6,000 US Marines and ARVN Rangers.[86] Khe Sanh provided the NVA an opportunity to decisively defeat the Americans as they had defeated the French at Dien Bien Phu fourteen years earlier.[87] The attack might also distract American forces as an estimated 80,000 NVA/VC launched their general offensive and general uprising into the major cities and provincial capitals across South Vietnam during the week-long Tet Holiday in late January and early February.[88]

[84] Bernard Nalty, *The War against Trucks: Aerial Interdiction in Southern Laos 1968–1972* (Washington, DC: Air Force History and Museums Program, 2005), 17–18; Polmar and Moraldo, *Naval Air War*, 55.

[85] Momyer, *Airpower in Three Wars*, 342–343; Bernard Nalty, *Air Power and the Fight for Khe Sanh* (Washington, DC: Office of Air Force History, 1986), 61–62.

[86] Westmoreland, *A Soldier Reports*, 339; Willbanks, *The Tet Offensive*, 23; Momyer, *Airpower in Three Wars*, 344; Hoopes, *The Limits of Intervention*, 138.

[87] Robbins, *This Time We Win*, 222–225; Pribbenow, *Victory in Vietnam*, 217.

[88] North Vietnamese sources do not indicate the North was attempting another Dien Bien Phu but do not provide reasons why the fighting at Khe Sanh occurred before the other attacks of the Tet Offensive. Guan, *The Vietnam War from the Other Side*, 130; Richard Camp and Leonard Blashol, *Ringed by Fire: U.S. Marines and the Siege of Khe Sanh 21 January to 9 July 1968* (Quantico, VA: History Division of Marine Corps University, 2019), 10.

The Battle of Khe Sanh: January 21–April 8, 1968

Positioned sixteen kilometers to the east of the Laotian border and twenty-five kilometers south of the DMZ, Khe Sanh was strategically important as it was located just north of the Shau Valley, a primary infiltration route into South Vietnam.[89] It also sat astride Highway 9, which ran eastward towards the cities of Quang Tri and Hue (Map 4.1).[90] The Marine base sat on a plateau along the mountain range, which ran north–south along the Vietnam–Laos border.[91] To the north lay seven hills situated west to east, protecting the NVA forces as they maneuvered toward Khe Sanh.[92] Alongside the base ran the Rao Quan River, which did not provide any defensive protection but supplied drinking water, significantly reducing resupply requirements.[93] For protection, the soil at Khe Sanh was suitable for digging, a feature essential to protecting the Marines from incoming artillery.[94] As a result, the Marines could hold their positions and, thus entrenched, call in airstrikes during conditions of danger close. The NVA could also take advantage of the pliable soil to dig trenches, which provided some cover as they slowly advanced toward the base.

The village of Khe Sanh had an American military presence as early as 1962 when special forces deployed into the region to monitor movement along the Ho Chi Minh Trail.[95] In 1967, the 27th Marine Regiment deployed to Khe Sanh and began expanding the combat base. In April, the Marines cleared NVA positions from a cluster of hills to the north and established on them four outposts resupplied by helicopter.[96] By October, combat engineers had lengthened the small runway to accommodate C-130s.[97] Within two months, the Marines detected the enemy concentrating around the base.[98]

89 Nalty, *Air Power and the Fight for Khe Sanh*, 4; Ian Horwood, *Interservice Rivalry and Airpower in the Vietnam War* (Ft Leavenworth, KS: Combat Studies Institute Press, 2006), 140.
90 Nalty, *Air Power and the Fight for Khe Sanh*, 2, 21.
91 Camp and Blashol, *Ringed by Fire*, 2, 3, 16.
92 Camp and Blashol, *Ringed by Fire*, 5–6; Nalty, *Air Power and the Fight for Khe Sanh*, 5; Project CHECO, *Battle of Khe Sanh and Operation Niagara* (HQ PACAF: Tactical Evaluation Team, 1968), 44.
93 Camp and Blashol, *Ringed by Fire*, 70–71; Nalty, *Air Power and the Fight for Khe Sanh*, 5.
94 Camp and Blashol, *Ringed by Fire*, 5; Nalty, *Air Power and the Fight for Khe Sanh*, 9; Pribbenow, *Victory in Vietnam*, 223.
95 John Prados and Ray Stubbe, *Valley of Decision: The Siege of Khe Sanh* (New York: Houghton Mifflin, 1991), 13; Camp and Blashol, *Ringed by Fire*, 7.
96 Davies, *US Marine Corps F-4 Phantom II Units of the Vietnam War*, 53; Nalty, *Air Power and the Fight for Khe Sanh*, 8; Westmoreland, *A Soldier Reports*, 337; Camp and Blashol, *Ringed by Fire*, 51–52.
97 Willbanks, *The Tet Offensive*, 20; Nalty, *Air Power and the Fight for Khe Sanh*, 8.
98 Nalty, *Air Power and the Fight for Khe Sanh*, 107.

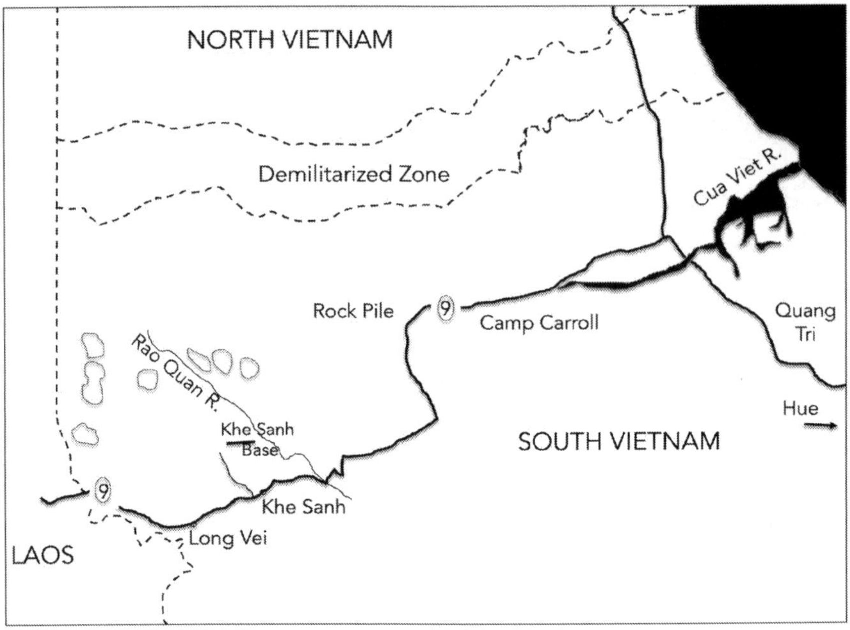

Map 4.1 Quang Tri province

The NVA began preparations for its general offensive in late 1967.[99] US intelligence, charged with tracking vehicle traffic along the Ho Chi Minh Trail, noticed the average number of 480 trucks per month rise sharply to 1,100 trucks in October, 3,800 in November, and 6,300 in December.[100] For the attack on Khe Sanh, the NVA dedicated two divisions, including their elite 304th, which had triumphed over the French at Dien Bien Phu. The 304th approached Khe Sanh from the northwest while the 325th maneuvered to the southwest.[101] In addition, the 320th and a regiment of the 324th crossed the DMZ to the east to cut off the Marines' sole LOC.[102] The NVA had 20,000 soldiers committed against Khe Sanh, with a total of 40,000 in the area.

[99] Pribbenow, *Victory in Vietnam*, 207, 214; Nguyen, *Hanoi's War*, 101.

[100] Project CHECO, *Battle of Khe Sanh and Operation Niagara*, 3; Pribbenow, *Victory in Vietnam*, 208.

[101] Pribbenow, *Victory in Vietnam*, 222; Project CHECO, *Battle of Khe Sanh and Operation Niagara*, 5; Willbanks, *The Tet Offensive*, 20; Walter Boyne, "Airpower at Khe Sanh" *Air Force Magazine*, 81:8, August 1, 1998, www.airandspaceforces.com/article/0898vietnam/; Nalty, *Air Power and the Fight for Khe Sanh*, 14; Thomas Pike, ed., *Military Records, February 1968 3rd Division: The Tet Offensive* (Charleston, SC: Pike Publishing, 2013), 13; Camp and Blashol, *Ringed by Fire*, 20.

[102] Willbanks, *The Tet Offensive*, 20; Project CHECO, *Battle of Khe Sanh and Operation Niagara*, 5; Nalty, *Air Power and the Fight for Khe Sanh*, 14; Pribbenow, *Victory in Vietnam*, 216.

The Soviet Union equipped the NVA with more firepower than the Americans had previously encountered.[103] The variety of weapons included artillery, rockets, and mortars.[104] Though their rate of fire could not match that of the Americans, the NVA still averaged over 160 rounds per day against Khe Sanh.[105]

Three battalions of the US 26th Marine Regiment, each with 1,200 men, defended Khe Sanh.[106] As reinforcement, in late January the Regiment received a fourth battalion and an ARVN Ranger battalion.[107] No further allied reinforcements were forthcoming.[108] As General Westmoreland watched the NVA build up along the DMV, he considered redeploying half of his combat battalions to support the Marines. He ultimately decided to rely instead on air power and artillery support.[109]

For firepower, the Marines operated three batteries of eighteen 105 mm artillery, a battery of six 155 mm artillery, and a battery of six 4.2-inch mortars. The base also had six tanks. In addition, at the Rock Pile and Camp Carroll, twenty and twenty-five kilometers to the east, sixteen 175 mm guns could support Khe Sanh.[110] On the first day of the battle, the Marines suffered a significant setback, however, when an NVA round hit their open ammo dump, igniting 1,500 tons of explosives and destroying 98 percent of their munitions.[111] The Marines required an extensive airlift effort to replenish their stores during the first week of the battle.[112] Throughout the siege, the United States fired 200,000 artillery shells, an average of 2,600 rounds per day, with 160,000 fired by the Marines at Khe Sanh.[113] Dedicated artillery, helicopters, and fixed-wing aircraft supported the Marines. A fire support coordination center, Marine forward air controllers, and a TPQ-10 radar at Khe Sanh directed strikes around the clock and in all weather conditions.[114] The TPQ-10 was similar to the

[103] Giap, *Big Victory Great Task*, 67, 69; Hoopes, *The Limits of Intervention*, 64–65.
[104] These were 75 mm, 105 mm, and 130 mm artillery; 122 mm rockets; and 60 mm, 82 mm, and 120 mm mortars. Nalty, *Air Power and the Fight for Khe Sanh*, 14.
[105] They fired 165 rounds a day in February and 167 in March. Project CHECO, *Battle of Khe Sanh and Operation Niagara*, 87.
[106] Camp and Blashol, *Ringed by Fire*, 11–17. [107] Pike, *Military Records*, 24.
[108] Nalty, *Air Power and the Fight for Khe Sanh*, 25–26.
[109] Willbanks, *The Tet Offensive*, 22; Westmoreland, *A Soldier Reports*, 336–339.
[110] Westmoreland, *A Soldier Reports*, 337; Nalty, *Air Power and the Fight for Khe Sanh*, iii, 4, 15; Boyne, "Airpower at Khe Sanh."
[111] Camp and Blashol, *Ringed by Fire*, 29; Willbanks, *The Tet Offensive*, 24; Boyne, "Airpower at Khe Sanh."
[112] Boyne, "Airpower at Khe Sanh."
[113] Nalty, *Air Power and the Fight for Khe Sanh*, 103, 105; Boyne, "Airpower at Khe Sanh."
[114] Davies, *US Marine Corps F-4 Phantom II Units of the Vietnam War*, 56; Nalty, *Air Power and the Fight for Khe Sanh*, 66–67; Horwood, *Interservice Rivalry and Airpower in the Vietnam War*, 149.

USAF's MSQ-77 Skyspot, except the TPQ-10 was more mobile and better integrated into Marine air operations.[115]

Air Superiority and the Battle of Khe Sanh

In January 1968, the air effort in Southeast Asia focused on Khe Sanh. In early January, a North Vietnamese SA-2 along the DMZ fired at a flight of B-52s, but overall neither SAMs nor MiGs played a significant role in the battle.[116] Instead, the enemy surface-to-air threat came from small arms and AAA up to 37 mm.[117] The danger was particularly acute for tactical airlift, the cargo planes charged with resupplying Khe Sanh. Aerial resupply continued throughout the siege at the cost of four cargo planes downed and another fifty-six damaged.[118]

Unlike at Dien Bien Phu, where the Vietminh had isolated the French troops, US tactical airlift implemented effective day/night, all-weather airdrops, delivering two-thirds of the 12,400 tons of supplies via parachute.[119] The airborne delivery method further reduced the vulnerability of cargo planes to ground fire. At Khe Sanh, the United States maintained air superiority throughout the battle, enabling air forces to perform their missions. Whereas air superiority had been eroded over North Vietnam by early 1968, the United States continued to enjoy air superiority over South Vietnam.

The Battle for Khe Sanh Begins

The preamble to the battle began on January 17 when the NVA attacked and briefly overran a Marine outpost on Hill 881 North (hills were numbered to indicate their elevation in meters). With supporting fire from the surrounding hilltop outposts, the Marines retook the hill and

[115] McCutcheon, "Marine Aviation in Vietnam, 1962–1970," 276; Davies, *US Marine Corps F-4 Phantom II Units of the Vietnam War*, 21–23; Camp and Blashol, *Ringed by Fire*, 39.

[116] Project CHECO, *War in Vietnam January–June 1967*, 73; Davies, *Marine Corps F-4 Phantom II Units of the Vietnam War*, 446.

[117] Nalty, *Air Power and the Fight for Khe Sanh*, 66.

[118] Another aircraft was destroyed on the runway by mortar fire. Project CHECO, *Battle of Khe Sanh and Operation Niagara*, 72; Horwood, *Interservice Rivalry and Airpower in the Vietnam War*, 144–146.

[119] Project CHECO, *Battle of Khe Sanh and Operation Niagara*, 74; Nalty, *Air Power and the Fight for Khe Sanh*, 20, 39–59, 108; Schlight, *The War in South Vietnam*, 285; Horwood, *Interservice Rivalry and Airpower in the Vietnam War*, 142; Robbins, *This Time We Win*, 230; Camp and Blashol, *Ringed by Fire*, 45.

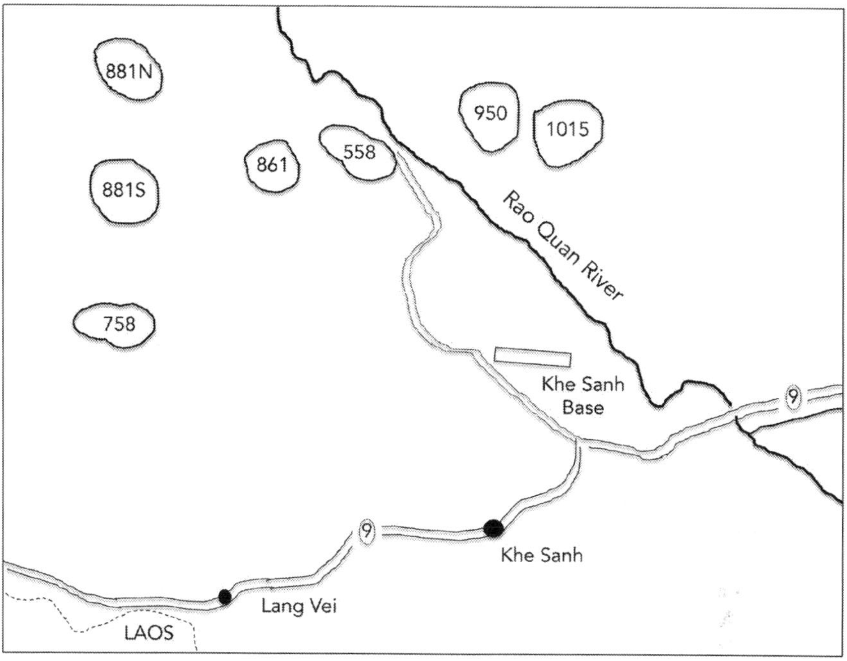

Map 4.2 Khe Sanh[120]

thereafter controlled the high ground surrounding Khe Sanh for the rest of the battle.[121]

The NVA commenced its main attack on January 21, pounding Hill 861 with mortar rounds, but the Marines repulsed the assault.[122] On February 5, the NVA attempted to take Hill 881 South and Hill 861 simultaneously but again were turned back (see Map 4.2).[123] Two days later, the NVA overran a US special forces camp at Lang Vei, five kilometers west of Khe Sanh.[124] In this assault, the NVA employed Soviet PT-76s, their first employment of tanks in the war.[125] The NVA charged Hill

[120] http://webdoc.sub.gwdg.de/ebook/p/2005/CMH_2/www.army.mil/cmh-pg/books/vietnam/fa54-73/ch5.htm.

[121] Willbanks, *The Tet Offensive*, 23.

[122] Camp and Blashol, *Ringed by Fire*, 27–28; Nalty, *Air Power and the Fight for Khe Sanh*, 23, 25; Shelby Stanton, *The Rise and Fall of an American Army* (San Francisco, CA: Presidio, 1985), 247–251.

[123] Camp and Blashol, *Ringed by Fire*, 24; Nalty, *Air Power and the Fight for Khe Sanh*, 31.

[124] Stanton, *The Rise and Fall of an American Army*, 250–254; Pribbenow, *Victory in Vietnam*, 222.

[125] Nalty, *Air Power and the Fight for Khe Sanh*, 33–34, 107; Project CHECO, *Battle of Khe Sanh and Operation Niagara*, 29, 35; Pike, *Military Records*, 33; Momyer, *Airpower in Three Wars*, 346; Camp and Blashol, *Ringed by Fire*, 55–58.

861 the following day, only to be turned back again.[126] There were no further attacks on the hills or main base camp in February, save a 1,000-round artillery barrage on February 23, which pre-staged a planned NVA assault that never materialized.[127]

At Khe Sanh, NVA tactics differed from their usual hit-and-run methods. Now the NVA held their ground; but as they concentrated, they became more vulnerable to air and artillery strikes.[128] Soldiers dug trenches in response and attempted to maneuver closer to the Marines, eventually reaching 350 feet from the base perimeter.[129]

With their assaults proving ineffective, in mid-February the NVA belatedly shifted artillery fire to the Khe Sanh airfield, vital for Marine supplies.[130] The most severe threat to the base had passed, and the improving weather in March allowed for more effective US airstrikes.[131] Even so, the NVA continued their offensive by expanding their trenchworks toward the base. They unsuccessfully attacked on the night of March 13 and again on March 21, pre-staging the latter effort with a 1,000-round artillery barrage. In response, the Americans concentrated over 1,000 tacair strikes, hundreds of B-52 Arc Light missions, and thousands of artillery rounds to neutralize both assaults.[132] By mid-March, US intelligence noticed a partial withdrawal of enemy troops from around Khe Sanh until, by the end of the month, only the 304th Division remained.[133] The North Vietnamese suffered heavily, with 10,000–15,000 troops dead or wounded.[134] While the enemy had fielded a capable conventional force, as predicted by TAP theory, it proved vulnerable to air attack when the NVA massed and maneuvered.

At the beginning of April, as the NVA withdrew, the Marines took the offensive while the Army's 1st Cavalry Division conducted a relief effort

126 Project CHECO, *Battle of Khe Sanh and Operation Niagara*, 43.

127 Project CHECO, *Battle of Khe Sanh and Operation Niagara*, 46; Pike, *Military Records*, 28; Momyer, *Airpower in Three Wars*, 343; Stanton, *The Rise and Fall of an American Army*, 255.

128 Pike, *Military Records*, 139.

129 Project CHECO, *Battle of Khe Sanh and Operation Niagara*, 20, 58, 73; Nalty, *Air Power and the Fight for Khe Sanh*, 38.

130 Project CHECO, *Battle of Khe Sanh and Operation Niagara*, 75.

131 Nalty, *Air Power and the Fight for Khe Sanh*, 38.

132 Project CHECO, *Battle of Khe Sanh and Operation Niagara*, 87, 91; Nalty, *Air Power and the Fight for Khe Sanh*, 96.

133 Nalty, *Air Power and the Fight for Khe Sanh*, 99, 107.

134 Robbins, *This Time We Win*, 234; Prados and Stubbe, *Valley of Decision*, 451; Boyne, "Airpower at Khe Sanh"; Nalty, *Air Power and the Fight for Khe Sanh*, 103; Momyer, *Airpower in Three Wars*, 347. For a discussion on communist casualty estimates in Tet see Moise, *The Myths of Tet*, 128, 162; Prados, *Vietnam: The History of an Unwinnable War*, 243.

which reopened Highway 9 on April 8, signaling an end to the siege.[135] US forces would remain at Khe Sanh until they abandoned the base in late June.[136] Overall, the Marines had demonstrated a formidable capability to withstand the NVA's attacks while coordinating the massive air and artillery effort to defeat the enemy's fielded forces. It took ground forces to hold the base, but the NVA would have quickly overrun the Marines had not air power provided firepower and resupply.

Impact of the Environment on the Battle of Khe Sanh

The weather was pivotal to air power effectiveness at the Battle of Khe Sanh.[137] The northeast monsoon, particularly severe in 1968, initially made air operations difficult.[138] The NVA took advantage of the low clouds and limited visibility to move two divisions to the South for the assault on the Marine base. Low clouds and limited visibility reduced the ability of reconnaissance flights to locate enemy positions, restricted tacair operations, and initially constrained aerial resupply efforts until the Americans introduced radar procedures for airdrops.[139] Even for the all-weather, day and night B-52 Arc Light missions, the poor weather impacted the quantity and the quality of intelligence in making valid targets available. The weather further diminished the ability of ISR platforms to perform battle damage assessment (BDA).[140]

Some tacair assets, such as the Navy and Marine A-6s, had onboard air-to-ground radars, which provided an all-weather capability. For most tacair, however, poor weather dictated radar bombing by the USAF's MSQ-77 or the Marines' TPQ-10 radars. For the first month of the battle, 65 percent of USAF tacair sorties employed ordnance under radar control.[141] The weather further limited the availability of CAS as the use of radar-guided bombing came with restrictions on how close to friendly positions attacks could be made.[142] Under marginal conditions, airborne FACs could operate where tacair could not. Under these conditions, the

135 Davies, *US Marine Corps F-4 Phantom II Units of the Vietnam War*, 58. The Army relief effort was Codenamed Pegasus. Camp and Blashol, *Ringed by Fire*, 77–83; Nalty, *Air Power and the Fight for Khe Sanh*, 99, 108–109; Stanton, *The Rise and Fall of an American Army*, 258.

136 Nalty, *Air Power and the Fight for Khe Sanh*, 109.

137 Camp and Blashol, *Ringed by Fire*, 5.

138 Project CHECO, *Battle of Khe Sanh and Operation Niagara*, 55.

139 Project CHECO, *Battle of Khe Sanh and Operation Niagara*, 28.

140 Project CHECO, *Battle of Khe Sanh and Operation Niagara*, 91.

141 Nalty, *Air Power and the Fight for Khe Sanh*, 60; Project CHECO, *Battle of Khe Sanh and Operation Niagara*, 23, 56–57.

142 Project CHECO, *Battle of Khe Sanh and Operation Niagara*, 19.

Marines summoned slower propeller-driven A-1s, A-26s, and T-28s to provide CAS and armed recce.[143]

Poor weather continued through February, and although US combat aircraft dropped 53,000 tons of bombs around Khe Sanh, only half of the airstrikes were conducted visually.[144] In March, the weather began to improve, exposing the NVA to more lethal airstrikes, with US air power growing in intensity and accuracy.[145]

In addition to the protection provided by cloud cover and nightfall, the NVA also took advantage of terrain features and utilized camouflage and the forest canopy to cover their maneuver. But as the battle continued, the sheer volume of fire from thousands of B-52 and tacair strikes deforested the terrain near Khe Sanh.[146] While the NVA dug trenchworks to provide some protection, there was not enough time to develop the deep triple-level tunnels to endure the B-52 strikes the way the Viet Cong had in the Iron Triangle near Saigon.

Air Power at Khe Sanh

Under cloud cover and the cloak of night, the NVA infiltrated troops across the DMZ. In response, General Westmoreland ordered the Marines to hold, confident that air power could decimate the NVA. At Khe Sanh, he finally got the decisive battle he had been hoping for over the previous two and a half years. Westmoreland relied upon all the services to provide firepower, with tacair from the Air Force, Navy, and Marine Corps, B-52 bombers from the Air Force, and artillery from the Marine Corps and Army.

However, the deconfliction of fire proved challenging due to the congestion and density of aircraft and artillery operating in such a confined air space. The simultaneous operation of three command and control systems further complicated the task. The Air Force operated two tactical air control systems (TACS), one for South Vietnam and another for "out of country" sorties in Laos and North Vietnam. Meanwhile, the Marine Corps maintained a direct air support center (DASC) co-located with their fire support coordination center (FSCC) for dedicated Marine air and artillery.[147] Around Khe Sanh, the

[143] Project CHECO, *Battle of Khe Sanh and Operation Niagara*, 46.
[144] Project CHECO, *Battle of Khe Sanh and Operation Niagara*, 27, 65.
[145] Project CHECO, *Battle of Khe Sanh and Operation Niagara*, 65.
[146] Project CHECO, *Battle of Khe Sanh and Operation Niagara*, 73; Nalty, *Air Power and the Fight for Khe Sanh*, 18.
[147] Project CHECO, *Battle of Khe Sanh and Operation Niagara*, 79–81; Robbins, *This Time We Win*, 220; McCutcheon, "Marine Aviation in Vietnam, 1962–1970," 274–275.

Americans divided the airspace into six fire zones, where the Marines controlled the four zones adjacent to and overhead the base.[148] As a result, most CAS sorties were flown by Marine tacair, while Air Force and Navy tacair and B-52s primarily conducted armed recce and Arc Light missions. Although the dual Air Force–Marine command and control procedures sufficed, the system increased the complexity of air operations, introduced inefficiencies, and was the source of constant complaints by Air Force leaders. Eventually, compromises streamlined the process, but only after the battle had been decided.[149]

General Westmoreland named the air operation Niagara.[150] Phase I was an intense intelligence-gathering effort to generate targets for Phase II, the airstrikes and artillery fire to destroy the NVA.[151] Air-to-ground doctrine for CAS assumes ground forces will provide the targeting information for airstrikes. At Khe Sanh, however, the Marines could not deploy their ground maneuver elements to find and fix the enemy because they were outnumbered and surrounded.[152] Instead, airborne ISR platforms produced targets for air and artillery strikes. Tactical reconnaissance flew 1,453 sorties over the course of the battle. Although clouds covered Khe Sanh for much of the time, fifty photo interpreters worked around the clock to analyze what film was available.[153] In addition, seismic and acoustic sensors were air-delivered at key locations to find and track enemy movement.[154] At the height of the battle, 213 personnel worked at the Intelligence Control Center (ICC) at Tan Son Nhut Air Base near Saigon. The ICC created daily target folders, then forwarded them to the 26th Marine Regiment fire support coordination center (FSCC) at Khe Sanh. The ICC averaged 150 targets a day but surged to 300 at the peak of the battle.[155] Given the poor

[148] Camp and Blashol, *Ringed by Fire*, 35–36; Boyne, "Airpower at Khe Sanh."

[149] Project CHECO, *Battle of Khe Sanh and Operation Niagara*, 79–81, 86; Schlight *The War in South Vietnam*, 287; Horwood, *Interservice Rivalry and Airpower in the Vietnam War*, 152–153, 156–160; Stanton, *The Rise and Fall of an American Army*, 256.

[150] Camp and Blashol, *Ringed by Fire*, 16.

[151] Westmoreland, *A Soldier Reports*, 339; Boyne, "Airpower at Khe Sanh"; Nalty, *Air Power and the Fight for Khe Sanh*, 15; Project CHECO, *Battle of Khe Sanh and Operation Niagara*, 4; Willbanks, *The Tet Offensive*, 22; Horwood, *Interservice Rivalry and Airpower in the Vietnam War*, 148; Robbins, *This Time We Win*, 219–220.

[152] The previous year the Marines had deployed maneuver elements at the Battle of Con Thien. Nalty, *Air Power and the Fight for Khe Sanh*, 14.

[153] Project CHECO, *Battle of Khe Sanh and Operation Niagara*, 49.

[154] Project CHECO, *Battle of Khe Sanh and Operation Niagara*, 29; Boyne, "Airpower at Khe Sanh"; Nalty, *Air Power and the Fight for Khe Sanh*, 95; Momyer, *Airpower in Three Wars*, 344; Dang Phong, *Five Ho Chi Minh Trails* (Hanoi: Gioi Publishers, 2012), 95–96; Sherwood, *Afterburner*, 38–39.

[155] Project CHECO, *Battle of Khe Sanh and Operation Niagara*, 49–52.

weather conditions for much of the fighting, finding viable targets remained the critical factor for successful air operations.

Four hundred tacair from across Southeast Asia converged on Khe Sanh at a rate of 429 sorties a day for the first week of fighting. By mid-February, Americans averaged 100 Marine, 100 Navy, and 150 Air Force tacair sorties a day.[156] In March, the daily total had slightly decreased, averaging 300.[157] All told, tacair flew 22,000 sorties and dropped 40,000 tons of general-purpose and anti-personnel bombs.[158] Due to the restricted nature of the airspace and close proximity to friendly positions, tacair could not employ their weapons independently but instead relied upon FACs, who flew over 1,000 sorties. FACs were responsible for coordinating with ground forces, deconflicting the air space, locating and identifying targets, marking and talking tacair aircrew eyes onto targets, controlling airstrikes, and providing BDA.[159] At times, tacair traffic was so voluminous that flights orbited in stacks as high as 35,000 feet, from which the strikers gradually descended until their turn to drop ordnance on the FAC's designated target.[160]

In addition to tacair, B-52s flew around the clock. Twenty-six B-52s deployed to Kadena, Okinawa, joining the sixty B-52s already operating from U Tapao, Thailand, and Guam.[161] Three-ship formations arrived overhead Khe Sanh on average every ninety minutes, providing sixteen missions and forty-eight strikes daily.[162] B-52s flew 2,548 sorties and dropped 60,000 tons of bombs, 60 percent of the total tonnage dropped in defense of Khe Sanh.[163]

To improve the precision of B-52s, the Air Force relocated a second MSQ-77 Skyspot radar closer to Khe Sanh, allowing the heavy bombers, previously restricted from dropping within three kilometers of friendly

156 Momyer, *Airpower in Three Wars*, 346.

157 Project CHECO, *Battle of Khe Sanh and Operation Niagara*, 28, 84, 90; Boyne, "Airpower at Khe Sanh"; Pribbenow, *Victory in Vietnam*, 222.

158 This included cluster bomb units, CBU-24. Project CHECO, *Battle of Khe Sanh and Operation Niagara*, 23, 90, 112–114; Nalty, *Air Power and the Fight for Khe Sanh*, 105; Boyne, "Airpower at Khe Sanh"; Pike, *Military Records*, 179; Phong, *Five Ho Chi Minh Trails*, 107.

159 Project CHECO, *Battle of Khe Sanh and Operation Niagara*, 31, 63.

160 Boyne, "Airpower at Khe Sanh"; Nalty, *Air Power and the Fight for Khe Sanh*, 64–65; Project CHECO, *Battle of Khe Sanh and Operation Niagara*, 9, 11.

161 Momyer, *Airpower in Three Wars*, 346. These additional bombers were part of the American response to the January 23 North Korean seizure of the *USS Pueblo*, now made available after the commencement of the Tet Offensive. The additional B-52s were made available on February 12. Nalty, *Air Power and the Fight for Khe Sanh*, 12, 105, 108.

162 Project CHECO, *Battle of Khe Sanh and Operation Niagara*, 68–69.

163 Nalty, *Air Power and the Fight for Khe Sanh*, iii, 88; Boyne, "Airpower at Khe Sanh."

forces, to drop as close as a kilometer.[164] In addition, a one-by-two-kilometer grid, each rectangle the size of a three-ship B-52 bomb pattern, was overlaid on the Marines' tactical maps.[165] This system, known as Bugle Note, streamlined and simplified the targeting process from sensor recognition through bomb release.

American air power demonstrated an impressive air-to-ground capability at Khe Sanh. Westmoreland's assessment of the vast air-to-ground assets he could bring to bear against massed NVA troops precipitated his decision to hold the combat base. As TAP theory explains, air power is most effective against fielded forces when they concentrate and maneuver, which is what happened at Khe Sanh. In the history of aerial warfare, Khe Sanh stands out for its military effectiveness wrought by the combined capacity for an air force to attrit an army. But it still took the courage and skill of a friendly ground force to hold its position and the willingness of an enemy army to endure such withering firepower over a sustained period.

Assessing Air Power at Khe Sanh

Poor weather and rugged terrain presented problems for US air power that allowed the NVA to maneuver and concentrate at Khe Sanh. As the battle continued, however, the Americans overcame most of these environmental challenges through technological innovation. Strikers and airlift utilized radar, while airdropped sensors located and tracked NVA forces. Through ingenuity, the Americans kept the NVA at bay. Still, it was ultimately the improvement in the weather that proved most decisive by significantly increasing the lethality of air-to-ground operations.

The Battle of Khe Sanh provided an essential test of TAP theory. An air force with air superiority and a significant air-to-ground capability in coordination with a competent, friendly ground force placed a larger, conventional enemy army at a considerable disadvantage. With the NVA vulnerable to air attack, TAP theory anticipated that enemy commanders would, when able, disperse and hide their troops. Instead, the NVA continued fighting under heavy fire.[166] At Khe Sanh, two enemy divisions maneuvered to concentrate their forces, converging on their mutual objective of the US Marine base outnumbered by over three to

164 Boyne, "Airpower at Khe Sanh"; Project CHECO, *Battle of Khe Sanh and Operation Niagara*, 70. In March, B-52s conducted 444 strikes inside three kilometers of friendlies. Nalty, *Air Power and the Fight for Khe Sanh*, 66–67, 86.

165 Nalty, *Air Power and the Fight for Khe Sanh*, 69; Project CHECO, *Battle of Khe Sanh and Operation Niagara*, 66–67.

166 Boyne, "Airpower at Khe Sanh," 82–88.

one. Though TAP theory did not anticipate the NVA would concentrate its forces under the lethal threat of air power, it did expect the enemy units that did mass would be decimated. The NVA continued to advance even under the persistent threat of massive airstrikes and artillery barrages. With around-the-clock US fire support and airlift resupply, the NVA offensive was eventually thwarted. The US combined arms operation demonstrated the lethality of air power and artillery, which inflicted as high as 75 percent attrition on the NVA.[167] The North Vietnamese endured these heavy losses partly because they did not anticipate the effects of the US airlift effort on the Marines' staying power and because the political objectives they hoped to achieve from a decisive victory outweighed their battlefield losses. Khe Sanh was part of the greater gamble by Hanoi of the Tet Offensive, an effort to achieve the ambitious goal of ending the war and reunifying the country under communist rule.

Tet Offensive: January 30–February 24, 1968

While the Battle of Khe Sanh held the attention of General Westmoreland and President Johnson, the NVA/VC launched the Tet Offensive across South Vietnam on January 31.[168] The Tet Offensive shocked the Americans and South Vietnamese by its scale and audacity.[169] In six major cities, the most prominent being Saigon and Hue, and in thirty-four provincial capitals, the Viet Cong emerged from the shadows to attack governmental and military facilities.[170] The NVA/VC committed 84,000 combat forces to the offensive, with the overall number of communist troops in South Vietnam numbering 200,000–250,000, of which 45,000–58,000 would be killed or injured.[171]

In Saigon, journalists reported attacks at the US embassy, the Presidential Palace, and various military headquarters and airfields. In the following days, photographs of the brutal street fighting appeared in American newspapers, the most indelible being the front page of the *New York Times*, capturing a South Vietnamese officer summarily executing a VC guerrilla.[172] The heaviest fighting in most cities and provincial

[167] Prados and Stubbe, *Valley of Decision*, 451. [168] Pribbenow, *Victory in Vietnam*, 217.
[169] Nalty, *Air Power and the Fight for Khe Sanh*, 29.
[170] Nalty, *Air Power and the Fight for Khe Sanh*, 28; Pribbenow, *Victory in Vietnam*, 218.
[171] Momyer, *Airpower in Three Wars*, 355–356; Nalty, *Air Power and the Fight for Khe Sanh*, 31, 35; Boyne, "Airpower at Khe Sanh"; Hoopes, *The Limits of Intervention*, 142, 155; Robbins, *This Time We Win*, 165. For a discussion on numbers of Communists in South Vietnam and casualty estimates see Moise, *The Myths of Tet*, 128, 162, 177, 207–208.
[172] "Guerilla Dies" Front Page, *New York Times*, February 2, 1968.

capitals lasted only a few days. Though the Communists were defeated within two weeks, sporadic attacks continued for several months.[173] Across South Vietnam, the ARVN, local militia, and police proved more resilient than the North Vietnamese had anticipated.[174]

At Hue, however, the fighting was more intense as the NVA/VC seized control of the city for twenty-five days. When the ARVN retook the ancient capital, 4,000 civilians lay dead, including 2,800 summarily executed by the Communists. The violence further created 90,000 refugees.[175] Poor weather limited airborne FACs and tacair support of friendly ground forces at Hue. The nature of the urban fighting also made CAS more challenging due to the danger of fratricide and collateral damage. These factors combined to limit the impact of air power in the battle.[176] Though the NVA/VC seized Hue, this city was the exception, as South Vietnamese ground forces held elsewhere. During the Tet Offensive, the Viet Cong were not only defeated, but the collapse of their infrastructure significantly reduced the effectiveness of the insurgency thereafter.

Air Power and the Tet Offensive

While air power was critical at Khe Sanh, with the exception of air mobility, US air forces proved largely irrelevant during the Tet Offensive. The United States had air superiority over South Vietnam and the ISR capability to identify the massing of conventional NVA forces. But ISR platforms could not track the movement of the dispersed VC as they infiltrated scores of cities and towns ahead of the offensive. Once the street fighting began, the allies could not utilize tacair and B-52s. Even if air power could have supported the effort, the friendly ground troops confronting the VC were local South Vietnamese Regional Forces and Popular Forces with limited ability to coordinate airstrikes.[177] Finally, the South Vietnamese did not need air support as they quickly defeated the NVA/VC once they emerged from the jungles and shadows. Unlike in the countryside, in the cities the VC did not have the support of the population. Without the advantage of mixing with the locals, the police and militia soon rounded up the insurgents.[178]

173 Rusk, *As I Saw It*, 476; Moise, *The Myths of Tet*, 3.
174 Andrew Wiest, *Vietnam's Forgotten Army: Heroism and Betrayal in the ARVN* (New York: New York University Press, 2008), 95–123.
175 Nalty, *Air Power and the Fight for Khe Sanh*, 30.
176 Nalty, *Air Power and the Fight for Khe Sanh*, 29; Pike, *Military Records*, 99, 101; Robbins, *This Time We Win*, 181–194.
177 Momyer, *Airpower in Three Wars*, 349–351.
178 Wiest, *Vietnam's Forgotten War*, 95.

During the Tet Offensive, airborne FACs flew during the day, and AC-47 gunships provided cover at night. Still, US air forces executed few CAS sorties, and those employed were limited to airstrikes outside cities. While fixed-wing airlifters and helicopters proved valuable in quickly moving troops, it was the South Vietnamese police and local militias that won the urban battles.

Even though the allies quickly beat back the NVA/VC, the ferocity of the fighting shocked America, which suffered 1,100 killed in action over two weeks.[179] Regardless of General Westmoreland's statements of military success, the images of urban street fighting and the reporting by disillusioned journalists told a different story. President Johnson's remaining domestic support evaporated during the Tet Offensive. On March 12, Eugene McCarthy, the peace candidate, emerged with 40 percent of the vote in the New Hampshire Democratic primary.[180] Johnson again turned to his "Wise Men," who, on March 25, reversed their position and now recommended negotiation.[181] Six days later, Johnson announced a de-escalation of the war by ending the bombing north of the 20th parallel. He also announced he would not seek reelection.[182] Two months later, in Paris, a North Vietnamese delegation attended the first meeting with the Americans, though subsequent negotiations made no progress toward peace.

Conclusion

From 1967 to 1968, the war in Vietnam witnessed the large-scale employment of air power in various operations. Rolling Thunder somewhat slowed the NVA but failed to stop the flow of troops and supplies to South Vietnam or impose sufficient costs upon Hanoi to reconsider its support of the Viet Cong. As anticipated by TAP theory, air power proved more effective in the direct attack of fielded forces in combined arms operations. In the face of lethal firepower, the NVA usually dispersed and concealed their troops, seeking only small-scale engagements in 1966 and 1967. When they did concentrate and fight at Khe Sanh, the Americans' joint, combined arms operation effectively employed air

179 James Wirtz, *The Tet Offensive: Intelligence Failure in War* (Ithaca, NY: Cornell University Press, 1991), 1.

180 Warren Weaver, "McCarthy Gets about 40%, Johnson and Nixon on Top in New Hampshire Voting" *New York Times*, March 13, 1968, 1.

181 Jonathon Kirshner, "When the Wise Men Failed" *New York Times*, October 31, 2017, www.nytimes.com/2017/10/31/opinion/lyndon-johnson-vietnam-war.html; Rusk, *As I Saw It*, 480.

182 Rusk, *As I Saw It*, 483.

power to soundly defeat the NVA. While TAP theory did not predict the NVA would continue to concentrate in the face of such an air threat, TAP theory does explain why and how air power could prove so lethal when a cooperative adversary continues to concentrate and maneuver.

Even though the allies won the battle at Khe Sanh and the Tet Offensive, these military victories did not translate into political success. North Vietnamese resolve remained undeterred. The Communists would continue to suffer more hardship for their nationalist goal of unification than the Americans would endure for their strategy of maintaining an allied South Vietnam as part of the broader Cold War grand strategy of containing communism. The next chapter continues the analysis of air power through the lens of TAP theory in Southeast Asia as the air interdiction campaign shifted from North Vietnam to southern Laos and Cambodia.

5 Commando Hunt I–III and Cambodia: 1969–1970

Because of enemy aerial reconnaissance each prescribed march objective had to be reached before daybreak at which time all men and animals had to be concealed in the most uncomfortable and inadequate accommodations imaginable. These night marches made great demands on the poorly fed troops.

Erwin Rommel on the October 1917 Tolmein Offensive[1]

As detailed in the previous chapter, the Battle of Khe Sanh demonstrated air power's lethality against a fielded force. A conventional army chose to concentrate and maneuver even under the lethal threat of air attack and was decimated. Poor weather, rugged terrain, and dense ground cover may have initially hindered air operations. But over time, American airmen adapted by employing new technologies and procedures to keep the pressure on the North Vietnamese Army (NVA) until the weather cleared and the enemy could be located and beaten back. Instead of dispersing and concealing their troops as they had in the past, and as predicted by tactical air power (TAP) theory, the value of the political object drove the North Vietnamese onward, even to military defeat.

Though the North Vietnamese did not succeed militarily at Khe Sanh or in the broader Tet Offensive, they obtained a political victory in the United States. President Lyndon Johnson reprioritized his foreign policy objective in Vietnam to an expedited peace agreement to get America out. While negotiations with Hanoi made no progress, the United States assisted the South Vietnamese in their pacification program. The United States also invested heavily in equipping and training Republic of Vietnam Military Forces (RVNMF) to replace US forces in what would become known as Vietnamization. US air power continued to try and slow the movement of troops and supplies along the Ho Chi Minh Trail (the Trail). When Rolling Thunder ended in October 1968, the interdiction effort shifted to southern Laos in a seasonal air campaign known as Commando Hunt. As a result of their military defeat in the Tet Offensive

[1] Erwin Rommel, *Infantry Tactics*, originally published 1937 (Lancaster, TX: Snowball Publishing, 2014), 169.

and several failed offensives thereafter, the weakened NVA and Viet Cong (VC) in South Vietnam reverted to guerrilla and terrorist tactics. By 1970, an empowered ARVN, with US air support, gained the initiative by expanding operations into the communist sanctuaries in Cambodia.

This chapter continues assessing US air power following the Tet Offensive through the cross-border incursion into Cambodia in the spring of 1970. Expanding the conflict denied the NVA/VC sanctuary and severed their southern lines of communication (LOC) through the port at Sihanoukville. Leading up to the Cambodian invasion, Commando Hunt I and III slowed the movement of supplies southward and imposed costs on the North to keep the Trail open. Commando Hunt did not halt troops making the journey on foot, but the direct attack of fielded forces as part of the combined arms operations in South Vietnam and Cambodia kept the NVA/VC dispersed and hidden. Keeping the Communists on the defensive, in turn, provided the time and space for South Vietnam's pacification program to take root. The additional time further allowed Vietnamization to generate a stronger RVNMF.

US air power performed well from the Tet Offensive through the Cambodian invasion. TAP theory argues that enemy ground forces are most vulnerable to air attack when they concentrate and maneuver. The NVA/VC usually reacted to the threat of air strikes by dispersing and hiding. Effective air and ground combined arms operations placed the Communists on the defensive, no longer able to hold territory. The enemy instead resorted to rocket and mortar fire and conducted terrorist attacks.

Meanwhile, air power in Rolling Thunder south of the 20th parallel through October 1968 and in Commando Hunt I and III in southern Laos effectively interdicted communist supplies heading south. While the threat of air strikes could not stop NVA reinforcements, it did compel soldiers to conduct the arduous journey along the Trail on foot. The overall result was that Commando Hunt I and III contributed to the success of US and ARVN combined arms operations in South Vietnam and Cambodia through 1970.

This chapter is divided into four sections. The first provides context for the political and military situation following the Tet Offensive. A description and history of the Ho Chi Minh Trail, the Communists' primary land LOC connecting North and South Vietnam, is also provided. Section two analyzes Commando Hunt I. The campaign included numerous technological and organizational innovations to target NVA forces and infrastructure along the Trail. Section three evaluates

Commando Hunt III, from late 1969 through spring 1970, to include American and North Vietnamese adaptation. Section four assesses the expansion of the war in Southeast Asia leading to the Cambodia incursion in April 1970.

A Tumultuous 1968

The Tet Offensive ushered in a turbulent year, as 1968 witnessed historic political and social upheaval in the United States and worldwide. On April 4 in Memphis, within a week of President Johnson announcing he would no longer seek reelection, an assassin's bullet struck down the leader of the civil rights movement, Reverend Martin Luther King. Two months later, presidential candidate Robert Kennedy was gunned down in a Los Angeles hotel. Also, a sit-in at Columbia University turned violent, ushering in a wave of anti-war protests. Meanwhile, even more violence surfaced in China as Chairman Mao "cleaned the class ranks" in his Cultural Revolution. The Sino-Soviet divide widened within the communist world as the Chinese and Soviets deployed combat troops along their shared and disputed border.[2] In August, Soviet tanks rolled into Czechoslovakia to reverse the political reforms that resulted from the Prague Spring. A few days later, on the streets of Chicago, protestors clashed with police outside a contentious Democratic national convention where Johnson's vice president, Hubert Humphrey, emerged as the candidate of a fractured party.[3] President Johnson ordered an end to Rolling Thunder on October 31, one week before Richard Nixon narrowly won the presidency.

Meanwhile, the North Vietnamese surprised the United States when they initially agreed to talks just days after President Johnson's March 31 speech. They met in Paris on May 13, but talks stalled as Hanoi was unwilling to negotiate from a position of military weakness. The Americans were also disinclined to make concessions after their victories at Khe Sanh and the broader Tet Offensive. Saigon also wanted nothing to do with any agreement that would decrease US support.[4]

Although defeated in the Tet Offensive, Hanoi stubbornly clung to its military strategy by sending more troops southward. An estimated 236,000 additional soldiers made the arduous journey along

[2] Ang Cheng Guan, *The Vietnam War from the Other Side: The Vietnamese Communists' Perspective* (New York: RoutledgeCurzon, 2002), 140.

[3] John Prados, *Vietnam: The History of an Unwinnable War, 1954–1975* (Lawrence: University Press of Kansas, 2009), 258–260.

[4] George Herring, *America's Longest War: The United States and Vietnam, 1950–1975, 4th Edition* (New York: McGraw, 2001), 230–231.

the Trail.[5] Over the next year, the NVA initiated three more offensives, the mini-Tet Offensive in late May, the Third Offensive in August, and the post-Tet Offensive the following February.[6] All these efforts resulted in heavy casualties, with each attack weaker than the one before.[7] Unable to take and hold territory, the NVA instead conducted sporadic attacks by fire, launching mortars and rockets to inflict casualties. VC units, no longer able to control territory, reverted to terrorist attacks.

In June 1968, General Creighton Abrams replaced General William Westmoreland as Military Assistant Command Vietnam (MACV) commander.[8] Abrams kept the pressure on the NVA/VC, but he transitioned away from Westmoreland's large-force operations. Instead, he expanded efforts to support the pacification program, a countrywide effort to increase the Thieu government's control over South Vietnam.[9] General Abrams also supervised the de-Americanization effort – what the Nixon administration would later call Vietnamization. This massive aid and training program raised over a million troops for the RVNMF to take over the responsibilities as the US military withdrew.[10]

In the late spring and summer of 1968, the Rolling Thunder air campaign, restricted by President Johnson's decision to refrain from bombing near Hanoi, continued to interdict the North Vietnamese LOC along the narrow panhandle south of the 20th parallel down to the DMZ. From July to October, airstrikes destroyed vital bridges, mined riverways, and cut the mountain passes into Laos.[11] Massed attacks against these chokepoints and heavy rains restricted truck traffic.[12] At the end of October, President Johnson ordered a near-complete bombing halt of North Vietnam.[13] US air forces then shifted their effort to southern Laos to interdict the Trail.[14]

[5] Lewis Sorley, ed., *The Abrams Tapes 1968–1972: Vietnam Chronicles* (Lubbock, TX: Texas Tech University Press, 2004), 130.

[6] Project CHECO, *Air War in Vietnam 1968–1969* (HQ PACAF: Tactical Evaluation Team, 1970), 31–33; Shelby Stanton, *The Rise and Fall of An American Army: U.S. Ground Forces in Vietnam 1965–1973* (New York: Ballantine, 1989), 273, 276.

[7] Guan, *The Vietnam War from the Other Side*, 134.

[8] General Westmoreland was named the Chief of Staff of the Army.

[9] Prados, *Vietnam: The History of an Unwinnable War*, 323–329.

[10] Herring, *America's Longest War*, 233; Henry Kissinger, *The White House Years* (New York: Simon & Schuster, 1979), 172; John Prados, *The Blood Road: The Ho Chi Minh Trail and the Vietnam War* (Hoboken, NJ: Wiley, 1999), 392.

[11] Sorley, *The Abrams Tapes*, 648.

[12] The mountain passes were closed 90 percent of the time. Sorley, *The Abrams Tapes*, 73; Project CHECO, *Air War in Vietnam 1968–69*, 38.

[13] There were occasional strikes north of the DMZ which were technically considered Rolling Thunder. This designation did not end until Linebacker.

[14] Bernard Nalty, *The War against Trucks: Aerial Interdiction in Southern Laos 1968–1972* (Washington, DC: Air Force History and Museums Program, 2005), 4.

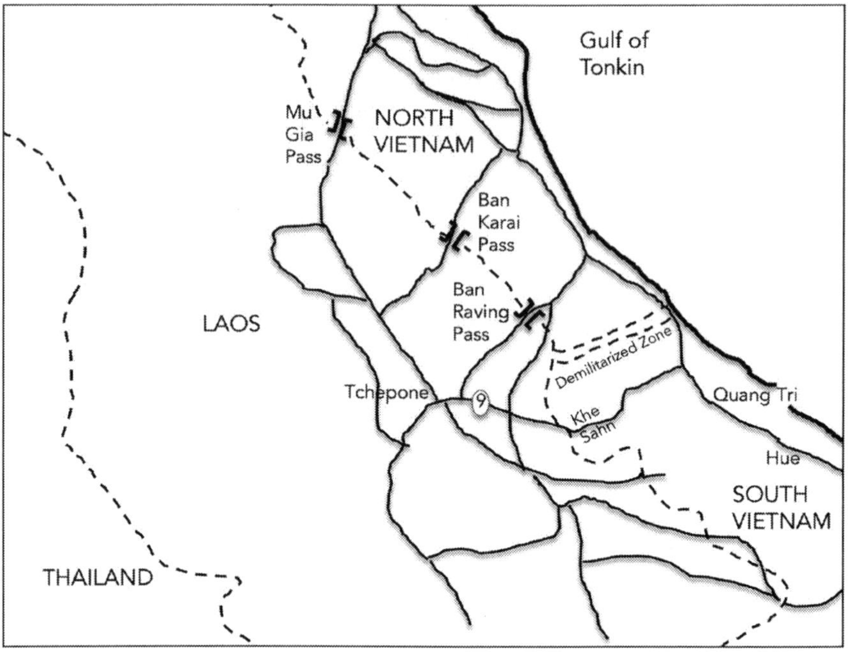

Map 5.1 Ho Chi Minh Trail

The Ho Chi Minh Trail

The Annamite Mountain Range runs north and south for 600 miles, creating a natural border dividing Vietnam and Laos. The Vietminh traveled along the western slope to avoid the French during the First Indochina War.[15] The network of dirt roads and footpaths, known in the West as the Ho Chi Minh Trail, originated in southern North Vietnam and crossed through the Nape, Mu Gai, and Ban Karai mountain passes (see Map 5.1).

The terrain in southern Laos opened into a sizable north–south plateau, lightly populated, with a few villages linked by interconnecting dirt roads and footpaths. A layered rainforest protected these trails, providing excellent cover for the concealment and movement of troops and supplies.[16]

[15] *The Hô Chí Minh Trail* (Hanoi: Gioi Publishers, 2008), 1–2, 43; Mark Eduard, *Aerial Interdiction in Three Wars* (Washington, DC: Center for Air Force History, 1994), 329–330.

[16] John Schlight, *The War in South Vietnam: The Years of the Offensive 1965–1968* (Washington, DC: Office of Air Force History, 1988), 56.

The NVA planted bushes and bamboo saplings to camouflage roadways, truck parks, and engineering and supply facilities.[17] They also stored supplies and sheltered personnel in large limestone caves, common throughout the region.[18]

In addition to the rugged terrain and heavy cover, the climate played a significant role in Commando Hunt. The dry season ran from November through April, with little cloud cover and good visibility favorable for air operations.[19] By contrast, heavy clouds and rain accompanied the summer monsoon from May through October. This poor flying weather resulted from the southwest weather pattern, with hot, humid air flowing up from the Indian Ocean.[20]

In May 1959, the North Vietnamese formed the 559 Military Transportation Group to expand their LOC through Laos in support of the VC in the South.[21] Over the next five years, the volume of troops and supplies gradually increased before surging in 1964, when supplies quadrupled as the insurgency intensified.[22]

In response, in late December 1964 the United States initiated Barrell Roll, an air operation assisting the Laotian government in suppressing the communist-supported Pathet Lao rebels. By April 1965, US air cover had expanded to southern Laos. Called Steel Tiger, this effort aimed to halt supplies moving along the Trail. At sea, in March 1965 the Navy and Coast Guard commenced Operation Market Time to cut off the North's sea lines of communication (SLOC). Market Time's success caused the North Vietnamese to depend even more on the Trail.[23]

In the summer of 1967, Secretary of Defense Robert McNamara ordered the construction of a barrier along the DMZ extending westward into Laos. Though the physical portion of "McNamara's Wall" never materialized, the US military developed a network of electronic sensors to monitor traffic flow along the Trail.[24] By late 1967, the arrival of the

17 John Sherwood, *Nixon's Trident: Naval Power in Southeast Asia, 1968–1972* (Washington, DC: Department of the Navy: Naval Historic Center, 2008), 7.

18 Nalty, *The War against Trucks*, 97. 19 Nalty, *The War against Trucks*, 97.

20 A lack of upwind weather observations from neighboring Cambodia further challenged US weather forecasting in southern Laos. Nalty, *The War against Trucks*, 32.

21 Dang Phong, *Five Ho Chi Minh Trails* (Hanoi: Theh Gioi Publishers, 2012), 56–75; Merle Pribbenow, *Victory in Vietnam: The Official History of the People's Army of Vietnam 1954–1975* (Lawrence: University Press of Kansas, 2002), 52; Guan, *The Vietnam War from the Other Side*, 34.

22 Pribbenow, *Victory in Vietnam*, 126.

23 Alex Larzelere, *The Coast Guard at War, Vietnam, 1965–1975* (Annapolis, MD: US Naval Institute Press, 1997); Peter Mersky and Norman Polmar, *The Naval Air War in Vietnam* (Mount Pleasant, SC: Nautical & Aviation Publishing Co. of America, 1981), 33.

24 Schlight, *The War in South Vietnam*, 57.

dry season allowed the North Vietnamese to double the influx of troops and supplies along the Trail, with their soldiers in South Vietnam increasing from 200,000 to 280,000 in preparation for the Tet Offensive.[25]

Following Tet, President Johnson restricted Rolling Thunder airstrikes to the south of the 20th parallel and halted all bombing of North Vietnam in late October. These air assets were then available for Commando Hunt, interdicting the Trail through southern Laos.

Commando Hunt I: November 1968–April 1969

On the first Tuesday in November 1968, Americans narrowly elected Richard Milhouse Nixon, who promised a new strategy for Vietnam that would "offer a fair and equitable settlement for all."[26] However, the first year of Nixon's presidency proved to be a continuation of Johnson's foreign policies in Southeast Asia. Though peace talks remained mired in Paris, progress continued in South Vietnam with the rapid expansion of the RVNMF as part of Vietnamization. At the same time, the pacification program increasingly brought stability and security to the countryside.

In mid-November, the start of Commando Hunt I coincided with the arrival of the dry season and the inflow of NVA supplies and personnel traversing the Trail.[27] Commando Hunt I did not start from scratch, as it inherited a command and control network, an array of sensors inserted in southern Laos, and a mature tactical air control system directing air operations in Laos since 1964. Also, the previous year's buildup for the Battle of Khe Sanh and Tet Offensive, combined with the end of Rolling Thunder, made available a plethora of US tactical aircraft (tacair) and bomber assets.[28]

To reduce the flow of enemy supplies, Commando Hunt I prioritized four target sets.[29] Phase I, which ran from November 1968 to early January, focused on choke points, including mountain passes and major road intersections. B-52s and tacair bombed these fixed targets and

[25] Pribbenow, *Victory in Vietnam*, 208, 210.
[26] "Republican Party Platform of 1968," August 5, 1968, www.presidency.ucsb.edu/documents/republican-party-platform-1968.
[27] The odd-numbered Commando Hunts (I, III, V, and VII) were active as they occurred during the dry season, while the even-numbered Commando Hunts (II, IV, and VI) accompanied the rainy season.
[28] Carl Berger, ed., *The United States Air Force in Southeast Asia, 1961–1973: An Illustrated Account* (Washington, DC: Office of Air Force History, 1984), 110.
[29] Berger, *The United States Air Force in Southeast Asia*, 109–110.

seeded the surrounding area with anti-personnel and anti-vehicular mines.[30] In early 1969, Phase II expanded operations adjacent to the North Vietnamese border, adding transportation facilities to the target list, including suspected truck parks and repair facilities. The third priority was attacking vehicles, and the last was suppressing the scattered anti-aircraft artillery (AAA) sites along the Trail.[31] From March to April, Phase III shifted bombing south to the NVA supply depots near the town of Tchepone, where the Trail's network of roads turned east toward the South Vietnamese border (Map 5.1).[32]

The following analysis separates operations by air superiority, air-to-ground capabilities, friendly ground force capabilities, and enemy ground force capabilities.

Air Superiority in Commando Hunt I

In late 1968, US air forces enjoyed air superiority over South Vietnam, Laos, and Cambodia, facing an air threat lower than that encountered over North Vietnam. In addition to tacair, more vulnerable aircraft, including B-52s, fixed-wing gunships, and propeller-driven FACs operated effectively over most of the Trail.[33]

The North Vietnamese People's Air Force (VPAF) MiGs did not have the range to patrol outside their border, and Hanoi initially kept its SA-2 surface-to-air missile (SAM) batteries north of the 20th parallel. The VPAF also had no radars in Laos. For early warning, they relied upon distant radars in North Vietnam, augmented by forward observers stationed atop mountains along the Laotian–South Vietnamese border.[34]

Given the limited MiG and SAM activity, the greatest threat in southern Laos came from small arms and AAA, with the 37 millimeter (mm) gun the most prolific surface-to-air weapon.[35] The NVA had an estimated 166 AAA pieces deployed along the Trail in November 1968, though this number rose steadily.[36] It prepared multiple AAA sites to neutralize US flak suppression efforts. In addition, the NVA set up dummy sites and concealed guns nearby to ambush aircraft when they

[30] Nalty, *The War against Trucks*, 106. [31] Nalty, *The War against Trucks*, 102.
[32] Nalty, *The War against Trucks*, 107.
[33] Even with air dominance, the USAF still suffered losses to ground fire, with fifty-six aircraft downed in Commando Hunt operations. Nalty, *The War against Trucks*, 102.
[34] Nalty, *The War against Trucks*, 97.
[35] USAF 7th Air Force, *Commando Hunt III* (May 1970), xxiv. AAA was primarily 23 and 37mm guns, with an effective tactical range of 5,000 feet. Schlight, *The War in South Vietnam*, 55.
[36] Nalty, *The War against Trucks*, 97; USAF 7th Air Force, *Commando Hunt III*, xxiii.

attacked the decoys.[37] AAA made the low-altitude regime dangerous over the Trail, but it did not prevent the United States from developing an effective air-to-ground capability.

Air-to-Ground Capability in Commando Hunt I

In 1968, the United States enhanced its air-to-ground capability in Commando Hunt I. The numerous improvements in command and control, sensor and intelligence technologies, air-to-ground aircraft, and specialized weaponry combined to make the air interdiction effort effective in curtailing the movement of supplies along the Trail.

Command and Control In the spring of 1968, Lieutenant General William Momyer, the commander of 7th Air Force, ordered a study to improve air operations over southern Laos. The USAF maintained a forward command post, call sign Sycamore, at Nakhon Phanom, Thailand.[38] Situated across from southern Laos, along the bank of the Mekong River, the base hosted the Infiltration Surveillance Center (ISC), a large complex housing two IBM 360-65 mainframe computers, the fastest in the world at the time.[39] The ISC received and processed signals from hundreds of sensors scattered along the Trail. The extensive computing capacity of the ISC allowed 400 intelligence analysts to estimate the size and predict the movement of vehicles in near real time, twenty-four hours a day.[40] General Momyer managed the subsequent integration of the ISC into the US Air Force (USAF) command and control system.[41]

In November 1968, the United States adjusted its daily air tasking order (ATO) to shift sorties to Commando Hunt I. Seventh Air Force controlled fixed-wing sorties in Southeast Asia through two tactical air control centers (TACC). One TACC directed missions in South Vietnam, and the other coordinated "out-of-country" sorties in North Vietnam, Laos, and Cambodia.[42] Previously, Rolling Thunder missions had launched in waves. However, such surges initially overwhelmed

[37] Nalty, *The War against Trucks*, 97. [38] Prados, *The Blood Road*, 267–268.

[39] Prados, *The Blood Road*, 269; William Rosenau, *Special Operation Forces and Elusive Enemy Ground Targets* (Santa Monica, CA: RAND Corporation, 2001), 11; Project CHECO, *Air War in Vietnam 1968–69*, 39; Sherwood, *Nixon's Trident*, 8.

[40] Nalty, *The War against Trucks*, 103; Sherwood, *Nixon's Trident*, 8.

[41] Project CHECO, *Air War in Vietnam 1968–69*, 4.

[42] Project CHECO, *Air War in Vietnam 1968–69*, 14. During the Battle of Khe Sanh, the Marines agreed to allow their aircraft on to the daily ATO so long as Marine air was assigned to support Marine operations. Nalty, *The War against Trucks*, 103.

Sycamore, which required a steady stream of aircraft around the clock to react immediately as perishable targeting information became available.

Sycamore tasked aircraft for the first few months of Commando Hunt I. Due to the large volume of air traffic and line-of-sight problems with its ground-based antennas, responsibility migrated to a C-130 airborne command and control center (ABCCC). Sycamore provided intelligence to the ABCCC, relaying the data to airborne forward air controllers (FACs) and fixed-wing gunships. In bad weather and at night, the ISC generated targets for Combat Skyspot and LORAN (Long-range navigation) ground-based radar systems for tacair and B-52 airstrikes.[43] ISC targeting was only as good as the intelligence behind it, and this depended upon the sensors available to detect the enemy's movement.

Sensors – Igloo White To support McNamara's 1967 decision to impede the movement of NVA supplies and troops, a program code-named Igloo White deployed various electronic sensors along the Trail.[44] Anti-vehicle sensors included acoustic, seismic, and engine ignition detecting devices.[45] Over time, 20,000 battery-powered units were delivered by air.[46] In addition, special forces planted smaller versions of the sensors by hand.[47] Sensors near choke points monitored the construction of bypasses and the diversion of traffic.[48] Other sensors strung out parallel to major roads monitored traffic flow. Nearby, orbiting EC-121 electronic surveillance aircraft received and retransmitted the sensors' low-powered emissions.[49] The input data fed the ISC's giant IBM mainframes, programmed to estimate convoys' size, movement, and predicted location.[50] The intelligence generated by Igloo White proved to be a crucial component of Commando Hunt I, as Sycamore could direct FACs and gunships to the most active areas along the hundreds of miles of trails. Though not precise enough to conduct strikes

[43] Nalty, *The War against Trucks*, 113; Project CHECO, *Air War in Vietnam 1968–69*, 40.

[44] The program was initially called Muscle Shoals. Project CHECO, *Igloo White Initial Phase* (HQ PACAF: Tactical Evaluation Team, 1968), 1.

[45] Nalty, *The War against Trucks*, 106. Also deployed were anti-personnel sensors. Project CHECO, *Igloo White Initial Phase*, 3 and figure 1.

[46] By F-4s, by the Navy's OP2-E Neptunes, and by helicopter. Sherwood, *Nixon's Trident*, 8; Mersky and Polmar, *The Naval Air War in Vietnam*, 174.

[47] From 1966 to 1971, the United States deployed 20,000 sensors. Rosenau, *Special Operation Forces*, 11.

[48] Nalty, *The War against Trucks*, 105.

[49] Project CHECO, *Igloo White Initial Phase*, 9.

[50] Nalty, *The War against Trucks*, 106.

against mobile targets, the intelligence enabled FACs and gunships to narrow their search.[51]

Many challenges arose in the daily operation of the Igloo White sensor array. First, the sensor strings had to be accurately delivered and their location validated before the ISC could trust the data. In practice, this necessitated low-altitude runs in the heart of small-arms and AAA fire, which distracted airmen and reduced the accuracy of sensor delivery. Second, the sensors needed constant replenishment due to limited battery life and frequent malfunctions. Third, the sensors required an EC-121 constantly orbiting to receive and relay their signals. Also, the ISC computers had to function correctly to store and process incoming data.[52] Even given the challenges of keeping these then-sophisticated technologies online, overall Igloo White proved functional, enhancing the ability to monitor, day and night, the flow of traffic along the Trail. However, Igloo White was no panacea as it still required aircrew flying dedicated air-to-ground sorties to perform the arduous task of locating and striking targets.

Air-to-Ground Aircraft The conclusion of Rolling Thunder in late October 1968 made available 420 tacair and 620 sorties a day for Commando Hunt I.[53] The number of US fixed- and rotary-winged aircraft in Southeast Asia peaked at 6,100, which remained steady through the end of 1969.[54] Tacair included Air Force F-4s and F-105s and Navy and Marine F-4s and A-6s, with 35 percent of their missions dedicated to Commando Hunt I.[55] In October, US air forces flew 4,000 tacair sorties in southern Laos, while in November this number tripled to 12,000.[56]

Tacair was survivable and carried a respectable weapons load, but the pilots flying these fast fighter-bombers could not locate targets hidden beneath the forest and jungle canopies. Instead, tacair relied on FACs flying slow, propeller-driven aircraft to perform visual reconnaissance and provide air strike control. For several years, Raven FACs, flying the O-1 Birddog, had conducted covert operations in the secret war in

51 Nalty, *The War against Trucks*, 113.
52 Project CHECO *Igloo White Initial Phase*, 21, 27.
53 Nalty, *The War against Trucks*, 97.
54 Project CHECO, *Air War in Vietnam 1968–69*, 16.
55 Project CHECO, *Air War in Vietnam 1968–69*, 40.
56 Berger, *The United States Air Force in Southeast Asia*, 110; Prados, *The Blood Road*, 270. Over 67,000 tacair sorties were flown in Commando Hunt I from November to April. Project CHECO, *Air War in Vietnam 1968–69*, 43.

Figure 5.1 O-2 Skymaster

Laos.[57] Ravens also interdicted the Trail along the Laotian and South Vietnamese border.[58] In addition to the O-1, the Air Force modified a commercial twin-engine Cessna 337, the O-2 Skymaster, with improved aircraft performance, better radios, and armed with white phosphorous (Willy Pete) rockets for target marking (Figure 5.1). The Marines introduced another FAC aircraft, the OV-10 Bronco, later adopted by the Air Force (Figure 5.2).[59] The Bronco had a significant increase in performance compared to the Birddog and Skymaster.[60] The OV-10, armed with

[57] The O-1 was a military version of the single-engine, propeller-driven Cessna 170. US support of the Laotian government was kept secret due to the 1954 Geneva Accords requiring Laos be neutral. It was an open secret, however, that both the North Vietnamese and the United States operated in Laos.

[58] Prados, *The Blood Road*, 269–270. For more on Raven operations in Laos see Christopher Robbins, *The Ravens: The Men Who Flew in America's Secret War in Laos* (New York: Crown, 1995); and Jim Roper, *Quoth the Raven* (Baltimore, MD: America House, 2001).

[59] Mersky and Polmar, *The Naval Air War in Vietnam*, 147.

[60] Keith McCutcheon, "Marine Aviation in Vietnam, 1962–1970" in *The Marines in Vietnam 1954–1973: An Anthology and Annotated Bibliography* (Washington, DC: History and

Figure 5.2 OV-10 Bronco

rockets and bombs, provided the FAC with an organic strike capability.[61] OV-10s would later carry the Pave Nail day and nighttime sensor with a designator for laser-guided bombs (LGBs).[62] In the higher threat areas near the North Vietnamese border, where these slow and vulnerable aircraft could not operate, the Air Force and Marine Corps employed two-seat tacair as fast FACs.[63]

In addition to tacair, B-52 bombers shifted operations from South Vietnam to support Commando Hunt I. In October 1968, B-52s flew 271 sorties in southern Laos. The B-52s bombed fixed targets, including mountain passes, road intersections, and suspected supply and repair facilities. In November, the number jumped to over 600 missions and remained high afterward. The B-52s executed 3,800 sorties by mid-April 1969.[64]

Museums Division Headquarters Marine Corps, 1985), 278; Peter Davies, *US Marine Corps F-4 Phantom II Units of the Vietnam War* (New York: Osprey, 2012), 68, 72.

61 Project CHECO, *Air War in Vietnam 1968–69*, 48.

62 7th Air Force, *Commando Hunt VII*, June 1972, Air Force Historical Research Agency (AFHRA), K740.430-6 Reel 42321, 46.

63 Nalty, *The War against Trucks*, 106; Project CHECO, *Air War in Vietnam 1968–69*, April 1, 1970, 6.

64 Project CHECO, *Air War in Vietnam 1968–69*, 43; Berger, *The United States Air Force in Southeast Asia*, 110; Prados, *The Blood Road*, 270.

All-Weather and Night Capabilities To overcome the inclement weather over southern Laos, the United States utilized several all-weather navigation capabilities, the most important being the MSQ-77 ground-to-air radar codenamed Combat Skyspot.[65] The USAF stationed five of these radar facilities in South Vietnam and Thailand.[66] Skyspot was most closely associated with B-52 Arc Light missions which relied almost exclusively upon Skyspot command guidance for flight path and weapons release cues. Ninety-five percent of the bombs dropped by B-52s in Commando Hunt were on Arc Light missions.[67] Sycamore supplied the targeting information to Skyspot, which then controlled an average of 27 B-52 strikes per day.[68] Tacair was also frequently directed by Skyspot during bad weather and at night. Aircraft on Igloo White sensor delivery sorties could utilize Skyspot. Ground-based radar bombing proved effective against area targets, such as mountain passes and road intersections. Even so, radar bombing was less accurate than the visual delivery methods of tacair.

Another all-weather radar bombing capability was LORAN, the long-range navigation system introduced in Southeast Asia in March 1969.[69] Though developed primarily as a navigational aid, aircrew with LORAN receivers could also follow cockpit cues to release bombs. LORAN was a poor substitute for Skyspot, though, as its longer radio wavelengths were not as accurate as those of the MSQ-77 radar. Still, LORAN had certain advantages, as it could employ at longer ranges. It also did not require ground-to-air radio communications to guide aircrew. Overall, LORAN accuracy proved sufficient for striking area targets and delivering Igloo White sensors.[70] Early in Commando Hunt I, the ISC became adept at generating near-real-time coordinates for these LORAN strikes in an operation known as Commando Bolt.[71]

In addition to radar navigation systems, the slower FACs could operate under poorer weather conditions, flying with ceilings as low as 300 feet and visibility as reduced as two miles compared to the 1,500-foot

[65] Schlight, *The War in South Vietnam*, 55.

[66] The B-52s could not accurately bomb with their airborne radars due to insufficient terrain contrast required to identify targets and radar offset points. HQ PACAF, *Summary Air Operations Southeast Asia Volume XCIII April 1972*, AFHRA K717.3063 (April 1972), A-4.

[67] Project CHECO, *Air War in Vietnam 1968–69*, 59–60.

[68] William Head, "Playing Hide-and-Seek with the 'Trail': Operation Commando Hunt, 1968–1972" *Journal of Third World Studies* 29:1 (2002), 103.

[69] Project CHECO, *Air War in Vietnam 1968–69*, 42.

[70] Nalty, *The War against Trucks*, 28. [71] Nalty, *The War against Trucks*, 108.

ceilings and five-mile visibility required for tacair.[72] Under conditions where tacair could not conduct visual attacks, FACs could still generate coordinates for radar-guided strikes.

In addition to operating in and under the weather, a creative effort during the summer monsoons encouraged mother nature. The USAF employed cargo planes to seed clouds along the Trail to induce heavy local rainfall to wash out dirt roads and trails.[73] In addition to seeding clouds, airlifters also conducted defoliation operations, utilizing Agent Orange to thin vegetation.[74] Such efforts proved marginally successful as the herbicide had only a local effect. The NVA diverted traffic along its parallel road network to circumnavigate exposed trails.

In addition to poor weather, the sanctuary of night concealed the enemy. Even before Commando Hunt I, daytime air operations had compelled the NVA to shift to moving supplies and personnel at night. The United States, with limited success, also flew FACs and tacair at night, dropping illumination flares to identify and strike targets.[75] The Navy and Marine Corps employed the all-weather A-6 Intruder, using its air-to-ground radar's moving target indicator (MTI) to identify trucks.[76] In Commando Nail, A-6s flew missions to radar map roads and returned at night to locate and attack truck convoys.[77] Overall, FACs and tacair harassed the enemy at night, but the development of a new combat system – the fixed-wing gunship – would prove the most prolific truck killer.

AC-47 gunships first flew missions along the Trail in December 1965. After losing several aircraft to enemy ground fire, these modified cargo planes only operated in South Vietnam. In Phase II of Commando Hunt I, in January 1969, four new AC-130As, callsign Spectre, ushered the return of the gunship over the Trail (Figure 5.3).[78] These aircraft operated at medium altitude at night, out of sight, and above the threat of small-arms and most AAA fire.

The AC-130 Spectre contained the latest night sensor technologies, including infrared and low-light cameras. The gunships could loiter for extended periods and, armed with 20 mm and later 40 mm and 105 mm cannons, proved lethal against trucks.[79] The gunship combined the roles

72 Project CHECO, *Air War in Vietnam 1968–69*, 60.
73 Nalty, *The War against Trucks*, 33.
74 Project CHECO, *Air War in Vietnam 1968–69*, 40; Nalty, *The War against Trucks*, 33.
75 Project CHECO, *Air War in Vietnam 1968–69*, 58.
76 Nalty, *The War against Trucks*, 107.
77 Navy and Marine A-6s claimed 11 percent of trucks destroyed or damaged on the Trail. Sherwood, *Nixon's Trident*, 9; John Sherwood, *Afterburner: Naval Aviators and the Vietnam War* (New York: New York University Press, 2004), 40; Mersky and Polmar, *The Naval Air War in Vietnam*, 170.
78 Schlight, *The War in South Vietnam*, 55; Nalty, *The War against Trucks*, 53–55.
79 Head, "Playing Hide-and-Seek with the 'Trail'," 103.

Figure 5.3 AC-130 Spectre

of ABCCC, FAC, and striker, able to receive intel from Sycamore on general convoy location and direction of movement, and with its then cutting-edge sensors and accurate cannons, identify, strike, and provide battle damage assessment (BDA). The gunship was the most prolific air-to-ground asset on the Trail, credited with 28 percent of all truck kills.[80] The Air Force soon deployed eighteen AC-130s and another sixteen AC-119Ks from the reserves.

In addition to the AC-130, other aircraft and tactics were utilized at night. One joint tactic was employing the Army's OV-1 Mohawk, with its side-looking air-to-ground radar (SLAR), teamed up with the AC-119K, upgraded with advanced sensors. They worked as a hunter-killer team, with the OV-1 locating moving trucks for the AC-119K to hit.[81]

Yet another improvement in all-weather and night operations was the Coordinated LORAN Sensor Strike System (COLOSSYS), which enabled LORAN-equipped F-4s and A-6s to display target data in their cockpits.[82] Once a Sycamore intel analyst had predicted a truck convoy's location and time of arrival, COLOSSYS could place bombs on target within twelve minutes.

Air-to-Ground Weapons All the specialized sensors, aircraft, and systems just described would have been ineffective without lethal air-to-ground weapons. From 1965 to 1968, the challenges facing air operations in Southeast Asia spurred the development of more accurate and

80 Sorley, *The Abrams Tapes*, 109; Nalty, *The War against Trucks*, 107; William Momyer, *Airpower in Three Wars* (Maxwell AFB, AL: Air University Press, 2003), 237.
81 Project CHECO, *Air War in Vietnam 1968–69*, 51.
82 Davies, *US Marine Corps F-4 Phantom II Units of the Vietnam War*, 70.

deadly weapons. Of these, the laser-guided bomb would prove to be one of the most revolutionary technologies for conventional air-to-ground warfare.

The employment of precision-guided munitions dates back to World War II.[83] The most significant advancement in bombing accuracy, however, did not occur until 1968 with the arrival of the Paveway system.[84] Over the next four years, the Air Force employed tens of thousands of these smart bombs along the Trail to cut roadways, bomb staging areas, destroy trucks, and suppress AAA.[85] The LGB proved easy to employ from medium altitude. A FAC could illuminate the target with a hand-held laser, which guided a bomb dropped by a strike aircraft.[86] The Paveway's seeker received the coded laser beam's reflection, which, in turn, actuated movable canards to adjust the bomb's trajectory to keep the projectile maneuvering toward the target. Relatively cheap and plentiful, the Air Force quickly attached the Paveway guidance kits to thousands of 500-, 1,000-, 2,000-, and 3,000-pound general-purpose bombs readily available in bomb dumps throughout Southeast Asia.

The Navy also introduced the Walleye, an air-to-ground glide bomb, and the Bull pup, an air-to-ground missile.[87] These munitions utilized a data link to send electro-optic (TV) signals to a cockpit display, enabling the aircrew to guide the weapon while the aircraft remained above the AAA threat envelope.[88]

In addition to new guided weapons, improvements to existing munitions included the M-36, a cluster bomb unit (CBU) that utilized the external casing of the M-30 but replaced its explosive submunitions with an incendiary bomblet to be more effective against petroleum oil lubricants (POL) and trucks. Another modification was the FMU-72 electronic fuze, which provided a pause feature for general-purpose bombs,

83 For a history of the development of precision-guided munitions, see Paul Gillespie, *Weapons of Choice: The Development of Precision Guided Munitions* (Tuscaloosa, AL: University of Alabama Press, 2006).

84 Sorley, *The Abrams Tapes*, 126; Paveway I and II were similar except Paveway II modified inputs to the bombs flight path guidance to be more efficient and accurate. Project CHECO, *Air War in Vietnam 1968–69*, 53.

85 HQ Seventh Air Force, *An Analysis of Laser Guided Bombs in SEA*, AFHRA K741–4 (June 28, 1973), 2; Nalty, *The War against Trucks*, 107.

86 AC-130 gunships also utilized laser designators.

87 Norman Polmar and Edward Moraldo, *Naval Air War: The Rolling Thunder Campaign* (Washington, DC: Department of the Navy, 2015), 8; Mersky and Polmar, *The Naval Air War in Vietnam*, 107; John Nichols and Barrett Tilman, *On Yankee Station: The Naval Air War over Vietnam* (Annapolis, MD: Naval Institute Press, 1987), 25.

88 Project CHECO, *Air War in Vietnam 1968–69*, 53.

turning them into time-delayed mines to hinder truck movement and road repairs.[89]

During Commando Hunt I, the United States invested heavily in intelligence surveillance and reconnaissance (ISR), specialized aircraft, and weapons to improve its air-to-ground capability. 7th Air Force also streamlined operations by reorganizing its command-and-control system. It enhanced its intelligence-gathering ability by deploying a vast sensor array to track NVA movement. Igloo White, combined with the immense computational capabilities at the ISC, provided all-weather, day and night surveillance to produce near-real-time, predictive intelligence, which enhanced the tactical effectiveness of the aerial armada of FACs, gunships, tacair, and B-52s interdicting the Trail. In Commando Hunt I, the Americans employed their air power based on phased and prioritized targeting, with 40 percent of missions striking mountain passes and roads, 35 percent attacking truck parks and storage facilities, 15 percent hitting vehicles, and 10 percent suppressing AAA.[90] The US investment in new technologies during Commando Hunt significantly improved its air-to-ground capability. Even though no friendly armies deployed to southern Laos, there were covert forces, considered next.

Friendly Ground Force Capabilities: Covert Operations

The United States conducted covert operations in Southern Laos. Per the 1954 Geneva Agreement, the United States agreed not to deploy forces into Laos. Instead, the Central Intelligence Agency (CIA) and US special forces conducted covert operations providing general intelligence and target information.[91] CIA road watch teams, as their name implied, monitored traffic flow. Though useful for an overall understanding of enemy operations, the intelligence could not produce near-real-time targets, and the teams' presence inhibited airstrikes near their locations.[92] Special operations units, known as Prairie Fire and later as OP35, were inserted by helicopter into Southern Laos along the South Vietnamese border. Their mission was to identify NVA positions and then call for airstrikes. Though a small operation, OP35 averaged thirty-seven missions a month in 1969 and controlled over 1,000 airstrikes. An OP35 team member flew alongside an O-2 FAC pilot to enhance air and

89 Project CHECO, *Air War in Vietnam 1968–69*, 53.
90 Project CHECO, *Air War in Vietnam 1968–69*, 40; Berger, *The United States Air Force in Southeast Asia*, 110.
91 Prados, *The Blood Road*, 274; Nalty, *The War against Trucks*, 30–32.
92 Sorley, *The Abrams Tapes*, 116; Nalty, *The War against Trucks*, 110.

ground coordination.[93] These covert missions located targets, but they were risky as OP35 teams suffered casualties on half their insertions.[94] Special operation units also could not maintain a permanent presence in Southern Laos and did not deploy sufficient firepower to threaten the enemy directly. The enemy, facing no significant threat from ground forces in southern Laos, did as TAP theory predicts. The NVA dispersed and hid its troops and supplies against the threat of airstrikes.

Enemy Ground Force Capabilities: North Vietnamese Response

In November 1968, the end of Rolling Thunder allowed the North Vietnamese to move their supply facilities south of the 20th parallel near the mountain passes where the Trail began. In reaction to Commando Hunt I, the North deployed another 20,000 Vietnamese and Pathet Lao laborers to 38 engineer battalions in Southern Laos.[95] Crews repaired roads, constructed bypasses, and dispersed repair facilities and truck parks while engineers built dummy truck parks and burned fuel to decoy infrared sensors.[96] Transportation units also camouflaged facilities and vehicles. They concealed their forces by day, when at most significant risk from tacair, and moved their vehicles at night. The North assigned over 10,000 trucks to its transportation units, which shuttled back and forth across their section of the Trail each night.[97] Adjacent truck units would replenish disabled vehicles, with requests for replacements trickling northward. Thanks to imports from communist allies, the North Vietnamese could reconstitute transportation units from the thousands of stockpiled trucks.

The cargo that survived the arduous journey was offloaded at supply depots near the border. These goods, when needed, would then be portered into South Vietnam by foot, bicycle, or oxcart. Overall, the North Vietnamese reacted to Commando Hunt I by significantly increasing their activity along the Trail.

In addition to supplies, the NVA also sent soldiers southward on foot, sufficient to replace their heavy casualties in South Vietnam. US aircrew

[93] Rosenau, *Special Operation Forces*, 21. [94] Rosenau, *Special Operation Forces*, 23.

[95] Schlight, *The War in South Vietnam*, 55; Nalty, *The War against Trucks*, 99. The NVA had an estimated 40,000 total working in Laos on the Trail. Sorley, *The Abrams Tapes*, 155.

[96] Nalty, *The War against Trucks*, 97; Dang Phong, *Five Ho Chi Minh Trails* (Hanoi: Gioi Publishers, 2012), 130.

[97] *The Ho Chi Minh Trail* (Hanoi: Gioi Publishers, 2001), 80; Sherwood, *Nixon's Trident*, 5–6.

had trouble locating and targeting the infiltration of troops, who hid under the forest canopy by day and marched only in small groups at night and in bad weather.[98] Commando Hunt I did, however, prevent the NVA from transporting troops by truck. As a result, it took up to 120 days for a soldier to make the arduous journey, with the attrition rate due to disease and injury estimated at 15 percent.[99]

Overall, along the Trail the NVA reacted as expected by TAP theory by dispersing and concealing its forces. Without a ground threat, the NVA was able to replace its troops in the South, but during Commando Hunt I it struggled to keep supplies moving southward to support the operations discussed next.

NVA/VC Operations in South Vietnam Following their military defeat in the Tet Offensive, and due to their extended LOC into South Vietnam, the NVA/VC were compelled to pre-position ammunition, supplies, and food in the vicinity where they intended to fight. While hiding and dispersing supplies reduced the vulnerability to air attack, pre-positioning reduced the flexibility of where the NVA/VC could operate. The forward-deployed caches were also vulnerable to allied ground patrols, particularly in areas where South Vietnamese intelligence could penetrate and exploit the Viet Cong infrastructure (VCI), the local insurgents responsible for pre-staging supplies.

On February 23, 1969, the NVA launched the post-Tet Offensive, its fourth and final offensive within a year. In preparation for this campaign, the NVA deployed to South Vietnam the same-sized force as it had had the previous year and conducted one-third more attacks than in the Tet Offensive. In the post-Tet Offensive, however, most of the NVA/VC attacks were by indirect fire, which inflicted casualties but were no longer designed to occupy territory or inspire insurrection. Most attacks included no more than a dozen sporadic rocket or mortar rounds aimed at villages or military installations. However, the offensive no longer involved ground assaults on cities, as the NVA no longer anticipated inciting the population. The NVA/VC had sufficient supplies in southern South Vietnam to launch the post-Tet offensive, but they could sustain their attacks for only a few days. Most attacks lasted less than a week, and in Saigon only thirty-four rockets fell on the city.[100]

With the failure of this fourth offensive, Hanoi finally recognized it could not win through conventional means and adjusted its strategy by

[98] Sorley, *The Abrams Tapes*, 134. [99] Sorley, *The Abrams Tapes*, 299.

[100] The Saigon rocket attacks were spread over three weeks. Sorley, *The Abrams Tapes*, 169.

resuming irregular warfighting tactics.[101] The North Vietnamese also reduced the infiltration of troops and supplies along the Trail over the summer of 1969. In September, they turned their attention to central Laos to support the Pathet Lao rebels.[102] In South Vietnam, the remaining NVA/VC refocused their effort to try and reverse the gains made in the countryside by the South Vietnamese government's pacification program.

Assessing Commando Hunt I

In 1969, the incoming Nixon administration ordered a review of US policy in Southeast Asia, which included an assessment of Commando Hunt I.[103] Intelligence agencies split over their evaluation of the air campaign. The Defense Intelligence Agency (DIA) and 7th Air Force intelligence concluded the interdiction operation had effectively reduced by 82 percent the supplies reaching South Vietnam.[104] The CIA reached a different verdict, maintaining that the NVA/VC in South Vietnam, which required fewer than fifteen truckloads a day, had received sufficient supplies to continue operations.[105] In addition, Commando Hunt I had not impacted the infiltration of NVA replacement troops, with soldiers continuing to march southward. Nor did air power affect the supplies that moved through the Cambodian port at Sihanoukville to support communist operations in southern South Vietnam.

Both DIA and CIA assessments were correct.[106] Commando Hunt I had not stopped the flow of men and supplies, but it had placed limits on what the NVA/VC could accomplish in South Vietnam and had compelled the North Vietnamese to invest more energy and resources to resupply them. TAP theory explains the North Vietnamese reaction to the threat of air strikes in both South Vietnam and along the Trail. In Commando Hunt I, air power performed above the expectations of TAP theory. Even without a capable, friendly ground force in Laos, the air interdiction program significantly inhibited the flow of supplies to the South. Although NVA reinforcements arrived in South Vietnam, they did not have the combat capability to mount and maintain effective operations. As a result, Commando Hunt I significantly delayed and

101 Pribbenow, *Victory in Vietnam*, 240–246; Sorley, *The Abrams Tapes*, 278, 709.
102 Pribbenow, *Victory in Vietnam*, 254.
103 Sorley, *The Abrams Tapes*, 118; Nalty, *The War against Trucks*, 108.
104 Of the 45,000 tons entering the Trail 8,500 made it to South Vietnam. 7th Air Force, *Commando Hunt VII*, June 1972, AFHRA K740.430-6 Reel 42321, 4; Nalty, *The War against Trucks*, 110, 112.
105 Nalty, *The War against Trucks*, 108; Project CHECO, *Air War in Vietnam 1968–69*, April 1, 1970, 43.
106 Sorley, *The Abrams Tapes*, 516–517.

reduced the severity of the 1969 post-Tet offensive. After this fourth offensive, Hanoi finally recognized the futility of further large-scale operations. It shifted back to guerrilla tactics and terrorist attacks in an effort to sustain a foothold in South Vietnam.[107] The reduction in pressure by the NVA/VC for the remainder of 1969 provided a critical window of opportunity for the pacification and Vietnamization programs to make progress.

US Foreign Policy in Southeast Asia: 1969

By June 1969, sufficiently satisfied with progress in Southeast Asia, President Nixon announced the immediate redeployment of 25,000 troops, with plans for a steady reduction thereafter.[108] The summer would see a lull as the North Vietnamese regrouped and repaired the Trail in preparation for the coming dry season. The NVA/VC in South Vietnam became even more reliant upon their southern LOC, which, unlike the Trail, had not been under significant pressure from airstrikes.[109] The Communists moved weapons, ammunition, and supplies from the Cambodian port of Sihanoukville to sanctuary bases and supply depots inside the border near Saigon.

Even with announcements in June and again in September of further reductions of 25,000 and 35,000 troops, any grace period President Nixon might have had with the anti-war movement ended in early autumn. Across the United States, large-scale protests returned. Collectively known as the Moratorium, these demonstrations on hundreds of college campuses and major cities, including Washington, drew hundreds of thousands.[110] Nixon responded with his "silent majority" address to the Nation on November 3, 1969, where he outlined the policy of Vietnamization while accusing the North Vietnamese of intransigence in both public and secret negotiations.[111] The speech worked, neutralizing protests through the following spring.

Diplomatically, there had been little progress since negotiations had commenced in Paris in May 1968. In August 1969, Nixon's National

107 Guan, *The Vietnam War from the Other Side*, 137.

108 Nalty, *The War against Trucks*, 109.

109 In March 1969, Nixon ordered the secret bombing of NVA/VC base camps and supply depots just across the Cambodian border. William Beecher, "Raids in Cambodia by U.S. Unprotested" *New York Times*, May 9, 1969, A1; Henry Kissinger, *The White House Years* (New York: Simon & Schuster, 1979), 247, 274.

110 Prados, *The Blood Road*, 294, 301; James Willbanks, *A Raid Too Far: Operation Lam Son 719 and Vietnamization in Laos* (College Station: Texas A&M University Press, 2014), 19.

111 Richard Nixon, "Address to the Nation over the War in Vietnam," November 3, 1969, https://millercenter.org/the-presidency/presidential-speeches/november-3-1969-address-nation-war-vietnam.

Security Advisor, Henry Kissinger met secretly with North Vietnamese representatives. However, Kissinger accomplished no more than the public talks as Hanoi remained adamant on two conditions for peace: the complete withdrawal of US troops and the replacement of the South Vietnamese government.[112]

Overall, TAP theory continued to explain successful air operations in Southeast Asia. US air power continued to be effective along the Trail, even with a decrease in overall tacair and B-52 availability, due to technological improvements in the AC-130 Spectre, which enhanced lethality at night. The North Vietnamese also adapted by improving their air defenses, expanding the number of roads along the Trail, and adjusting their tactics for moving supplies. In addition, while the NVA/VC continued to struggle in South Vietnam, the North Vietnamese expanded the war into Laos and Cambodia.

Commando Hunt III: November 1969–April 1970

Commando Hunt II, conducted over the summer rainy season of 1969, began to see a reduction in sortie availability. By September, the United States decreased tacair and bomber sorties by 15 percent.[113] In November, the arrival of the dry season kicked off Commando Hunt III, with the return of an intensified air interdiction effort to stem the surge of NVA supplies heading south along the Trail. Meanwhile, in South Vietnam, the continued lull in fighting allowed pacification and Vietnamization to make progress, such that by the end of 1969 Nixon announced another 50,000 troops would be returning home. No longer fearing large-scale offensives by the NVA, General Creighton Abrams dispersed his remaining ground forces to support the pacification program. For emergencies, he relied upon tacair and B-52s as a strategic reserve.

The remainder of this section analyzes Commando Hunt III, including air superiority along the Trail, improvements of air-to-ground capabilities, and adaptation by the North Vietnamese.

Air Superiority

Over time, the VPAF increased the number of MiGs operating in North Vietnam from 50 fighters in June 1969 to 130 by the end of

[112] Henry Kissinger, *The White House Years* (New York: Simon & Schuster, 1979), 283.
[113] The decrease in sortie availability resulted from congressional budgetary pressure to speed the withdrawal. Project CHECO, *Air War in Vietnam 1968–69*, April 1, 1970, 47.

December.[114] In January 1970, a squadron of MiG-21s deployed south of the 20th parallel to an airfield near Vinh. Later that month, the MiGs demonstrated their lethality by downing a rescue helicopter over southern Laos.[115] An SA-2 battery near the Laotian border fired on a B-52 flight in February, restricting bomber and fixed-wing gunship operations near the Mu Gai and Ban Karai mountain passes.[116]

By early 1970, the NVA had doubled the AAA operating along the Trail. As Commando Hunt III continued, the NVA grew more aggressive, increasing ammunition expenditures by 45 percent.[117] By April 1970, the NVA actively employed 75 percent of the 1,000 AAA pieces deployed along the Trail.[118] As a result, US combat loss rates over southern Laos increased marginally from 0.63 to 0.74 losses per 1,000 sorties compared to the previous dry season. The loss of 60 aircraft, with another 310 damaged, was not, however, prohibitively high compared to the losses previously incurred during Rolling Thunder. US air forces dedicated 12 percent of their tacair sorties to escort and flak suppression.[119] Although the United States maintained air superiority over the Trail, the increasing threat from the North Vietnamese air defenses compelled aircrew to take countermeasures. They flew at higher altitude, dedicated more tacair missions for escort and flak suppression, and restricted B-52s, AC-130s, and slow prop-driven FACs from operating near the North Vietnamese border.[120]

Air-to-Ground Capability

The return of the dry season allowed US air forces to reengage the North Vietnamese LOC in southern Laos. Though the United States reduced the number of aircraft, it still generated 53,000 tacair sorties for Commando Hunt III.[121]

114 USAF 7th Air Force, *Commando Hunt III*, May 1970, 14. Of the 262 VPAF MiGs, half remained based in China. Project CHECO, *Air War in Vietnam 1968–69*, April 1, 1970, 18.

115 USAF 7th Air Force, *Commando Hunt III*, May 1970, 48.

116 USAF 7th Air Force, *Commando Hunt III*, May 1970, 139. US intelligence identified eighteen SA-2 sites during Commando Hunt III. USAF 7th Air Force, *Commando Hunt III*, May 1970, 139.

117 USAF 7th Air Force, *Commando Hunt III*, May 1970, xxiii.

118 USAF 7th Air Force, *Commando Hunt III*, May 1970, iii, 25.

119 Ten percent in Commando Hunt I and 12 percent in Commando Hunt III. USAF 7th Air Force, *Commando Hunt III*, May 1970, xxiv.

120 USAF 7th Air Force, *Commando Hunt III*, May 1970, xxiv.

121 They were 58 percent by the Air Force, 36 percent by the Navy, and 5 percent by the Marine Corps. Another 7,500 tactical reconnaissance sorties were flown, as were 4,100 B-52 Arc Light missions. USAF 7th Air Force, *Commando Hunt III*, May 1970, xi–xii.

US air-to-ground capabilities continued to improve steadily. Despite the raised threat from North Vietnamese air defenses and the decreased availability of sorties, Commando Hunt III increased efficiency due to new sensors, weapons, and tactics. For night operations, the most significant improvement was the arrival of the "Surprise Package," a single, highly modified AC-130A Spectre carrying an assortment of new sensors and weapons, allowing it to operate well above AAA tactical effective range. The Surprise Package nearly doubled the truck kill rate compared to the other AC-130 Spectres, up from 4.34 to 7.34 trucks claimed per sortie.[122] The Surprise Package had the further advantage of recording video footage to validate BDA. As a result of the superior performance of the Surprise Package, over the next year the Air Force modified its other five AC-130As. The Air Force also ordered the procurement of new AC-130Es with a greater payload to incorporate even more sensor and weapon upgrades.[123]

Though the AC-130 killed more trucks, this did not mean it was the greatest threat to the enemy. With FACs and tacair patrolling the Trail by day and Spectres by night, the NVA chose to operate at night, indicating that the more significant threat came from daytime strikes. FACs and tacair denied using the Trail during the day, compelling the North Vietnamese to operate for fewer hours and with reduced efficiency at night.

The two chief limitations of the AC-130 were that it still needed clear weather to operate and, being big and slow, it proved vulnerable to ground fire, which precluded flying during the day or at twilight. The NVA partially countered the gunship by adjusting operations to move during the hours around sunrise and sunset. However, doing so further limited the time available each night to transport supplies.[124] During the dry season, the threat from tacair, which deterred the NVA during the day, along with the new Spectres flying at night, had a significant impact on the ability to move supplies along the Trail, causing the NVA to react.

NVA Response to Commando Hunt III

During the first weeks of the dry season in late 1969, the North Vietnamese focused on repairing and expanding the road networks in

[122] Gunship kill claims were above the tacair average of half a truck per sortie. Fixed-wing gunships accounted for 58 percent of truck kills flying just 8 percent of sorties; tacair had 39 percent of truck kills. USAF 7th Air Force, *Commando Hunt III*, May 1970, xvii; Sorley, *Abrams Tapes*, 496, 523.

[123] The AC-130Es would become operational in Commando Hunt VII in 1971–72. Jack Ballard, *Development and Employment of Fixed-Wing Gunships 1962–1972* (Washington, DC: Office of Air Force History, 1982), 145–147, 159, 162.

[124] Head, "Playing Hide-and-Seek with the 'Trail'," 103.

southern Laos and reinforcing their air defenses.[125] Truck movement along the Trail in November 1969 was up 23 percent from the previous year.[126] When the United States commenced heavy strikes on the Mu Gia and Ban Karai passes, the NVA opened an alternative pass, which crossed into Laos just north of the DMZ.[127] The new route had the added benefit of reducing the exposure time of trucks to airstrikes.[128] In January 1970, the number of convoys surged, tripling goods entering the Trail, up to 131 tons per day. The rush to move supplies southward during good weather continued through February, peaking at 216 tons per day.[129] This activity exposed truck convoys to air strikes, particularly gunship attacks. Even though facing this lethal air threat, the combination of an expanded road network, dispersed supply facilities, and the surge of trucks meant a third of the supplies which entered the Trail reached South Vietnam, up from 20 percent the year before.[130]

In addition to providing supplies, the Trail continued to be the primary means for NVA reinforcements to reach South Vietnam. The Communists in South Vietnam had suffered high attrition, beginning in 1969 with 267,000 troops, of which an estimated 154,000 had died. The North replaced the heavy losses; 103,000 reinforcements made the trip on foot down the Trail. By the end of 1969, the NVA/VC had an estimated 226,000 soldiers in the South.[131] In 1970, however, the infiltration to South Vietnam dropped precipitously as the North Vietnamese diverted troops to fight alongside the Pathet Tao in Laos and the Khmer Rouge in Cambodia.[132]

Preparing for these twin operations in Laos and Cambodia produced a personnel shortfall in South Vietnam, where the NVA/VC struggled.[133] Unable to launch offensives as in the past, they conducted sporadic attacks by fire and terrorist activities to impose costs, where they could, on the South Vietnamese government and US forces.[134] This extended lull in enemy operations in South Vietnam allowed pacification and

125 Sorley, *The Abrams Tapes*, 317.
126 USAF 7th Air Force, *Commando Hunt III*, May 1970, i–ii.
127 Sorley, *The Abrams Tapes*, 293.
128 USAF 7th Air Force, *Commando Hunt III*, May 1970, ii.
129 USAF 7th Air Force, *Commando Hunt III*, May 1970, v–vii, 24. Of 54,000 tons entering the Trail 19,000 reached South Vietnam. USAF 7th Air Force, *Commando Hunt VII*, 5.
130 USAF 7th Air Force, *Commando Hunt III*, May 1970, xxviii.
131 Sorley, *The Abrams Tapes*, 303, 299.
132 Pribbenow, *Victory in Vietnam*, 257; Sorley, *The Abrams Tapes*, 329; Lien-Hang Nguyen, *Hanoi's War: An International History of the War for Peace in Vietnam* (Chapel Hill, NC: University of North Carolina Press, 2012), 154. MACV estimated 53,600 NVA infiltrations for 1970. Sorley, *The Abrams Tapes*, 516.
133 Sorley, *The Abrams Tapes*, 710.
134 Sorley, *The Abrams Tapes*, 337.

Vietnamization to expand and enabled the allies to conduct a cross-border offensive into Cambodia.

Overall, air power, though not as effective as Commando Hunt I, still prevented most supplies from entering South Vietnam. Commando Hunt III and Hanoi's decision to divert troops into Laos and Cambodia further weakened NVA/VC operations in South Vietnam. TAP theory helps to explain why the NVA continued to struggle under a lethal air threat and why it chose to continue to disperse and conceal its forces.

Expansion of the Ground War into Laos and Cambodia: 1970

In 1970, the war spilled across the border into Laos and Cambodia. In Laos, a civil war between the US-supported Royal Laotian government and the North Vietnamese-backed Pathet Lao rebels had been ongoing since the early 1960s. In February 1970, Pathet Lao and NVA troops pushed westward across the Plaine Des Jarre into central Laos. To blunt the communist offensive, the United States diverted hundreds of tacair and B-52 sorties from the Trail to support their Laotian allies.[135] In March, the ouster of King Sihanouk in Cambodia by a pro-American Cambodian government resulted in the communist Khmer Rouge rebels, backed by Hanoi, surrounding the capital of Phnom Penh.[136]

The turmoil in Cambodia provided General Abrams the opportunity he had been waiting for. President Nixon approved sending US and ARVN troops across the border to attack enemy base camps, including the COSVN (Central Office of South Vietnam), the VC's headquarters. Allied ground forces also captured enemy supplies and interdicted the Sihanouk Trail. Though most NVA/VC avoided contact by retreating deeper into Cambodia, the Americans and South Vietnamese considered the operation a success. The capture of tons of sensitive documents, rice, weapons, and ammunition stockpiles set back enemy plans in southern South Vietnam for more than a year. The permanent loss of the Sihanouk Trail also made the Trail even more vital for the Communists.[137]

[135] Berger, *The United States Air Force in Southeast Asia*, 131. In March 1969, the White House ordered B-52s to secretly bomb base camps and supply depots just across the Cambodian border. Beecher, "Raids in Cambodia by U.S. Unprotested"; Henry Kissinger, *The White House Years* (New York: Simon & Schuster, 1979), 247, 274.

[136] Nguyen, *Hanoi's War*, 181; Prados, *Vietnam: The History of an Unwinnable War*, 362–363.

[137] Prados, *The Blood Road*, 299.

On April 20, 1970, President Nixon announced the planned withdrawal of another 150,000 troops. Any domestic political relief this might have provided evaporated ten days later when he disclosed allied troops had crossed into Cambodia. This revelation set off another wave of domestic protests. May included student strikes on hundreds of college campuses followed by massive demonstrations after Ohio National Guardsmen killed four students at Kent State University.[138] Nixon ordered all US troops out of Cambodia to preempt a Democratic-controlled Congress debating placing restrictions on military operations in Southeast Asia.

US Ground Activity in South Vietnam Leading Up to the Cambodian Incursion

Following the Tet Offensive, US ground troops focused on controlling territory in support of the South Vietnamese pacification program. Army divisions were divided into smaller maneuver units to conduct patrols to identify the VCI, the local insurgents responsible for forward-positioning caches of supplies. General Abrams spread his combat forces across South Vietnam and, for a strategic reserve, depended upon air power, which could mobilize quickly to support operations anywhere in the country.[139] In addition to this change in ground tactics, Vietnamization showed promise as new RVNMF units were activated. South Vietnamese regional and police forces also improved their ability to maintain security in rural areas.

Until the spring of 1970, friendly ground forces showed limited ability to threaten the NVA/VC outside South Vietnam. While covert activity continued in southern Laos, US and ARVN leaders planned a more substantive cross-border operation into Cambodia. US force levels in South Vietnam continued to draw down to 344,000 from the wartime peak of 543,000 the previous April.[140] Vietnamization, however, had somewhat offset the drawdown such that by spring, the South Vietnamese could test their new capabilities in Cambodia. On April 29, ARVN troops moved across the border into the Parrot's Beak.[141] This geostrategic territory, named after the unique shape of the border, lay thirty-five miles west of Saigon and was a base area for NVA/VC

[138] Prados, *The Blood Road*, 302. In addition, Mississippi police officers killed two students at Jackson State University.
[139] Sorley, *The Abrams Tapes*, 142.
[140] Sorley, *The Abrams Tapes*, 300; Willbanks, *A Raid Too Far*, 23.
[141] Andrew Wiest, *Vietnam's Forgotten Army: Heroism and Betrayal in the ARVN* (New York: New York University Press, 2009), 198–199.

operations. Two days later, US and ARVN forces maneuvered sixty miles northwest of Saigon into the area known as the Fishhook, where the allies suspected the VC of having its headquarters.

In May, the air effort shifted southward from the Trail to eastern Cambodia to support the combined cross-border incursion. Embedded USAF and RVNAF Air Liaison Officers (ALOs) and airborne FACs coordinated and controlled 7,800 preplanned tacair strikes and another 1,700 immediate strike requests. In addition, 380 fixed-wing gunship sorties supported friendly troops at night. At the same time, 653 B-52 Arc Light missions prepared the battlefield and conducted strikes beyond where friendly ground forces were permitted.[142] C-130 airlifters also contributed to the combined arms effort, dropping twenty 15,000-pound Commando Vault, BLU-82 bombs, with the massive bomb blasts instantaneously clearing helicopter landing zones.[143] As TAP theory would anticipate, this effective combined arms effort caused the NVA/VC to disperse and hide.

Ever since the overthrow of the Cambodian King Sihanouk, the North Vietnamese had expected such a cross-border incursion. Still, they had not anticipated the magnitude and speed of the allied advance.[144] The NVA/VC had orders to avoid heavy losses by conducting a measured retreat into Cambodia. However, they did not have the time or means to remove the large caches of supplies stockpiled.[145] By the end of June, when US troops withdrew from Cambodia, they had seized or destroyed 22,600 weapons, 1,800 tons of ammunition, and 6,800 tons of rice, sufficient to arm and feed 25,000 soldiers for a year.[146]

In addition to denying the NVA/VC sanctuary, the destruction of the stockpiles and blockade of the Cambodian port sealed off the Sihanouk Trail.[147] The North Vietnamese would thereafter depend upon the Trail as the sole means of supply for all operations in South Vietnam. The closure of the Sihanouk Trail would particularly impact NVA/VC operations near Saigon and the Mekong Delta.

Even though most of the enemy troops in Cambodia had escaped, the ARVN had performed relatively well in its first large-scale operation,

142 A 30-kilometer restriction was placed on US ground forces. MACV Official History, Volume III, 1970 (Saigon: MACV Military History Branch, 1971), C-32.

143 MACV Official History, Volume III, 1970, C-128, 131, 132; Robert Sanders, *Invasion of Laos, 1971, Lam Son 719* (Norman: University of Oklahoma Press, 2014), 111.

144 MACV Official History, Volume III, 1970, C-28.

145 Sorley, *The Abrams Tapes*, 321.

146 In addition, the allied forces reported 10,000 enemy killed and 1,000 captured at the cost of 1,000 friendly killed. MACV Official History, Volume III, 1970, C-47.

147 MACV Official History, Volume III, 1970, C-1.

viewed as a validation of Vietnamization.[148] Still, the test had been partial. The ARVN had deployed its best troops and had had the advantage of embedded US Army advisors and Air Force liaisons to coordinate extensive air support. As important, the NVA/VC chose not to stand and fight in Cambodia.[149]

Assessment of US Air Operations Southeast Asia: November 1968–June 1970

Overall, the results of air operations in Southeast Asia from the end of Rolling Thunder through the Cambodian incursion of 1970 were positive but not decisive. Commando Hunt I and III had a significant impact on the ability of the NVA to resupply its forces in northern South Vietnam. But so long as the Sihanouk Trail remained open, air interdiction of the Ho Chi Minh Trail had little impact on NVA/VC activity near Saigon and the Mekong Delta. It would take a combined arms offensive, with allied troops invading Cambodia, to shut down the Sihanouk Trail. Further, Commando Hunt I and III had little impact on the infiltration of NVA troops.

In contrast to Commando Hunt I and III, where there were no friendly ground forces, in South Vietnam US air and ground forces could coordinate action. As expected by TAP theory, enemy fielded forces were consistently defeated and compelled to disperse and hide. Unable to conduct large-force operations, the NVA/VC reverted to intermittent attacks by fire and terrorist attacks. Air power, employed as a strategic reserve, allowed friendly ground forces to disperse to support South Vietnamese pacification efforts, which further allowed the Thieu government to make significant inroads, denying the VC the ability to reestablish control of the countryside.

Strategically, South Vietnam continued to make strides with pacification and Vietnamization. For the North Vietnamese, the loss of the Sihanouk Trail and sanctuary in Cambodia seriously undermined operations in the southern regions of South Vietnam. Hanoi had begun to show signs of war-weariness, as evidenced by the decision to call off further offensives in South Vietnam. Still, Hanoi's Communist Party, under the thumb of Le Duan, remained resolute in its policy of uniting the North and South by force.[150] On a positive note for the Communists,

148 MACV Official History, Volume III, 1970, C-107–108.

149 Willbanks, *A Raid Too Far*, 22. On the role of US advisors see Weist, *Vietnam's Forgotten War*, 84–91.

150 Nguyen, *Hanoi's War*, 156.

the North Vietnamese continued to make political gains in America with the reemergence of widespread protests in the spring of 1970. Congressional action further threatened to cut war funding, even as President Nixon rapidly drew down hundreds of thousands of combat troops from South Vietnam. Since the Tet Offensive, the threat of funding cuts and troop redeployments put the allies' military gains at risk. As will be revealed in the next chapter, the clock was ticking for South Vietnam to defend itself, and this pressure would, in part, lead to its fateful decision to launch Lam Son 719, the ARVN's ill-advised raid into southern Laos in 1971.

6 Commando Hunt V–VII and Lam Son 719: 1971–1972

The tactical air power (TAP) theory introduced in Chapter 2 explains why, after the Tet Offensive, the combination of lethal US air power and capable allied ground forces placed the North Vietnamese in a dilemma. Should the North Vietnamese Army and Viet Cong (NVA/VC) concentrate and maneuver against allied ground forces, as it had at Khe Sanh, or instead disperse and hide against the air threat as it had in the past? The NVA/VC initially attempted the former. However, after being repeatedly beaten back in the mini-Tet, third Tet, and 1969 post-Tet offensives, they eventually adopted the latter option by shifting to guerrilla tactics and terrorist attacks. The Commando Hunt I and III air interdiction campaign in southern Laos slowed supplies moving along the Ho Chi Minh Trail. Still, it could not stop the infiltration of the small clusters of NVA troops traveling on foot. The cross-border combined arms operations in Cambodia in early 1970 further denied the Communists sanctuary and cut off their southern supply route. These actions bought precious time and space for the South Vietnamese pacification program to gain more control over the population. At the same time, Vietnamization expanded the capacity of the Republic of Vietnam Military Forces (RVNMF) as it replaced the departing American combat units.

This chapter continues to assess the impact of air power through the lens of TAP theory. Following the Cambodian invasion, an emboldened Army of the Republic of Vietnam (ARVN) shifted its offensive northward into Laos. The objective was the complete interdiction of the Ho Chi Minh Trail – which US air power had not been able to achieve. Instead, the ill-fated Lam Son 719 raid revealed significant shortcomings in allied air-to-ground coordination and the ARVN's combat capabilities. Without its US advisors, the ARVN could not leverage air power to defeat the enemy. Instead, the NVA massed and maneuvered to drive the South Vietnamese from Laos.

In the United States, the Cambodian incursion had brought a resurgence of anti-war sentiment, with heated congressional debate over restricting military operations in Southeast Asia. Though the Cooper–Church amendment failed in June 1970, as did the McGovern–Hatfield amendment in September, the Nixon administration continued to face intense domestic pressure to abandon Saigon. Through his National Security Advisor, Henry Kissinger, President Nixon responded with a secret peace initiative, offering an immediate ceasefire followed by a complete American withdrawal from South Vietnam. Hanoi responded by reiterating its long-held position that a communist-approved government must first replace South Vietnamese President Thieu's regime.[1] In an October 7, 1970 speech to the Nation, Nixon offered an immediate ceasefire, a prisoner of war (POW) exchange, followed by a complete US withdrawal.[2] Nixon's speech drew praise in the West but was rejected by Hanoi as it did not mention installing a new government in Saigon. In November congressional elections, the Democrats widened their antiwar caucus in the House and maintained a slim majority in the Senate. At the end of the year, Congress finally voted Cooper–Church into law, forbidding US ground troops from operating beyond South Vietnamese borders.

In mid-October 1970, the early arrival of the dry season ushered in Commando Hunt V. As in previous years, B-52 and tactical aircraft (tacair) strikes initially targeted the entry points where the Ho Chi Minh Trail crossed the Annamite Mountain Range into Laos.[3] Meanwhile, senior American and South Vietnamese military leaders began planning a cross-border raid into southern Laos. The allies anticipated the invasion, Lam Son 719, would achieve what the Cambodian incursion had the previous spring, denying the enemy sanctuary and severing the Communists' lines of communication (LOC). In preparation for Lam Son 719, US troops marched north to secure Khe Sanh as a staging base. In early February 1971, the ARVN, minus US advisors and tactical air controllers, pushed across the Laotian border, moving westward along Route 9. Their objective was to reach the town of Tchepone, a critical juncture along the Ho Chi Minh Trail (see Map 5.1). However, the cross-border offensive was soon bogged down: the ARVN was outnumbered more than two to one as heavily armed NVA reinforcements arrived.[4] In response, the ARVN, after reaching

[1] Henry Kissinger, *The White House Years* (New York: Simon & Schuster, 1979), 976–979.

[2] Richard Nixon, *Address to the Nation on a New Initiative for Peace*, October 7, 1970, www.youtube.com/watch?v=-sPWyGYDJvM&ab_channel=RichardNixonPresidentialLibrary.

[3] 7th Air Force, *Commando Hunt V* (Saigon, Republic of Vietnam, May 1971), preface.

[4] James Willbanks, *A Raid Too Far: Operation Lam Son 719 and Vietnamization in Laos* (College Station: Texas A&M University Press, 2014), 121.

Tchepone, curtailed operations and hastily withdrew. Though both sides claimed victory, the North held the ground.

In addition to the invasion of Laos, President Nixon's decision to place Lieutenant William Calley under house arrest after his March conviction for the Mai Lai massacre set off another wave of anti-war protests.[5] In late April 1971, the Vietnam Veterans against the War and other anti-war movements gathered on the Mall in Washington. A week later, DC police and federal troops broke up protests and arrested 7,000. On June 13, the *New York Times* published segments of the Pentagon Papers, exposing the secret history of US administration decision-making in Southeast Asia.[6] In Hanoi, over the summer, Le Duan, the aggressive North Vietnamese Communist Party leader, determined that the ARVN's poor performance in Lam Son 719 indicated that Vietnamization had failed. He ordered preparations for another general offensive for the following dry season.

This chapter analyzes the decreasing effectiveness of air power in Commando Hunt V, Lam Son 719, and Commando Hunt VII from the fall of 1970 to the lead-up to the Easter Offensive in early 1972. In Commando Hunt V, the air interdiction campaign continued to impede supplies reaching South Vietnam but had little impact on the infiltration of NVA troops into Laos. During Lam Son 719, unlike what TAP theory would have predicted, air power did not deter the NVA from concentrating and maneuvering. US advisors, forbidden by law from entering Laos, were not embedded in ground units to coordinate airstrikes. As a result, the outnumbered ARVN withdrew. After Lam Son 719, the North Vietnamese built up their air defenses along the demilitarized zone (DMZ). The resultant reduction in US air superiority, in turn, significantly degraded the impact of Commando Hunt VII, allowing the NVA to deploy a dozen mechanized divisions in preparation for the Easter Offensive.

Commando Hunt V: October 1970–February 1971

In 1970, following the loss of the Sihanouk Trail in Cambodia, the NVA/VC in South Vietnam relied solely on the Ho Chi Minh Trail (the Trail)

[5] Richard Nixon, *The Memoirs of Richard Nixon* (New York: Simon & Schuster, 1978), 500; George Herring, *America's Longest War: The United States and Vietnam, 1950–1975, 4th Edition* (New York: McGraw, 2001), 256; John Prados, *Vietnam: The History of an Unwinnable War, 1954–1975* (Lawrence: University Press of Kansas, 2009), 424–425.

[6] Nixon, *The Memoirs*, 508.

for supplies.[7] For reinforcements, they also depended on a steady stream of troops to replace the heavy losses since 1968. Attrition had been so high that by 1970 three-quarters of VC units were manned by northern soldiers.[8] In late fall, the North Vietnamese again surged trucks down the Trail once the rains receded.[9] This increased activity, however, made their supply lines vulnerable to air attack. The NVA therefore deployed additional air defenses into southern Laos. Engineers also widened roadways to accommodate the increased traffic and constructed 400 miles of new roads, expanding the Trail to the west. Road improvements allowed convoys to drive faster and in all weather conditions, thus decreasing exposure to airstrikes.[10] This section assesses US air superiority and air-to-ground capabilities during Commando Hunt V.

Air Superiority in Commando Hunt V

In late 1970, at the beginning of Commando Hunt V, North Vietnamese air defenses were less intense than they had been the previous year. As a result, US air losses fell by half.[11] MiG-21s continued to operate from their southern airfield at Vinh but rarely entered Laos or South Vietnam.[12] The SA-2s in southern North Vietnam continued to harass aircraft along the border, and in March 1971, US aircrew sighted several surface-to-air (SAM) batteries in southern Laos.[13] The SAM threat, however, was only a minor irritant. Occasionally the United States diverted its B-52s, but the only losses to SAMs were two tacair, with another three damaged, while flying near the DMZ.[14] The United States neutralized the threat with suppression of enemy air defense (SEAD) missions and dedicated strikes against suspected SAM sites.[15]

[7] Robert Sanders, *Invasion of Laos 1971: Lam Son 719* (Norman: University of Oklahoma Press, 2014), 82; Lewis Sorley, ed., *The Abrams Tapes 1968–1972: Vietnam Chronicles* (Lubbock: Texas Tech University Press, 2004), 599.

[8] Nguyen Duy Hinh, *Lam Son 719* (Washington, DC: US Army Center of Military History, 1979), 24.

[9] 7th Air Force, *Commando Hunt V*, 38.

[10] Duy Hinh, *Lam Son 719*, 16, 18; 7th Air Force, *Commando Hunt VII*, 6.

[11] In Commando Hunt III, 310 aircraft were hit, with 60 lost for a 0.74 loss per 1,000 sorties, while in Commando Hunt V, 179 aircraft were hit, with 25 lost for a 0.27 loss per 1,000 sorties. 7th Air Force, *Commando Hunt V*, 93, 129.

[12] E. Hartsook and Brian Gunderson, *The Air Force in Southeast Asia: Shield of Vietnamization and Withdrawal 1971* (Washington, DC: Office of Air Force History, 1976), 21.

[13] 7th Air Force, *Commando Hunt V*, 95–96, 249, 251.

[14] 7th Air Force, *Commando Hunt V*, 243.

[15] 7th Air Force, *Commando Hunt V*, 32, 80, 102; Hartsook and Gunderson, *The Air Force in Southeast Asia*, 22.

Given the limited MiG and SAM activity, the greatest threat to air operations in Laos remained small arms and anti-aircraft artillery (AAA). The Communists had reduced the number of active AAA sites by 17 percent by 1970. As a result, the number of allied aircraft reacting to AAA fire decreased by 14 percent from the previous year.[16] Even so, US air forces, including Air Force, Navy, and Marine Corps aviation, increased the dedicated sorties for flak suppression from 10 to 15 percent.[17] On these missions, tacair equipped with laser-guided bombs (LGBs) surgically attacked AAA when identified or dropped cluster bomb units (CBU) and napalm on suspected sites.[18]

Air-to-Ground Capability in Commando Hunt V

In October 1970, Commando Hunt V commenced with the early arrival of the dry season. As with Commando Hunt I and III before it, B-52s and tacair bombed mountain passes and other vital chokepoints.[19] One difference from previous Commando Hunts was a significant decrease in tacair sorties, with fewer than half the combat aircraft available compared to the year before.[20] Even with this decrease, the ability to destroy trucks improved as the "Surprise Package," augmented by five additionally retrofitted AC-130As, more than made up for the loss in tacair.[21] In addition, eleven B-57Gs, modified twin-engine Canberra bombers, deployed to Southeast Asia to conduct night operations. With its forward-looking infrared (FLIR), the Canberra could employ laser-guided, cluster, incendiary, and general-purpose bombs against mobile targets.[22] US air forces dedicated nearly a quarter of the 57,000 sorties flown in Commando Hunt V to killing trucks. Due to these enhanced air-to-ground capabilities, intelligence estimated that only 14 percent of supplies entering the Trail reached South Vietnam.[23]

Overall, Commando Hunt V's success in interdicting supplies, in conjunction with the permanent shutdown of the Sihanouk Trail, constrained the availability of supplies, weapons, and ammunition to support the NVA/VC in South Vietnam. These shortages contributed to the

16 7th Air Force, *Commando Hunt V*, 93, 234.

17 7th Air Force, *Commando Hunt V*, 78, 93.

18 7th Air Force, *Commando Hunt V*, 93.

19 7th Air Force, *Commando Hunt V*, 7–12.

20 7th Air Force, *Commando Hunt V*, 3.

21 7th Air Force, *Commando Hunt V*, 39.

22 7th Air Force, *Commando Hunt V*, 40, 62, 269–274.

23 Even with the increase in the NVA supply effort, only 7,000 of the 60,000 tons that entered the Trail reached the South. 7th Air Force, *Commando Hunt V*, 6, 54, 129; Project CHECO, *Commando Hunt VI* (HQ PACAF: Tactical Evaluation Team, 1972), 40; Sorley, *The Abrams Tapes*, 612, 637.

Communists continuing only to conduct sporadic rocket/mortar fire and terrorist attacks. Though air interdiction could impede the flow of supplies, without friendly ground forces on the ground, air power alone had little ability to stop enemy troops from operating in Laos or infiltrating South Vietnam. These limitations of air interdiction resulted in the allied decision to conduct a raid into Laos.

Lam Son 719: February–April 1971

The previous year's success in closing the Sihanouk Trail and denying sanctuary to the Communists in Cambodia prompted the allied decision to conduct a similar raid into southern Laos in 1971.[24] There were several distinctions, however, between Cambodia and Laos. First, the Communists had chosen not to stand and fight in Cambodia, and as a result, the ARVN had not been tested in the conduct of large, combined arms operations.[25] In southern Laos, however, the NVA held its ground because it had to keep the remaining LOC open to continue the war in the South.[26] In Laos, the NVA had the advantage of shorter lines of operation, which allowed it to bring forward reinforcements quickly.[27] The terrain also favored the NVA, while the ARVN operated in unfamiliar territory.[28] ARVN mechanized units struggled along Route 9, washed out in numerous places.[29] A prominent escarpment to the south and a river to the north further narrowed the roadway, making it easy for the NVA to interdict.[30] By contrast, the NVA had long operated in southern Laos, where it was well acquainted with the terrain and utilized ground cover to conceal the movement of its infantry and armor to mount a counterattack.

Second, security concerns over leaking information about the impending offensive to the enemy and press curtailed the detailed planning required for such a complex raid.[31] Third, Cooper–Church, which

[24] Nixon, *The Memoirs*, 498; Kissinger, *The White House Years*, 990–991; Jeffrey Kimball, *Nixon's Vietnam War* (Lawrence: University of Kansas Press, 1998), 241; Duy Hinh, *Lam Son 719*, 8.

[25] Sanders, *Invasion of Laos*, 95, 97; Lewis Sorley, *A Better War: The Unexamined Victories and Final Tragedy of America's Last Years in Vietnam* (New York: Harcourt, 1999), 245.

[26] Willbanks, *A Raid Too Far*, 55.

[27] Initially, the NVA had 15,000 infantry and 12,000 support troops around Tchepone. In March, the arrival of five regiments brought its combat strength up to 35,000 compared to ARVN's 17,000. 7th Air Force *Commando Hunt V*, 66–67.

[28] Willbanks, *A Raid Too Far*, 54.

[29] Andrew Weist, *Vietnam's Forgotten Army: Heroism and Betrayal in the ARVN* (New York: New York University Press, 2009), 201.

[30] Duy Hinh, *Lam Son 719*, 28.

[31] Duy Hinh, *Lam Son 719*, 54; Willbanks, *A Raid Too Far*, 52.

made it unlawful for US soldiers to operate outside South Vietnam, impacted operations.[32] The allies planned a sequential attack, first with US forces retaking Khe Sanh, to establish a staging and resupply base.[33] Next, the ARVN would cross into Laos and maneuver toward Tchepone. The objectives were to interdict the Trail and destroy NVA supply bases in the area (Map 5.1).[34] However, the ARVN, stripped of US advisors and tactical air controllers, was handicapped in its ability to coordinate air support, and, as a result, the offensive faltered.[35] Finally, the South Vietnamese proved more risk-averse than the North Vietnamese.[36] President Thieu intervened early in the planning of Lam Son 719, ordering the ARVN commanding officer to limit combat losses.[37] As a result of poor leadership and the reluctance to take casualties, the ARVN lost momentum in its initial push toward Tchepone.[38] The resulting delay provided the opportunity for the NVA to bring forward reserves.[39] Though the ARVN would eventually reach Tchepone, it quickly withdrew.[40] Poor planning and coordination by US and ARVN leaders, along with political intervention by Thieu, undermined Lam Son 719.[41]

By contrast, the North Vietnamese had anticipated an enemy offensive into southern Laos. By late December 1970, the NVA had deployed 22,000 soldiers to the region, including 7,000 combat troops who received alert orders in January.[42] When ARVN mechanized units crossed into Laos on February 8, 1971, the NVA's defenses were initially weak, but within four days the North Vietnamese began to fight back.[43] With the ARVN unable to suppress enemy artillery fire, and as enemy combat forces surged to over 24,000, the NVA overran the ARVN's northern firebases, threatening Route 9 by late February.[44] Two weeks

[32] Kissinger, *The White House Years*, 992; Wiest, *Vietnam's Forgotten Army*, 199, 203.
[33] Willbanks, *A Raid Too Far*, 33; Sanders, *Invasion of Laos*, 87, 98.
[34] Duy Hinh, *Lam Son 719*, 33–39; 7th Air Force, *Commando Hunt V*, 67; Willbanks, *A Raid Too Far*, 54.
[35] Wiest, *Vietnam's Forgotten Army*, 211–212. [36] Willbanks, *A Raid Too Far*, 112.
[37] Lien-Hang Nguyen, *Hanoi's War: An International History of the War for Peace in Vietnam* (Chapel Hill: University of North Carolina Press, 2012), 203; Sanders, *Invasion of Laos*, 124; Wiest, *Vietnam's Forgotten Army*, 210; John Prados, *The Blood Road: The Ho Chi Minh Trail and the Vietnam War* (Hoboken, NJ: Wiley, 1999), 413.
[38] Wiest, *Vietnam's Forgotten Army*, 205.
[39] Willbanks, *A Raid Too Far*, 90; Sanders, *Invasion of Laos*, 125, 200.
[40] 7th Air Force, *Commando Hunt V*, 70. [41] Willbanks *A Raid Too Far*, 160.
[42] Duy Hinh, *Lam Son 719*, 25; Willbanks, *A Raid Too Far*, 61, 64–65; Sanders, *Invasion of Laos*, 106.
[43] Willbanks, *A Raid Too Far*, 82; Wiest, *Vietnam's Forgotten Army*, 205.
[44] William Head, "Playing Hide-and-Seek with the 'Trail': Operation Commando Hunt, 1968–1972" *Journal of Third World Studies* 29:1 (2002), 104; Willbanks, *A Raid Too Far*, 111; Sanders, *Invasion of Laos*, 140; Sorley, *A Better War*, 249; Wiest, *Vietnam's Forgotten Army*, 206–209.

later, the NVA, now strengthened to over 34,000, launched a counter-offensive. Heavy fighting continued until all ARVN forces had retreated to South Vietnam by March 24.[45]

The remainder of this section analyzes why during Lam Son 719 US air power was ineffective against a fielded enemy army. Without sufficient air superiority and unable to coordinate with friendly ground forces, US air power could not stall and scatter the NVA as they had in Cambodia.

Air Superiority in Lam Son 719

In contrast to the overall air superiority enjoyed by US air forces over the Trail, during Lam Son 719 airmen were compelled to take greater risks to protect ARVN troops. As a result, the United States lost seven fixed-wing aircraft to AAA and small arms; a loss rate double that of the rest of Commando Hunt V.[46] The rotary-wing losses to fierce NVA ground fire were even more troubling.[47]

Throughout the Vietnam War, the helicopter had been the workhorse for the Army, Marine Corps, and ARVN. For years in South Vietnam helicopters had delivered troops and supplies to the battlefield, had conducted close air support (CAS), and had provided command and control for ground commanders. In Lam Son 719, the ARVN assumed a similar level of support as it planned to establish a series of firebases on the high ground to the north and south of Route 9.[48] These firebases served the same purpose as the Army and Marine defensive positions along the DMZ, to provide overlapping fire support. Once in place, the firebases would protect the flanks of the ARVN as they drove west along Route 9. To remain active, the firebases' artillery required constant aerial resupply. The NVA took advantage of its numerical advantage by surrounding these isolated positions.[49] As helicopters approached, the NVA opened fire with small arms and AAA. US and ARVN helicopters incurred heavy casualties during these resupply missions, compelling the evacuation of the northernmost firebases. The US Army lost 107

[45] By the end of combat operations, the NVA had an estimated 60,000 troops in the area. Willbanks, *A Raid Too Far*, 69, 133, 143; 7th Air Force, *Commando Hunt V*, 69–71; Head, "Playing Hide-and-Seek with the 'Trail'," 104; Sanders, *Invasion of Laos*, 125.

[46] Carl Berger, ed., *The United States Air Force in Southeast Asia, 1961–1973: An Illustrated Account* (Washington, DC: Office of Air Force History, 1984), 116.

[47] Sanders, *Invasion of Laos*, 229–232; Willbanks, *A Raid Too Far*, 92; Hartsook and Gunderson, *The Air Force in Southeast Asia*, 16.

[48] Willbanks, *A Raid Too Far*, 49; Wiest, *Vietnam's Forgotten Army*, 201, 211.

[49] Willbanks, *A Raid Too Far*, 103.

helicopters, with an additional 600 damaged, during Lam Son 719.[50] Unable to secure the northern flank, the firebases fell one by one, exposing the ARVN's sole LOC. With Route 9 cut off, the ARVN vanguard and the remaining firebases were even more dependent on helicopter support for mobility and resupply.[51]

In sum, the requirements for air superiority differed in Lam Son 719 compared to Commando Hunt V because friendly ground forces depended upon helicopters that flew slowly and at low altitude, vulnerable to small arms and AAA.

Air-to-Ground Ineffectiveness in Lam Son 719

In February 1971, Commando Hunt V shifted to supporting Lam Son 719.[52] To better coordinate tacair and B-52 Arc Light strikes, 7th Air Force established a Direct Air Support Center (DASC) at Quang Tri, collocated with the US Army's XXIV Corps headquarters.[53] The 7th Air Force initially assigned two airborne forward air controllers (FACs) to support Lam Son 719, tasking them to control strikes for the two-ship tacair flights scheduled to arrive every thirty minutes. Eventually, six FACs would manage triple this sortie rate, with tacair flights checking in every ten minutes. In addition, B-52s expanded from twenty-seven to forty sorties per day.[54]

In the late dry season, the weather conditions in southern Laos were typically good for air operations once the morning fog lifted. However, low ceilings in the mountainous terrain made helicopter and FAC operations treacherous.[55] To improve all-weather and night operations, the deployment of an additional Combat Skyspot radar improved the accuracy of radar bombing for B-52s and tacair. At the same time, the Black Crow sensor, which tracked engine ignition emissions, provided AC-130 Spectres with a non-visual means to target trucks.[56]

50 Sorley, *The Abrams Tapes*, 577; Berger, *The United States Air Force in Southeast Asia*, 116; Willbanks, *A Raid Too Far*, 127; Hartsook and Gunderson, *The Air Force in Southeast Asia*, 15.

51 Duy Hinh, *Lam Son 719*, 55; Sanders, *Invasion of Laos*, 122.

52 7th Air Force, *Commando Hunt V*, 32; Hartsook and Gunderson, *The Air Force in Southeast Asia*, 12.

53 Hartsook and Gunderson, *The Air Force in Southeast Asia*, 10; 7th Air Force, *Commando Hunt V*, 67–68; Willbanks, *A Raid Too Far*, 42.

54 7th Air Force, *Commando Hunt V*, 67; Willbanks, *A Raid Too Far*, 47.

55 Duy Hinh, *Lam Son 719*, 30–31; Sanders, *Invasion of Laos*, 115.

56 7th Air Force, *Commando Hunt V*, 184, 257. One NVA countermeasure was to cover the ignition of truck engines with aluminum foil. John Sherwood, *Afterburner: Naval Aviators and the Vietnam War* (New York: New York University Press, 2004), 61.

From February 8 to April 8, US air forces flew 1,300 FAC, 8,500 tacair, 1,358 B-52, 430 tactical reconnaissance (tac recce), and 2,800 tac airlift sorties in support of Lam Son 719.[57] In addition, C-130s dropped twenty-eight seven-and-a-half-ton Commando Vault bombs to instantaneously clear helicopter landing zones.[58] Overall, US intelligence credited airstrikes with a third of NVA casualties.[59]

Even with this intense air-to-ground effort, the ARVN offensive soon faltered. The expectation of having the devastating firepower available to the Marines at Khe Sanh in 1968 had been a primary reason why both US and South Vietnamese leadership had agreed to Lam Son 719.[60] However, two reasons explain allied overconfidence in air power's ability to neutralize the enemy army's numerical advantage. First, during the Battle of Khe Sanh the Marines fought from fortified, defensive positions. The NVA, forced to maneuver and concentrate on the offensive, was vulnerable to air power. In Lam Son 719, the reverse was true as the ARVN marched into NVA territory. Only at the end of Lam Son 719, once the ARVN began to withdraw, was the NVA exposed to airstrikes as it attempted to exploit the ARVN's hasty retreat.[61] As anticipated by TAP theory, only when the NVA massed and maneuvered along the border was it exposed to US air power. Second, at Khe Sanh air and land action had been well-coordinated, with dedicated Marine Corps aviation providing CAS to their brethren on the ground. In addition, the Air Force and Navy coordinated their air forces to directly attack NVA forces beyond the range of CAS through a mature TACS/AAGS (tactical air control system/army air ground system). By contrast, when the ARVN crossed into Laos, it left behind US military advisors and tactical air controllers. The ARVN had previously relied upon these critical components to coordinate airstrikes for operations in South Vietnam and Cambodia. As a result of the disconnect between air and ground forces in Laos, air power could not effectively support the offensive or blunt the NVA's counterattack until it reached South Vietnam. As troubling as the lack of air-to-ground coordination during Lam Son 719 was the inability of the air interdiction effort of Commando Hunt V to slow the movement of tens of thousands of heavily armed NVA reinforcements as they rapidly massed against the ARVN.

57 7th Air Force *Commando Hunt V*, 74, 81.
58 7th Air Force, *Commando Hunt V*, 81; Sanders, *Invasion of Laos*, 111.
59 Berger, *The United States Air Force in Southeast Asia*, 115; 7th Air Force, *Commando Hunt V*, 74.
60 Willbanks, *A Raid Too Far*, 56; Sanders, *Invasion of Laos*, 92, 209.
61 Sorley, *A Better War*, 256; Sanders, *Invasion of Laos*, 190; Hartsook and Gunderson, *The Air Force in Southeast Asia*, 14, 15.

Implications of Lam Son 719

In addition to forcing the ARVN withdrawal, the NVA inflicted 8,000 casualties, including 3,800 killed. But the NVA suffered even more, with an estimated 14,000 casualties.[62] Furthermore, the destruction of their supply bases surrounding Tchepone delayed communist plans in South Vietnam by a year.[63] Despite these setbacks, Hanoi viewed its defense against the ARVN as a success, signifying to it the failure of Vietnamization. The victory encouraged Le Duan to order a general offensive for the following dry season.[64] During the summer rains of 1971, while the United States reduced its flying operations in Commando Hunt VI, the North Vietnamese busily labored to expand and improve their road networks, deployed hundreds of additional AAA pieces, constructed dozens of SA-2 sites in Southern Laos, and deployed more MiGs to their southern airfields.[65]

The Vietnam War: May 1971–March 1972

Following Lam Son 719, anti-war protests and congressional action pressured President Nixon to announce additional troop withdrawals. Meanwhile in Paris, the North Vietnamese and American delegations remained at loggerheads. The diplomatic impasse over Vietnam, however, did not preclude the Nixon administration from making significant foreign policy gains in 1971, most notably a thawing of relations with the Soviet Union and China. On May 26, the United States and the Soviet Union signed the Strategic Arms Limitation Talks Agreement (SALT I).[66] In early July, Henry Kissinger traveled to Beijing to negotiate a presidential trip to China for the following year. Similarly, the Soviets agreed to a subsequent presidential visit to Moscow, announced by Nixon in October.

Unfortunately for the United States, diplomatic success with the Soviets and Chinese did not translate to progress with North Vietnam. In May, June, twice in July, August, and again early in September 1971, Kissinger met secretly in Paris with the stubborn North Vietnamese delegation. Kissinger offered to redeploy all US forces from South

62 Wiest, *Vietnam's Forgotten Army*, 224.

63 Sorley, *The Abrams Tapes*, 576, 600; Willbanks, *A Raid Too Far*, 63.

64 Nguyen, *Hanoi's War*, 206; Merle Pribbenow, *Victory in Vietnam: The Official History of the People's Army of Vietnam 1954–1975* (Lawrence: University Press of Kansas, 2002), 283.

65 Head, "Playing Hide-and-Seek with the 'Trail'," 105.

66 Nixon, *The Memoirs*, 523.

Vietnam without requiring a similar withdrawal by the North Vietnamese. However, the sticking point for Hanoi remained the US backing of the Thieu government.[67] With the Paris talks mired and the steady NVA buildup along the border, a frustrated Nixon ordered airstrikes across the DMZ in mid-September.

In Saigon in October 1971, President Thieu solidified his grip on power with a landslide victory in a controversial, uncontested election.[68] Simultaneously in Hanoi, encouraged by Lam Son 719, Le Duan ordered final preparations for another major offensive. Commando Hunt VII commenced with the arrival of the dry season, but the US drawdown constrained air strike availability at a critical time as the enemy ramped up troops and supplies heading southwards.

In November, Nixon publicized another withdrawal, to be down to 139,000 American troops in South Vietnam by February 1972. This drawdown was announced even as intelligence agencies predicted another NVA offensive. In addition to massing along the DMZ, the NVA moved into the Central Highlands; it was the first time so many troops had been observed there since the Tet Offensive.[69] Unconcerned with defending North Vietnamese territory, the NVA committed fourteen of its fifteen divisions to the offensive. An estimated 300,000 communist troops deployed to southern Laos, Cambodia, and South Vietnam (see Map 6.1).[70] By early January 1972, Military Assistance Command Vietnam (MACV) intelligence had indications of a third NVA buildup further south in Cambodia, threatening Saigon and the Mekong Delta.[71] However, the initial warnings of a general offensive during the coming Tet holiday proved premature. Eventually, the NVA would attack at the end of March, in what would be known in the West as the Easter Offensive.

The remainder of this chapter analyzes the effectiveness of air power during Commando Hunt VII by examining US air superiority, air-to-ground capabilities, friendly ground force capabilities, and enemy ground force capabilities.

67 Herring, *America's Longest War*, 269.

68 Though the United States continued to support Thieu, the disqualification of his primary challenger, General Nguyen Cao Ky, marred the election results as the other candidate, the Communists' preference, General Duong Van Minh, refused to run. Kimball, *Nixon's Vietnam War*, 265–282; Herring, *America's Longest War*, 270; Sorley, *The Abrams Tapes*, 676, 682, 717.

69 Sorley, *The Abrams Tapes*, 693, 696, 704, 713.

70 The one division not committed was a training unit. Sorley, *The Abrams Tapes*, 719.

71 Sorley, *The Abrams Tapes*, 740.

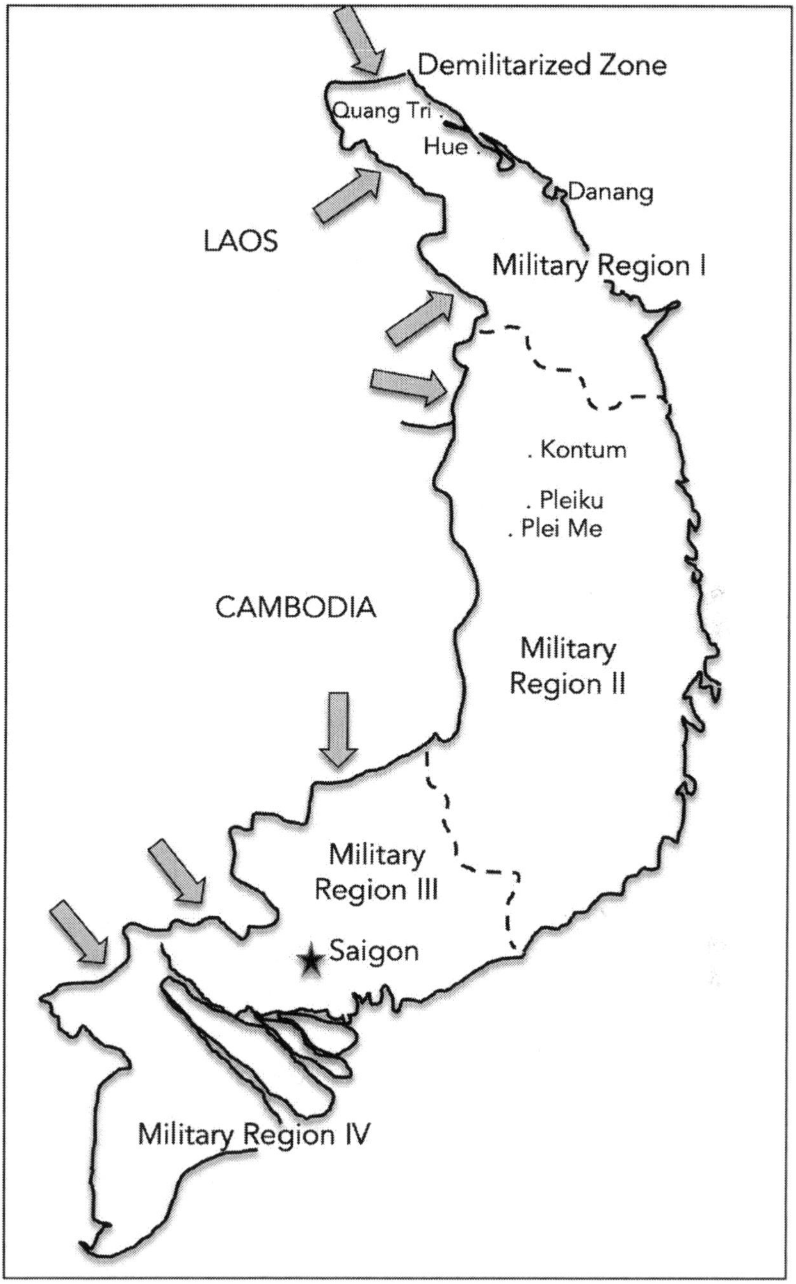

Map 6.1 The Easter Offensive

Air Superiority Commando Hunt VII

By late 1971, the North Vietnamese had significantly upgraded and expanded their integrated air defense system (IADS), extending radar coverage into southern Laos and across the DMZ. MiG, SAM, and AAA activity increasingly contested US air superiority over the Trail. Since airstrikes had ceased in North Vietnam after the end of Rolling Thunder in October 1968, Hanoi had taken full advantage of the curtailment of the air-to-air threat to replenish and improve the Vietnam People's Air Force (VPAF). The North Vietnamese bolstered their fighter force from 150 to 265 MiGs, including a near tripling of the higher-performance MiG-21s.[72] The VPAF also trained a new cadre of pilots and adapted tactics for low-altitude intercepts, which shielded MiGs from early radar detection. The VPAF further expanded its ground control interceptor (GCI) radar coverage, a critical element for successful air-to-air engagements.[73] The VPAF also improved existing airfields and built new runways in the southern panhandle, such that by October, MiG-21s staged from four bases south of the 20th parallel.[74] The MiG activity along the DMZ and in southern Laos put at risk the B-52s, AC-130s, and slow FACs.[75] Responding to the enhanced air threat, the US Air Force redeployed EC-121Ts to improve air-to-air radar coverage. It also deployed eight F-4Ds, upgraded with the latest APX-80 Combat Tree interrogator. Combat Tree could identify friend or foe (IFF), which allowed F-4D aircrew to satisfy stringent rules of engagement (ROE) criteria for beyond visual range (BVR) shots with their AIM-7 radar-guided missiles.[76]

In the aerial combat that ensued, the North Vietnamese drew first blood when, on December 18, 1971, a MiG-21 downed an Air Force F-4.[77] While supporting the subsequent combat search-and-rescue mission, two more F-4s crashed from fuel starvation after being engaged by MiGs.[78] The USAF responded to these embarrassing losses by deploying five more F-4 squadrons to Southeast Asia. In addition, on December

[72] The VPAF increased their MiG-21 force from thirty-eight to ninety-four. Marshall Michel, *Clashes: Air Combat over North Vietnam 1965–1972* (Annapolis, MD: Naval Institute Press, 1997), 188.

[73] 7th Air Force, *Commando Hunt VII* (Saigon, Republic of Vietnam, 1972), 10, 21.

[74] 7th Air Force, *Commando Hunt VII*, 10, 21, 236; Michel, *Clashes*, 190, 193; Hartsook and Gunderson, *The Air Force in Southeast Asia*, 24; Sorley, *The Abrams Tapes 1968–1972*, 677.

[75] Hartsook and Gunderson, *The Air Force in Southeast Asia*, 29; Michel, *Clashes*, 193.

[76] Michel, *Clashes*, 193–194.

[77] 7th Air Force, *Commando Hunt VII*, 141.

[78] Bernard Nalty, *The War against Trucks: Aerial Interdiction in Southern Laos 1968–1972* (Washington, DC: Air Force History and Museums Program, 2005), 233–234; Michel, *Clashes*, 195; Hartsook and Gunderson, *The Air Force in Southeast Asia*, 33.

26, the United States launched Proud Deep Alpha: five days and 1,000 airstrikes against North Vietnamese airfields, radars, and supply facilities.[79] However, poor weather largely frustrated this effort, with only twenty-nine airstrikes conducted under visual conditions. The remaining strikers dropped their bombloads through the clouds, utilizing long-range navigation (LORAN) guidance with degraded bombing accuracy.[80] MiG-21 incursions into Laos occurred on fifty-four occasions during December and January, with the VPAF suffering no MiG losses through mid-January 1972.[81] The inability of US fighters to engage MiGs resulted mainly from the VPAF only attacking under favorable conditions, combined with its new terrain masking techniques that precluded US early-warning radars from detecting the MiGs. On the rare occasions when fighters did manage to track down a MiG, the abysmal performance of US air-to-air missiles negated the attacks.[82]

In addition to the MiGs, SA-2 activity rose along the DMZ and in southern Laos.[83] In December, the NVA fired twenty-two missiles, compared to only three launches during November and December the prior year.[84] The North Vietnamese also adapted tactics by linking GCI radars to the SAMs.[85] GCI radars, previously only employed with the MiGs, could now provide tracking information to the SA-2s so that SAM operators could delay illumination of their Fansong radars until missile launch. This tactic denied US aircrew cues from their radar warning receivers (RWR).[86] In mid-December, utilizing these new methods, SAMs downed an F-105 Wild Weasel, and, a week later, an F-4 pilot ejected after losing aircraft control while reacting to a missile.[87] SAMs continued to threaten air operations, with 163 observed missile launches

79 7th Air Force, *Commando Hunt VII*, 144; Michel, *Clashes*, 196.

80 Hartsook and Gunderson, *The Air Force in Southeast Asia*, 33; Michel, *Clashes*, 196.

81 On January 19, 1972, the first MiG kill since 1968 was by a Navy F-4 with a heat-seeking AIM-9 missile. US aircraft would go on to shoot down three MIGs in March, two by USAF F-4s and one by a USN F-4. 7th Air Force, *Commando Hunt VII*, 141–142.

82 Michel, *Clashes*, 196; Sorley, *The Abrams Tapes*, 677, 726. The US scored four air-to-air kills with a USN F-4 kill against a MiG-21, with an AIM-9 rear-aspect shot on January 19, 1972, a USAF F-4 AIM-7E-2 nose-aspect shot on February 21, another USAF F-4 AIM-9 kill on the night of March 1, and a USN F-4 AIM-9 kill against a MiG-17 on March 6. Michel, *Clashes*, 197–198.

83 7th Air Force, *Commando Hunt VII*, 9, 20; William Momyer, *Airpower in Three Wars (WWII, Korea, Vietnam)* (Maxwell AFB, AL: AU Press, 2003), 240–241.

84 7th Air Force, *Commando Hunt VII*, 140.

85 Project CHECO, *Rules of Engagement November 1969–September 1972* (HQ PACAF: Tactical Evaluation Team, 1973), 41.

86 Sorley, *The Abrams Tapes*, 722; Hartsook and Gunderson, *The Air Force in Southeast Asia*, 31; 7th Air Force, *Commando Hunt VII*, 235.

87 Michel, *Clashes*, 192; Nalty, *The War against Trucks*, 218.

downing 9 aircraft during Commando Hunt VII, including the loss of an AC-130 and its 14 crew members on March 28, 1972.[88]

In addition to MiGs and SAMs, North Vietnam was more aggressive with its AAA, increasing by 20 percent the number of guns along the Trail from 1970 to 1971.[89] In November 1971, the NVA had 365 active AAA guns, which doubled to 748 by the end of March 1972.[90] The 57 millimeter (mm), with its extended range and increased lethality, now replaced the 37 mm as the NVA's most widely deployed air defense weapon. In addition, the NVA deployed even larger 85mm and 100mm radar-guided AAA near critical locations, such as mountain passes and other major chokepoints.[91] AAA claimed thirteen aircraft during Commando Hunt VII, including another AC-130, the second Spectre lost in three days, downed on March 30, 1972.[92]

The impact of the improved North Vietnamese defenses was more than the number of aircrew and aircraft lost. A significant effect was prohibiting vulnerable, non-tacair, aircraft from operating over the most critical sections of the Trail.[93] In reaction to the air threat, 7th Air Force Commander General John Lavelle repeatedly lobbied Washington for additional authorities to preemptively strike enemy airfields, radar, and SAM positions in southern North Vietnam, to little avail.[94] Overall, the erosion of air superiority over the Trail had a cascading, adverse effect on US air-to-ground operations.

Air-to-Ground Capability in Commando Hunt VII

Heavier than normal rains in the fall of 1971 delayed Commando Hunt VII until early November, when thick clouds further degraded air

[88] 7th Air Force, *Commando Hunt VII*, 140–141, 157; Nalty, *The War against Trucks*, 218–219; Craig Whitney, "U.S. Plane Downed by Missile in Laos; Crew of 14 Missing" *New York Times*, March 30, 1972; Sorley, *The Abrams Tapes*, 804.

[89] 7th Air Force, *Commando Hunt VII*, 9, 20.

[90] 7th Air Force, *Commando Hunt VII*, 134, 157, 227.

[91] 7th Air Force, *Commando Hunt VII*, 134.

[92] Nalty, *The War against Trucks*, 215, 218–219; Stephen Randolph, *Powerful and Brutal Weapons: Nixon, Kissinger, and the Easter Offensive* (Cambridge, MA: Harvard University Press, 2007), 54; 7th Air Force, *Commando Hunt VII*, 51, 71, 134–135.

[93] 7th Air Force, *Commando Hunt VII*, 15, 60, 70–71, 136; Sorley, *The Abrams Tapes*, 799, 809–810; Nalty, *The War against Trucks*, 216, 218; Hartsook and Gunderson, *The Air Force in Southeast Asia*, 30.

[94] Sorley, *The Abrams Tapes*, 751, 768. General Lavelle was recalled to Washington and relieved of command by Chief of Staff of the Air Force, General John Ryan, on March 26, 1972. Mark Clodfelter, *Violating Reality: The Lavell Affair, Nixon, and Parsing the Truth* (Washington, DC: National Defense University Press, 2016), 38; Project CHECO, *Rules of Engagement*, 2, 46.

operations. It would not be until February that the weather cleared sufficiently for US air forces to operate consistently under visual conditions.[95] The North Vietnamese benefited from the bad weather. In addition to taking advantage of the cloud cover, the NVA improved its roadways, including constructing a secret "green road," a hidden trail that ran under the jungle canopy and along dry stream beds. The North Vietnamese further built decoys and added AAA sites to abandoned roads so they appeared active.[96] Overall, the NVA could better move troops and supplies under clouds and at night along the upgraded roadways.[97]

While the NVA ramped up activities, by the end of 1971 US air-to-ground capability, as measured by the number of aircraft, had declined from 545 tacair and 89 B-52s in Commando Hunt III to only 226 and 54 by Commando Hunt VII. Tacair sorties per month for Southeast Asia dropped from 14,000 to 10,000, of which two-thirds were assigned to the Trail.[98] In addition to fewer strike aircraft, a cutback of EC-121s to retransmit Igloo White sensor signals reduced by a third the capability to monitor vehicle movement along the Trail.[99] Even the ability to process the sensor data had been constrained as the Infiltration Surveillance Center at Nakhon Phanom now had only one IBM mainframe. Its computing capacity was overwhelmed when NVA activity surged.[100]

However, in anticipation of the coming NVA offensive, additional air assets deployed to Southeast Asia over the winter. By early 1972, B-52 availability had expanded from 1,000 to 1,200 sorties per month, and the number of Navy carriers doubled from two to four by March.[101] The availability of AC-130 Spectres also rose, tripling from six to eighteen, with 700 gunship sorties available per month.[102]

When Commando Hunt VII commenced, the plan had been for B-52s to cut the Mu Gia, Ban Karai, and Ban Raving passes as they had done at

95 7th Air Force, *Commando Hunt VII*, 50.
96 Randolph, *Powerful and Brutal Weapons*, 42; 7th Air Force, *Commando Hunt VII*, 225.
97 Nalty, *The War against Trucks*, 211, 213.
98 B-52s would remain at 1,000 per month as they had the previous year. Sorley, *The Abrams Tapes*, 716, 753; Nalty, *The War against Trucks*, 213, 223; Michel, *Clashes*, 196; 7th Air Force, *Commando Hunt VII*, 58, 149, 201.
99 EC-121 coverage shrank from twenty-four to eighteen hours a day. Sorley, *The Abrams Tapes*, 787; 7th Air Force, *Commando Hunt VII*, 67.
100 Nalty, *The War against Trucks*, 229.
101 During Commando Hunt VII the Navy flew 10,000 tacair sorties. Sherwood, *Afterburner*, 62; Sorley, *The Abrams Tapes*, 781; 7th Air Force, *Commando Hunt VII*, 90, 218; John Sherwood, *Nixon's Trident* (Washington, DC: Naval History and Heritage Command, 2009), 36.
102 7th Air Force, *Commando Hunt VII*, 14, 22; Nalty, *The War against Trucks*, 213.

the outset of previous dry seasons.[103] The increased MiG and SAM threat interrupted bomber operations, however, just as the North Vietnamese began pushing thousands of trucks and personnel onto the Trail.[104] Airstrikes soon shifted to engage mobile vehicles further to the south, with claims of over 10,000 trucks destroyed or damaged from November through March.[105] This assertion came under scrutiny, however, as the figure was higher than the intelligence estimate of the total number of trucks on the Trail.[106] In February 1972, General Lavelle noted the discrepancy between the number of truck kills claimed and the supplies delivered to the South. 7th Air Force intelligence estimated that while supplies entering the Trail was down by 15 percent from the previous year, what reached South Vietnam and Cambodia was up by 15 percent.[107] Most of the supplies, weapons, and equipment transported along the Trail were not immediately destined for South Vietnam but for the staging areas north of the DMZ, in Laos, and in Cambodia in preparation for the coming invasion. The North Vietnamese, by contrast, estimated an attrition rate of only 10 percent of the supplies that entered the Trail during Commando Hunt VII, a much lower loss rate than previous years.[108]

Prior Commando Hunts had focused on interdicting NVA supply lines. But in Commando Hunt VII, Task Force Alpha at Nakhon Phanom, Thailand inaugurated Operation Island Tree, the first coordinated effort to target the infiltration of enemy troops. US intelligence had noted that the supply and infiltration routes, which ran in parallel, merged at specific points, presumably at troop way stations. By monitoring radio transmissions, Task Force Alpha predicted the timing and location of these stops. F-4s dropped acoustic sensors nearby for Task Force Alpha to nominate targets for B-52 strikes. The B-52s then seeded the area with thousands of time-delayed, anti-personnel CBUs.[109] The sensors then recorded strike audio. Throughout Commando Hunt VII, B-52s struck 186 of the 355 targets nominated by Task Force Alpha.[110] As with the truck kills, providing meaningful BDA for Island Tree proved difficult. Even so, MACV General Abrams ordered the attacks to

[103] 7th Air Force, *Commando Hunt VII*, 15; Nalty, *The War against Trucks*, 229.
[104] Nalty, *The War against Trucks*, 218; Sorley, *The Abrams Tapes*, 688.
[105] 7th Air Force established a series of blocking belts at choke points. 7th Air Force, *Commando Hunt VII*, 44, 49, 61; Nalty, *The War against Trucks*, 231; Randolph, *Powerful and Brutal Weapons*, 55; Sherwood, *Afterburner*, 58–59.
[106] Nalty, *The War against Trucks*, 221; Randolph, *Powerful and Brutal Weapons*, 55.
[107] Sorley, *The Abrams Tapes*, 786. [108] Randolph, *Powerful and Brutal Weapons*, 56.
[109] Sorley, *The Abrams Tapes*, 743, 773; Nalty *The War against Trucks*, 200–201.
[110] Nalty, *The War against Trucks*, 201.

continue as there was no other way to attrit the enemy troops flooding south.[111]

TAP theory claims air forces are lethal against enemy ground forces when they concentrate and maneuver, but this proved not to be the case in Commando Hunt VII. Reduced air superiority, poor weather, and constrained air-to-ground capabilities neutralized the impact of air power as the NVA prepared for its offensive. With most US combat ground forces having departed South Vietnam, it would be left to the ARVN to shoulder the brunt of the ground battle that was to come.

Friendly Ground Force Capability in Early 1972

Commando Hunt interdicted North Vietnamese supplies moving along the Trail into southern Laos for three years. During this period, US troop levels decreased from 540,000 in 1968 to only 95,000 by early 1972. As Americans departed, the remaining personnel focused on providing intelligence and communication support for the RVNMF, which had expanded rapidly to over a million personnel, with 414,000 on active duty.[112] The United States armed the South Vietnamese with heavier weapons, and over the previous two years, the ARVN had gained valuable combat experience in Cambodia and Laos. The biggest advantage the South Vietnamese would have going forward, however, was that they would be fighting on their own soil.

Though the ARVN grew stronger, its poor showing during Lam Son 719 undermined the deterrent value such a sizeable force might have had on the North Vietnamese decision to launch another general offensive.[113] Further troubling was the deficiency in the quality of some ARVN senior leaders, as many division commanders had been selected not based on merit but on their personal loyalty to President Thieu.[114] Across South Vietnam, the ARVN took over the duties of the departing US combat forces, which stretched ARVN units thin. Their ability to defend against the anticipated NVA offensives near the DMZ and the Central Highlands was particularly troubling.[115]

Air support for ARVN units had also shifted to the RVNAF (Republic of Vietnam Air Force) such that, by February 1972, RVNAF aircrew

[111] Sorley, *The Abrams Tapes*, 749, 785.
[112] Sorley, *The Abrams Tapes*, 749, 772; A. J. C. Lavalle, ed., *Airpower and the 1972 Spring Invasion* (Washington, DC: Office of Air Force History, 1985), 1–2.
[113] Pribbenow, *Victory in Vietnam*, 283; Randolph, *Powerful and Brutal Weapons*, 24.
[114] Sorley, *The Abrams Tapes*, 741. [115] Sorley, *The Abrams Tapes*, 725–726.

conducted 3,300 of the 4,000 in-country strike sorties.[116] While the RVNAF had the means and experience to support counterinsurgency operations, it could not blunt a conventional offensive. The RVNAF command and control system was also inadequate to coordinate the massive number of US sorties made available during the Easter Offensive. In addition, RVNAF assigned units to specific military regions. This division of labor made sense for fighting an insurgency, but the decentralized organization meant it was challenging to reallocate sorties to regions needing additional air support.[117]

As with Vietnamization, pacification also had made headway, expanding President Thieu's control over South Vietnam.[118] The VC's inability to be a threat across most of the country and the recognition of the steady decline of communist influence was one of the reasons Hanoi decided to launch its offensive even while US combat forces were still withdrawing.[119]

Overall, the ARVN had grown into a sizeable conventional ground force, but it would soon have to face the enemy on the ground on its own, with the question unanswered as to whether it could now coordinate for the vital US air support that it had been unable to utilize the previous year during Lam Son 719. The increasingly capable NVA conventional forces would soon test the ability of the ARVN and US air forces to conduct combined arms operations.

Enemy Ground Force Capability in Early 1972

After the tepid performance by the ARVN in the Lam Son 719 raid, Hanoi committed to another general offensive for the following dry season.[120] Serious preparations commenced in the second half of 1971, with the Soviet Union and China supplying vast quantities of trucks, weapons, armor, ammunition, fuel, and supplies.[121] North Vietnam inducted 150,000 men into the military in 1971, of which five-sixths would eventually march south.[122] The North Vietnamese raised fifteen divisions from these recruits and veterans, of which fourteen would be

[116] During Commando Hunt VII, the RVNAF flew 67 percent of sorties in South Vietnam, 37 percent in Cambodia, 30 percent overall in Southeast Asia. 7th Air Force, *Commando Hunt VII*, 11; Lavalle, *Airpower and the 1972 Spring Invasion*.

[117] Sorley, *The Abrams Tapes*, 747. [118] Sorley, *The Abrams Tapes*, 718.

[119] Sorley, *The Abrams Tapes*, 719, 723, 757; Randolph, *Powerful and Brutal Weapons*, 26.

[120] Pribbenow, *Victory in Vietnam*, 283; Sorley, *The Abrams Tapes*, 693.

[121] Nalty, *The War against Trucks*, 214–215; Randolph, *Powerful and Brutal Weapons*, 34; Pribbenow, *Victory in Vietnam*, 285; Sorley, *The Abrams Tapes*, 785.

[122] Randolph, *Powerful and Brutal Weapons*, 38.

committed to the offensive.[123] To move their troops, equipment, and supplies, the NVA expanded the Trail with an additional 400 miles of all-weather roadways for a total of 2,700 miles in Laos. This effort extended the road network further west into Laos to operate along six parallel routes, which ran toward South Vietnam and Cambodia.[124] In addition, the expansion of their POL pipelines and rice cultivation in Laos reduced the overall supply requirements for the North Vietnamese truck fleet from the previous year by 40 percent.[125] As for personnel, by late November 1971 MACV estimated the NVA infiltration rate had doubled from the last dry season, which, along with captured enemy intelligence, indicated plans for a major offensive for early 1972.[126]

With the arrival of Soviet tanks and artillery, the NVA began preparing for mechanized operations, adapting the Soviet doctrine to its experience in Lam Son 719. The result was basic combined arms tactics for armor, infantry, and artillery but did not include the air force.[127] The overall North Vietnamese military strategy was like the Tet Offensive: a general offensive conducted by NVA forces. The difference now was that they had more and heavier armed divisions, and Hanoi no longer depended upon the VC to incite a popular uprising. The NVA divided its forces along three fronts; across the DMZ in the Quang Tri province; in the Central Highlands; and near Saigon (see Map 6.1).[128] Hanoi wanted the main attack axis to put direct pressure on Saigon. However, delays in the movement of supplies forced a later start date for the offensive. No longer having access to the Sihanouk Trail, the NVA struggled to move its men, weapons, and supplies to southeastern Cambodia.[129] Of the 31,000 tons of supplies entering the Trail, only 5,000 tons (16 percent) would reach South Vietnam or Cambodia.[130] By early March 1972, Hanoi realized that the Central Office of South Vietnam (COSVN) in Cambodia was not prepared to be the vanguard for the general offensive. As a result, the North Vietnamese changed their strategy, making the DMZ the primary

[123] US intelligence estimated that the NVA deployed 300,000 to South Vietnam, southern Laos, and Cambodia, along with another 30,000 in northern Laos. Sorley, *The Abrams Tapes*, 734, 746, 757.

[124] Sorley, *The Abrams Tapes*, 636; Randolph, *Powerful and Brutal Weapons*, 42; Pribbenow, *Victory in Vietnam*, 285–286; 7th Air Force, *Commando Hunt VII*, 224.

[125] 7th Air Force, *Commando Hunt VII*, 67, 149.

[126] 7th Air Force, *Commando Hunt VII*, 164, 223; Randolph, *Powerful and Brutal Weapons*, 49; Sorley, *The Abrams Tapes*, 707, 759.

[127] Pribbenow, *Victory in Vietnam*, 284.

[128] Pribbenow, *Victory in Vietnam*, 283–285; Sorley, *The Abrams Tapes*, 792.

[129] Sorley, *The Abrams Tapes*, 793, 798, 803; Pribbenow, *Victory in Vietnam*, 289.

[130] 7th Air Force, *Commando Hunt VII*, 61.

attack axis by committing more air defenses, tanks, and artillery to support this northernmost front.[131]

The North Vietnamese had raised a large, heavily armed, conventional army and deployed it to the South Vietnamese border, even if it had taken longer than anticipated. The primary front would now cross the DMZ into Quang Tri province, though this was the one area where the South Vietnamese had the strategic depth to recover from a major setback. Furthermore, the NVA's conventional tactics were untested. It was yet unknown how well it could coordinate a combined arms effort to maintain the momentum beyond the range of its artillery and air defenses.

Conclusion

From late 1968 through 1971, Commando Hunt had impeded the movement of supplies, though not troops, along the Trail. The invasion of Cambodia in 1970 had further cut off the Sihanouk Trail, denying the VC sanctuary and supplies for operations in southern South Vietnam. These two campaigns frustrated North Vietnamese efforts to support the VC, which declined in power and influence across South Vietnam. Meanwhile, pacification and Vietnamization expanded Saigon's ability to control and defend itself. However, the allied decision for the ARVN to invade Laos in 1971 proved a critical turning point in the war. Lam Son 719 may have set back NVA/VC operations by a year, but it failed to close off the Trail. The inadequacy of the ARVN, minus its US military advisors and tactical air controllers, proved to be a critical factor in its defeat. During Lam Son 719, US air power, weakened by the drawdown of aircraft along with improved North Vietnamese air defenses in Laos, could not stop NVA reinforcement, resulting in the ARVN's hasty retreat in the face of the fierce enemy counterattack. The NVA's success lent Le Duan the confidence to gamble again with another general offensive. In the coming battles of 1972, the question would be whether US air power could coordinate with friendly ground forces in the manner it had done with the Marines at Khe Sanh or as it had failed to do in Lam Son 719.

This chapter illuminates both the strengths and limitations of tactical air power. A sufficient degree of air superiority was necessary to conduct effective air-to-ground operations. The United States enjoyed air superiority over the Trail from Commando Hunt I through V. But in 1971, with the North Vietnamese buildup along the DMZ and into southern

131 Pribbenow, *Victory in Vietnam*, 289.

Laos, US political leaders would not grant airmen the latitude to preemptively degrade the North Vietnamese air defense system. Neither would the Air Force risk some of its most lethal but vulnerable air-to-ground assets, its heavy B-52s and AC-130 gunships. Whereas North Vietnam was willing to accept heavy losses and take high risks to achieve its objectives, the United States was not.

In addition to having air superiority, to be effective at air-to-ground operations US air forces procured new sensors, adapted intelligence systems, and deployed specialized aircraft, weapons, and tactics. The United States invested in new technologies to improve its ability to target mobile targets, with some success. Commando Hunt I–V reduced the flow of supplies to South Vietnam, but the North Vietnamese adapted by improving their air defenses and logistics capabilities. As Commando Hunt VII demonstrates, effective air interdiction can be difficult to maintain.

The lack of friendly ground forces to threaten the NVA in Laos allowed the North Vietnamese to disperse and hide. Air interdiction delayed the Communists and required additional resources to secure the Trail. The time and space Commando Hunt I–V provided from late 1968 to early 1971 was vital to pacification and Vietnamization success. But the indirect attack of the enemy LOC did not deter a determined ground force. The NVA overcame the challenges imposed by air interdiction by pre-positioning supplies, surging resupply efforts, and developing resilient and redundant supply lines. The decision by the United States and South Vietnam to invade Laos provides evidence of the frustration of friendly ground commanders with the effectiveness of Commando Hunt.

During Lam Son 719, when the ARVN deployed into southern Laos, US air power proved ineffective. TAP theory anticipates that the combination of competent air and ground forces places the enemy in a dilemma over whether to disperse against the air threat or concentrate against the ground threat. However, the congressional mandate that no US troops accompany the ARVN across the border precluded the embedding of military advisors, air liaison officers, and tactical air controllers who could have provided the vital linkage between air forces and armies. As a result, US air power proved ineffective as the NVA massed against the ARVN.

Commando Hunt VII further demonstrates the challenge of air power to engage mobile targets. It was not difficult for intelligence to identify fixed positions, such as mountain passes, key choke points, and truck parks. Over time, Igloo White even allowed US air forces to target the NVA's truck convoys. However, even with this cutting-edge intelligence system, US air forces could never stop the infiltration of hundreds of thousands of NVA troops, which marched southward in small, dispersed packets. By 1972, Commando Hunt VII could not even halt the movement of armor, artillery, and SAM batteries deployed into southern Laos and Cambodia in preparation for the Easter Offensive.

Environmental factors also played a role in restricting air operations along the Trail and throughout Southeast Asia. TAP theory anticipates that air forces overhead can locate a massed and maneuvering army. However, the annual monsoon seasons produced heavy cloud cover, which significantly impaired air operations over Laos for half the year. Unable to identify targets visually, airstrikes devolved to all-weather Arc Light and LORAN strikes. Radar bombing could attack area targets, but these airstrikes were only as good as the intelligence provided. In addition, rugged terrain, forests, and jungles provided ample concealment for the NVA/VC. As MACV General Abrams pointed out, B-52 strikes without good intelligence was just killing monkeys and tigers.[132] Though US air forces struggled under the challenges of Lam Son 719 and Commando Hunt VII, the Easter Offensive, assessed in the next chapter, would demonstrate how air power, as part of a combined arms campaign, could defeat a fielded force.

[132] Sorley, *The Abrams Tapes*, 638.

7 Easter Offensive and Linebacker I & II: 1972–1973

The tactical air power (TAP) theory introduced in Chapter 2 explains when air forces can effectively attack fielded forces. As demonstrated in the previous four chapters, the North Vietnamese Army and Viet Cong (NVA/VC) proved vulnerable to air power when they massed and maneuvered. The NVA/VC usually reacted by dispersing and hiding. Taking such defensive measures, however, came at the cost of not executing the North's preferred strategy of concentrating its forces at the decisive point. The greatest threat to the NVA/VC occurred when the allied air and ground forces worked together. These combined arms operations placed the enemy army in a dilemma. Did it concentrate against US and South Vietnamese ground forces, only to be vulnerable to air attack, or instead disperse its troops only to be left open to a ground assault? The North Vietnamese usually did not engage in large battles but they had done so at Khe Sanh and would again in the Easter Offensive.[1]

Over six years, the Rolling Thunder and Commando Hunt air interdiction campaigns had slowed the movement of supplies and imposed costs on North Vietnam. However, these independent air campaigns had not convinced Hanoi to change its policy of unifying Vietnam under communist rule, nor had they curtailed the infiltration of the NVA into the South. This chapter concludes the examination of air power in the Vietnam War during the Easter Offensive and the Linebacker I and II air campaigns. The relative lull over South Vietnam from 1969 to 1971 provided time and space for Thieu's regime, through pacification, to expand government control over the countryside. Vietnamization further increased the capability of the Republic of Vietnam Military Forces (RVNMF) to take over security responsibilities as US combat forces departed. When the NVA launched another general offensive, the

[1] This chapter is a revision and extension of the article by Phil Haun and Colin Jackson, "Breaker of Armies: Air Power in the Easter Offensive and the Myths of Linebacker I and II in the Vietnam War" *International Security* 40:3 (Winter 2015/16), 139–178.

relevant question remained whether the Army of the Republic of Vietnam (ARVN) could incorporate the hard-earned lessons from Lam Son 719 (see Chapter 6). Could it now coordinate with US air power in an effective combined arms operation to defend South Vietnam?

The chapter consists of four sections. The first analyzes the Easter Offensive with the three battles at Quang Tri, An Loc, and Kontum. The second assesses the Linebacker I air interdiction campaign. The third analyzes the ARVN's retaking of Quang Tri, which ended the Easter Offensive. It also provides an overall assessment of air power in the Easter Offensive and Linebacker I. The final section examines diplomatic negotiations, the Linebacker II strategic bombing campaign, and the Paris Accords, signed in January 1973, which led to the US withdrawal from Vietnam.

The Easter Offensive

The North Vietnamese decision in late March 1972 to launch the Nguyen–Hue Offensive, known in the West as the Easter Offensive, was in reaction to an array of opportunities and threats. Their success the previous year against the ARVN's Lam Son 719 raid suggested that a major conventional offensive into South Vietnam might succeed. The steady withdrawal of US combat units also meant that the ARVN would have to fend for itself on the ground. There were reasons for Hanoi also to fear that the window of opportunity to unify North and South might be closing. In the aftermath of the Tet Offensive, the South Vietnamese had made steady progress suppressing VC resistance. President Richard Nixon's negotiating détente with China and the Soviet Union further jeopardized Hanoi's relationship with both patrons. Unless they moved swiftly, North Vietnam faced the prospect of a stronger Saigon while having diminished support from its communist allies.

Le Duan, the strong Communist Party leader, supported a conventional offensive to resolve these dilemmas. At a minimum, such an offensive would upset the Nixon administration's progress in isolating Hanoi from its Sino-Soviet sponsors; at best, it might break the ARVN and trigger the southern uprising the VC had failed to achieve during the Tet Offensive.[2] North Vietnam viewed the destruction of large ARVN forces and the seizure of major cities and towns as the means to shatter

[2] Lien-Hang Nguyen, *Hanoi's War: An International History of the War for Peace in Vietnam* (Chapel Hill: University of North Carolina Press, 2012), 232–234.

pacification and Vietnamization, strengthen their hand in the Paris negotiations, and precipitate the collapse of Thieu's regime.[3]

The NVA committed fourteen of its fifteen divisions, 130,000–150,000 troops, to accomplish these sweeping goals.[4] This new army was equipped with the latest conventional weaponry, included tanks, armored fighting vehicles, long-range artillery, advanced air defense systems, and antitank guided missiles.[5] The NVA planned to attack along three axes: a main attack across the demilitarized zone (DMZ), a second from eastern Cambodia toward Saigon, and a third from southern Laos and northern Cambodia into the Central Highlands (see Map 6.1).[6] The distribution of these separate fronts would presumably divide South Vietnamese forces. The NVA planned to combine long-range artillery preparatory fire followed by the shock of tanks to smash through ARVN lines that would be exploited by infantry and mechanized units.[7]

Opposing the NVA was the ARVN, which fielded eleven infantry divisions, fifty-eight artillery battalions, and nineteen armor battalions. In addition, throughout South Vietnam 550,000 personnel of the Regional Forces and Popular Forces defended against VC insurgents. However, this combined friendly force of over a million in arms faced four problems.[8] First, the departure of US ground troops thinned the South's defensive lines. Along the DMZ, the focus of the North Vietnamese main effort, 80,000 US soldiers and marines had been replaced by 25,000 ARVN to defend the same territory.[9] Second, the geography of South Vietnam provided the North Vietnamese an opportunity to strike at multiple points from the DMZ, southern Laos, and Cambodia. Third, the quality of ARVN leadership varied widely.

[3] Nguyen, *Hanoi's War*; James Willbanks, *Abandoning Vietnam: How America Left and South Vietnam Lost Its War* (Lawrence: University Press of Kansas, 2004), 124–127; *The Nguyen–Hue Offensive*, MACDI Study 73-01, January 12, 1973, C-1.

[4] Andrew Wiest, *Vietnam's Forgotten Army: Heroism and Betrayal in the ARVN* (New York: New York University Press, 2009), 243.

[5] The vanguard of the NVA offensive was 1,200 tanks. Thomas McKenna, *Kontum: The Battle to Save South Vietnam* (Lexington: University Press of Kentucky, 2011), 60–61; Willbanks, *Abandoning Vietnam*, 127.

[6] For a discussion of North Vietnamese debates over the main effort, see Nguyen, *Hanoi's War*, 245.

[7] Lam Quang Thi, *The Twenty-Five Year Century: A South Vietnamese General Remembers the Indochina War to the Fall of Saigon* (Denton: University of North Texas Press, 2001), 266–267; Jack Ballard, *Development and Employment of Fixed Wing Gunships* (Washington, DC: Government Printing Office, 1982), 236.

[8] Wiest, *Vietnam's Forgotten Army*, 231–232.

[9] Ngo Quang Truong, *The Easter Offensive of 1972* (Washington, DC: US Army Center of Military History, 1977), 16.

President Thieu's domestic struggle to maintain power led to countless political compromises that placed incompetent generals in critical command positions.[10] Fourth, for years the ARVN had primarily conducted counterinsurgency rather than conventional warfighting. While this had contributed to gains in pacification, it also meant that they lacked combined arms experience, as evidenced during Lam Son 719.[11]

By late March 1972, the United States had withdrawn almost all its combat ground units. However, MACV (Military Assistance Command Vietnam) headquarters remained, as did Air Force tactical aircraft (tacair) and B-52s based at airfields in South Vietnam and Thailand. Also, the US Navy launched tacair from carriers off the coast.[12] The MACV commander, General Creighton Abrams, observed the North Vietnamese buildup in the fall of 1971 and correctly assessed the coming offensive would be a massive affair.[13] Abrams planned to use the North Vietnamese offensive as another opportunity, as had General Westmoreland at Khe Sanh, to employ firepower to defeat the NVA.[14] Stripped of US ground forces, Abrams planned to use tacair and B-52s as a mobile reserve to support the ARVN. American advisors deployed alongside local commanders would provide the requisite air–ground coordination absent during Lam Son 719. At the same time, airborne forward air controllers (FACs) would locate and target enemy forces.[15]

Commando Hunt VII, conducted over the winter of 1971–72, had not stopped the infiltration of NVA divisions into southern Laos. Still, the loss of the Sihanouk Trail, the southern supply route, had delayed the communist timetable for requisite supplies reaching southeast Cambodia. Hanoi, therefore, postposed the start date for the invasion until the end of March. To take advantage of shorter lines of operation, the NVA further shifted the primary attack axis, aimed initially at Saigon, toward the Quang Tri province adjacent to the DMZ.[16]

This section evaluates the impact air power had on the three major battles at the outset of the Easter offensive: the fall of Quang Tri, the defense of An Loc, and the defense of Kontum. The outcome of all three

[10] John Prados, *Vietnam: The History of an Unwinnable War, 1954–1975* (Lawrence: University Press of Kansas, 2009), 335.

[11] Truong, *The Easter Offensive of 1972*, 166.

[12] Three US Marine F-4 squadrons returned to DaNang in early April. John Sherwood, *Afterburner: Naval Aviators and the Vietnam War* (New York: New York University Press, 2004), 256.

[13] Lewis Sorley, ed., *The Abrams Tapes 1968–1972: Vietnam Chronicles* (Lubbock: Texas Tech University Press, 2004), 729, 733–734, 740–741, 745–756, 775, 803.

[14] Sorley, *The Abrams Tapes*, 568, 779, 782, 784.

[15] Sorley, *The Abrams Tapes*, 782, 807.

[16] The 316 Division was operating in Laos. Truong, *The Easter Offensive of 1972*, 13.

battles was determined before the Linebacker I air interdiction campaign could have an effect. Instead, air power was limited to the direct attack of fielded forces by armed recce (reconnaissance) and close air support (CAS). As anticipated by TAP theory, at An Loc and Kontum, air power was decisive in stopping the offensive and destroying large portions of the NVA. However, the fall of Quang Tri is the story of bad weather and a lack of air superiority preventing US air power from halting the NVA's advance.

Weather played a critical role at the outset of the Easter Offensive. At the end of March, the NVA took advantage of poor visibility and low cloud cover to cross the DMZ. The North Vietnamese concentrated and maneuvered armor and infantry with immunity across an open area where they otherwise would have been vulnerable to airstrikes. The local weather in Quang Tri during the first two weeks of fighting was harsh, with continuous heavy rain and overcast skies. These conditions proved worse than further south in the Central Highlands and near Saigon.[17] The United States employed all-weather B-52 Arc Light missions and, along the coast, naval gunfire to some effect.[18] Still, the lack of accurate and timely coordinates and the adjustment of fire, usually provided by forward observers or FACs, hampered the heavy bombers and artillery. By the time the weather improved in mid-April, additional airstrikes to halt the NVA assault on the city of Quang Tri proved too little and too late.

In addition to bad weather, allied air forces had to contend with a degradation of air superiority. In the leadup to the invasion, the US and South Vietnamese air forces enjoyed air superiority throughout South Vietnam, except along the DMZ. Though the Vietnam People's Air Force (VPAF) MiGs did not present a threat in South Vietnam, the North Vietnamese increased their surface-to-air threat by relocating SA-2 surface-to-air missile (SAM) batteries near and, in some cases, across the DMZ. During the first weeks of the invasion, the NVA fired 1,000 SA-2 missiles.[19] It also deployed large numbers of medium and heavy caliber anti-aircraft artillery (AAA). As a result of the increased threat, AC-130 gunships could not operate near Quang Tri. The threat environment near the DMZ also proved lethal for the low and slow-flying FACs.[20] Even the high-flying B-52s were restricted north of Quang Tri

[17] HQ PACAF, *Summary Air Operations Southeast Asia, Volume XCIII, April 1972,* AFHRA K717.3063 April 1972, 6-2; Truong, *The Easter Offensive,* 38.
[18] Sherwood, *Afterburner,* 253.
[19] 8th Tactical Fighter Wing, *History of the 8th TAC Fighter Wing, 1 April through 30 June 1972, Supporting Documents* AFHRA K-WG-8-HI April–June 1972, V.2.
[20] 8th Tactical Fighter Wing, *History of the 8th TAC Fighter Wing,* 24.

City after an SA-2 struck one of the heavy bombers.[21] Tacair continued to operate along the DMZ, but not without losses, as the North downed seven jets in April alone.[22]

Even well south of the DMZ, besides the constant threat of small arms and light AAA, the surface-to-air threat in the low-altitude regime also increased with the deployment of the Soviet's latest SA-7 manpads (man-portable air defense system). These infrared-guided, shoulder-launched missiles were lethal against FACs, helicopters, and gunships.[23] Their introduction at An Loc forced the withdrawal of the more vulnerable aircraft from the immediate battle area.[24]

The Fall of Quang Tri

On March 30, 1972 the battle opened with a massive artillery barrage aimed at ARVN positions south of the DMZ. Taking advantage of their longer-range artillery, the NVA fired over 5,000 rounds in the first twenty-four hours.[25] This fusillade silenced ARVN artillery arrayed across twelve firebases, which allowed NVA infantry to encircle the isolated outposts. From the north and the west, 40,000 troops of the 304th and 308th Divisions, supplemented by three additional infantry regiments, and supported by 200 tanks, enveloped the ARVN frontline positions.[26]

The defenders were ill prepared for the scale and intensity of the combined arms assault. The ARVN were spread thin across a series of firebases initially established by the Americans to interdict supplies, halt the infiltration of enemy troops, and stave off attacks from the NVA's southern Laotian sanctuary to the west.[27] The newly formed ARVN 3rd Division, numbering 11,000, protected the northernmost province.[28] Before the offensive, ARVN leaders had been confident that artillery and air power would be sufficient to defeat any assaults launched across the DMZ's open terrain.[29] While such a defense was plausible, the 3rd

[21] HQ PACAF, *Summary Air Operations Southeast Asia*, 2-7.
[22] HQ PACAF, *Summary Air Operations Southeast Asia*, 4-1.
[23] Peter Davies, *US Marine Corps F-4 Phantom II Units of the Vietnam War* (New York: Osprey, 2012), 72.
[24] Project CHECO, *Battle for An Loc* (HQ PACAF: Tactical Evaluation Team, 1972), 57–59; Truong, *The Easter Offensive of 1972*, 129.
[25] G. H. Turley, *The Easter Offensive: Vietnam, 1972* (Novato, CA: Presidio Press, 1985), 46–47, 65; McKenna, *Kontum*, 63.
[26] Willbanks, *Abandoning Vietnam*, 127.
[27] Thi, *The Twenty-Five Year Century*, 267; McKenna, *Kontum*, 64.
[28] Turley, *The Easter Offensive*, 23; Wiest, *Vietnam's Forgotten Army*, 236–238.
[29] Turley, *The Easter Offensive*, 29; Truong, *The Easter Offensive of 1972*, 22–23.

Division had no detailed plan to respond to such an invasion.[30] The division had further ignored specific warnings of an impending attack. It was instead engaged in rotating two of its three regiments on the day of the invasion.[31]

A successful allied defense would have required the timely application of heavy firepower and strong resistance by frontline units. For several reasons, neither of these actions came to pass. First, accurate enemy fire silenced ARVN artillery; without their artillery, the ARVN could not attrit the attacking columns. Second, bad weather prevented significant tacair support for a week. During this critical phase of the battle, the only source of fire were B-52 Arc Light missions and naval gunfire from US Navy ships offshore. Third, the NVA moved substantial air defenses into the forward area; these weapons, including SA-2s, led to the withdrawal of B-52s, FACs, and AC-130 gunships. And critically, as part of the Vietnamization process, the US Air Force (USAF) had just withdrawn its Tactical Air Control System (TACS) from the northern Military Region I. For the first month of the Easter Offensive, difficulties in coordinating airstrikes hampered allied air forces being employed near the DMZ.

Under these dire conditions, the forward ARVN defense crumbled by the third day.[32] Once the enemy breached the forward firebases, the ARVN scrambled to reestablish a defensive line along the Cua Viet River (see Map 7.1). Fortunately for the ARVN, difficulties in the NVA coordinating a second armored assault, along with delays in bringing artillery forward, temporarily paused their advance. On April 14, General Lam, the senior ARVN commander in Military Region I, took this opportunity to launch a counteroffensive.[33] Unfortunately, Lam lacked the reserves and coordinated air support to advance against the numerically superior NVA; instead, the 3rd Division counterattack weakened its position and set the stage for its final collapse.[34]

On April 27, the enemy renewed its offensive with another artillery barrage followed by a tank assault. Once again, weather severely limited the effectiveness of allied tacair. The ARVN was driven back from the Cua Viet River and encircled in the provincial capital of Quang Tri. A flurry of contradictory orders from General Lam to withdraw and then

30 Turley, *The Easter Offensive*, 50; Truong, *The Easter Offensive of 1972*, 20.
31 Turley, *The Easter Offensive*, 30.
32 Turley, *The Easter Offensive*, 73; Wiest, *Vietnam's Forgotten Army*, 251–264.
33 Wiest, *Vietnam's Forgotten Army*, 265.
34 Dale Andrade, *America's Last Vietnam Battle: Halting Hanoi's 1972 Easter Offensive* (Lawrence: University Press of Kansas, 2001), 106; Truong, *The Easter Offensive of 1972*, 36–37.

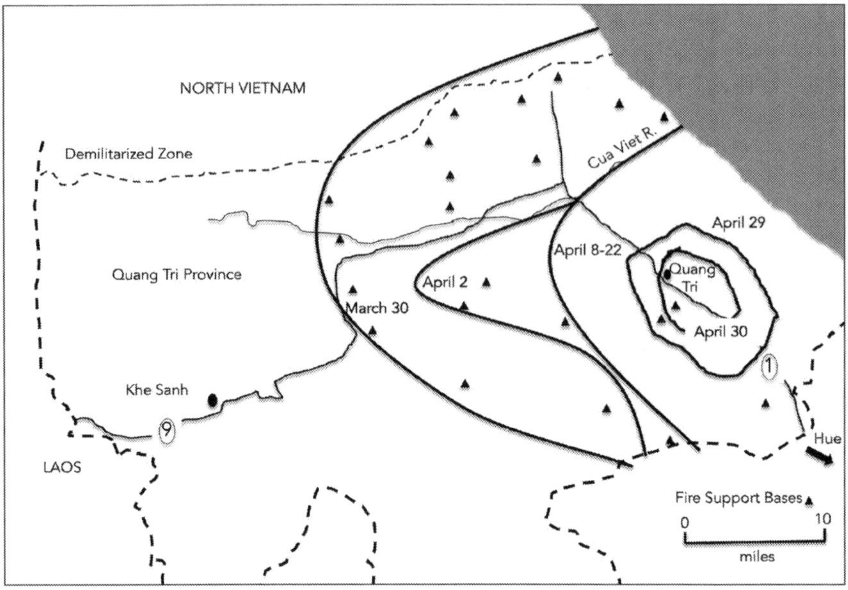

Map 7.1 Fall of Quang Tri
Source: Truong, *The Easter Offensive of 1972*, 42.

hold in place contributed to the disintegration of the South Vietnamese defenses, resulting in a retreat southward toward the ancient city of Hue. By May 2, the ARVN 3rd Division had been destroyed, and the Communists occupied Quang Tri province.[35]

The Role of Air Power in the Fall of Quang Tri

Even with the influx of additional tacair, B-52s, and gunships into Southeast Asia, with the resultant surge in sortie availability, air power could not prevent the fall of Quang Tri. This failure was due to three reasons: effective NVA air defenses deployed along the DMZ, bad flying weather, and an ineffective Republic of Vietnam Air Force (RVNAF) tactical air control system (TACS).

A primary reason air power proved ineffective in the defense of Quang Tri was the result of the Vietnamization of the TACS. The TACS was the air force organization responsible for integrating air power to support

[35] Andrade, *America's Last Vietnam Battle*, 45.

friendly ground units. The TACS in South Vietnam consisted of three levels. Overall responsibility for allocating air power fell to the Tactical Air Control Center (TACC) near Saigon, staffed by RVNAF and USAF personnel. The TACC planned and coordinated air operations and, when necessary, diverted air assets to the four military regions. The second level of control was the Direct Air Support Centers (DASCs) in each military region. DASCs were tasked with distributing air assets to ground units. They had radio contact with aircrew, who checked in on frequency to verify assigned missions or be diverted to higher priority requests. The third level of air control was Air Liaison Officers (ALOs) and tactical air control parties (TACP) assigned directly to ARVN units. ALOs coordinated and initiated airstrike requests, while TACPs, embedded in frontline units, provided air strike control.[36]

By the end of 1971, the RVNAF had assumed sole operation of Military Region I's DASC at Quang Tri City, responsible for supporting the ARVN 3rd Division. By contrast, the transition to RVNAF's exclusive control of the DASCs in Military Regions II and III was not scheduled until June 1972.[37] The Vietnamese-only DASC had the daunting task of handling hundreds of English-only-speaking US aviators crowding the airwaves. This job proved to be unmanageable due to the poor coordination between the RVNAF ALOs, the 3rd Infantry Division planning staff, and inexperienced RVNAF airborne FACs. Inadequate equipment and training left the FACs unprepared to perform the critical tasks of visual reconnaissance and air strike control.[38]

Problems with South Vietnamese ALOs and FACs can be traced back to the rapid expansion of the RVNAF as a part of Vietnamization. A shortage of qualified pilots left many ALO billets vacant or manned by junior-ranking, inexperienced personnel. Also, unlike the American FACs, RVNAF FACs were not pilots but observers who flew alongside inexperienced pilots assigned to fly the O-1 Birddog. The breakdown of the TACS in Military Region I meant the RVNAF could not efficiently coordinate airstrikes, nor could the FACs effectively employ tacair even when the weather allowed.[39]

[36] Project CHECO, *Vietnamization of the Tactical Air Control System* (HQ PACAF: Tactical Evaluation Team, 1974), 2–9.

[37] Project CHECO, *Vietnamization of the Tactical Air Control System*, 44–46.

[38] Project CHECO, *Vietnamization of the Tactical Air Control System*, 75–77; Earl Tilford, *Crosswinds: The Air Force's Setup in Vietnam* (College Station: Texas A&M University Press, 1993), 145.

[39] Project CHECO, *Vietnamization of the Tactical Air Control System*, 23–29.

Allied Response to the Fall of Quang Tri

In late April, the collapse at Quang Tri compelled General Abrams to intercede with President Thieu to demand General Lam be replaced by the more competent Lieutenant General Ngo Quang Truong.[40] Truong quickly prepared a defensive line along the My Chanh River north of Hue and to the west in the A Shau Valley.[41] The ARVN losses over the month had been severe. In addition to the disintegration of the 3rd Division, the South Vietnamese had suffered 50 percent casualties in its ranger units and had lost 140 artillery pieces and over 200 armored vehicles.[42] Though the ARVN suffered this major defeat in the north, they fared better in the south.

The Siege of An Loc

As the battle raged along the DMZ, the NVA/VC launched a second offensive into Military Region III, a thrust from Cambodia toward Saigon. After a feint toward the more densely populated Tay Ninh Province, the Communists sought to destroy the northernmost ARVN stronghold at Loc Ninh and then isolate and destroy the South Vietnamese position at An Loc.[43] If the NVA/VC could capture An Loc, they would only have forty-seven miles of open road to Saigon.[44] The NVA/VC committed 35,000 soldiers from three infantry divisions, an artillery division, and a tank regiment to this southern front (Map 7.2).[45]

Only the ARVN 5th Division stood between the NVA/VC and Saigon. Two infantry battalions and two artillery batteries dug in at Loc Ninh. The remainder of the 5th remained at An Loc or was assigned to fire support bases along its northern and western flanks.[46] As the enemy attack unfolded, the local province chief committed an additional 2,000

40 Andrade, *America's Last Vietnam Battle*, 141–142.
41 Thi, *The Twenty-Five Year Century*, 279; Willbanks, *Abandoning Vietnam*, 149.
42 Truong, *The Easter Offensive of 1972*, 61.
43 Lam Quang Thi, *Hell in An Loc: The 1972 Easter Invasion and the Battle that Saved South Viet Nam* (Denton: University of North Texas Press, 2009), 41–42; Truong, *The Easter Offensive of 1972*, 112.
44 Military Assistance Command Vietnam (MACV), *Command History, March 1972–March 1973, Volume II* (Saigon: Military History Branch, 1968), J-3.
45 James Willbanks, *The Battle of An Loc* (Bloomington: Indiana University Press, 2005), 33.
46 Willbanks, *The Battle of An Loc*, 30–31, 44.

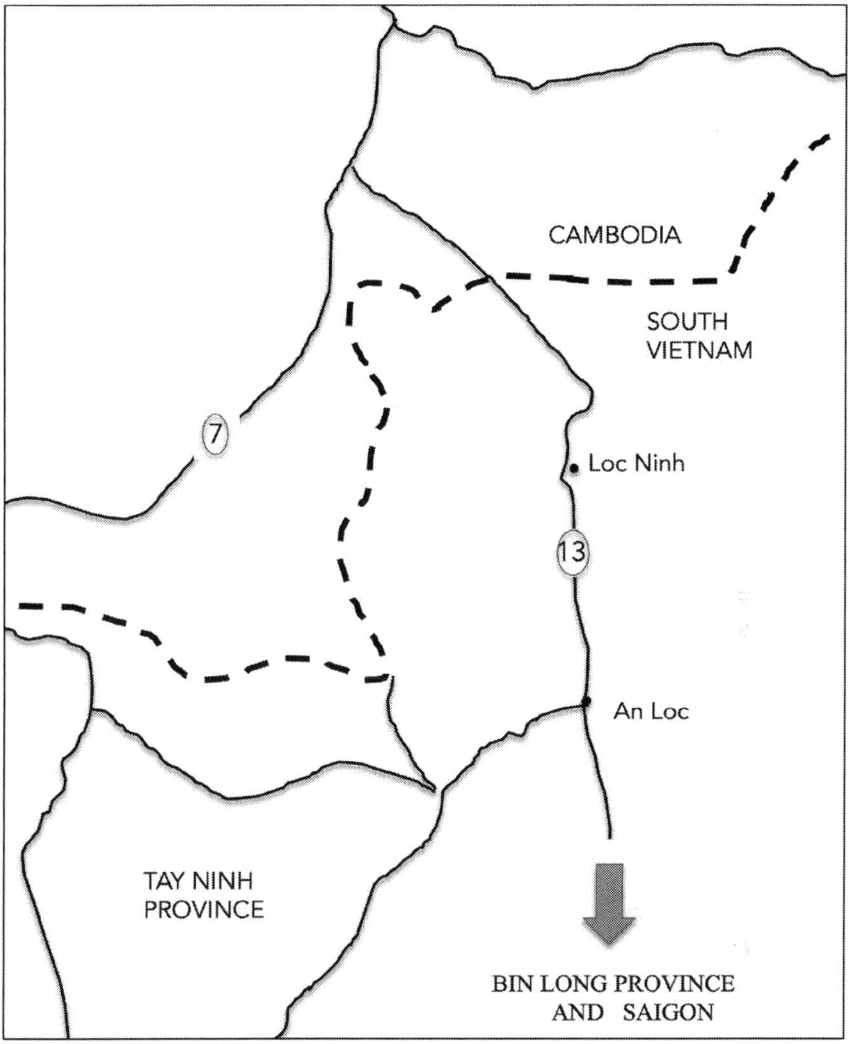

Map 7.2 Battle of An Loc
Source: Truong, *The Easter Offensive of 1972*, 111.

Regional Force and Popular Force personnel to the defense of An Loc, bringing the total inside the town to 6,200 Vietnamese troops accompanied by 25 US military advisors.[47]

[47] Tran Van Nhut, *An Loc: The Unfinished War* (Lubbock: Texas Tech University Press, 2009), 110–111.

While the NVA/VC feint toward the firebases to the west in Tay Ninh province had inflicted losses on the local defenders, intelligence indicated the main thrust would come along Route 13, the road which stretched through the Binh Long province toward Saigon.[48] On April 5, the 5th VC division struck Loc Ninh with heavy artillery fire, tank assaults, and the infiltration of infantry. US TACPs called in continuous tacair strikes, Cobra helicopter attacks, and fixed-wing gunship missions to break the initial assault. While ARVN resistance and aerial firepower stalled the enemy's advance for three days, these measures ultimately proved insufficient to hold off the attackers. As TACPs and FACs sought to apply supporting fire, the complexity of orchestrating artillery, attack helicopters, fixed-wing gunships, tacair, and B-52s tested ground and airborne controllers.[49]

ARVN resistance at Loc Ninh had, however, bought time for An Loc to organize a defense. The senior US Advisor in Military Region III, Lieutenant General Hollingsworth, articulated how he planned to employ air power to offset the numerical advantage of the attackers: "Once the Communists decided to take An Loc, and I could get a handful of soldiers to hold and a lot of American advisers to keep them from running off, that's all I needed … Hold them and I'll kill them with airpower; give me something to bomb and I'll win."[50] This joint combined arms formula would define the allied strategy in all the defensive battles of the Easter Offensive. ARVN troops willing to fight, while US advisors, TACPs, FACs, and a TACS orchestrated massive amounts of firepower to repel and destroy the mechanized formations that outnumbered the defenders by more than three to one.

The first ground assault on An Loc commenced April 13. The ARVN, now cut off from the south by the NVA 7th Division, was subjected to a 7,000-round, 15-hour artillery barrage followed by an assault by two infantry regiments accompanied by two dozen T-54 and PT-76 tanks.[51] The ARVN had dug into the town center, with a rectangular-shaped perimeter measuring one by two kilometers. The ARVN repelled attacking tanks and infantry throughout the day by utilizing only small arms and M-72 LAW antitank rockets.[52] US and Vietnamese air support proved pivotal in stopping the NVA advance. Having lost almost all their artillery to NVA counter-battery fire, the defenders depended solely on airstrikes.

48 Andrade, *America's Last Vietnam Battle*, 350. 49 Willbanks, *The Battle of An Loc*, 50.
50 Lieutenant General Hollingsworth as quoted in Willbanks, *The Battle of An Loc*, 66.
51 Project CHECO, *Battle for An Loc*, 16; Willbanks, *The Battle of An Loc*, 72.
52 Willbanks, *The Battle of An Loc*, 28.

Building on the experience at Loc Ninh, US advisors, TACPs, and FACs applied air power in a layered approach. B-52s carpet-bombed the enemy's staging and assembly areas while US and RVNAF tacair provided CAS near the perimeter.[53] Cobra attack helicopters delivered the closest fire, as did the AC-119 and AC-130 gunships orbiting overhead.[54] The allies multiplied the sorties available by operating a forward base at Bien Hoa to rearm and refuel strike aircraft originating from carriers and airbases in South Vietnam and Thailand.[55]

After two days of heavy fighting, the NVA/VC had seized the northern half of An Loc, but at a terrible price, losing twenty-three tanks and numerous infantry, which forced them to regroup.[56] Brigadier General Giffert, the number two US Army advisor in Military Region III, was blunt in his assessment of this first wave: "I really believe that without these [B-52 strikes and pre-planned tacair] the city would have fallen."[57] As they weathered the first assaults, the ARVN received critical reinforcements on April 14 as helicopters inserted the 1st Airborne Brigade onto the high ground south of the town.[58]

The NVA renewed its assault on April 19 with simultaneous thrusts at the newly arrived Airborne units and the dug-in 5th Division in the town. After fierce resistance, the Airborne troops were driven off the southern high ground, abandoning their artillery in the process, once again leaving the defenders at An Loc with no artillery support. This second battle raged from April 19 to 22 in much the same manner. The NVA battered the town with artillery, tanks, and infantry assaults, while the ARVN, armed only with light weapons, ordered airstrikes to repel the attackers.

After another week-long pause, the NVA/VC made their final effort to destroy the garrison at An Loc on May 11. The 5th VC and 7th NVA divisions threw seven infantry regiments against the northeastern and western flanks of the ARVN position, which had shrunk to a postage stamp-shaped perimeter measuring a mere one by one and a half kilometers. The enemy again relied on artillery, firing 7,500 rounds in the first four hours and another 10,000 in the twelve hours after sunrise.[59]

The last NVA assault, however, collided with the allies' heaviest and best-orchestrated aerial fire. Acting on indicators of an impending attack, Lieutenant General Hollingsworth interceded with General Abrams to secure the maximum available air support on May 11. MACV diverted

[53] Sherwood, *Afterburner*, 259. [54] Willbanks, *The Battle of An Loc*, 77–78.
[55] Willbanks, *The Battle of An Loc*, 88.
[56] Truong, *The Easter Offensive of 1972*, 123; Nhut, *An Loc*, 123.
[57] MACV, *Command History, Volume II 1968*, J-13. [58] Nhut, *An Loc*, 126.
[59] Willbanks, *The Battle of An Loc*, 117.

300 tacair and 30 B-52 Arc Light sorties to An Loc on May 11 alone. Over the next four days, an average of 260 airstrikes a day hammered the NVA and its nearby assembly areas. Desperate to maximize the effects of their munitions, US advisors cleared B-52 strikes as close as 600 meters to their perimeter.[60] Confronted by these withering fire, the last big NVA push ground to a halt.

While the NVA continued to shell the town with 2,500 rounds per day from May 13 to 16, the greatest danger had passed. Communist losses from airstrikes had enabled the ARVN to hold An Loc. By June 15, the Airborne units were strong enough to push back onto the high ground and lift the siege.[61]

By this time, An Loc had been reduced to rubble and ash: 78,000 rounds of enemy artillery, more than 700 B-52 Arc Light sorties, and thousands of tacair strikes destroyed the town. The NVA lost three divisions, with an estimated 10,000 killed and 15,000 wounded. The ARVN defenders had also lost 2,300 dead and 3,100 wounded.[62]

As anticipated by TAP theory, air power had been decisive in defeating the NVA when it concentrated and maneuvered. The circumstances of the siege made An Loc a natural experiment on the effectiveness of air power in combined arms operations. In contrast to the battles of Quang Tri and Kontum, the defenders of An Loc never enjoyed artillery support or naval gunfire. Instead, they relied on massive amounts of US and South Vietnamese airstrikes.[63] For the duration of the siege, the defenders also depended almost entirely on resupply by parachute from fixed-wing airlift.[64]

ARVN commanders were unequivocal about the importance of direct attack missions in the outcome at An Loc. In his postwar study of the battle, ARVN Lieutenant General Truong explained the result in these terms: "An Loc had held against overwhelming odds. To a certain extent this feat could be attributed to the sheer physical endurance of ARVN defenders ... But the enemy's back had been broken and An Loc saved only because of timely B-52 strikes."[65] Captured enemy documents revealed similar opinions. A handwritten letter seized on April 18 from

[60] MACV, *Command History, Volume II*, J-23–25.
[61] MACV, *Command History, Volume II*, J-29.
[62] Willbanks, *The Battle of An Loc*, 146–147; Project CHECO, *Battle for An Loc*, 63–65.
[63] Project CHECO, *Battle for An Loc*, 55. [64] Project CHECO, *Battle for An Loc*, 26–36.
[65] Truong, *The Easter Offensive of 1972*, 131. Lam Quang Thi, Truong's wartime deputy, came to similar conclusions in his history of the battle of An Loc: "What then were the causes of success of the defense of An Loc? First, it was the air support available that made the biggest difference between An Loc and Dien Bien Phu. Day after day, B-52 sorties hit NVA assembly areas, logistical installations, even the first echelon assault units." Thi, *Hell in An Loc*, 209.

a political commissar of the 9th VC Division to Central Office of South Vietnam (COSVN) Headquarters explained the failure in terms of their inability to coordinate tanks and infantry and "the effects of tactical air and B-52 strikes [that] were unbelievably devastating."[66]

Still, applying such a volume of airstrikes would not have been possible without effective air–ground coordination. US advisors, working with American and Vietnamese FACs, focused these on the enemy while minimizing fratricide. During the battle, FACs developed increasingly effective procedures for controlling the variety and volume of aircraft in the battle area.[67] While less visible than the hardware or munitions employed, the organizational and procedural control helps explain the success at An Loc in contrast to the failure to defend Quang Tri.

Even though air power had been decisive at An Loc, it could not have been effective without the resistance of ARVN forces augmented by US advisors. On the third day at Loc Ninh, the collapse of ARVN resistance spoiled plans to hold its position with airstrikes. At An Loc, by contrast, the encircled ARVN forces fought tenaciously. As General Abrams aptly summarized: "I *doubt* the fabric of this thing could have been held together without U.S. air. But the thing that had to happen before that is the Vietnamese, some numbers of them, *had* to stand and fight. If they did not do that, *ten times* the air would not have stopped them."[68]

The North Vietnamese concurred with Abrams' assessment as their postwar internal histories point to US air power and the renewed strength of the ARVN due to aerial resupply as nearly insurmountable obstacles:

> Even though we had concentrated the maximum possible amount of our air defense forces for the key, decisive battle in Binh Long [An Loc], we were unable to prevent the enemy from being able to constantly resupply his forces and to replace and replenish his personnel. Although Binh Long was surrounded and we had blocked the road from Chon Thanh up to Binh Long, the enemy continued to be able to bring in reinforcements so his strength constantly increased. Fire support provided by tactical aircraft and B-52s played the decisive role in repelling our assaults and enabling the enemy to defend Binh Long. The reality of the situation clearly demonstrated one thing: since we did not have sufficient strength to disrupt the enemy's air superiority, even if we had all of the enemy's ground access routes sealed off tightly, it would still be difficult for us to prevent the enemy from bringing in additional forces and adding additional firepower to rescue the enemy's surrounded and threatened position.

[66] MACV, *Command History, Volume II*, J-15.

[67] For a detailed discussion of the FAC system at An Loc see Project CHECO, *Battle for An Loc*, 19.

[68] Sorley, *The Abrams Tapes*, 826.

Under those conditions, the decision to try a second time to assault and overrun the Binh Long province capital was not a good decision for us to have made.[69]

At An Loc, the joint combined arms defense had held, and Saigon spared. So too, in the Central Highlands, a similar defense prevented the division of South Vietnam by a third NVA offensive.

The Siege of Kontum

With the battles in Quang Tri and An Loc underway, the NVA launched a third attack from northeastern Cambodia and southern Laos into the thinly populated Central Highlands. If the NVA could seize Kontum and Pleiku and destabilize the coastal area, it would divide South Vietnam. The NVA invested 20,000 troops in three infantry divisions, heavy artillery, and 400 tanks for this offensive.[70]

The NVA's plan proceeded in three phases. First, infantry would infiltrate to the east and cut the flow of supplies from the coast to the ARVN's forward positions in the highlands at Tac Canh/Dak To, Kontum, and Pleiku (see Map 7.3). Second, it would seize Rocket Ridge, the strip of high ground that dominated both Tan Canh/Dak To and Kontum. Holding the high ground, the NVA could isolate and destroy the ARVN garrisons in sequence, opening a gateway to the sea.

The forces that stood in the way of the NVA were considered the weakest of South Vietnam's four corps. US advisors regarded II Corps Commander General Dzu and his regimental commanders as ineffectual. US military leaders were pessimistic about their ability to withstand an attack.[71] Still, the US senior advisor, John Paul Vann, hoped that even moderate ARVN resistance would allow air power to break the NVA's bid to seize the Central Highlands.[72]

Vann sought first to use B-52s to disrupt the buildup. The limiting factor for these spoiling attacks would be not having direct observation of enemy forces. Many ARVN commanders were reluctant to patrol

[69] "The Nguyen Hue Offensive Campaign in Eastern Cochin China, 1972 – For Internal Distribution Only" [Chien Dich Tien Cong Nguyen Hue Mien Dong Nam Bo Nam 1972 – Luu Hanh Noi Bo], Editorial Direction: Colonel General Hoang Minh Thao, Major General Cao Pha, Senior Colonel Vo Cong Luan. Author: Senior Colonel Le Buoi. Editor: Senior Colonel Ho Ban, Military History Institute of the Ministry of Defense, Hanoi, 1988 (Translation by Merle Pribbenow), 87.

[70] Project CHECO, *Kontum: Battle for the Central Highlands 30 March–10 June 1972* (HQ PACAF, Directorate of Operations Analysis, 1972), 3; Willbanks, *Abandoning Vietnam*, 139.

[71] Andrade, *America's Last Vietnam Battle*, 207–208; Sorley, *The Abrams Tapes*, 730–731.

[72] McKenna, *Kontum*, 47; Andrade, *America's Last Vietnam Battle*, 214–215, 217.

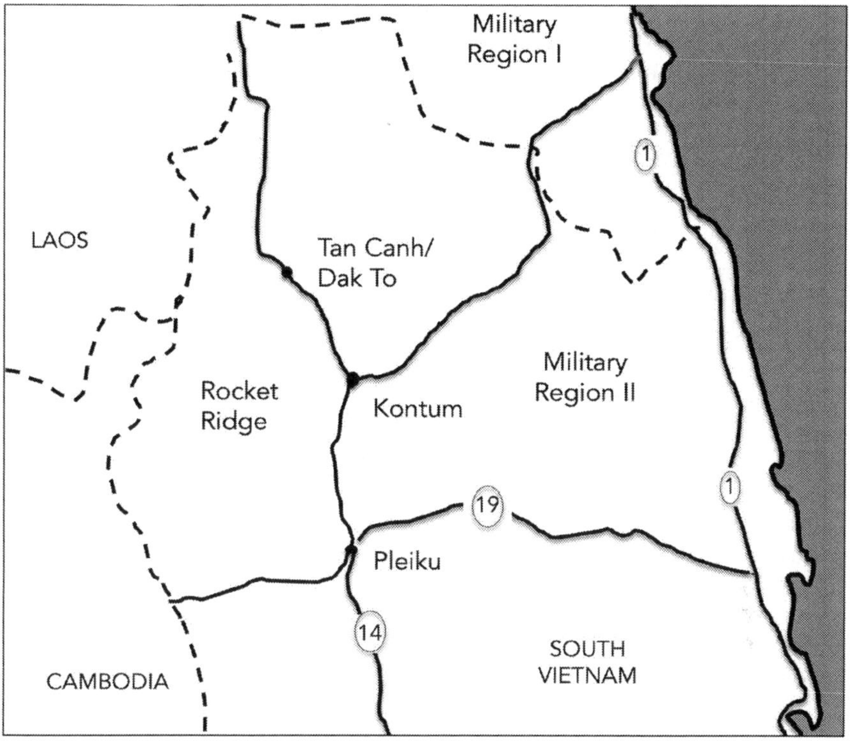

Map 7.3 Battle of Kontum
Source: Truong, *The Easter Offensive of 1972*, 79.

aggressively and pin down enemy positions.[73] Even so, in the first two months, B-52s had been employed against the NVA in western Military Region II, with more than 100 Arc Light sorties servicing the Central Highlands.[74] Later, prisoner reports revealed that these unobserved strikes had inflicted significant attrition on the NVA. As one prisoner from the 320th Division testified, his regiment of 2,500 had suffered 1,200 casualties before it even conducted its first attack. Equally important, these airstrikes delayed the offensive. This postponement meant that the third NVA front would not open until after the other two had culminated.[75] The NVA's postponement in the Central Highlands would allow the United States to focus the total weight of its air power.

[73] MACV, *Command History January 1972–March 1973, Volume I*, K-1; Andrade, *America's Last Vietnam Battle*, 213; McKenna, *Kontum*, 29, 87.
[74] McKenna, *Kontum*, 53, 98. [75] McKenna, *Kontum*, 53, 193–194.

Despite the disruption caused by the B-52 strikes, the preparatory phases of the NVA attack were broadly successful. In early April, the NVA seized An Khe Pass and cut the primary supply line from the coast to the highlands; it would take ARVN and allied South Korean forces a month to clear this roadblock. At the same time, diversionary attacks in coastal Binh Dinh province allowed the VC to seize control of several villages.[76] Most importantly, in early April, the NVA began isolating and attacking the ARVN firebases strung out from north to south along Rocket Ridge. While these firebases held for a time, they began to withdraw by the last week of April.[77] Once established on the dominating heights, the NVA positioned its artillery and assembled its troops to launch deliberate attacks on Tan Canh/Dak To and Kontum.[78]

On April 23, the first blow fell on two regiments of the ARVN 22nd Division at Tan Canh/Dak To. Neither was prepared for the scale and ferocity of the assault. Two enemy divisions attacked the regiments. In addition to heavy artillery and tanks, the NVA employed AT-3 Sagger antitank missiles. The Saggers quickly dispatched ARVN tanks and contributed to the disintegration of the regiments.[79] By April 24, Tac Canh/Dak To had fallen, the 22nd Division shattered, and the allied plan of a forward defense lay in tatters. In the collapse, the ARVN lost heavy artillery, which fell intact into the hands of Communists, who would soon turn the guns on Kontum.[80]

The commander at Kontum convinced his superiors to deploy three regiments of the 23rd Division to defend the city, bringing the total garrison to 5,000. Anticipating a high volume of US and South Vietnamese airstrikes, the defenders reorganized their airborne command and control through a single air boss in an Army OH-58 helicopter, who acted as an airborne traffic cop.[81] As important, a US ALO reorganized the air effort at the II Corps headquarters in Pleiku. In contrast to the situation at Quang Tri, the II Corps DASC had not transitioned to only South Vietnamese personnel, which made restoring US control over air operations simpler.[82] As the volume of air support increased, the cooperation between USAF controllers and US Army

[76] McKenna, *Kontum*, 74, 132; Andrade, *America's Last Vietnam Battle*, 220–227.
[77] MACV, *Command History, Volume I*, K-5.
[78] Truong, *The Easter Offensive of 1972*, 85; Andrade, *America's Last Vietnam Battle*, 232.
[79] The 22nd Division 42nd and 47th Regiments. McKenna, *Kontum*, 100–103, 107.
[80] The losses included twenty-three 105 mm howitzers, seven 155 mm howitzers, ten M-41 tanks, and 14,000 rounds of artillery ammunition. Andrade, *America's Last Vietnam Battle*, 250; McKenna, *Kontum*, 120.
[81] McKenna, *Kontum*, 126–127.
[82] Project CHECO, *Kontum: Battle for the Central Highlands*, 33.

ground advisors proved the key to the successful direct attack of fielded forces.

After the battle for Tac Canh/Dak To, the NVA paused for three weeks to prepare for Kontum. In the intervening period, the 23rd Division dug in north of the city to block the anticipated NVA southward thrust. Unlike at An Loc, the defenders enjoyed the support of a full complement of artillery.[83] Further north and west, ARVN Ranger units clung to two positions hoping to slow the NVA.[84]

The battle at the gates of Kontum opened on May 14. The Rangers' defense had bought valuable time to orchestrate airstrikes. On May 12 alone, seventy-eight tacair and twenty-five B-52s bombed the approaching attackers. Whether out of bluster or necessity, the NVA dispensed with its traditional, multiday artillery barrage and instead committed 3,000 troops, supported by tanks, in a bid to repeat the victory at Tan Canh/Dak To.[85]

The combination of stiff ARVN resistance and massive airstrikes held the attackers at bay from May 14 to 16. The 23rd Division poured small-arms and artillery fire onto the attacking columns as hunter-killer infantry teams armed with M-72 LAWs knocked out the tanks that managed to breach the frontlines. The US Army brought in its newest tank killer, the XM-26 "Hawk Claw," a UH-1B Huey helicopter armed with BGM-71 TOW (tube-launched, optically tracked, wireless-guided) antitank missiles. Two experimental aircraft, firing from medium altitude, knocked out seven of ten enemy tanks on the first day alone. At the same time, the hourly B-52 Arc Light strikes hammered the attacking formations and wreaked havoc with NVA artillery and supply.[86]

While the NVA attacked again on May 19, the cumulative damage to its forces was immense. As one prisoner taken on May 23 recounted, the strength of his company had fallen to ten men, and the regiment was critically short of food and ammunition. The NVA had no more than twenty-five functioning tanks by May 24.[87]

A week later, the NVA launched a second wave of attacks. This time it managed to suppress ARVN artillery as five regiments of infantry, an understrength battalion of tanks, and three sapper battalions simultaneously hit the northern and southeastern sides of the ARVN perimeter.[88] Exploiting seams in the defenses, the NVA drove a deep salient into

[83] The firepower included forty-four 105 mm and four 155 mm howitzers. McKenna, *Kontum*, 135.

[84] MACV, *Command History, Volume I*, K-14; Andrade, *America's Last Vietnam Battle*, 257.

[85] Andrade, *America's Last Vietnam Battle*, 287. [86] McKenna, *Kontum*, 173, 197.

[87] McKenna, *Kontum*, 207, 209.

[88] Truong, *The Easter Offensive of 1972*, 102; Andrade, *America's Last Vietnam Battle*, 301.

Kontum. The North Vietnamese held half the city by the night of May 27, forcing the ARVN to draw into a tighter perimeter. With lousy weather grounding most forward air controller (FAC) and tacair, the B-52s and the attack helicopters played the leading role in halting the NVA advance. Fifty Arc Light missions supported Kontum on May 28 alone. With some trepidation, US advisors had the B-52s strike within 700 meters of the friendly lines.[89] The helicopters, for their part, also played a critical role in blunting the tank assaults in weather conditions that grounded fixed-wing aircraft.[90]

The NVA offensive culminated on May 29. While it had managed to break into the ARVN lines, the cumulative effect of air power and ARVN resistance stopped the momentum. Unable to dislodge the NVA with airstrikes alone, the ARVN launched a weeklong counterattack to clear the town.[91] By June 5, Kontum was entirely in ARVN hands, and the siege was over.

As at An Loc, the costs of a successful defense at Kontum were enormous. Estimates of NVA casualties ranged as high as 16,000, with a minimum of 5,700 dead. According to prisoners and defectors, many NVA regiments had fought until only 400 of 2,500 men remained. The official ARVN losses were more modest but likely understated as it reported 400 dead and 1,600 wounded.[92]

As at An Loc, and in sharp contrast with Tan Canh/Dak To, the defenders at Kontum had held their ground in the face of superior numbers, numerous tank assaults, and withering artillery fire. Without ARVN resistance and absent US ground advisors, FACs, and the II Corps DASC, the NVA would have driven to the coast, dividing South Vietnam in half. The role of air power in defeating the NVA attack on Kontum was indisputable.[93] The remainder of this section analyzes the US and RVNAF air-to-ground capabilities during the Easter Offensive.

[89] McKenna, *Kontum*, 232, 240.

[90] The UH1-B/TOWs knocked out ten tanks on the first day and two on the second; their precision fire also destroyed targets inside the city. John Burns, *XM-26 TOW: The Birth of the Helicopter as a Tank Buster* (Quantico, VA: United States Marine Corps Command and Staff College, 1994), 74.

[91] "Fierce fighting, much of it was brutal, hand-to-hand combat, raged between the [ARVN and NVA] bunkers. Hand grenades flew and rifles fired point blank. It was the only way for the South Vietnamese to win the battle … It was ironic that in the final hours of the battle for Kontum airpower was unable to defeat the North Vietnamese, although it had done much to blunt their offensive. No one would deny that airpower had saved the Central Highlands, but it took infantry to punctuate the victory." Andrade, *America's Last Vietnam Battle*, 317.

[92] McKenna, *Kontum*, 263.

[93] B-52 Arc Light strikes had shredded the NVA, destroyed its supplies, and neutralized its artillery. Between May 14 and June 8, 300 B-52 Arc Light strikes had dropped bombs in

US and RVNAF Air-to-Ground Capabilities in the Easter Offensive

By 1972, the RVNAF maintained a fleet of O-1 FACs and A-1 and A-37 attack aircraft squadrons.[94] At the beginning of the Easter Offensive, the USAF also had over 180 FACs, 200 tacair, 23 fixed-wing gunships, and 30 B-52s deployed to South Vietnam, Thailand, and Guam.[95] In April and May, additional deployments brought the number of Air Force and Marine Corps tacair up to 417 fighter-bombers and 171 B-52s.[96] In addition, the Navy deployed 180 tacair aboard two carriers. The number of carriers increased to four in April and later to six, with naval aviation providing the majority of tacair sorties through April until additional USAF squadrons were redeployed to Southeast Asia.[97] The air order of battle by May totaled over 600 tacair, 171 B-52s, and 28 gunships, a force sufficient to provide air support for all three battle fronts at Quang Tri, An Loc, and Kontum, as well as Linebacker I operations in North Vietnam.[98]

Tacair proved the most available and flexible strike asset. The fast jets carried various air-to-ground munitions: 500- to 2,000-pound general-purpose and laser-guided bombs (LGBs), rockets, napalm, and cluster bombs. Attacks were most effective during the day and under clear weather conditions. Pilots could visually identify and engage targets, or, if not, airborne FACs could mark their targets. Under such conditions,

the vicinity of Kontum. McKenna, *Kontum*, 257. John Paul Vann's private assessment to General Abrams on May 29 was that "The consensus is that Arc Light results greatly exceed kills by all other means. My personal synthesis of all available information indicates that most enemy units are at 50% or less of their entry strength in early 1972. Nearly all PW and Hoi Chanh [defectors] reports indicate average company strength around 20–25." McKenna, *Kontum*, 239. For similar opinions by other US sources, see HQ MAC-V, *The Nguyen Hue Offensive MACDI Study 73-01 12 January 1973*, 7 and HQ PACAF, *Evaluation Report for the NVN Offensive (April–August 1972)*, AFHRA K717.04-9 19720401-19720831, V.II-2.

94 Sherwood, *Afterburner*, 260.

95 A. J. C. Lavalle, ed., *Air Power and the 1972 Spring Invasion* (Washington, DC: Office of Air Force History, 1985), 39; HQ PACAF, *Evaluation Report for the NVN Offensive*, III-7, IV-1.

96 HQ Seventh Air Force, *History of Linebacker I Operation 10 May 1972–23 October 1972*, AFHRA K740.04-24 72/05/10-72/10/23, figure 3; HQ PACAF, *Summary Air Operations in Southeast Asia*, 2–7.

97 John Sherwood, *Nixon's Trident: Naval Power in Southeast Asia, 1968–1972* (Washington, DC: Naval History & Heritage Command, 2009), 36; Peter Mersky and Norman Polmar, *The Naval Air War in Vietnam*, 2nd ed. (Baltimore, MD: Nautical and Aviation Publishing Co of America, 1986), 195, 197; Sherwood, *Afterburner*, 254, 256, 261, 263.

98 HQ Seventh Air Force, *History of Linebacker I Operation 10 May 1972–23 October 1972*, AFHRA K740.04-24 72/05/10-72/10/23, figure 3; HQ PACAF, *Summary Air Operations in Southeast Asia*, 2–7.

tacair was lethal against mobile targets, including tanks, artillery, and troops in the open. While F-4s with new Pave Knife pods would designate their targets for LGB attacks in the North, as will be discussed later, in the South forward ground observers and FACs employed handheld lasers to guide LGBs onto enemy armor and artillery.[99] The USAF reported 389 tanks destroyed and another 289 damaged from LGB strikes.[100]

In contrast to FACs and tacair, controlled through the TACS, the B-52s had a separate command and control system. As a Senior Fighter Duty Officer at II DASC later explained:

> TACAIR is used with FACs. FACs go out and look for targets, or the ground commander will direct them to a target [CAS] or give them an area to check out [armed recce]. He calls back here with the coordinates to be cleared, and also requests air at the same time. We clear the target here by going through ARVN channels. After that's done, we have our incoming air that's been fragged to us; we parcel it out to the FAC depending on what priority target he's got … [As for the B-52s] Frankly, that's no longer an Air Force weapon. We fly the airplanes, but the (U.S.) Army puts in the target request; they handle the clearing, etc.[101]

By 1972, B-52s on Arc Light missions were sufficiently accurate to employ within a kilometer of friendly positions.[102] From March 31 to October 23, B-52s flew 6,000 missions, 88 percent south of the DMZ, with 10 percent north of the DMZ in Route Package I and fewer than 2 percent north of Route Package II (see Map 3.2).[103] During the battles of Quang Tri, An Loc, and Kontum, in April and May, B-52s flew 1,360 sorties in Southeast Asia, of which 42 percent supported the Battle of Kontum.[104]

The B-52s offered distinct advantages for attacking fielded forces. First, as previously discussed, the bombers provided a day and night,

99 HQ Seventh Air Force, *The U.S. Air War against Tanks*, AFHRA K740.041-2 20 May 1973, ii; HQ Seventh Air Force, *US Air Forces vs the 130MM Field Gun April–November 1972*, AFHRA K740.041-1 April–November 1972, ii.

100 HQ Seventh Air Force, *The U.S. Air War against Tanks*, 28.

101 Project CHECO, *Kontum: Battle for the Central Highlands*, 33–34.

102 HQ PACAF, *Evaluation Report for the NVN Offensive*, VII-1. For additional details on the development of Arc Light tactics, see Project CHECO, *ARC LIGHT: June 1967–December 1968* (HQ PACAF: Tactical Evaluation Team, 1969).

103 Missions consisted of three B-52 sorties. The missions in Route Pack I began after July once Wild Weasels suppressed the SA-2s. Two sources on the B-52 missions have total missions between 5,600 and 6,600, the lower number coming from the THOR database from March 31, 1972 to October 23, 1972 and the higher figure from the HQ PACAF, *Summary Air Operations Southeast Asia*.

104 HQ PACAF, *Summary Air Operations Southeast Asia*, A-4, 5.

all-weather capability, a significant edge over tacair and gunships. Second, a B-52 mission packed a lethal punch. A single bombing run could destroy most supplies and troops within its vast bomb pattern. During the Easter Offensive, NVA/VC units were on the move and, as a result, did not have the time to dig in to neutralize the impact of the heavy airstrikes. Third, the B-52s operated above 30,000 feet, well above most NVA air defenses.[105]

For all its capability, the B-52 did have limitations. First, airstrikes were only as good as the quality and timeliness of intelligence. Because of poor weather and a lack of forward observers, intelligence was inadequate during the Battle of Quang Tri but much improved at An Loc and Kontum. Second, as anticipated by TAP theory, the NVA reacted to the threat of airstrikes by dispersing troops and supplies. Dispersal increased survivability but made it more difficult for the NVA to conduct offensive operations. Third, B-52 attacks, while lethal against soft targets, were much less so against armor, artillery, or even trucks.[106] Precision strikes by tacair and AC-130 gunships were more effective against these more hardened targets. The B-52 was a blunt instrument best suited for area targets, and it was problematic to employ B-52s for most troops in contact situations given the higher likelihood of fratricide. Finally, B-52s were not immune to SA-2s and were restricted from flying in the contested airspace until the SAM threat was suppressed.

Even more vulnerable than the B-52s were the gunships. Though they could safely operate above small-arms fire and light AAA, gunships were vulnerable to SAMs and heavy AAA.[107] In late March, the loss of two AC-130 Spectres shifted gunship operations away from Quang Tri. During the battles of An Loc and Kontum, gunships were heavily relied upon for CAS as they could loiter for prolonged periods over friendly positions. Because of the reduced air threat, gunships could provide precise, around-the-clock firepower during the most critical days and nights of these two battles.[108]

From March 31 to October 23, 1972, the Air Force, Navy, Marine Corps, and RVNAF conducted 18,610 strikes over Southeast Asia. Of these missions, 94 percent would be classified as direct attack, either

[105] HQ PACAF, *Summary Air Operations Southeast Asia*, 554; Davies, *US Marine Corps F-4 Phantom II Units of the Vietnam War*, 73.

[106] HQ MAC-V, *The Nguyen Hue Offensive MACDI Study 73-01 12 January 1973*, 8.

[107] HQ PACAF, *Evaluation Report for the NVN Offensive*, VI-6. On March 28, an AC-130 was downed by an SA-2, on March 30 by 57 mm AAA, and on June 8 by an SA-7.

[108] History of the 8th TAC Fighter Wing, v.1 "Narrative," AFHRA K-WG-8-H1 April–June 1972, v.1, 24; HQ PACAF, *Evaluation Report for the NVN*, VI-1.

armed recce or CAS.[109] Air power significantly contributed to successful allied combined arms operations over most of South Vietnam. At An Loc and Kontum, allied air power decimated NVA forces that outnumbered and outgunned their ARVN opponents. However, as previously discussed, at Quang Tri, air power faltered due to enemy air defenses, bad weather, and an inadequate command and control system. Air power would not be effective at Quang Tri until the summer, when the ARVN proved to be a more capable, friendly ground force.

Linebacker I: May 10–October 23, 1972

In reaction to the fall of Quang Tri, and with battles at An Loc and Kontum ongoing, in early May President Nixon ordered the mining of Haiphong Harbor and air attacks against North Vietnam's railways and supply distribution system.[110] The objective of the Linebacker air interdiction campaign, named after the president's penchant for American football, was to stall the offensive by denying the resupply of NVA troops.[111] This section examines Linebacker I by first describing the North Vietnamese transportation network, then evaluating US air interdiction against Hanoi's supply lines, and finally assessing the impact these airstrikes had on NVA operations in South Vietnam.

North Vietnam's Transportation System

Two major supply routes provided North Vietnam with imports. Soviet ships offloaded at Haiphong Harbor, with goods then transported to storage facilities near Haiphong and Hanoi. Chinese supplies arrived via a fifty-mile rail line connecting China and Hanoi, while a northwest railway provided a tertiary route (see Map 3.2).[112] The Haiphong,

[109] Sixteen thousand were flown south of the DMZ in South Vietnam, Laos, and Cambodia, while another 1,000 were conducted in Route Package I. During Linebacker I, US air forces flew another 1,250 missions in the North Vietnamese panhandle in Route Pack II, III, and IV between the 18th and 20th parallel. Only 360 strikes were flown north of the 20th parallel, near Hanoi, Haiphong, and the Chinese border. THOR DATABASE March 31–October 23, 1972, courtesy of Jenns Robertson, USAF Lt. Col. (ret.).

[110] CINCPAC, *Command History 1972, Volume II*, Air Force Historical Research Agency, K712.01 1972 v.2, 538–539; Sherwood, *Afterburner*, 208–212; Norman Polmar and Edward Moraldo, *Naval Air War: The Rolling Thunder Campaign* (Washington, DC: Department of the Navy, 2015), 61; Mersky and Polmar, *The Naval Air War in Vietnam*, 198.

[111] HQ Seventh Air Force, *History of Linebacker I*, preface.

[112] HQ Seventh Air Force, *Commanders' Conference 18–19 July 1972*, AFHRA K168.06-228 72/07/18-72/07/19, 3.

northeast, and northwest railways converged north of Hanoi, where a single rail line crossed the Red River over the Paul Doumer Bridge. Spanning a mile and a half, the massive bridge handled both rail and road traffic and had been repeatedly attacked during Rolling Thunder. Once they passed Hanoi, trains traveled south through Thanh Hoa, where another bridge provided a second major choke point. The trains then continued on to Vinh, where supplies were moved via truck, boat, or on foot across the DMZ or westward into Laos along the Ho Chi Minh Trail.

In addition to the rail network, the North Vietnamese road system roughly paralleled the railways. In addition, the Communists constructed a series of pipelines to transport fuel from China to North Vietnam and then further south to base areas in Laos. These pipelines made the fuel supply network, which had previously been transported in barrels by trucks, more resilient to US air attacks.[113]

US Air Operations

In response to the March 31 invasion of South Vietnam, the United States conducted a series of airstrikes, codenamed Freedom Train, against North Vietnamese transportation, storage, and military facilities below the 18th parallel.[114] Airstrikes escalated significantly, however, with the commencement of Linebacker I on May 10. This air interdiction campaign was designed to dismantle the entire North Vietnamese transportation system.[115]

A significant operational innovation of Linebacker I was the US Air Force's employment of the new Pave Knife targeting pod. The space-stabilized device allowed F-4 strike aircraft to maneuver in high-risk areas while guiding LGBs against transportation, power generation, and industrial targets.[116] LGB strikes, however, could only be conducted

[113] HQ PACAF, *CORONA HARVEST: USAF Air Operations in Southeast Asia 1 July 1972–15 August 1973*, v.II, AFHRA K717.0423-23 July 1, 1972–August 15, 1973, v.2, IV-84–85; John Prados, *The Blood Road: The Ho Chi Minh Trail and the Vietnam War* (New York: Wiley & Sons, 1999), 339.

[114] CINCPAC, *Command History 1972, Volume I*, AFHRA K712.01 1972, v.1, 151–154; HQ Seventh Air Force *History of Linebacker I*, 7; History of the 8th TAC Fighter Wing, v.1 "Narrative," 36; Tilford, *Crosswinds*, 146.

[115] HQ CINCPAC, *Command History 1972*, v.II, 538. Airstrikes in North Vietnam rose from 1,644 in April to 5,438 in May. Stephen Randolph, *Powerful and Brutal Weapons: Nixon, Kissinger, and the Easter Offensive* (Cambridge, MA: Harvard University Press, 2007), 282.

[116] Due to restrictions for carrier operations, the Navy did not employ a large number of laser-guided bombs. It used electro-optic guided weapons, as did the Air Force, but these missiles did not prove to be as effective as laser-guided bombs. As a result, most

during the daytime due to the Pave Knife, having only an electro-optic (TV) sensor.[117]

On May 10, a dozen Air Force F-4s dropped twenty-two 2,000-pound LGBs, disabling the Paul Doumer bridge.[118] Employing precision munitions had the added benefit of minimizing collateral damage, which, in turn, allowed airstrikes against targets located nearer civilians.[119] Increased accuracy, coupled with larger warheads, inverted the calculus of planners from determining the number of airstrikes required to destroy a given target to the number of targets assigned to a single mission. Precision bombs dropped from medium altitude further reduced the risk to aircrew now kept above the reach of small arms, AAA, and manpads.[120]

Despite a healthy supply of LGBs, the Air Force had only six Pave Knife pods in Southeast Asia, all flown by F-4s out of Ubon, Thailand. By July, losses reduced the pods to four, further limiting strike availability for high-threat areas.[121] Due to this shortage, the Air Force designed strike packages to protect the aircraft carrying these precious devices. Combat air patrol (CAP) and escort fighters shielded the strikers from MiGs. At the same time, other F-4s dispensed chaff corridors over target areas to disrupt enemy search radars, and F-105 Wild Weasels on suppression of enemy air defenses (SEAD) missions launched preemptive anti-radiation missiles to deter SA-2 operators from turning on their radars. Strike missions had as many as 100 aircraft, including tankers, electronic jammers, and search-and-rescue assets tasked to support a handful of strikers.[122]

With this additional protection, the initial LGB strikes of Linebacker I were operationally remarkable, disabling the Paul Doumer Bridge on

Navy strikes utilized free-fall bombs. For area targets, such as rail yards, the Air Force also employed unguided bombs.

117 HQ PACAF, *Evaluation Report for the NVN Offensive*, V-5; Tilford, *Crosswinds*, 157–158.

118 HQ Seventh Air Force, *History of Linebacker I*, 10. In addition, the raid dropped seven 2,000-pound television-guided bombs. Due to signal interference and lower altitude releases, during Linebacker I, the USAF only conducted two electro-optical guided strikes. The Navy also conducted a limited number of precision strikes with electro-optic weapons.

119 History of the 8th TAC Fighter Wing, v.2 "Supporting Documents," AFHRA K-WG-8-H1 April–June 1972, v.2, 7; HQ Seventh Air Force, *History of Seventh Air Force 1 July 1971–30 June 1972*, 301.

120 History of the 8th TAC Fighter Wing, v.1 "Narrative," 39.

121 HQ Seventh Air Force, *History of Linebacker I*, 54.

122 HQ Seventh Air Force, *History of Linebacker I*, 13.

May 10 and the Thanh Hoa Bridge on May 13.[123] These airstrikes cut the North Vietnamese rail system into thirds, forcing the shuttling of goods from the Chinese border to Hanoi, Hanoi to Thanh Hoa, and Thanh Hoa to Vinh.[124] From May through July, the Air Force primarily conducted precision-guided attacks in northern North Vietnam in Route Packs V and VI (see Table 7.1). In addition to these surgical strikes, over 1,000 armed recce missions were flown by Air Force and Navy jets dropping free-fall munitions on rail yards, rolling stock, bridges, and storage facilities. The combination of precision and conventional bombing disabled the North Vietnamese rail system.[125]

The Impact of Weather on Linebacker I

Weather played a significant role in Linebacker I, becoming so crucial that daily target selection for Air Force strike packages occurred only after the forecast had been provided.[126] For all their advantages, LGBs had drawbacks, one of the biggest being the requirement for clear skies.[127] Lasers do not penetrate clouds, and given the weather patterns in Southeast Asia, this limited laser-guided bombing. Strike packages flew at medium altitude for optimal weapons employment, and mid-level clouds could disrupt a strike. Weather conditions remained relatively good from May through July, when the Air Force flew 60 percent of the precision-guided strike packages scheduled.[128]

The arrival of the monsoon season in August brought a reduction in the availability of good weather days available for laser-guided bombing, forcing reliance instead on less accurate long-range navigation (LORAN)

[123] Tilford, *Crosswinds*, 150. The Navy had been assigned attacking the Thanh Hoa bridge and had dropped 128 tons of ordnance on the bridge during Rolling Thunder. Despite several direct hits it had not been able to drop a span. Sherwood, *Afterburner*, 268, 270; Mersky and Polmar, *The Naval Air War in Vietnam*, 109.

[124] John Vogt, "Speech Delivered by General John W. Vogt, CINCPACAF, To Air Force Association," Honolulu, HI, November 15, 1973, AFHRA K168.06-234 73/11/15-73/12/04, 10; HQ Seventh Air Force, *History of Seventh Air Force 1 July 1971–30 June 1972*, AFHRA K740.01-25 197110701-19720630, v.1, 302.

[125] Randolph, *Powerful and Brutal Weapons*, 287; A. J. C. Lavalle, ed., *The Tale of Two Bridges and the Battle for the Skies over North Vietnam* (Washington, DC: Office of Air Force History, 1985), 84.

[126] Project CHECO, *Linebacker Overview First 120 Days* (HQ PACAF: Tactical Evaluation Team, 1973), 50, 67.

[127] HQ Seventh Air Force, *An Analysis of Laser Guided Bombs in SEA* (June 28, 1973), K741–44, AFHRA, 6.

[128] The USAF conducted nineteen Linebacker missions in May, eighteen in June, and fourteen in July. HQ Seventh Air Force *History of Linebacker I*, 73.

Table 7.1 *USAF major strike activity in Linebacker I*[1]

Month	Laser-guided missions	Free-fall missions
May (21 days)	40	5
June	46	5
July	42	15
August	21	22
September	25	120
October (23 days)	7	97
Total (447)	183	264

[1] Data on fixed target attacks from April to October from Pacific Air Force Headquarters (HQ PACAF) monthly Summary of Air Operations South East Asia. Not included are two electro-optic guided bombing missions in May and July.

and air-to-ground radar bombing against area targets.[129] The NVA had yet to show signs of calling off the Easter Offensive, prompting the White House to pressure the Air Force and Navy to increase the bombing near Hanoi, Haiphong, and along the Chinese border.[130] As a result, they increased the number of airstrikes, but with overcast skies, most bombs were dropped unguided through the clouds.[131] Table 7.1 denotes the USAF shift from precision to conventional bombing due to poor weather and political pressure.

Air Superiority over North Vietnam

When US air forces returned over Hanoi in the spring of 1972, they met fierce resistance from North Vietnamese air-to-air and surface-to-air defenses, just as they had previously encountered during Rolling Thunder.[132] The primary US fighter, the F-4, though a more powerful and technologically advanced aircraft, had the disadvantage of being a large platform. Its size and the dark smoke trailing its twin engines made it easier to acquire than the smaller MiGs. Also, in the case of the USAF, the combination of inexperienced aircrew, inadequate air combat training, unreliable air-to-air missiles, a lack of ground-controlled

[129] HQ Seventh Air Force, *History of Linebacker I*, 25; HQ PACAF, *Summary Air Operations Southeast Asia*, 4-1.

[130] HQ Seventh Air Force, *History of Linebacker I*, 25; "Message from the Chairman of the Joint Chiefs of Staff (Moorer) to the Commander in Chief, Pacific (McCain)," *FRUS, 1969–1976 Volume VIII, Vietnam*, January–October 1972, Document 230.

[131] HQ PACAF, *Summary Air Operations Southeast Asia*, Volume 97, 4-2.

[132] The first attack on Hanoi was a single strike on April 16, 1972, during the Freedom Train raids. Project CHECO, *Linebacker: Overview of the First 120 Days*, 13.

interception (GCI), and overall poor radio communications all contributed to mediocre air combat performance. The Air Force downed forty-eight MiGs during Linebacker I and II while losing twenty-four for a two-to-one kill ratio.[133] By contrast, the Navy performed better. The Navy had developed superior tactics and training through its Top Gun fighter weapon school, improved its AIM-9 heat-seeking missile, had better GCI from its ship-based radars, and faced older, poorer-performance MiG-15 and 17s.[134] As a result, Navy fighter pilots enjoyed a six-to-one kill ratio (twenty-four to four).[135] The VPAF adapted by launching fewer MiGs at the Navy raids along the coast, relying instead on SAMs and AAA. At the same time, the more sophisticated MiG-21s attacked the larger USAF strike packages aimed at Hanoi.[136]

To counter the MiG threat, the USAF assigned more F-4s for air-to-air duty, while the SAM threat compelled additional F-4s to be sent ahead of strike packages to lay large chaff corridors to clutter the SA-2's Fansong radar scope. The USAF also allocated specialized aircraft to jam enemy radio and radar frequencies and dedicated SEAD aircraft to attack SAM sites. As a result, a strike package might have five to ten times the number of aircraft to protect and support less than a dozen strikers.

In Linebacker I, the USAF gradually improved its air-to-air performance, one reason being the introduction of Teaball, a GCI that incorporated highly classified real-time intelligence of enemy radio transmissions.[137] Throughout the summer, the USAF air-to-air kill ratio increased from less than one to one in early July to four to one by August.[138]

While the Air Force was tasked with striking targets near Hanoi and therefore faced a more significant air-to-air threat, the Navy, which

[133] Marshall Michel, *Clashes: Air Combat over North Vietnam 1965–1972* (Annapolis, MD: Naval Institute Press, 1997), 202–278.

[134] Polmar and Moraldo, *Naval Air War*, 63; Sherwood, *Afterburner*, 219–221, 231, 241; Project CHECO, *Linebacker: Overview of the First 120 Days*, 45; Carole Reardon, *Launch the Intruders: A Naval Attack Squadron in the Vietnam War, 1972* (Lawrence: University of Kansas Press, 2005), 121; Mersky and Polmar, *The Naval Air War in Vietnam*, 106.

[135] Michel, *Clashes*, 277; Sherwood, *Afterburner*, 219. The Marine Corps, which operated mainly in the South, had a single MiG kill during the entire war. Two USMC pilots also had air-to-air kills while serving on exchange tours in USAF squadrons. Davies, *US Marine Corps F-4 Phantom II Units of the Vietnam War*, 17, 25, 77.

[136] During the Vietnam War the Air Force confirmed a total of 137 MiGs downed while the Navy confirmed 59 MiGs. Mersky and Polmar, *The Naval Air War in Vietnam*, 207. VPAF MiGs killed seventy-six US aircraft. John Nichols, *On Yankee Station* (Annapolis, MD: Naval Institute Press, 1987), 67.

[137] In addition, Combat Tree, a highly classified IFF interrogator improved enemy and friendly aircraft identification. Tilford, *Crosswinds*, 157.

[138] Project CHECO, *Linebacker: Overview of the First 120 Days*, 68–69.

dropped unguided bombs from lower altitudes, faced more lethal SAMs and AAA. Overall, the two services' attrition rates were roughly the same, with thirty-two USAF and thirty USN aircraft lost between May 10 and September 10. However, losses came from different sources. The Navy lost only three aircraft to MiGs compared to eighteen by the Air Force. However, the Navy lost thirteen aircraft to SA-2s while the Air Force lost only seven. Similarly, the Navy lost fourteen aircraft to AAA compared to seven by the Air Force.[139]

Though US aircrew continued to strike their assigned targets, North Vietnamese air defenses limited Linebacker I to tacair only (i.e., no FACs, B-52s, or AC-130s). The increased air threat compelled the Air Force and Navy to dedicate a large portion of each strike package for force protection.

Evaluating Linebacker I

Linebacker I's precision strikes immediately impacted North Vietnamese rail traffic, creating a backlog of trains at the Chinese border.[140] Hanoi diverted labor to repair the damaged rail, roadways, and bridges.[141] Attacks on petroleum oil lubricants (POL) forced the dispersal of stockpiles, increasing the difficulty of storing and moving fuel south. The air interdiction campaign increased the time and cost for the North Vietnamese to resupply their forces.[142]

An assessment of Linebacker I conducted by Pacific Air Force (PACAF) headquarters at the beginning of June was optimistic, estimating that the limited supplies flowing south would not support sustained NVA operations.[143] In early August, a mixed review by the Joint Chiefs of Staff (JCS) concurred that Linebacker I had substantially disrupted the enemy's transportation and distribution system. However, they concluded Hanoi continued to pursue its goals in the South and called for an escalation of the air war in the North.[144] By October, another PACAF report was more pessimistic, estimating that the North Vietnamese had now generated the capacity to import 10,000 tons of cargo daily from

139 Project CHECO, *Linebacker: Overview of the First 120 Days*, 71–72.
140 HQ Seventh Air Force, *Commanders' Conference 18–19 July 1972*, 1.
141 "The 1972 Quang Tri Offensive Campaign, (Secret)" (Hanoi: Military Art Faculty of the Military Science Institute, 1976), 76 (from Lessons Learned section).
142 HQ PACAF, *CORONA HARVEST: USAF Air Operations in Southeast Asia*, v.2, AFHRA K717.0423-23, July 1, 1972–August 15, 1973, IV-59.
143 HQ Seventh Air Force, *History of Seventh Air Force 1 July 1972–29 March 1973*, v.I, AFHRA740.01-25 July 1, 1972–March 29, 1973, v.1, 121.
144 HQ PACAF, *CORONA HARVEST: USAF Air Operations in Southeast Asia*, v.2, IV-16.

China by truck. These imports doubled what North Vietnam had been able to muster by ship and rail before Linebacker I.[145] An internal Air Force evaluation of Linebacker I conducted in the fall of 1972 concluded that: "[I]n spite of the substantial U.S. air effort devoted to the Linebacker operation, we were unsuccessful in our objective of isolating NVN [North Vietnam] from its outside sources of supply. We should have recognized that this objective was unattainable, without politically unacceptable changes in the rules of engagement."[146] A MACV study concurred with the Air Force findings and provided insight into why Linebacker I did not have more impact. The report noted that the NVA had stockpiled in South Vietnam before the invasion. These reserves proved critical to the NVA enduring shortfalls in resupply during the four to six weeks it took for Hanoi to adapt from rail to roads. As a result, the NVA was never forced to cancel or alter its major operations.[147] Stockpiles neutralized the initial impact of Linebacker I, as only airstrikes in South Vietnam could affect the resupply of the NVA troops fighting at the front.

In sum, Linebacker I increased the costs and time for North Vietnam to send supplies to the South. However, the combination of already having its divisions deployed to South Vietnam, its stockpiling of stores before the invasion, and its transition from rail to dispersed road transport negated the overall impact of the air interdiction campaign.

In contrast to the limitations of Linebacker I, the next section assesses the influence of air power in the direct attack of fielded forces in the retaking of Quang Tri, which brought the Easter Offensive to a conclusion and, in so doing, compelled Hanoi to seek a ceasefire.

Retaking Quang Tri, May–September 1972

If the story of the fall of Quang Tri was one of the inability of air power to stem the NVA advance, then its recapture is a story of adaptation with air power as a decisive factor in the largest South Vietnamese counteroffensive of the war. Changes in ARVN leadership, improved weather, and the restoration of critical coordination and control mechanisms set the stage for a dramatic shift in the military balance of power.

The assumption of command by General Truong after the fall of Quang Tri paid immediate dividends. Not content to secure the defense

[145] HQ PACAF, *CORONA HARVEST: USAF Air Operations in Southeast Asia*, v.2, IV-81–82.
[146] HQ PACAF, *Evaluation Report for the NVN Offensive*, V-3.
[147] HQ MAC-V, *The Nguyen Hue Offensive MACDI Study 73–01 12 January 1973*, A-1–3.

of Hue, he instituted significant changes in the organization and focus of I Corps. Troung recognized that coordinating air strikes and artillery fire was the key to a counteroffensive. He established a Fire Support Coordination Center (FSCC) to centralize requests for all allied fire and a Target Acquisition Element to produce targets. He pushed Vietnamese ALOs and TACPs to the various divisions in I Corps to improve their capability to designate targets and control strikes.[148]

Within two days of taking command, Truong launched a local counterattack to stabilize the front.[149] By mid-May, the ARVN launched multi-battalion airmobile and amphibious raids to keep the NVA off-balance.[150] At the same time, he announced "Loi Phang" (Thunder Hurricane):

> Loi Phang ... was a sustained offensive by fire conducted on a large scale. The program scheduled the concentrated use of all available kinds of firepower, artillery, tactical air, Arc Light strikes, naval gunfire for each wave of attack and with enough intensity as to completely destroy every worthwhile target detected, especially those files of enemy personnel and materials that were streaming toward staging areas near Hue.[151]

Whereas the NVA had used preparatory artillery fire and the speed of its tank assaults to capture Quang Tri, Truong envisioned his counteroffensive not as a blitzkrieg but as a methodical and overwhelming application of firepower, particularly air power.[152]

Improving weather and the enemy's overextension beyond the protection of the SA-2 missile rings amplified the effects of US airstrikes. B-52s could operate outside the range of the SAMs, and once the clouds had lifted, tacair was free to hammer the artillery, staging areas, and supply lines in the communist-held territory.[153] As the NVA units massed and maneuvered in the hopes of seizing Hue, as TAP theory predicts, their offensive exposed them to ever-increasing volumes of air, artillery, and naval gunfire.

By late June, the ARVN was ready to push north. Having received two elite units, the Vietnamese Marine Division and the Airborne Division, Truong was confident he could retake Quang Tri. He opened the Lam Son 72 offensive on June 28 with an elaborate deception operation and a two-day-long air and artillery bombardment. The Marines and Airborne

148 Truong, *The Easter Offensive of 1972*, 53, 76.
149 Wiest, *Vietnam's Forgotten Army*, 269.
150 Andrade, *America's Last Vietnam Battle*, 165, 170; Truong, *The Easter Offensive of 1972*, 57.
151 Truong, *The Easter Offensive of 1972*, 54–55.
152 Truong, *The Easter Offensive of 1972*, 65.
153 Thi, *The Twenty-Five Year Century*, 279; Truong, *The Easter Offensive of 1972*, 76.

drove north, coordinating tacair and B-52 strikes to weaken remnants of NVA units. In just over a week, South Vietnamese troops reached Quang Tri's outskirts.[154] However, this rapid advance came to a halt as it became clear that the North would attempt to hold the city at all costs. The NVA rotated elements of six divisions throughout the city to block the Marine and Airborne advance. Truong responded by placing the fresher Marine division in the lead and increasing air and artillery fire. With the battles of An Loc and Kontum resolved, the B-52 fleet could bring its full weight to bear. In August, most of the 3,407 B-52 sorties flown were directed to decimate the NVA at Quang Tri.[155]

On September 8, after two months of bombardment, Truong unleashed a final wave of air and artillery before launching five battalions of Marines against the Quang Tri Citadel. With the Marines fighting step by step through the rubble, they drove out the defenders and reclaimed the Citadel on September 16. Over the previous ten days, the NVA had suffered 2,767 dead while the Marines lost 1,500.[156] The blood costs on both sides had been high, and the final price for retaking the Citadel had been its destruction.

Assessing the Retaking of Quang Tri

What role did air power play in the Lam Son 72 counteroffensive, and why was it more effective than the defense of Quang Tri in April? Several factors stand out. The first was the weather. Bad weather shielded the NVA from airstrikes for the first weeks of the Easter Offensive. But by May, the weather had improved and, with it, the availability and utility of tactical air power. Second, Truong and US advisors reassembled a system to coordinate air power, artillery, and naval gunfire. Third, the enemy had broken itself in its bid to take Quang Tri. The losses suffered in the April attacks, and even more so in the NVA's stubborn insistence on maintaining the offensive in May and June, tilted the balance in favor of the allied counterattack. Fourth, the successful conclusion of the battles at An Loc and Kontum meant air power could focus on Quang Tri. Finally, Truong's aggressive leadership and acute understanding of how to employ air power ensured it would be the centerpiece of Lam Son 72.

Postwar North Vietnamese accounts underscore the impact of their overextension and the massive amounts of firepower applied against

[154] MACV, *Command History, Volume I*, 73.
[155] MACV, *Command History, Volume I*, 70.
[156] Truong, *The Easter Offensive of 1972*, 70–71.

them. In its conclusions on the Quang Tri offensive and ARVN counter-attack, a 1987 Ministry of Defense study emphasized the costs of under-estimating US firepower:

> The enemy's situation had fundamentally changed. The puppet army had ... moved up two mobile divisions from his strategic reserve forces, the Marine Division and the Airborne Division, and to these were added a large number of pieces of heavy technical equipment that directly participated in the battle. A point that requires special note and a full and adequate assessment is the direct participation of U.S. Air Force and the U.S. Navy fire support forces in large numbers to provide very intense and massive fire support (this was the heaviest amount of American firepower provided to support a single campaign in the entire history of the American aggression against South Vietnam, including even campaigns fought primarily by American ground forces; in terms of B-52s alone, during June 1972 the enemy flew an average of 135 B-52 bombing sorties per day, and more than 200 sorties on one day when the sortie level was the highest).[157]

The history was equally emphatic about the costs of these mistakes to the NVA:

> We suffered heavy losses in six enemy counterattacks. Many of our units needed to be regrouped and reconstituted. We lost a large quantity of technical equipment and weapons but received no replacements for these losses (this was the phase in which we suffered our heaviest losses, larger than either of the two previous waves of attacks [March 30–April 9 and April 27–May 2]).[158]

Airstrikes and artillery could blunt conventional attacks, but the friendly ground force's transition to the offense demanded infantry attacks and the casualties they entailed. The South Vietnamese Marines suffered 5,000 casualties in their three-month bid to retake Quang Tri. Firepower alone could not root out the NVA defenders of the Quang Tri Citadel if the South Vietnamese were unwilling to fight and die. At Kontum, An Loc, and in the retaking of Quang Tri, they were.[159]

Assessment of Air Power in the Easter Offensive and Linebacker I

In sum, the results of air power in the direct attack of enemy fielded forces in the three initial battles of the Easter Offensive were mixed. Unable to stop the fall of Quang Tri, air power was constrained by the

[157] "The Tri Thien Strategic Offensive Sector, 1972," Military History Institute of Vietnam/Ministry of Defense, Hanoi, 1987 (Translation by Merle Pribbenow), 173.
[158] "The Tri Thien Strategic Offensive Sector, 1972," 174.
[159] Andrade, *America's Last Vietnam Battle*, 196.

combination of bad weather, the lethality of enemy air defenses, and a friendly ground force unable to hold ground and coordinate airstrikes. By contrast, at An Loc and Kontum, air power proved decisive, operating as TAP theory would predict when the enemy army concentrated and maneuvered. In a moderate threat environment, an operative US TACS and advisors embedded in friendly ground forces, and air power integrated well into the ARVN's defensive scheme of maneuver combined to destroy the NVA. The retaking of Quang Tri also demonstrated that air power could be effective against enemy fielded forces even in defensive positions. Several factors contributed to the victory: the rollback of the enemy air defenses, the application of overwhelming firepower, better weather, the reintroduction of a US TACS system, a capable ARVN leader who prioritized firepower, and the willingness of the South Vietnamese to shed blood to retake their land. It also helped that the NVA refused to give ground and stubbornly massed its forces, leaving them vulnerable to airstrikes.

The retaking of Quang Tri in September marked the end of the Easter Offensive and the beginning of Hanoi's earnest search for a diplomatic settlement to terminate the American presence in South Vietnam.[160] In October, North Vietnamese foreign minister Le Duc Tho agreed to terms with Henry Kissinger. However, South Vietnamese President Thieu's dissent would delay a peace deal until January 1973.[161]

Air power played a significant role in the defeat of the NVA in the Easter Offensive. The most compelling evidence for the impact of direct attack of fielded forces comes from the US Army advisors and North and South Vietnamese accounts. These groups had no compelling interest in the bureaucratic struggles over the importance of air power and its proper employment. They all emphasized the role that tacair and B-52s played in defeating the NVA. On May 5, General Abrams captured this sentiment in his remarks to the MACV staff:

> On this question of the B-52s and tac air, it's very clear to me that – as far as my view on this is concerned – that this government would now have fallen, and this country would now be gone, and we would not be meeting here today, if it had not been for the B-52s and the tac air. There's absolutely no question about it.[162]

In strikingly similar terms, a 1976 internal North Vietnamese history of the Battle of Quang Tri acknowledged the distinct role of air power in upsetting the NVA advance:

> During combat, with the increased American fire support, the puppet was able to erode our troop strength and equipment levels to a greater extent, increasing the

[160] Nguyen, *Hanoi's War*, 270. [161] Tilford, *Crosswinds*, 160–163.
[162] Sorley, *The Abrams Tapes*, 833.

ferocity and complexity of the battle and having an enormous impact on the combat strength of our troops. *In practical terms, the intensity of U.S. firepower, which had been reinforced to the highest level possible, had a decisive impact and rescued the puppet army from complete collapse.*

Although we anticipated that the United States might resume bombing, we did not fully anticipate the capabilities and the full impact U.S. air and naval firepower would have on the progress of the campaign. For that reason, our assessments of the puppet army were sometimes subjective, simplistic, one-sided, and not in tune with the developing situation, and sometimes our battle plans were not sufficiently based on reality...[163]

Lieutenant General Truong, the savior of ARVN fortunes in Military Region I, was equally adamant about the impact of US air power on the outcome of the offensive:

The role of the U.S. Air Force was decisive in several instances. The support provided by U.S. tactical air and the B-52s on all major fronts was timely and most effective; it not only destroyed many enemy formations but also sustained the morale of the ARVN soldiers. If laudatory words are used here to describe the U.S. Air Force's contributions to the RVNAF success in repelling the enemy's biggest offensive to date, they certainly should not be construed as flattery ... Quang Tri certainly could not have been retaken, nor could ARVN forces have held at Kontum and An Loc, had it not been for the support provided by the U.S. Air Force ... The only adverse effect that can be attributed to the use of B-52s was that in time, ARVN forces became too dependent on them.[164]

The effective use of air power in the Easter Offensive hinged on the control and coordination of fire. The combination of US ground advisors, FACs, and the American-administered TACS made possible the victories at An Loc, Kontum, and the retaking of Quang Tri. By contrast, the absence of a functioning US TACS in Military Region I played a prominent role in the failure of air power in the opening month of the NVA offensive against Quang Tri.

It is hard to imagine a successful ARVN defense without US air forces. With it, the defeat of the Easter Offensive was possible, and that outcome left Hanoi with few alternatives to a negotiated settlement. Battlefield defeat, in turn, brought the North Vietnamese to accept the "peace with honor" terms necessary to prompt the United States to withdraw its remaining forces from Vietnam. It was not Linebacker I's air interdiction

[163] "The 1972 Quang Tri Offensive Campaign, (Secret)" [Chien Dich Tien Cong Quang Tri 1972, Mat], Military Art Faculty of the Military Science Institute, Hanoi, 1976, 76 [NOTE: In addition to being marked "Secret" [Mat], this document is also marked "Document for Internal Distribution Only" [Tai Lieu Luu Hanh Trong Noi Bo]] (Translation by Merle Pribbenow).

[164] Truong, *The Easter Offensive of 1972*, 172.

campaign that compelled the North Vietnamese; instead, it was air power's direct attack of the NVA fielded forces in the South that allowed the ARVN to hold at An Loc, at Kontum, and that turned the tide at Quang Tri.

In contrast to the success of US air power in thwarting the Easter Offensive, the indirect attack of fielded forces in Linebacker I proved to be another ineffective air interdiction campaign, as had Rolling Thunder and Commando Hunt V and VII. Linebacker I did introduce the technologically sophisticated operational employment of modern air power with specialized command and control, air-to-air, SEAD, jamming, and precision-strike missions. Combined, these mass strike packages over Hanoi appeared to fulfill the USAF's long-held dream of penetrating air defenses and precisely striking the critical nodes of an enemy's infrastructure.[165] The Air Force precision strikes were remarkably successful in May in cutting North Vietnamese rail lines, thus slowing the enemy's lines of communication (LOC) and imposing costs upon the North. The effect, however, was no more than to temporarily halt the flow of supplies southward as the North Vietnamese soon adapted.

Unfortunately, many have mistakenly accepted Linebacker I as an example of the strategically effective use of air power. Bureaucratic politics and institutional biases can partially explain this continued misconception. The Air Force has little institutional interest in telling the story of how independent air operations in North Vietnam failed. At the same time, armed recce and CAS succeeded as part of an allied combined arms campaign. The direct attack of fielded forces compelled Hanoi to seek peace, not Linebacker I. Likewise, the Army has little to gain by emphasizing how the largest battle of the Vietnam War was won not by US ground troops but by a weaker ally supported by a handful of their military advisors and ALOs who coordinated overwhelming US firepower to tip the scales in their favor.

The October Agreement, Linebacker II, and the Paris Peace Accords

In September, the recapture of Quang Tri caused Hanoi to seek a diplomatic solution. According to American-Vietnamese historian Lien-Hang Nguyen, "Only after his military plans failed with the ARVN's recapture of Quang Tri City did Le Duan accept that the diplomatic struggle had to prioritize 'American troop withdrawal' first and foremost."[166]

[165] Phil Haun, *Lectures of the Air Corps Tactical School and American Strategic Bombing in World War II* (Lexington: University Press of Kentucky, 2019).

[166] Nguyen, *Hanoi's War*, 270.

On October 8, 1972, North Vietnamese Foreign Minister Le Duc Tho met in Paris with President Nixon's national security advisor, Henry Kissinger. Tho announced that Hanoi was willing to negotiate a ceasefire so long as North Vietnamese troops were allowed to remain in South Vietnam and US forces withdraw from Vietnam. In exchange, US prisoners of war (POWs) would be repatriated.[167] These terms, which no longer mentioned as a precondition the removal of the South Vietnamese government, were the same as proposed by Nixon back in May.[168] By October 18, Tho and Kissinger had settled on the specific terms of the agreement, and on October 26, Kissinger proclaimed, "peace is at hand."[169] Saigon, however, had been excluded from the talks. President Thieu was first made aware of its specifics in late October. He refused to sign any agreement allowing the NVA to remain in the South, which led to a three-month delay in the peace deal.[170]

Nixon took no action until after his November reelection. By then, Hanoi, feeling duped by the Americans, had begun to question the degree of control the White House had over Saigon. When further negotiations in Paris went nowhere, Nixon ordered Linebacker II to start just before Christmas. Meanwhile, to assuage Thieu, Nixon promised billions in military aid and assurances that the United States would punish North Vietnam for any infractions of the peace treaty. Nixon also issued an ultimatum that the United States would withdraw and cut off all support if Saigon did not sign.[171]

Linebacker II consisted of eleven nights of airstrikes highlighted by B-52 attacks on rail yards, power plants, and airfields near Hanoi and Haiphong Harbor.[172] The USAF lost fifteen B-52s in the process.[173] By the tenth night of bombing, the North Vietnamese had run out of surface-to-air missiles to defend their skies.[174] On December 28, Hanoi indicated a willingness to resume talks. Nixon ordered a bombing halt the following night, and talks resumed in early January. On January 27,

[167] Henry Kissinger, *The White House Years* (New York: Simon & Schuster, 1979), 1343.

[168] Kissinger, *The White House Years*, 1345.

[169] Kissinger, *The White House Years*, 1355; Pierre Asselin, *A Bitter Peace: Washington, Hanoi, and the Making of the Paris Agreement*, Appendix A (Chapel Hill: University of North Carolina Press, 2002), 191–201; and Bernard Gwertzman, "Kissinger Asserts That 'Peace Is At Hand'; Saigon Says It Will Agree to a Ceasefire" *New York Times*, October 26, 1972.

[170] Tilford, *Crosswinds*, 163–170.

[171] Kissinger, *The White House Years*, 1459–1460.

[172] For operational details of Linebacker II, see Marshall Michel, *The Eleven Days of Christmas* (New York: Encounter Books, 2002). Tacair was also employed to suppress enemy air defenses including airfield attacks. Sherwood, *Afterburner*, 285, 287; René J. Francillion, *Tonkin Gulf Yacht Club: U.S. Carrier Operations off Vietnam* (London: Conway Maritime Press, 1988), 70.

[173] Tilford, *Crosswinds*, 164–167.

[174] Tilford, *Crosswinds*, 169.

1973, all parties signed the Paris Peace Accords with terms virtually identical to the October 1972 agreement.[175]

Whereas Linebacker I had done little to stop the Easter Offensive, Linebacker II did compel the North Vietnamese to return to Paris but only to sign the peace agreement to which they had already agreed. More important, it had been air power employed in coordination with South Vietnamese ground forces, which had defeated the NVA in the Easter Offensive, and this had, in turn, compelled Hanoi to seek a peace deal.

The Paris Peace agreement would prove bittersweet. Nixon had gotten his "peace with honor" with the return of POWs and the US disentanglement from Southeast Asia. However, the resignation of Nixon following the Watergate scandal and his impending impeachment meant US air support would not be available in 1975 when the South Vietnamese collapsed under the weight of yet another North Vietnamese offensive.

The willingness of the NVA to continue to mass and maneuver against enemy ground forces helps explain the effectiveness of air power in the Easter Offensive and the ineffectiveness of Linebacker I. In the Easter Offensive, even under the lethal threat of the direct attack by allied air forces, the NVA chose to mass and maneuver as it had previously done at the battle of Khe Sanh. Le Duan's willingness to sacrifice his armies led to a short-term military defeat but ultimately long-term political victory, as the American withdrawal in 1973 set the stage two years later for the unification of Vietnam under communist rule. In hindsight, the continuation of the NVA to their destruction at Khe Sanh and again in the Easter Offensive in an effort to achieve Le Duan's nationalist ambitions was an unnecessary waste of life and treasure. As TAP theory predicts, most armies disperse and conceal when under the lethal threat of airstrikes. Khe Sanh and, to a greater degree, the Easter Offensive provide two examples of the destructive capability of air power to destroy fielded forces when armies ill-advisedly mass and maneuver.

The next chapter expands analysis of modern air warfare after Vietnam to include an overall assessment of TAP theory. It also develops a typology of the operational and environmental factors that impact the effectiveness of air power and then assesses their impact on the outcome of twenty-three modern air wars.

[175] To appease Thieu, the name that the North Vietnamese had given to their troops remaining in South Vietnam, the Provisional Revolutionary Government of the Republic of South Viet-Nam, had been removed from the document's main text and appeared only one of the signature pages. The full wording for the two agreements is in Asselin, *A Bitter Peace*, appendices A and B; Tilford, *Crosswinds*, 171.

8 Analysis and Conclusion

Tactical air power (TAP) theory explains why armies are most vulnerable to air attack when they mass and maneuver. Air and ground forces conducting effective combined arms operations place enemy fielded forces on the horns of a dilemma. Do they concentrate only to be left vulnerable to airstrikes, or disperse and be susceptible to ground attack? More often, armies choose the latter. The defeat of the North Vietnamese Army (NVA) at Khe Sanh and again in the Easter Offensive are exceptional cases that demonstrate how air power can destroy an army that chooses to mass and maneuver in the open.

Instead of directly attacking fielded forces, air power can target the enemy's lines of communication (LOC) to hinder the flow of supplies and reinforcements. In practice, however, indirect attack does not significantly impact the enemy's strategy. Though airstrikes may cause delay and impose costs, armies usually offset the adverse effect of air interdiction by stockpiling, repairing damage, and utilizing alternative supply routes. Likewise, independent strategic bombing campaigns have seldom succeeded. Linebacker II being an exception, where B-52 raids compelled Hanoi to accede to an American peace plan, which set the conditions for the eventual unification of Vietnam under communist rule. The terms, however, were identical to those previously agreed after the NVA's defeat in the Easter Offensive.

The previous five chapters assessed the effectiveness of US air power in the Vietnam War. Overall, the evidence supports the premise of TAP theory that air forces are most effective in directly attacking fielded forces which deters the enemy army from adopting its preferred strategy of concentrating at the decisive point. In Vietnam, the United States first gained experience in modern air warfare. The threat of escalation to nuclear war with the Soviet Union contained the fighting to a regional conflict. The new radar-guided air-to-air and surface-to-air missiles made North Vietnam's integrated air defense systems (IADS) lethal. To a varying degree, the North Vietnamese contested US air superiority during eight bitter years of fighting and through thirteen air campaigns.

The US Air Force (USAF), Navy, and Marine Corps responded to the air threat by shifting from the bomber to tactical aircraft (tacair) as the primary combat aircraft. In Vietnam, the United States further refined the joint air and ground, combined arms warfighting doctrine it employs today.

This chapter begins by providing a brief history of modern US air warfare since Vietnam (Appendix B provides more detailed assessments of each of these ten additional air campaigns).[1] The second section introduces four operational and five environmental factors which impact air power effectiveness. A summative assessment follows, which correlates these nine conditional factors with the military and political outcomes for all twenty-three modern US air campaigns (Table 1.1). In the fourth section, nine general observations concerning modern air power are considered.

Air Warfare after the Vietnam War

Unfortunately, the US Air Force largely ignored the critical lesson from Vietnam: the direct attack of fielded forces being the most effective way to employ conventional air power. From an organizational viewpoint this oversight is understandable. After World War II, the USAF was founded on the promise that strategic bombing would win wars.[2] Independent air operations justified an air force. Service bias influenced airmen's interpretation of how the Vietnam War ended, in part to validate their separate service status. Doing so also bolstered the hopes for the future of strategic bombing. To airmen, Rolling Thunder illustrated the dangers of political interference. By contrast, Linebacker I demonstrated the potential for precision strike, and Linebacker II made good on the promise of strategic bombing.

After the Vietnam War, airmen flocked to the Nevada desert to fly in Red Flag exercises and attend the Fighter Weapon School. Unburdened by the operational and environmental constraints that had plagued them over Southeast Asia, airmen honed their air-to-air skills, penetrated simulated IADS, and recreated the large-force packages they had flown over Hanoi.[3] Neglected were the hard-earned lessons from Khe Sanh,

[1] For chapter-length analysis for these wars see Phil Haun, Colin Jackson, and Timothy Schultz, eds., *Air Power in the Age of Primacy: Air Warfare Since the Cold War* (Cambridge: Cambridge University Press, 2021).

[2] James Forrestal to President Harry Truman, "Functions of the Armed Forces and the Joint Chiefs of Staff" JCS 1478 Series, April 21, 1948.

[3] For more on USAF and USN dissimilar air combat training during and after the Vietnam War see Michael Weaver, "Missed Opportunities before Top Gun and Red Flag" *Air*

Lam Son 719, and the Easter Offensive on the need to maintain a joint air and ground capability to defeat an enemy army.[4]

In October 1973, just months after the US withdrawal from Vietnam, the fourth Arab–Israeli War highlighted the lethality of modern combat. The Israeli Air Force (IAF), which had decimated Arab air forces in the Six Day War just six years before, suffered heavy losses imposed by Egyptian and Syrian surface-to-air missiles (SAMs) and anti-aircraft artillery (AAA). IAF losses were masked by an emergency relief effort to replenish its F-4 and A-4 squadrons with aircraft taken directly from US Air Force and Navy units.[5] Similarly, Israeli armor endured staggering casualties at the hands of Egyptian infantry employing the latest Soviet anti-tank weapons. The US Air Force and Army recognized the deadly character of modern warfare exhibited during the Yom Kippur War and what this might portend for a conventional battle against the Soviet Red Army in central Europe.

The enormous arsenals of the United States and the Soviet Union had made a nuclear war between the two superpowers unlikely. Still, whether the United States could extend deterrence to its allies remained uncertain.[6] The lack of credible forces in Europe motivated the US military in the late 1970s to develop and deploy new conventional weapon systems to bolster North Atlantic Treaty Organization (NATO) defenses. The intent was to enhance deterrence through a denial strategy that planted seeds of doubt in the minds of the Soviets as to the probable success of a preemptive offensive. Cooperation between soldiers and airmen resulted in the US Army's AirLand Battle doctrine, which closely paralleled the follow-on forces attack (FOFA) doctrine adopted by NATO. The Army's mechanized divisions, armed with their new Abrams tanks and supported by close air support (CAS) provided by Air Force A-10s, would hold off the frontal assault by the Warsaw Pact armies. Meanwhile, F-15s would clear the skies as F-16s conducted deep strikes

Power History 60:4 (Winter 2013), 18–31; Ronald Rusing, *Prepare the Fighter Force-Red Flag/Composite Force* (Ft. Leavenworth, KS: US Army Command and General Staff, 1980) 8, https://apps.dtic.mil/sti/pdfs/ADA094982.pdf.

4 In 1981 the USAF did create Air Warrior (now known as Green Flag-West) to provide CAS for the US Army's national training exercise at Ft. Irwin, California. Air Warrior, however, never was given the priority or conducted to the scale of Red Flag or the Weapon School's large-force employment exercises.

5 Edgar Puryear, *George S. Brown, General, U.S. Air Force: Destined for Stars* (San Francisco, CA: Presidio, 1983), 223.

6 Each side had over 20,000 nuclear warheads by the mid-1970s. Federation of American Scientists, "Status of World Nuclear Forces," https://fas.org/issues/nuclear-weapons/status-world-nuclear-forces/.

to halt the advance of the Red Army's Operational Maneuver Groups held in reserve.[7]

The Air Force reintroduced the armed recce (reconnaissance) mission into its doctrine, renamed battlefield air interdiction (BAI). Still, Air Force leaders were not comfortable with BAI or the underlying premise of AirLand Battle.[8] AirLand Battle required air power to support ground forces, something the Air Force was loathe to do. Still, an agreement with the Army had garnered the older sister service's backing within the Pentagon to procure thousands of hi-tech F-15 and F-16 fighters.[9] Once it obtained its new tacair fleet, the Air Force began pushing back against the new combined arms doctrine. The rejection of AirLand Battle was revealed in Desert Storm in 1991, when the Air Force did not identify any BAI missions on its air tasking orders and thus avoided having to coordinate target prioritization decisions with ground commanders.[10]

In Desert Storm, the United States simultaneously conducted a strategic bombing and air interdiction campaign, but neither proved effective (see Appendix B). Instead, most missions were armed recce against Iraqi fielded forces. The threat from air power kept the Iraqi Army in dispersed and static positions as the US-led coalition ground forces quickly liberated Kuwait. Remarkably few coalition casualties occurred during the 100-hour ground campaign, after which the coalition's combined arms effort had destroyed two-thirds of the Iraqi Army. However, the US unilateral decision to impose a ceasefire prior to cutting off the Iraqi retreat allowed half of the Republican Guard, which Saddam Hussein needed to retain power, to escape.

After Desert Storm, conflict continued between the United States and Iraq. Throughout the 1990s, the US-led coalition enforced a southern no-fly zone and northern safe area while, over time, international sanctions collapsed the Iraqi economy. The impact of sanctions eventually compelled Saddam Hussein to partially comply with UN Security Council resolutions over weapons of mass destruction (WMD). For several years, air power and sanctions constrained Iraqi military power. However, by 1998 the weakening of sanctions, and frustration by US and UN leaders over Iraq's "cheat and retreat" tactics regarding WMD

7 Phil Haun, "Peacetime Military Innovation through Interservice Cooperation: The Unique Case of the U.S. Air Force and Battlefield Air Interdiction" *Journal of Strategic Studies* 43:5 (2020), 15.

8 Haun, "Peacetime Military Innovation," 11–12.

9 The Army also benefited from this partnership by acquiring the technologically sophisticated M1A1 tank.

10 Thomas Keaney and Eliot Cohen, *Gulf War Air Power Survey: Summary Report* (Washington, DC: US Government Printing Office, 1993), 50.

inspections, led the United States to elevate its foreign policy objective for Iraq from containment to regime change.

Meanwhile, crises in the Balkans in the early 1990s resulted from the breakup of Yugoslavia. In Bosnia, during the summer of 1995, following three years of a civil war that involved evidence of brutal ethnic cleansing, US-led NATO air forces directly targeted the Bosnian Serb Army. Air power played a role in pressuring the Bosnian Serbs, but it was the Bosnian Muslim–Croatian offensive that retook Bosnian Serb-held territory. Eventually, the warring parties agreed to split the country in a treaty brokered by the United States and Serbian President Slobodan Milosevic.

Four years later, a new crisis emerged in the Serbian semi-autonomous region of Kosovo as insurgents targeted Serbian police and paramilitaries. The heavy-handed response by the Serbs generated hundreds of thousands of Kosovar Albanian refugees, which, in turn, garnered international condemnation. NATO air power intervened in late March 1999. Encountering poor weather and without a capable deployed ground force, US airborne forward air controllers (AFACs) and NATO tacair flying armed recce missions struggled to locate and engage the dispersed Serbian fielded forces in Kosovo.[11] Instead, a strategic bombing campaign paralyzed a weak Serbian economy.[12] After seventy-eight days, and with no relief in sight, Milosevic conceded after Russia withdrew its diplomatic support. The case of Kosovo is unique, however, as it is the sole case in modern air warfare where strategic bombing succeeded in gaining a major territorial concession.

In 2001, the character of warfare changed with the September 11 terrorist attacks on the World Trade Center. The subsequent war in Afghanistan was not a modern air campaign as defined in this book, as the United States did not face an enemy IADS with advanced air-to-air or surface-to-air weapon systems. Still, air power proved vital in tilting the military balance of power on the ground. Only after the insertion of US special operation forces, which coordinated and controlled airstrikes, did the Afghan rebels topple the Taliban. Strategic bombing, air interdiction, and armed recce missions were not effective in Afghanistan. Instead, CAS helped defeat the Taliban and afterward would support allied counterinsurgency operations for two decades.

In 2002, while American leaders debated the threat of Iraqi WMD, US air forces (including Air Force, Navy, and Marine Corps aviation)

[11] The author was the A-10 Weapons Officer for the 81st Fighter Squadron, which flew most of the daytime airborne forward air control (AFAC) missions over Kosovo.

[12] There remains some doubt as to the primary cause for Milosevic's decision to concede Kosovo. See Appendix B for further discussion.

systematically began to roll back Iraq's IADS. By early 2003, with the risk of another war on the rise, Saddam Hussein prioritized the survival of his army against airstrikes. As anticipated by TAP theory, he ordered his forces to disperse and hide instead of concentrating them in strategic positions to defend against an invasion. Air power, flying armed recce missions, had significantly affected the ground war before the first American boot touched Iraqi soil. After the conventional warfighting, CAS proved critical for counterinsurgency operations.

In 2011, after a decade of counterinsurgency and counterterrorism operations in Afghanistan and Iraq, US air forces and NATO partners imposed a no-fly zone over Libya. This air operation was in response to threats made by Muammar Qaddafi to suppress rebels. These groups had taken to the streets during the Arab Spring protests that swept the Arab world. However, the UN-sanctioned no-fly zone quickly morphed into a no-drive zone, as the US objective shifted from protecting civilians to regime change. NATO promptly gained air superiority and then conducted armed recce missions, which kept Qaddafi's forces dispersed, immobile, and vulnerable to rebel attack. Many Libyan troops switched their allegiance to the rebel coalition, which eventually toppled what remained of Qaddafi's regime. Soon afterward, however, the fragile rebel alliance fragmented and, without international peacekeepers on the ground, Libya disintegrated.

As with the Vietnam War, operational and environmental factors contributed to the effectiveness or ineffectiveness of US air power in these modern air wars. The following section identifies and discusses nine significant factors.

Operational and Environmental Factors that Affect Modern Air Warfare

Of the twenty-three modern air campaigns introduced in Chapter 1, Table 1.1, air power did not always achieve US military and political objectives. Context mattered in each war, regarding the level of objectives being sought and how operational and environmental factors affected the application of air power.

Operational Factors

Four operational factors impact the ability of air forces to conduct air-to-ground operations: air superiority, air-to-ground capabilities, friendly ground force capabilities, and enemy ground force capabilities. Table 8.1 provides a template for how and what to assess for each factor, the first being air superiority.

Table 8.1 *Operational factors affecting air operations*

Operational factors	How to estimate	What to assess
Air superiority	– Degree to which air forces operate over surface forces with acceptable risk and sustainable losses – Comparison of the relative strengths and weaknesses of own and enemy air defense capabilities	– Offensive air capabilities: early warning, command and control, air-to-air interceptors, SEAD, electronic warfare, jammers, self-defending strikers – Defensive air capabilities: integrated air defense system (IADS), early warning, command and control, interceptors, surface-to-air missiles, and AAA
Air-to-ground capability	– Quality and quantity of ISR dedicated to air-to-ground operations – Quality and quantity of platforms, weapons, and sensors – Quality of the doctrine, training, and aircrew experience	– Air-to-ground aircraft – Weapons effective against moving targets, armor, and large formations – Sensors to locate and identify mobile targets – Command and control – Intelligence to process targeting information – Air-to-ground doctrine to include CAS and armed recce – Training and exercises attacking fielded forces – Relevant combat experience
Friendly ground force capability	– Ground force organic capabilities – Integration with air forces	– Ability to independently threaten enemy ground forces – Combined arms doctrine, air–ground system, and training to integrate air power
Enemy ground force capability	– Composition, doctrine, training to operate under air threat	– Quantity, quality, and types of ground forces: mechanized, infantry, guerrilla – Quality of training, doctrine, and experience operating under air threat

Air Superiority

A prerequisite to successful air-to-ground operations is to gain sufficient air superiority to be able to employ with acceptable losses. There are two types of air superiority forces. First are aircraft designed for offensive purposes, capable of projecting power across borders and long distances. Modern air superiority forces have most of the following capabilities. They have an early warning and command and control system, such as AWACS (airborne warning and control system), to conduct long-range surveillance to provide intelligence on enemy air activity and control air-to-air engagements. They also include long-range sensors to detect enemy ground-based air defense systems, the most lethal being radar-guided SAMs. Second, air-to-air engagements require fighters with onboard sensors, including radar and infrared search-and-track (IRST) systems. Tacair are armed with radar and infrared-guided air-to-air missiles. Third, suppression of enemy air defense (SEAD) and electronic warfare systems deter, suppress, and destroy the early warning and guidance radars for enemy SAMs and AAA. Fourth, air- and space-borne sensors monitor and disrupt enemy command and control communication networks. Finally, strike aircraft employ self-protection devices, including radar warning receivers, electronic countermeasure (ECM) pods, chaff, and flares to confuse and decoy enemy weapons. The latest generation aircraft also utilize stealth technology in airframe design to reduce radar and heat signatures. These platforms, sensors, weapons, and jammers increase the likelihood that a strike force can penetrate enemy defenses and conduct air-to-ground operations with acceptable risk.

In response to the threat of air attack, modern nations employ IADS to deny or deter offensive air forces from conducting strikes. IADS include early warning radars to identify incoming enemy aircraft and communicate this information through a command-and-control network. Radar-guided SAMs and air-to-air interceptors engage enemy air forces. But even when the enemy's radars can be jammed, and its air-to-air interceptors and radar SAMs neutralized, the low-altitude regime remains a contested environment given the proliferation of small arms, AAA, and man-portable air defense system (manpads). A well-designed IADS covers all altitudes, both day and night. Even when an IADS cannot defeat an enemy air force, air defenses may compel strike packages to invest scarce resources to gain and maintain air superiority. Such efforts, in turn, limit the employment of more vulnerable combat aircraft, reduce the availability of tacair for air-to-ground missions, and restrict the freedom of action for those assigned on strike missions.

Gaining air superiority, however, is not enough. In *On War*, Clausewitz insists that one must convert the advantage of the high ground into battlefield results.

> In reality, the occupation [of the high ground] is nothing but a raised arm, and the position itself only a lifeless tool, a mere potentiality that needs an object for its realization, a simple plus or minus sign without a value attached. The real

thrust and blow, the object, the value is *victory in battle*. It is the only thing that really counts and can be counted on, and one must always bear it in mind, whether it be in passing judgment in books or in taking action in the field.[13]

Concerning air warfare, Clausewitz's point on the potential value of occupying the high ground suggests that gaining air superiority is a necessary but insufficient condition for achieving military and political objectives.[14] Exploiting the advantage air superiority provides requires the ability to conduct air-to-ground operations.

Without air superiority, air forces must stand off at a safe distance, vertically or laterally, which reduces their ability to locate and strike targets. Alternatively, aircrew may be compelled to fly inside the range of enemy air defenses, diverting attention for self-preservation, which then reduces the precious time available for air-to-ground strikes. There is thus a direct relationship between an aircraft's ability to survive and its lethality, which is considered next.

Air-to-Ground Capability

Engaging ground targets requires an air force to complete the targeting cycle by locating, identifying, striking, and conducting battle damage assessment (BDA). This ability requires intelligence surveillance and reconnaissance (ISR) assets to identify targets and then communicate this vital information to strike forces. The ISR requirement includes air and space-borne electro-optic, infrared, radar, and electromagnetic spectral sensors, and open source and classified human intelligence to develop accurate targeting data. For the large, fixed targets of strategic bombing, this information includes not only coordinates and elevation but also collateral damage estimates. While fixed targeting is challenging, it is less so than the direct attack of mobile targets, which requires constant surveillance and updates.

An example of near-real-time ISR required for dynamic targeting occurred in Commando Hunt when the USAF utilized thousands of Igloo White sensors deployed along the Ho Chi Minh Trail. In the 1980s, the US military increased its ability to monitor enemy traffic by developing the Joint Surveillance Target Attack Radar System (JSTARS).[15] JSTARS utilized a Boeing 707 airframe with an airborne

[13] Carl Von Clausewitz, *On War* (Princeton, NJ: Princeton University Press, 1975), 354.

[14] The exception would be purely defensive objectives, such as the Battle of Britain in 1940, where air superiority deterred the German invasion.

[15] John Holly, "The Forgotten Dimension of AirLand Battle" *Military Review* 65:8 (August 1985), 23.

battlefield management command-and-control center dedicated to analyzing and sharing data gathered from its large synthetic aperture radar and moving target indicator (MTI) mounted on the side of the aircraft.[16] The all-weather, day and night JSTARS platform monitored enemy movement out to 150 miles. It could also conduct broad area searches and, once located, track vehicles.[17]

In addition to near-real-time ISR, attacking fielded forces requires strike aircraft with air-to-ground sensors that can validate target information, conduct precision strikes, and provide video imagery of BDA. Since Vietnam, the AC-130 gunship has utilized its onboard sensor array for this purpose. Gunships have been employed at night in low-threat environments, conducting counterinsurgency and counterterrorist operations. Recent advancements in targeting pods have provided similar sensor capabilities for tacair to identify, track, and engage mobile targets during the day and at night.

In addition to air-to-ground sensors, strike aircraft must also be equipped with accurate weapon delivery systems and carry the proper mix of munitions. During Vietnam, the US Air Force invested in weapon systems designed against armored forces, including the Maverick air-to-ground missile and the Mk 20 "Rockeye" CBU (cluster bomb unit). For US air forces to remain lethal against ground forces requires the resources to upgrade existing weapon systems and take the lessons from combat to generate the requirements for the next generation of platforms, sensors, and munitions.

Just as important as the equipment, aircrew must be well versed in air-to-ground doctrine and experienced with the unique challenges of directly attacking armies. Organizations need to be structured such that the precious knowledge and expertise gained in combat can be handed down from generation to generation. Keeping communities of experts with a shared history and culture is vital to ensure the lessons learned from combat are not forsaken but instead used to adapt doctrine and update training. In peacetime, exercises and training must be realistic and not overlook the most challenging task for attacking enemy forces: target location and identification. In addition to combat squadrons with qualified and experienced aircrew, air forces must invest in the manning and

[16] US General Accounting Office, "The Army's Standoff Target Acquisition System – A Program Having Development Difficulties" (February 18, 1981).

[17] U.S. Air Force "Fact Sheet: E8C Joint Stars" (September 23, 2015); Even with its capabilities JSTARS has struggled to integrate into combat operations. It has had challenges in target identification of dispersed and concealed forces. JSTARS's requirements were to identify the large convoys of the Soviet's Operational Maneuver Groups as envisioned by AirLand Battle doctrine.

training of competent air liaisons and tactical controllers to integrate air into the ground scheme of maneuver through a functioning tactical air control system (TACS). The TACS structure remains a vital but often neglected aspect of an air force, especially during peacetime. Yet the TACS remains the primary means by which an air force coordinates with a friendly ground force. The appropriate quantity and quality of equipment, personnel along with a functioning TACS are the critical components for integrating air with friendly ground forces, which is considered next.

Friendly Ground Force Capability

A third operational factor impacting air-to-ground operations is the competence of friendly ground forces. While ground forces are not applicable for independent strategic bombing and air interdiction campaigns, they are vital for the direct air attack of fielded forces. The two attributes most important for friendly ground forces are their lethality as a fighting force and their ability to integrate air power into combined arms operations.

To be lethal, ground forces must have the maneuverability and firepower to detect and engage the enemy. When friendly air and ground forces threaten an army, TAP theory identifies the enemy's dilemma of whether to concentrate and maneuver against the opposing army, only to be vulnerable to air attack, or instead disperse and hide but be left defenseless against a ground attack. During Desert Storm, Iraqi forces faced this situation and decided on the latter, to remain in static defenses rather than maneuver to challenge coalition ground forces. As a result, the Iraqis were quickly routed. Even so, as with the South Vietnamese army in the retaking of Quang Tri, the US-led coalition would not have liberated Kuwait had not its ground forces been able and willing to maneuver and engage the Iraqi Army.

The second attribute of effective ground forces is the ability to coordinate with air forces. Friendly armies provide target prioritization and intelligence for armed recce missions at the theater level, while tactical air controllers coordinate CAS strikes near friendly positions. The cooperation of army and air commanders, the integration of army and air force operational centers, the exchange of liaisons, and the utilization of trained and experienced tactical air controllers are the critical enablers of air–ground cooperation. The development of joint air-to-ground doctrine, the training of airmen, sailors, soldiers, and marines in air-to-ground tactics, and combat experience create a synergy that magnifies the impact of air power against fielded forces.

The most straightforward situation for integrating air and ground is when these forces reside in the same service. The Marine Corps has long committed to combined air-and-ground operations and consistently demonstrated a high level of proficiency. The next most manageable air and ground relationship is between sister services, such as the Air Force and Army. Though divided by service culture, air and ground forces share political leadership and therefore have the same overarching national security objectives. More challenging is maintaining air and ground relations between countries with long-standing alliances, those which have developed multinational doctrine for air-to-ground operations, such as NATO. Such doctrine is difficult to create and has the additional challenge of clearing multiple national political hurdles.[18] Finally, proxy ground forces, especially nonstate groups, are least likely to integrate air power effectively. Additional factors, including language and cultural barriers, inhibit coordination. Specific steps may overcome some of these impediments, such as embedding army advisors, special operations teams, or navy ANGLICOs (Air Naval Gunfire Liaison Company) and providing tactical air controllers, as the United States did in South Vietnam and Afghanistan. The most challenging condition for air-to-ground operations is when there are no deployed friendly forces, allowing the enemy to focus solely on defending against air attacks. Such a condition can significantly reduce air power effectiveness, as occurred in Kosovo and most air interdiction campaigns.[19]

Enemy Ground Force Capabilities

The fourth operational factor is the composition and capabilities of the enemy force.[20] Mechanized armies have a large footprint, making them easier to locate and identify from the air. By contrast, infantry units are more challenging to observe from above. Guerrilla forces and insurgents are even more difficult to locate. Irregular forces mix with the population, which may restrict air operations for various moral, legal, political, and strategic reasons.[21]

In addition to the type of enemy troops, the doctrine, training, experience, and skill of commanders also matter. Stephen Biddle in *Military*

18 For an example, see the challenges of battlefield air interdiction (BAI) versus follow-on force attack (FOFA) with NATO. Haun, "Peacetime Military Innovation."

19 Chris Haave and Phil Haun, eds., *A-10s over Kosovo* (Maxwell AFB, AL: Air University Press, 2003).

20 This factor excludes the enemy's air defenses considered under air superiority.

21 Stephen Biddle, *Nonstate Warfare: The Military Methods of Guerillas, Warlords, and Militias* (Princeton, NJ: Princeton University Press, 2021).

Table 8.2 *Environmental factors affecting air operations*

Environmental factors	How impair target identification and attack	Physical characteristics
Weather	Visibility	Clouds and humidity
Lighting	Visibility and contrast	Sunlight, moon or flare illumination, day, dusk, night
Geography and terrain	Line of sight	Vertical changes and features
Civilians	Sorting challenges and collateral damage potential	Urban environment and concentration of civilians
Concealment and cover	Line of sight, impact on weapons effects	Deserts, forests, jungles, urban areas

Power maintains that it is challenging for conventional ground forces to adopt a modern-system doctrine to reduce exposure to survive on the battlefield.[22] As this final operational factor highlights, the effectiveness of air power is relative, as it depends upon the capabilities of friendly and enemy ground forces. Air power effectiveness also depends upon the following five environmental factors.

Five Environmental Factors

The ability of air forces to project power onto land also depends on environmental conditions. Although technologies have, over time, improved an air force's capabilities, environmental factors still have a significant impact. Table 8.2 lists the five environmental factors, physical characteristics, and effects on target identification and strike.

Weather The first environmental factor that affects air-to-ground operations is the weather, with conditions that reduce visibility being the most critical consideration.[23] The altitude and thickness of clouds and

[22] Stephen Biddle, *Military Power: Explaining Victory and Defeat in Modern Battle* (Princeton, NJ: Princeton University Press, 2006), 3.

[23] Temperature also affects aircraft performance, with colder temperatures improving engine performance for takeoff, allowing for increased combat loads and improved aircraft performance. Concerning rain, aircraft prefer dry climates as electrical systems are less subject to maintenance issues. Calm winds are usually preferred to windy and stormy conditions, with crosswinds affecting takeoff, landing, navigation, and weapons delivery. Under certain conditions, however, even calm winds can be distracting, such as when conducting multiple strikes or battle damage assessment where the debris cloud from a bomb blast may obscure the target. Thunderstorms can also be dangerous, with strong winds making takeoffs and landings risky, and lightning strikes may damage aircraft. Overall, modern aircraft have adapted to these conditions, with the impact of

the humidity and suspended particles determine inflight visibility. The dry, clear climate over Kuwait, Iraq, Afghanistan, Libya, and Syria has proven conducive for air operations for most of the year. In contrast, the cloudy seasonal weather of central Europe and East Asia has been more problematic.

Airmen early on developed instrument flying and navigational aids to conduct operations in adverse weather. However, flying under such conditions and being able to locate and engage targets are different matters. Low-level clouds and fog provide refuge for ground forces. For example, cloud cover over North Vietnam during the monsoon season in August and September of 1972 essentially negated the ability of USAF tacair to perform medium-altitude, laser-guided precision strikes.

Inclement weather has not precluded all air forces from employing accurate air-to-ground weapons. During Vietnam, ground-based radar controllers vectored B-52 Arc Light missions around the clock in all weather conditions. More recently, GPS-guided munitions allow accurate weapons delivery through the clouds. Still, such all-weather weapons have a limit in that strike effectiveness depends on the accuracy of the coordinates and timeliness of the intelligence. In modern air warfare, the availability of such detailed near-real-time data has been rare. For most airstrikes, aircrew have been responsible for final target identification. The key to success remains aircraft overhead (either crewed or uncrewed) with eyes and sensors on the target. To do this requires good inflight visibility and proper lighting.

Lighting Flight visibility requires not only adequate weather conditions but also appropriate lighting. Daytime operations rely on sunlight, while nighttime missions depend on other forms of illumination, either naturally by moonlight or artificially with flares. Daytime operations are usually more efficient, but it comes at a price as enemy air defenses are also more lethal during the day, particularly small arms, AAA, and manpads, which visually identify and engage aircraft.

Nighttime air operations have generally been less lethal against ground forces so long as enemy troops maintain light discipline. Still, technological advancements, including night vision devices, low light sensors, infrared targeting systems, air-to-ground radar, and moving targeting indicators, have enhanced nighttime air effectiveness. One of the most successful aircraft at night has been the AC-130 gunship

temperature, winds, and storms being relatively minor compared to the effect clouds and humidity have on inflight visibility.

because it combines sensors and weapons in a persistent platform. Since the Cold War, tacair has also improved night operations by mounting infrared targeting pods on aircraft flown by aircrew wearing night vision goggles (NVGs).[24] An advantage of flying at night is that, while it is more difficult to find targets, it is also more difficult for the enemy to locate and engage aircraft, particularly with non-radar-guided surface-to-air weapons. Yet even with such improvements in sensors and a reduced surface-to-air threat, nighttime operations have usually been less effective as it is more challenging to locate, identify, and attack in the dark.

Reviewing the combat results from the Vietnam War, it might not be evident that daylight air attacks were more lethal than nighttime strikes. During Commando Hunt, the air interdiction campaign of the Ho Chi Minh Trail from 1968 to 1972, AC-130 gunships killed more trucks than did tacair. However, the threat from airborne FACs and tacair deterred the NVA from moving during the day. Though the AC-130s destroyed more vehicles, the gunships were not the most significant threat as the NVA preferred to face them at night rather than tacair during the day.

A final note on lighting conditions is that aircraft are the least lethal and most vulnerable at dawn and dusk. When day meets night, aircraft are illuminated by the sun while the surface remains cloaked in darkness. Neither aircrew nor their nighttime sensors operate well under these transient conditions. Evidence of aircraft vulnerability at twilight includes the losses of two AC-130 gunships over Laos at the onset of the Easter Offensive and an AC-130 downed by a manpad during Desert Storm.[25]

Geography and Terrain In addition to weather and lighting, a third environmental factor that impacts air-to-ground operations is geography and terrain: the physical features of the land, with the rate of vertical change being the most crucial consideration. Overall, flat, open terrain is best suited for air-to-ground operations so long as there are

[24] In 1991, the author flew the A-10 over Iraq with only an IR Maverick air-to-ground seeker for a night device. Nine years later, over Kosovo, the author flew with night vision goggles (NVGs). Five years later, in 2004 over Afghanistan the author had the advantage of an advanced lighting targeting pod and NVGs, which provided a significant enhancement in night strike capability.

[25] Kelly Humphries, "The Tragedy of Spirit 03: 'They Became the True Ghostriders'," January 30, 2016, www.nwfdailynews.com/story/news/military/2016/01/30/tragedy-of-spirit-03-they-became-true-ghostriders/32592068007/. An AC-130 stayed on station engaging Iraqi vehicles until sunrise during the Battle of Khafji.

sufficient ground features for navigation and target reference. It is no coincidence that the United States' premier air-to-ground training ranges are in the Nevada and Mojave Deserts.[26] By contrast, rapid vertical changes in terrain interrupt the air-to-ground line of sight from the cockpit to the target. Aircrew attempting to locate targets do not fly directly over the target but instead offset such that even relatively minor elevation changes may mask the enemy's position.

Mountainous terrain introduces further difficulties. Elevation changes rapidly, which masks targets and makes it more difficult to deliver weapons accurately. Attack run-in axis may also be more restricted, elevation estimates less accurate, and laser designators more challenging to keep on-target. Mountainous terrain, however, may present some advantages for air operations if it funnels ground forces along predictable lines of operation, as occurred in Bosnia.

Civilians Civilians are not technically an environmental factor, but the infrastructure created to support dense populations introduces complexities for air-to-ground operations. In urban areas, the line of sight is broken by vertical structures, making target identification more difficult. Also, the presence of civilians introduces collateral damage concerns that may place political, legal, and humanitarian constraints on airstrikes. As a result, the population density affects the ability of air forces to locate, identify, and engage targets and enhances the opportunities for enemy ground forces to utilize civilians and urban infrastructure for concealment and cover.

Concealment and Cover The final environmental factor affecting air-to-ground operations is concealment and cover, which have two related attributes. Concealment is the ability to hide. Forests, jungles, and urban terrain break the line of sight, introducing challenges for locating targets. While concealment hides the enemy, cover affords protection.[27] Heavy vegetation, caves, trenches, tunnels, and buildings provide physical protection from munition effects. Dirt and concrete absorb the energy of bomb blasts, fragmentation patterns, and slows projectiles. The availability of cover, and the time to create and seek cover, can significantly reduce the impact of airstrikes. For example, the Viet Cong dug expansive triple-layer tunnels in the Iron Triangle northeast

[26] USAF Nellis Test and Training Range is in Nevada, and the US Navy's China Lake facility is in California.

[27] Webster's Dictionary, www.merriam-webster.com/dictionary/cover.

of Saigon. From deep underground, they could absorb even the bomb blasts from B-52 strikes.

Table 8.3 provides the coding (plus or minus) for each of the nine operational and environmental factors for the twenty-three modern US air campaigns identified in Table 1.1. The thirteen air campaigns during the Vietnam War have been extensively examined in Chapters 3–7. Appendix B provides individual summaries and assessments of the ten air campaigns since Vietnam. Correlating these conditional factors with modern air wars' military and political outcomes helps explain when tactical air power has been most effective.

A Summative Assessment of Modern Air Power

An examination of the air campaigns listed in Table 8.3 provides several observations as to the effectiveness of US air power in modern wars. First, almost half of the air campaigns (eleven of twenty-three) have been direct attack against fielded forces. Nine of these eleven cases have been militarily successful, and over half (five of nine) of these military victories further contributed to achieving the desired political goals. This outcome compares favorably to the approximately quarter of air campaigns conducted independently as strategic bombing (six of twenty-three) or air interdiction (six of twenty-three). Strategic bombing only achieved its political objectives a third of the time (two of six), while interdiction succeeded militarily once (one of six) and politically never.[28] The first observation is that the United States utilizes direct attack strategies more often than strategic bombing or air interdiction with a higher degree of military and political success (see the following list of general observations on modern US air warfare):

1. Direct attack occurs more often than strategic bombing or air interdiction and with a higher rate of military and political success.
2. Military victory does not always translate to political success, especially for coercive strategies where the enemy must make concessions and where success depends on the level of demands made.
3. Operational factors favor direct attack over strategic bombing or air interdiction.
4. Air superiority is relatively easier to obtain over the battlefield for direct attack than strategic bombing or air interdiction missions that must penetrate enemy IADS.

[28] Strategic bombing has no intermediary military objectives.

Table 8.3 *Coding operational–environmental factors and military–political outcomes for modern US air campaigns*

Air campaign	Date	Air superiority	Air-to-ground cape	Friendly ground cape	Enemy ground cape	Weather	Lighting	Geography/ terrain	Civilians	Conceal/ cover	+/total mil/pol outcome
Rolling Thunder Strat bombing	Mar–Jul 65	+	–	–	–	–	–	+	+	–	3/9 Failure
Rolling Thunder Interdiction	Mar 65–Dec 66	+	–	–	–	–	–	+	+	–	3/9 Failure
South Vietnam Direct attack	Jul 65–Dec 66	+	+	+	+	–	–	–	+	–	5/9 Suc/fail
Rolling Thunder Interdiction	Jan 67–Mar 68	–	–	–	–	–	–	+	+	–	2/9 Failure
Khe Sanh Direct attack	Jan 67–Mar 68	+	+	+	+	–	–	–	+	–	5/9 Suc/fail
Rolling Thunder Strat bombing	Apr–Dec 67	–	–	–	–	+	–	+	–	+	3/9 Failure
Commando Hunt Interdiction	Nov 68–Jun 70	+	+	–	+	+	+	+	+	–	7/9 Suc/fail
Cambodia Direct attack	Apr–Jun 70	+	+	+	+	+	+	–	+	–	7/9 Suc/fail
Commando Hunt Interdiction	Nov 70–Mar 72	–	–	–	–	+	+	–	+	–	3/9 Failure
Lam Son 719 Direct attack	Feb–Mar 71	–	–	–	–	+	+	–	+	–	3/9 Failure
Easter Offensive Direct attack	Mar–Oct 72	+	+	+	+	+	+	–	+	–	7/9 Success
Linebacker I Interdiction	May-Sep 72	–	+	–	–	–	–	–	–	+	2/9 Failure
Linebacker II Strat bombing	Dec 72	–	+	–	–	+	+	+	–	+	5/9 Success

Table 8.3 (*cont.*)

Air campaign	Date	Air superiority	Air-to-ground cape	Friendly ground cape	Enemy ground cape	Weather	Lighting	Geography/ terrain	Civilians	Conceal/ cover	+/total mil/pol outcome
Instant Thunder Strat Bombing	Jan–Feb 91	+	+	–	–	+	+	+	–	–	5/9 Failure
Desert Storm Interdiction	Jan–Feb 91	+	+	–	–	+	–	–	+	+	5/9 Failure
Desert Storm Direct attack	Jan–Feb 91	+	+	+	+	+	+	–	+	+	8/9 Success
No Fly Zones, WMD Direct attack	Apr 91–Oct 98	+	–	–	–	+	+	+	+	–	5/9 Suc/fail
Bosnia Direct attack	May–Sep 95	+	+	+	–	+	–	+	–	–	5/9 Success
Serbia Strat bombing	Mar–Jun 99	+	+	–	–	+	+	+	–	+	6/9 Success
Kosovo Direct attack	Mar–Jun 99	+	+	–	–	–	–	–	+	–	3/9 Failure
Iraq Strat bombing	Mar 03	+	–	–	–	+	+	+	–	–	4/9 Failure
Iraq Direct attack	Mar 03	+	+	+	+	+	+	+	–	–	7/9 Success
Libya Direct attack	Mar 11	+	+	–	+	+	+	–	–	+	6/9 Success
Summation of Direct attack	+/total 11/23	10/11	9/11	7/11	8/11	7/11	7/11	2/11	8/11	2/11	Suc/total 9/11 Mil 5/11 Pol
Summation of Strat bombing	+/total 6/23	4/6	3/6	0/6	0/6	4/6	4/6	6/6	1/6	3/6	Suc/total 2/6
Summation of Interdiction	+/total 6/23	3/6	3/6	0/6	1/6	3/6	2/6	3/6	5/6	1/6	Suc/total 1/6 Mil 0/6 Pol

5. Combined arms operations work better than independent air campaigns. Air power is more effective in direct attack when a capable, friendly ground force is present.
6. The impact of environmental factors depends on where and when air campaigns are fought. Tropical and temperate climates are less favorable than arid ones, and dry seasons are more favorable than wet seasons.
7. Environmental factors have less impact on strategic bombing due to its large, fixed target sets, which are easier to attack in all weather conditions, at night, and where terrain and cover play lesser roles.
8. Technologies including radar, GPS, advanced infrared sensors, and night vision devices have enhanced all-weather and nighttime capabilities.
9. Collateral damage concerns place more constraints on strategic bombing.

Second, military victory does not always translate into political success.[29] When coercion is attempted, variables other than military power may contribute to determining political success or failure. Military victory directly translates into political success for brute force invasions, such as Kuwait and Iraq. In Desert Storm, the allied invasion liberated Kuwait in 1991, and the invasion of Iraq in 2003 ousted Saddam Hussein from power. By contrast, for the coercive air campaigns conducted in North Vietnam, Bosnia, and Kosovo, the enemy's willingness to make concessions was closely linked to the level of demands. In 1965, the United States demanded Hanoi abandon its ambition to unite Vietnam under communist rule. By 1972, demands had been significantly lowered to allow the US military to withdraw from South Vietnam. Conceding to these latter demands was not only less onerous for Hanoi but even assisted the Communists as the departure of American forces shifted the balance of military power back in North Vietnam's favor, setting the stage for their final victory in 1975. Military success, therefore, does not necessarily translate directly to political success for coercive strategies, as enemy concessions depend heavily on the demands made.

Examining the operational factors considered in the previous section can further help explain the success of direct attack (see bottom three rows of Table 8.3). The third observation is that, overall, operational factors favored direct attack over strategic bombing or air interdiction. In

[29] For additional information on why US coercion does not always succeed see Phil Haun, *Coercion, Survival, and War: Why Weak States Resist the United States* (Palo Alto, CA: Stanford University Press, 2015).

the eleven direct attack campaigns, operational factors favored air power on average 75 percent (three of four) of the time, compared to just 25 percent (one of four) for strategic bombing or air interdiction. As will be discussed next, having both air superiority and a capable ground force enhances the effectiveness of joint, combined arms operations compared to independent air campaigns.

US air forces obtained air superiority in 91 percent (ten of eleven) of direct attack cases, all but the Lam Son 719 ARVN raid into Laos. The North Vietnamese could not effectively operate their MiGs and SAMs in South Vietnam, southern Laos, and Cambodia. Instead, the NVA relied more on small arms, AAA, and manpads, which did not threaten tacair except when forced to fly at low altitude. By contrast, over the contested air space where strategic bombing and air interdiction most often took place, the United States gained air superiority in two-thirds (four of six) of strategic bombing campaigns and half (three of six) of air interdiction campaigns. As a result of having air superiority, direct attack missions could expend less effort on aircrew survivability and focus more on locating and engaging targets. Air superiority also allowed more vulnerable combat aircraft to operate, such as bombers, gunships, and propeller-driven FACs. The fourth observation is that it is relatively easier to obtain air superiority over the battlefield for direct attack than strategic bombing and air interdiction campaigns that must penetrate an enemy's IADS.

A fifth observation is the synergy when capable air and ground forces work together in combined arms operations. Competent, friendly ground forces were present in seven of eleven direct attack campaigns. All seven of the combined arms operations achieved their military objectives, and four of seven obtained their political goals. By contrast, of the four direct attack campaigns absent capable, friendly ground forces, these campaigns succeeded militarily only half the time (two of four) and obtained US political aims once (one of four). In practice, rather than being assigned as CAS, these joint combined arms operations employed air forces primarily as armed recce that made their greatest contribution by dispersing and immobilizing the enemy army.

The sixth observation is that the impact of environmental factors depends on the geographic region. In general, the arid Middle East is more conducive for air operations than tropical Southeast Asia and temperate Europe. Likewise, seasons dictate when air operations are most effective. The impact of weather was most apparent during Commando Hunt when both US air forces and North Vietnamese ground forces timed their offensives around the arrival and departure of the monsoon seasons.

Although environmental factors impact all air campaigns, the seventh observation is that they have less impact on strategic bombing (overall 60 percent favorable) than either direct attack or air interdiction (47 percent favorable for both). The advantage of strategic bombing is the nature of the target set. Large, fixed sites such as factories and power plants are easier to locate and strike in any weather and lighting condition. Likewise, terrain and concealment have less impact on these big target arrays. Air interdiction, by contrast, has both fixed targets, such as railways, roads, bridges, and associated infrastructure, and smaller, mobile targets that traverse the lines of communication.

An eighth observation is that, over time, US air forces have developed and deployed technologies that reduce the impact of clouds and limited visibility. Combat Skyspot's ground-based radars made possible accurate all-weather B-52 Arc Light strikes in South Vietnam. Thirty years later, B-2 stealth bombers dropped GPS-guided bombs on Serbia when all other aircraft were grounded. Though technology has improved the ability to conduct all-weather and nighttime strikes, these are still most effective against large-area and fixed targets. Smaller, mobile targets additionally require near-real-time intelligence.

Airborne sensors have also affected night operations, as evidenced by the variety of sensor arrays on the AC-130 "Special Package" gunship during Commando Hunt. Later, infrared targeting pods on tacair and the widespread utilization of NVGs after Desert Storm have further improved the ability of tacair to operate in the dark. The eighth observation is that new technologies have, over time, enhanced air operations in all weather conditions and at night.

The final observation is that collateral damage concerns have had less impact on direct attack (favorable in eight of eleven cases) and air interdiction (favorable in five of six cases) compared to strategic bombing (favorable in one of six cases). For direct attack and air interdiction in Vietnam and Iraq, collateral damage was less of a factor because enemy armies and most choke points were well away from urban areas. However, this has not always been the case, as in the Tet Offensive, Bosnia, Kosovo, and Libya, when US air forces operated under more restrictive rules of engagement to limit civilian casualties. However, the impact of civilians has been even more pronounced for strategic bombing.[30] For example, collateral damage resulting from the attack

[30] During the first Rolling Thunder strategic bombing campaign, the United States attempted to use gradual escalation by targeting primarily military and transportation targets in the southern panhandle of North Vietnam and gradually increasing strikes further north. Collateral damage concerns had an impact on the type of targets selected.

on the Al Firdos bunker during Desert Storm curtailed strikes around Baghdad, as did restraints placed around Belgrade after the bombing of the Chinese Embassy.

Assessing Tactical Air Power Theory

The eleven direct attack campaigns support the central insight of TAP theory that a capable air force has its most significant effect by denying an army its preferred strategy of concentrating at the decisive point. In seven of the nine successful direct attack campaigns, the primary contribution of air power was to disperse the enemy. Only at Khe Sanh and during the Easter Offensive did the NVA continue to concentrate and maneuver under the lethal threat of airstrikes. And in these cases, when the NVA did not disperse, air power played the decisive role in their defeat, as TAP theory predicts. In these two battles, the North Vietnamese took enormous risks and were willing to sacrifice their armies in an attempt to knock the United States out of the war. By contrast, in Lam Son 719 the ARVN, stripped of US advisors and tactical air controllers, could not coordinate air power to halt the NVA counterattack. Without the threat of coordinated airstrikes, the NVA could mass and maneuver to drive the ARVN from Laos. In the other failed case of direct attack in NATO's air war over Kosovo in 1999, as again anticipated by TAP theory, the Serbians dispersed their soldiers. However, without facing a capable opposing ground force, the Serbians swapped their tanks for civilian automobiles and continued their ethnic cleansing while NATO air forces circled helplessly overhead.[31] Even though direct attack campaigns have not always dispersed enemy armies, nor have they always succeeded, their outcomes have most often been as TAP theory predicts. Well-integrated combined arms operations cause the enemy to scatter and hide, only to be at a significant disadvantage against the opposing ground force. On rare occasions, enemy armies ignore the air threat only to be destroyed. In sum, joint air and ground operations achieve military and political objectives more often than strategic bombing, air interdiction, or independent direct attack.

Direct Attack: Armed Recce and Close Air Support

A better understanding of how air power works in attacking fielded forces can be made by comparing the two direct attack missions of CAS and

[31] The author flew thirty-nine combat missions over Kosovo as an A-10 forward air controller. Haave and Haun, *A-10s over Kosovo*.

armed recce. There are times when CAS is critical, such as during the perilous stages at Khe Sanh, An Loc, and Kontum. The availability of on-call CAS has also been crucial for counterinsurgency operations in Vietnam, Afghanistan, and Iraq when friendly ground forces, dispersed to control territory, did not have the organic firepower to counter isolated insurgent attacks.

In modern air warfare, however, the direct attack of fielded forces has primarily not been by CAS, conducted near friendly ground forces requiring detailed coordination and deconfliction. Instead, it has been on armed recce sorties, referred to in Marine doctrine as deep air support (DAS). DAS is flown "against enemy targets at such a distance from friendly forces that detailed integration of each mission with fire and movement of friendly forces is not required." Unlike air interdiction strikes against known targets, an armed recce mission "finds and attacks targets of opportunity in assigned areas."[32] Armed recce missions are flown beyond the frontlines, beyond the range of CAS, where airborne FACs and tacair have been charged with locating and attacking fielded forces without the aid of ground tactical air controllers. This situation repeatedly proved to be the case in most direct attack missions flown over Vietnam, Kuwait, Bosnia, Kosovo, Iraq, and Libya.

Armed recce has been the direct attack mission more often employed and has proven more effective than CAS, strategic attack, or air interdiction. Yet the Air Force no longer recognizes armed recce as a separate mission, instead categorizing it as a subset of air interdiction.[33] On two occasions, the USAF expunged armed recce, called battlefield interdiction and battlefield air interdiction, from its doctrine. In 1966, during major combined arms operations in South Vietnam, battlefield interdiction was removed from USAF doctrine, and again after Desert Storm BAI disappeared. Four reasons help explain why the Air Force has never embraced the direct attack missions of armed recce and CAS. First, armed recce and CAS support joint air and ground operations and, as a result, unlike strategic bombing, do not justify an independent

[32] US Marine Corps, *Aviation Operations MCWP 3-2* (Washington, DC: Marine Corps Headquarters, 2018), 2-1, 2-2.

[33] "The Air Force defines air interdiction as air operations conducted to divert, disrupt, delay, or destroy the enemy's military potential before it can be brought to bear effectively against friendly forces, or to otherwise achieve joint force commander's objectives, and conducted at such distance from friendly forces that detailed integration of each air mission with the fire and movement of friendly forces is not required." USAF, *Air Force Doctrine Publication 3-03: Counterland Operations*, October 21, 2020, 6, www.doctrine.af.mil/Portals/61/documents/AFDP_3-03/3-03-AFDP-COUNTERLAND.pdf.

air force. Second, armed recce and CAS are apportioned to Army commanders while air interdiction and strategic attack remain under Air Force control. Eliminating BAI from doctrine and defining the direct attack of fielded forces beyond the fire support coordination line (FSCL) as a subset of air interdiction, as in current Air Force doctrine, allows the Air Force leaders to control all its strike missions, except the limited number dedicated to CAS.[34]

A third reason the Air Force has not embraced armed recce is that locating and attacking a fielded army is challenging. It requires a dedicated airborne capability to provide timely ISR and then combat aircrew in real time, to locate, identify, strike, and conduct BDA. This mission requires specialized weapons designed against armored vehicles and personnel, such as air-to-ground missiles and cluster bomb units (CBUs). The tactics, techniques, and procedures (TTPs) to conduct direct attack require specialized training. In addition, aircrew expertise is significantly enhanced by actual combat experience.

Armed recce, like CAS, also requires coordination with friendly ground forces as strikes often occur inside the FSCL. The FSCL has the dual function of preventing fratricide and delineating where targeting requires coordination with the ground commander's scheme of maneuver.[35] Unlike CAS missions, which rely on tactical air control parties (TACPs) to provide targeting information, armed recce missions typically do not have the advantage of real-time army intelligence, nor are TACPs available to find and mark targets. Without friendly ground forces to identify enemy positions, aircrew must locate and attack targets independently, which is one of the most difficult tasks.

The US Air Force has further not appreciated the armed recce mission because when most effective, the enemy disperses and hides. The number of bombs dropped and targets destroyed decreases where tacair has its most significant impact of deterring the enemy army from concentrating at

[34] Current USAF doctrine identifies BAI-type missions of strike coordination and reconnaissance (SCAR) as an air interdiction mission. USAF, *Air Force Doctrine Publication 3-03:: Counterland Operations*, October 21, 2020, 11.

[35] Historically, deconfliction was based on the bomb line, which was renamed the fire support coordination line (FSCL) during Vietnam. The bomb line was initially introduced as a practical safety measure to avoid fratricide. Any strike that occurred short of the FSCL required ground commander coordination. While in theory, direct attack of fielded forces could take place on either side of the FSCL, in practice most airstrikes have been flown short of the FSCL. David Zook, *The Fire Support Coordination Line* (Leavenworth, KS: School of Advanced Military Studies thesis, 1992); Terrance McCaffrey, *What Happened to BAI?* (Maxwell AFB, AL: Air University Press, 2002) 18; Merrill McPeak, "TACAIR Missions and the Fire Support Coordination Line" *Air University Review* 36:6 (September–October 1985), 65–72.

the decisive point.[36] The armed recce mission is hard, but when it works, it is also frustrating for aircrew because the enemy scatters to neutralize the air threat. When most successful, armed recce does not heavily attrit an enemy army but instead causes it to disperse, thus shaping the battlefield in favor of friendly ground forces. Successful direct attack operations have sometimes even drawn criticism from military analysts who measure air power effectiveness by the number of tanks destroyed rather than by the impact air power has had on the enemy's strategy.[37] From a service perspective, why would Air Force leaders support a mission with the primary purpose of setting conditions for the Army to claim victory?

In sum, direct attack does not justify an independent air force, and it requires Air Force commanders to include the Army in the target selection process. The armed recce mission is also challenging, requiring resources to develop and maintain ISR and strike capabilities. Finally, when most successful, the Air Force drops fewer bombs while the Army takes the credit. Therefore, it is not surprising that the Air Force has largely sought to avoid investing in the direct attack of fielded forces in peacetime and, as a result, at times, has struggled during war.[38]

By contrast, Marine Corps aviation, whose mission is to support fellow marines, has consistently recognized the importance of armed recce.[39] Marine aviation doctrine more accurately differentiates armed recce from air interdiction. The US military would be better poised for the requirements of direct attack if it adopted the Marine aviation doctrine as joint doctrine.

Final Thoughts

TAP theory explains how air power has worked most often in modern US air warfare, which began in Vietnam. These conflicts have not been like the great power wars of the first half of the twentieth century, which the threat of nuclear Armageddon has so far deterred. Instead, modern air wars have been limited, regional conflicts characterized by the increased lethality of radar-guided air defenses, which caused US air forces to shift from relying on heavy bombers to more survivable tactical aircraft. In the Vietnam War and those that followed, the direct attack of fielded forces

[36] This challenge of measuring the effectiveness of tacair is similar to that of general deterrence, where it is difficult to provide proof when nothing happens.
[37] Stephen Biddle, "Victory Misunderstood: What the Gulf War Tells Us about the Future of Conflict" *International Security* 21:2 (Fall 1996), 152.
[38] As discussed earlier in this chapter, the exception was conventional deterrence in Europe in the 1980s.
[39] US Marine Corps, *Aviation Operations MCWP 3-2*, 2-2.

in joint, combined arms operations mostly succeeded, while independent air campaigns largely failed. TAP theory does not explain every outcome, such as why the NVA continued to concentrate under withering airstrikes at Khe Sanh and during the Easter Offensive. But TAP theory still better explains why, how, and when air power has been effective compared to other theories (see Appendix A). Armed recce missions conducted as part of joint, combined arms operations disperse enemy ground forces, which, in turn, provide friendly ground forces an asymmetric advantage. While military victory does not always translate into political success, it does so more often with joint air and ground operations than independent air campaigns.

Though this concludes the discussion of tactical air power in the modern air wars the United States has fought over the past sixty years, the epilogue addresses the so-what questions of why, how, and when TAP theory remains relevant today and for future conflicts in an emerging era of near-peer competition.

9 Epilogue

As the international security environment shifts away from the United States unipolar moment, the risk of a general war may increase. Still, the enormous costs associated with nuclear conflict will likely continue to constrain nuclear powers. As the stability–instability paradox suggests, even as the United States deters nuclear war, it should also prepare for the more probable conventional and irregular wars as it has fought over the past six decades.[1] This epilogue explores several topics regarding the future of air warfare. The first section offers recommendations for how the United States can better prepare its air and ground forces. The second section considers air power in counterinsurgency and counterterrorism operations. The third section anticipates the role of air power in extended deterrence. The fourth section assesses the Russian Air Force's performance in the invasion of Ukraine through the lens of tactical air power (TAP) theory. The final section considers additional challenges facing the United States against China and Russia during this emerging era of near-peer competition.

Maintaining US Tactical Air Power

The first recommendation is for the US Air Force (USAF) to deemphasize its preparations for conventional strategic bombing campaigns that rarely work and instead create domestic and international blowback that harms broader US interests. As was their primary responsibility in the Cold War, US strategic forces should focus instead on maintaining an assured second-strike capability to enhance the stability of nuclear deterrence. Also, conventional bomber forces, such as the B-52s in Vietnam, should retain the capacity to conduct direct attack missions against conventional armies and counterinsurgents. The heavy bombers'

[1] Robert Jervis, *The Illogic of American Nuclear Strategy* (Ithaca, NY: Cornell University Press, 1984), 31.

extended range, long loiter time, and expansive weapons load make it an effective weapon in certain low-threat scenarios.

1. Stop conducting conventional strategic bombing campaigns and instead employ strategic forces in peacetime for nuclear deterrence, in modern air wars for direct attack, and in counterinsurgencies for CAS.
2. Stop conducting independent air campaigns but instead plan, equip, and train for joint and multinational combined arms operations.
3. Reprioritize air superiority resources to suppress enemy air defenses (SEAD) with less emphasis on air-to-air combat training.
4. Invest more in intelligence, surveillance, and reconnaissance (ISR) capabilities to target enemy fielded forces.
5 Invest in air-to-ground strike capability to include networks, sensors, weapons, and aircraft.
6. Recruit, promote, and retain air-to-ground expertise in active and reserve forces.
7. Invest in more realistic, joint training for the direct attack of fielded forces, including live, virtual, and constructive (LVC) combined arms scenarios.
8. Invest in the specialized air-to-ground coordination functions in peacetime, including forward air controllers (FACs) and joint tactical air controllers (JTACs) embedded in dedicated air-to-ground squadrons. Maintain a functional tactical air control system (TACS) to include the air support operations center (ASOC) and embedded air liaison officers (ALOs).
9. Maintain the capacity to integrate with allied ground forces.
10. Adopt Marine Corps aviation doctrine as joint doctrine by accepting armed recce (reconnaissance) as a direct attack mission.
11. Invest in capable, friendly ground forces, including a functional army air–ground system (AAGS) and military advisors assigned to allied armies.

A second, related recommendation is for US air forces (including Air Force, Navy, and Marine Corps aviation) to conduct joint operations instead of independent air campaigns. Strategic bombing and air interdiction are usually ineffective because air power, without the dual threat from coordinated ground attack, presents the enemy with too few dilemmas. So too independent direct attack air campaigns, as evidenced by Kosovo, have been unsuccessful when there has not also been a capable friendly ground force. While organizational incentives lead services to prefer to operate autonomously, this usually leads to failure. Instead of independent action, US air forces should plan, equip, and train primarily for joint and multinational combined arms operations, which present the enemy with numerous problems across multiple domains.

Still, political leaders may find it difficult to refrain from ordering independent air campaigns if they view air power as a cheap substitute for boots on the ground.[2] However, when national interests are insufficient to warrant risking American lives, it is also less likely the United States will have the will and capability to win with air power alone. In such situations, it is up to military leaders to convince their civilian bosses of what air power alone can and cannot accomplish.

A third recommendation, derived from examining the operational factor of air superiority discussed in the previous chapter, is that US tactical aircrew should deemphasize their obsession with air-to-air combat and expend more effort in defeating radar-guided surface-to-air missiles (SAMs). Enemy fighters are less of a threat than SAMs. Emphasis placed on the suppression of SEAD, jammers, and self-protection measures would allow the current tactical aircraft (tacair) fleet to function in most foreseeable modern air wars. The Russian Air Force's recent inability to suppress Ukrainian SAMs, examined in more detail later, demonstrates how not having a robust SEAD capability can lead to failure. Realigning dedicated air superiority squadrons to include more SEAD responsibility and reprioritizing the development of associated sensors, platforms, and munitions could enhance the ability to provide air superiority where it is needed most, over the battlefield.

As substantial as changing the acquisition priority given to SEAD is a reduction in the ratio of air-to-air to air-to-surface training. Tacair units have historically spent a significant portion of flight training maintaining air-to-air skills rarely utilized in combat. The focus on air-to-air remains a cultural bias within the US Air Force and Navy tactical air forces, which have long identified air-to-air expertise as the acme of fighter pilot skill. Yet, in the two modern air wars with numerous air-to-air engagements over North Vietnam and Iraq, aerial combat supported strategic bombing and air interdiction, not direct attack operations. The third recommendation is not to do away with all air-to-air capabilities but instead reprioritize scarce resources and shift acquisition and training priority more towards SEAD to better protect the air-to-ground assets considered next.

[2] Eliot Cohen, "The Mystique of U.S. Air Power" *Foreign Affairs* (January/February 1994), www.foreignaffairs.com/articles/1994-01-01/mystique-us-air-power; Anthony Schinella, *Bombs without Boots: The Limits of Airpower* (Washington, DC: Brookings, 2019).

Air-to-ground capabilities for direct attack consist of three categories: the intelligence surveillance and reconnaissance to locate and identify targets; the networks, sensors, weapons, and aircraft to strike targets; and the personnel, training, and doctrine to conduct armed recce and close air support (CAS). First, ISR units must have dedicated platforms for collecting visual imagery and electronic emissions/transmissions. They also should be integrated into joint and multinational intelligence organizations tasked with receiving, processing, evaluating, and prioritizing data in near real time. The USAF's Infiltration Surveillance Center (ISC) at Nakhon Phanom, Thailand, during Commando Hunt is an example of a proactive intelligence organization that performed this critical function. In recent years, dedicated air intelligence centers have likewise led counterterrorism campaigns by operating global networks and processing data, such as that generated by remotely piloted aircraft (RPA), into actionable intelligence.[3] Considering ISR organizations as equal partners is essential for more effective direct attack operations. Efficient teamwork requires ISR personnel to work alongside tacair units in daily training and exercises. Too often, ISR and strike units first meet in combat where, only over time, they develop the cooperation, trust, and respect required to be effective. The fourth recommendation is to continue to invest in ISR capabilities, enhance peacetime training, and mature the requisite doctrine to integrate ISR and tacair units to better target enemy fielded forces.

The fifth recommendation is to continue to invest in air-to-ground capabilities, including networks, sensors, weapons, and strike aircraft. Maintaining and enhancing communication networks, such as Link 16, is critical for manned and remotely piloted strike aircraft to remain connected with command and control (C2) networks and intelligence centers. Advanced targeting pods with electro-optic and infrared video links now allow tactical aircrew to perform some ISR duties. These sensors can also generate coordinates for GPS strikes or provide target designation for laser-guided weapons at medium altitude and at night. Strike recordings can later verify battle damage assessment (BDA), an essential function for measuring tactical effectiveness.[4]

Along with onboard sensors, special-purpose anti-armor and anti-personnel weapons enhance the lethality of air attacks against armies.

[3] Timothy Schultz, "Remote Warfare: A New Architecture of Air Power" in Phil Haun, Colin Jackson, and Timothy Schultz, eds., *Airpower in the Age of Primacy: Air Warfare since the Cold War* (Cambridge: Cambridge University Press, 2021).

[4] During Desert Storm, intelligence estimates gave more weight to F-111 and F-15E LGB strikes because of the available video evidence.

Two examples include cluster bombs with precision-guided anti-tank submunitions and laser-guided rockets with small warheads designed to reduce collateral damage.[5]

In addition to air-to-ground sensors and weapons, strike aircraft must have the performance and self-protection measures to fly with acceptable risk for extended periods above enemy air defenses. Aircrew must be able to focus on finding and striking targets and dedicate less time to self-protection measures. In sum, to be effective against small and mobile targets requires a communications suite for combat aircraft to receive and transmit data, air-to-ground sensors for day and night operations, and the capability to deliver the specialized weapons necessary to destroy fielded forces.

One area where ISR and strike missions have merged is with RPAs. In low-threat areas conducting counterinsurgency and counterterrorism operations, RPAs have proven to be a vital capability, adding persistence as a characteristic of modern air power. The USAF's MQ-1 Predator was initially an ISR-only platform, but over time it and its replacement, the MQ-9 Reaper, added precision strike. Other RPAs, such as the stealthy RQ-170 Sentinel and the RQ-4 Global Hawk, are capable of longer-range ISR. Still, RPA limitations, particularly in aircraft performance and self-protection measures, must improve before they can conduct the complex mission of direct attack in contested threat environments.

As important as having the right equipment for conducting the direct attack mission are personnel with the proper experience, training, and doctrine. Smart, creative, and experienced air leaders are vital to articulating the requirements, acquiring the resources, and organizing and training air forces in peacetime to be able to fight effectively. The sixth recommendation is to prioritize the recruitment, development, and promotion of air-to-ground experts to ensure that intelligent-minded and capable warriors are tasked with this essential airpower mission. One measure for maintaining this talent that has worked has been to sustain reserve and guard units filled with combat veterans with emphasis on retaining highly trained personnel such as weapons officers. These units can retain corporate expertise key for acquisition decisions and provide an experienced surge capability. Emphasis should be on making sure

[5] The Wind Corrected Munitions Dispenser guidance system provides precision delivery for combined effects munitions (CBU-103) and the sensor-fuzed weapons (CBU-105). Against ISIS in northern Iraq, USAF A-10s employed modified 2.75-inch rockets with the APWKS (Advanced Precision Weapons Kill System) laser-guidance kit, providing precision strike capability with lower collateral damage potential for urban combat operations. Stephen Renner, "Air Power in the Battle of Mosul" in Haun et al., eds., *Airpower in the Age of Primacy*.

these veterans systematically share their knowledge with less experienced active duty personnel.

Also critical are realistic training and joint exercises exposing aircrew to the additional challenges of directly attacking fielded forces. Current tactical air-to-ground ranges have fixed target arrays, well-known by aircrew provided with excellent imagery and precise coordinates. However, these intentionally easy-to-locate training aids assume away the most challenging aspect of air-to-ground combat: locating the target. Placing as much emphasis on target identification as weapons delivery is one way to improve the ability to conduct direct attack. Aircrew exposure to the challenges of target identification can be increased to expand joint combined air and ground training such as that available at the National Training Center at Fort Irwin, California, and the Joint Multinational Readiness Center at Hohenfels, Germany. Live, virtual, and constructive simulation is another way to simulate combat conditions at a lower cost, so long as LVCs involve combined arms scenarios. The seventh recommendation is to invest in more realistic live and virtual training for direct attack missions.

The eighth recommendation is to invest in specialized air-to-ground personnel, including forward air controllers and joint tactical air controllers. Embedding FACs and JTACs in air squadrons ensures they maintain their technical skills, and it exposes aircrew in their daily training to the vital link connecting air and ground forces. Often neglected in peacetime are these integrators of air power, not only FACs and JTACs but also the tactical air control system operated by the air support operations center and air liaison officers. These critical air elements, inserted in ground units, ensure air and ground forces coordinate operations. Though these air tasks are less glamorous than flying a fighter, they serve the vital role of coordinating air and ground actions which, as demonstrated in Vietnam, is key to air power success.

While air and ground coordination has often proven to be a challenge and the cause of friction between services, coordination within coalitions is even more problematic. Cultural and language barriers and the lack of shared doctrine and training make cooperation between US air and allied ground forces difficult. One means of overcoming the problem of working with new partners is to adopt the "Afghan model," inserting US special forces alongside allied ground units. Here they played multiple roles of ASOC, ALO, military advisor, and JTAC. The ninth recommendation is to maintain the specialized capability to coordinate air operations with allied ground forces that do not have Army air–ground systems.

The tenth recommendation is to elevate Marine Corps aviation doctrine to joint doctrine. The Air Force acknowledging armed recce as a separate mission would help to reprioritize the resources and personnel discussed in the previous recommendations. It would also make explicit the requirement that US air forces conduct joint operations, including sharing targeting prioritization and responsibility with ground commanders. Armed recce requirements differ from those of either air interdiction or CAS. Air interdiction primarily attacks fixed targets, such as bridges and railways, or the mobile trucks and trains operating along known and predictable lines of communication. CAS missions rely upon ground forces to locate and identify targets. Yet, as pointed out repeatedly in this book, target identification is the biggest challenge for directly attacking fielded forces. Aircrew on armed recce missions are responsible for identifying and striking mobile targets over a large battlespace, often obscured by weather, terrain, and cover. Armed recce is one of the most demanding air missions for which ISR and strike aircrew must prepare with the proper doctrine and training before encountering the enemy in combat.

The eleventh recommendation is to invest in friendly ground force capability. US and allied armies must be capable of operating a serviceable AAGS. This coordination capability includes ground liaison officers (GLOs) allocated to air units during peacetime. The Army and the Marine Corps should continue to train with and assign military advisors to allied armies, so these ground forces prepare to operate with US air forces. A capable and coordinated friendly ground force is necessary for effective air-to-ground operations.

Implementing these eleven recommendations would enhance the ability of US air forces to conduct direct attack operations in future modern air wars. In addition, air forces must be ready to contribute to the counterinsurgency and counterterrorism operations as they have for the past two decades, as discussed next.

Air Power in Counterinsurgency and Counterterrorism Operations

Just as air forces need to remain prepared for modern warfare, they should also be ready for counterinsurgency and counterterrorism operations, which continue long after conventional fighting. In counterinsurgencies, ground forces disperse to control territory. Under such situations, occupiers rely upon air power for various support, including ISR, C2, emergency CAS, resupply, and medical evacuation. Air forces have the flexibility to react quickly across a vast territory.

Counterinsurgency air support allows friendly ground forces to operate with a lighter footprint, being less disruptive and better positioned for positive civic engagement while retaining the ability to call upon air power when needed.

Counterinsurgency operations differ from the modern air wars considered in this book. Air superiority is not contested, and enemy armies do not have the conventional capability to threaten friendly ground forces. Instead, guerrillas organize hit-and-run raids, conduct mortar and rocket attacks, plant improvised explosive devices (IEDs), and terrorize the population. The direct attack missions of armed recce and CAS require specific air power skills that can translate well for counterinsurgency operations. Direct attack depends on capable real-time ISR networks. The ISR challenge for direct attack is identifying enemy forces that mask their location and movement utilizing weather, night, terrain, and cover. By contrast, for counterinsurgency operations, the problem is more often how to differentiate insurgents and their supporters from the local population. Irregular forces blend in with civilians to avoid detection and raise potential collateral damage and political blowback from air attacks. Counterinsurgency operations rely more on human intelligence (HUMINT), which requires language and cultural skill sets unique to local forces. Thus, a key to airpower success in counterinsurgencies has been a flexible ISR organization and strike forces prepared to transition from conventional to irregular warfare.

For air power to be effective in counterinsurgency operations, US air forces must integrate with the friendly ground force scheme of maneuver. While the number of strike missions is usually not as large as conventional warfighting, strike aircraft still need advanced sensors and specialized weapons to target insurgents while minimizing risks of collateral damage. Unlike direct attack in modern air warfare, CAS is a more important mission in counterinsurgency operations than armed recce. Airstrikes occur less frequently, usually reserved for troops in contact (TIC) situations. The objective in a counterinsurgency is to control the population and provide security. The resort to violence, particularly airstrikes, is a negative indication of how well the counterinsurgency is going. One means of constraining the undesirable effects of airstrikes is to educate ISR, JTACs, FACs, and strike aircrew. For counterinsurgencies, the objective is *not* to employ force but instead reserve the use of force to deter insurgent activity. Pre-deployment training is essential to understand air power's role and that a good mission does not equate to dropping ordnance. The objective of a counterinsurgency is to deter bad things from happening. When successful, air forces are present but do not have to employ. The constraint and patience required can be challenging as it contradicts Air Force culture and its motto "to fly, fight, and win."[6]

As discussed briefly in the previous section, RPAs have added a new air power capability for counterinsurgency and counterterrorism. Counterterrorism has several of the same traits as counterinsurgencies, emphasizing ISR and HUMINT and restraint in the employment of firepower. Counterterrorism involves specialized units, including US special forces and the Central Intelligence Agency (CIA). Counterterrorism operations use specialized aircraft that combine ISR and strike capability, such as AC-130 gunships or armed RPAs, such as the MQ-9 Reaper, for targeted strikes.[7]

Over the past two decades, the US military and intelligence communities have invested significant resources to develop expertise to combat non-state actors. While insurgents and terrorist groups remain a threat, it is not apparent that the priority and level of resources given to these missions will continue. The United States now faces a changing international security environment, as evidenced by the Russian invasion of Ukraine.

The Russo-Ukrainian War and the Battle of Kyiv

On February 24, 2022, Russia invaded Ukraine. Widespread expectations for a quick victory, however, never materialized. Instead, the Ukrainians held off the advance on Kyiv, which concluded by the beginning of April. The Battle of Kyiv provides the case of a recent conflict which can help demonstrate how TAP theory can predict the likely effectiveness of air power in current and future modern air wars. TAP theory claims an air force can defeat a massed and maneuvering fielded army. Most defenders of Kyiv, however, were not massed mechanized forces but infantry and armed civilians. These dispersed units would prove difficult to target from

[6] Secretary of the Air Force Public Affairs, "Air Force Unveils New Mission Statement," April 8, 2021, www.af.mil/News/Article-Display/Article/2565837/air-force-unveils-new-mission-statement/. An example of the USAF culture preferencing kinetic force occurred in the summer of 2004 in Afghanistan. Then commanding an A-10 squadron, the author submitted a squadron pilot for an individual award for displaying constraint in support of a high-impact mission where he identified and tracked insurgents leaving a compound raided by friendly special operations forces. The pilot did not strike the insurgents but instead tracked them and then radioed ground units to the insurgents' location, where special forces detained, questioned, and extracted valuable intelligence. The award write-up was later disapproved in the Air Force awards process because the pilot had not dropped ordnance on the mission.

[7] See Schultz, "Remote Warfare," and Colin Jackson, "Retrospect and Prospect" in Haun et al., eds., *Airpower in the Age of Primacy.*

the air.[8] In addition to this fundamental insight, five of the nine operational and environmental factors negatively impacting air power effectiveness could have provided *ex ante* indications that the Russian Aerospace Force (*Vozdushno-kosmicheskiye sily* – VKS) might struggle. The most apparent operational factor that would challenge the VKS at the onset of the war was air superiority, considered next.

Air Superiority

One of the most glaring weaknesses exhibited by the VKS has been its inability to gain air superiority over Ukraine. With more than a ten-to-one advantage in tacair, materially the VKS dominated the Ukrainian Air Force (UKAF). At the outset of the war, the Russians had an estimated 1,200 tacair, 350 deployed for operations over Ukraine.[9] By comparison, the UKAF fielded 100 tacair inherited from the Soviet Union.[10]

Initially, aerial engagements gained international attention, yet few air-to-air kills have been confirmed.[11] Instead of being contested in the air, the advanced air-to-air radars and long-range missiles of the Russian Su-30SM and Su-35S Flankers outmatched and deterred the older Ukrainian fighters.[12] With the war ongoing at the time of this writing, validation of the number and type of air kills remains speculative. Even so, the UKAF likely lost several aircraft to VKS interceptors over the first few days of fighting when there were active air-to-air engagements. By contrast, the UKAF has had no confirmed air-to-air kills to date. While the VKS maintained the advantage in air-to-air fighting, the more lethal threat came from Ukrainian ground-based air defenses (GBAD).

Though several factors played a role in the struggle for air superiority, the primary and predictable reason the VKS failed over Kyiv was its

[8] Only a single Ukrainian mechanized brigade was dedicated to protect the capital. Paul Sonne and Isabella Khurshudyan, "Battle for Kyiv:Valor vs. Hubris: Ukrainians' Profound Will to Fight and Kremlin Blunders Combined to Save the Capital" *Washington Post*, August 24, 2022, A9.

[9] This included fighters in Su-27, Su-30SM, and Su-35S Flankers; fighter/bombers in MiG-29 Fulcrums, Su-24 Fencers, and Su-34 Fullbacks; and attack aircraft in the Su-25 Frogfoots; Flight International, "Russian Air Forces" *2022 World Air Forces*, 28, www.flightglobal.com/download?ac=83735; "Chapter Five: Russia and Eurasia" *The Military Balance* 121:1 (2021), 198; Justin Bronk, Nick Reynolds, and Jack Watling, "The Russian Air War and Ukrainian Requirements for Air Defence: Special Report" *Royal United Services Institute* (November 7, 2022), 6.

[10] These included similar, but older model Su-27s, MiG-29s, Su-24s, and Su-25s. Flight International, "Ukrainian Air Forces."

[11] BBC, "How Ukraine's 'Ghost of Kyiv' Legendary Pilot Was Born," May 1, 2022, www.bbc.com/news/world-europe-61285833.

[12] Bronk et al., "The Russian Air War," 9–10.

inability to suppress the Ukrainian's mobile SAMs. By April, the VKS had lost at least eight tacair to SAMs or pilot error.[13]

The Ukrainians inherited hundreds of SAMs from the Soviet Union. The foundation of the Ukrainian integrated air defense system (IADS) has been its radar-guided S-300s (SA-10 Grumble and SA-12 Gladiator), Buk-M1/2s (SA-11 Gadfly and SA-17 Grizzly), and S-125 (SA-3 GoA) SAMs. The Ukrainian Army also fielded more mobile SAMs, including the 9K33M3 OSA-ASM (SA-8 Gecko), 9K35 Strela-10 (SA-13 Gopher), the 2K22 Tunguska (SA-19 Grison), along with a variety of manpads (man-portable air defense systems). In addition, most Ukrainian ground units employ small arms, anti-aircraft artillery (AAA), and manpads.[14]

Since the Russian annexation of Crimea in 2014, Ukrainian air defenses have been improving, refining, and developing their capabilities. Even so, initially the Russians effectively suppressed the Ukrainian IADS by launching hundreds of air and missile strikes, including attacks against early-warning radars and other fixed C2 targets.[15] In addition, the VKS electronically jammed Ukrainian radar-guided SAMs, which left the UKAF fighters no option but to confront the VKS in the brief and one-sided air-to-air battles previously mentioned.[16] After these temporary setbacks, however, the Ukrainians quickly recovered by dispersing their mobile air defenses and adjusting their equipment and tactics to minimize Russian interference.[17] After the first three days of fighting, the increased lethality of Ukrainian radar-guided SAMs compelled VKS

[13] Sebastian Roblin, "An Unexpected Air-to-Air Battle Is Raging over Ukraine. Here's What We Know about the Losses on Both Sides" *Business Insider*, September 5, 2022, www.businessinsider.com/whats-known-about-russian-and-ukraine-losses-in-aerial-combat-2022-9. By September 2022, an estimated fifty-five VKS aircraft, including seventeen night-capable Su-34 Fencers, along with hundreds of drones, had been downed by Ukrainian GBAD. Paul McLeary, "Ukraine Has Shot Down 55 Russian Warplanes, U.S. General Says" *Politico*, September 19, 2022, www.politico.com/news/2022/09/19/ukraine-has-shot-down-55-russian-warplanes-00057569; General James B. Hecker, Commander US Air Forces Europe and Africa, "Air Force Association Interview," October 6, 2022, www.airandspaceforces.com/watch-read-top-usaf-commanders-on-countering-russian-aggression/; Bronk et al., "The Russian Air War," 19. For a list of reported destroyed aircraft see Stijn Mitzer, "List of Aircraft Losses during the 2022 Russian Invasion of Ukraine" *Oryx*, March 20, 2022, www.oryxspioenkop.com/2022/03/list-of-aircraft-losses-during-2022.html.

[14] "Chapter Five: Russia and Eurasia," 209–211.

[15] Bronk et al., "The Russian Air War," 25–26.

[16] Sonne and Khurshudyan, "Battle for Kyiv," A11.

[17] Tyson Wetzel, "Ukraine Air War Examined: A Glimpse at the Future of Air Warfare" *Atlantic Council*, August 30, 2022, www.atlanticcouncil.org/content-series/airpower-after-ukraine/ukraine-air-war-examined-a-glimpse-at-the-future-of-air-warfare/. The Ukrainian IADS was assisted when VKS jammers also significantly degraded communications of friendly ground troops as their offensive quickly stalled outside Kyiv. After two days of confusion, the VKS was appreciably scaled by jamming, which,

strikers to fly at low altitude in the heart of the small arms, AAA, and manpad threat.[18]

In contrast to its air-to-air prowess, the VKS has not demonstrated the capability of suppressing enemy air defenses (SEAD) to the same level employed by the US and NATO.[19] Based on an assessment of both belligerents' air defense capabilities and the analysis provided in this book, it could have been predicted that the VKS would not gain sufficient air superiority to prosecute an effective air campaign against the Ukrainian Army. Because of the continued Ukrainian surface-to-air threat, Russian aircrews have instead prioritized survivability over lethality, as evidenced by their shift to employing more cruise missiles and RPAs.

In addition to its inability to gain air superiority, the VKS also demonstrated limited air-to-ground capabilities against enemy ground forces. Also, the VKS and Russian Army were incompetent in coordinating combined arms operations, and the Ukrainians proved adept defenders. However, these three latter operational factors were less likely to have been predicted before the war than air superiority and the environmental factors considered next.

Environmental Factors

At the end of February, the cloud conditions over Kyiv were overcast half the time and mostly cloudy 70 percent of the time. Conditions only gradually improved by early April.[20] Such poor flying weather impacted the VKS, making it challenging to implement the medium-altitude tactics it had successfully employed over Syria.[21] Poor weather also inhibited ISR missions, particularly by high-altitude and orbital

in turn, allowed the Ukrainian SAMs to target Russian tacair. Bronk et al., "The Russian Air War," 11–13.

[18] Bronk et al., "The Russian Air War," 20.

[19] Alexander Mladenov, "Investigating Russia's Lack of SEAD Capabilities over Ukraine" *Key.Aero*, August 19, 2022, www.key.aero/article/investigating-russias-lack-seaddead-capabilities-over-ukraine. Through March, Su-30M and Su-35S Flankers on combat air patrols did carry anti-radiation missiles (ARMs) to launch at radiating SAMs with apparently some success in suppressing mobile Ukrainian air defense systems. Also, only after the Battle of Kyiv did the VKS compel Ukrainian SAMs to radiate by employing Orian-10 drones in conjunction with Russian ARMs. Bronk et al., "The Russian Air War," 16.

[20] By early April, clouds over Kyiv were overcast 45 percent of the time and mostly cloudy 60 percent of the time. Weather Spark, "Climate and Average Weather Year Round in Kiev," https://weatherspark.com/y/96633/Average-Weather-in-Kiev-Ukraine-Year-Round.

[21] Ralph Shield, "Russia's Air War in Syria: A Kinetic Approach to Counterinsurgency" in Haun et al., eds., *Air Power and the Age of Primacy.*

platforms. Low ceilings further impaired tacair by compelling flight at lower altitudes, where VKS aircrew could not loiter over targets given the threat from ground fire.

In addition to the poor weather, lighting conditions offered challenges to most VKS tacair, with only the Su-34 Fullback having a significant nighttime capability. However, due to cumulative losses, the Su-34 eventually had to limit its low-altitude night operations.[22] The sanctuary of the dark allowed the Ukrainians to reposition air defenses and ground forces without the fear of VKS detection and interference.

The decision to attack Kyiv from the north through Belarus further disadvantaged the VKS. Geography and terrain funneled the Russian mechanized units into river valleys, providing concealment and cover for Ukrainian infantry and irregulars. Also, as the Russians approached the outskirts of Kyiv, the defenders utilized their capital's sprawling urban terrain.[23]

The sole environmental factor that did not negatively affect VKS operations was the density of the Ukrainian population. Unlike US and NATO air forces, which have consistently attempted to minimize civilian casualties, Russian forces showed little regard for civilian suffering, as previously demonstrated in Syria and would again be revealed throughout Ukraine.[24]

Overall, if conducted before the war, the previous TAP analysis could have revealed that most of the operational and environmental factors did not favor the VKS against the Ukrainian fielded forces. This analysis does not suggest that TAP theory could have predicted the eventual outcome of the Battle of Kyiv, as Russian air power was but one of several factors that affected the battle. Instead, the argument is that it would have contributed to a better *ex ante* understanding of the military balance and likelihood of a successful Russian invasion. It should have been no surprise that Ukrainian SAMs and poor flying weather compelled VKS tacair to fly at low level, where they suffered losses. Limited night capability was also always going to limit the usefulness of most Russian tacair. Further, the Ukrainian infantry and irregular forces would defend in terrain that concealed and protected their positions from VKS observation and air strikes. The Battle of Kyiv complements the other modern air wars examined in this book. It provides additional evidence of the value of TAP theory for understanding why, how, and when air power, even for non-US air forces, is, or is not, likely to be effective against enemy fielded forces.

[22] Bronk et al., "The Russian Air War," 17.
[23] Sonne and Khurshudyan, "Battle for Kyiv," A11.
[24] Shield, "Russia's Air War in Syria."

The Relevance of Tactical Air Power in an Era of Great Power Competition

How has the reemergence of great power competition affected the requirements for US air power today and tomorrow? The potential gains from a major war with Russia or China remain overshadowed by the catastrophe all sides would suffer should such a conflict escalate into a nuclear war. While deterring a nuclear attack against the United States may not seriously be in question, there remains the concern, as was the case in the Cold War, of how to extend deterrence to allies. In the early 1980s, the United States introduced AirLand Battle and NATO's equivalent Follow-on Forces Attack as a conventional denial strategy to create doubt in the minds of Soviet political and military leaders as to whether a preemptive offensive into western Europe would succeed. Having US forces deployed to Europe bolstered the credibility of NATO capability and resolve to fight if attacked, which, in turn, had the intended effect of deterring the Soviet Union. Are there analogous conventional strategies that could extend deterrence to US allies now threatened by Russia or China?

US war plans must factor in the risk of nuclear war. Conventional airstrikes aimed at Russia or China could trigger escalation dynamics should the US target their nuclear forces or C2. Any strategic bombing campaign penetrating the enemy's IADS and threatening their homeland runs similar dangers of escalation. US threats to retaliate for aggression against an ally with punitive strikes against the Russian or Chinese nuclear forces, population, economy, or leaders are less credible because of the risk of escalation. Would the United States risk Washington over Warsaw or Los Angeles over Taipei?

In contrast to extended deterrence by punishment, a more viable denial strategy threatens to respond to an attack on an ally by threatening Russian and Chinese fielded forces.[25] As this book has argued, a multinational, combined arms defense, where US air forces focus on attacking enemy armies or navies and not on strategic bombing, should be more effective against and less threatening to Russia and China. The force structure required for conducting direct attack differs from independent air campaigns, which can reduce the risks of misperception by opponents that threatened airstrikes will be punitive or decapitating. Such a combined arms force structure could, in turn, potentially stabilize security

[25] The one aspect of a defense of Taiwan from a Chinese invasion is the possibility for an effective interdiction campaign against Chinese sea lines of communication. This interdiction campaign would not, however, be independent but only conducted as part of the combined arms defense of Taiwan.

dilemmas as Russia and China would be less likely to view US air forces in direct attack roles as an existential threat. Such a constrained denial strategy would be less likely to escalate into a nuclear war. The United States could therefore be more willing and capable of defending its allies with conventional forces, which, in turn, would make extended deterrence more credible.

In addition to the risk posed by nuclear weapons, the second technological development of the modern air era has been the advancement in radar technologies, which has significantly enhanced the lethality of air-to-air and surface-to-air missile systems. These guided weapon systems compelled the Air Force in the 1960s to shift from bombers to more survivable tacair. In the late 1970s, the introduction of phased-array radars mated to high-speed, long-range, maneuverable missiles made it more challenging for even high-performance fighters to operate in contested airspace. The SA-2 in the 1960s changed the calculations of the type of aircraft that could operate over enemy territory. Likewise, the introduction of the Soviets' S-300 (SA-10 Grumble) compelled the United States to rethink the viability of its tacair. The Air Force adapted by developing stealth aircraft less detectable to these advanced enemy radars. Today, the lethality of Russian and Chinese modern SAMs calls into question US air superiority and the ability of fourth-generation tacair, such as F-15s, F-16s, and F-18s, to operate with acceptable risk in contested air space. Even stealthy F-22s, F-35s, B-2s, and future B-21s will likely be wary of where and how long aircrew can conduct combat operations within modern SAM threat rings. US air forces cannot assume they will achieve sufficient air superiority against Russian and Chinese air defenses to conduct tacair missions as they have in the past.

In addition to the enhanced lethality of modern SAMs, long-range anti-access/area denial (A2/AD) surface-to-surface missile systems have introduced another challenge: theater access. Over the horizon radars and space-based sensors have made it possible for Chinese ISR to target airfields in the region, including mobile Navy carriers. Denying land- and sea-based tacair and ISR aircraft the ability to base operations in theater would significantly reduce the response and loiter time for US air forces. This delay, in turn, could undermine the deterrent value for denial air strategies designed to provide an immediate response against Chinese aggression.

The template utilized since the Vietnam War of having tacair secure air superiority followed by a direct attack against the enemy's enemy fielded forces may not be a credible deterrent for a Chinese assault against Taiwan. An alternative strategy, which acknowledges the increased risk to air operations for conventional and stealth aircraft, would instead rely on multi-domain ISR capabilities to include advanced sensors on air, surface, and subsurface platforms. These sensors would network in a C2 system providing near-real-time targeting information for a quick response by long-range strikes against mobile targets.[26] Unlike air interdiction campaigns against land lines of communication, the interdiction of sea lines of communication is more likely to be successful, such as Operation Market Time in the Vietnam War.[27] A combination of multi-domain ISR mated with long-range strike capability could threaten the Chinese sea lines of communication if they contemplated an invasion of Taiwan. Chinese planners must factor these risks into war plans for any amphibious operation.

In this Chinese scenario, such a multi-domain ISR and long-range strike capability would be like the Assault Breaker concept demonstrated by the Defense Advanced Research Projects Agency (DARPA) in the late 1970s.[28] Assault Breaker combined the ISR capability of long-range airborne sensors with data quickly processed and then shared with medium-range surface-to-surface missiles. These weapon systems utilized anti-armor submunitions with semi-autonomous seekers to strike mobile targets. Assault Breaker never became operational largely because the Air Force disapproved of this concept as it excluded a role for its strike aircraft.[29] Still, it demonstrated the potential for an ISR capability against mobile vehicles, which led to the development of JSTARS (Joint Surveillance Target Attack Radar System). JSTARS mounted a synthetic aperture radar and moving target indicator along the side of a Boeing 707 capable of tracking vehicles out to 150 miles. Additionally, though never fielded due to technological challenges at the time, the Precision Location and Strike System utilized electronic detection sensors mounted on TR-1s (a U-2 variant) to triangulate and track radio emissions of mobile Soviet ground units at similar ranges.[30] During the Cold War, for US long-range missiles to be lethal against Soviet armor required a specialized anti-armor submunition with semi-autonomous

[26] Owen Cote, "One If by Invasion, Two If by Coercion: US Military Capacity to Protect Taiwan from China" *Bulletin of Atomic Scientists*, March 10, 2022, https://thebulletin.org/premium/2022-03/one-if-by-invasion-two-if-by-coercion-us-military-capacity-to-protect-taiwan-from-china/.

[27] Judy Erdheim, *Market Time: CRC 280 Center for Naval Analyses* (Arlington, VA: Center for Naval Analyses, 1975), www.history.navy.mil/research/library/online-reading-room/title-list-alphabetically/m/market-time-u-crc280.html.

[28] Robert Tomes, "The Cold War Offset Strategy: Assault Breaker and the Beginnings of the RSTA Revolution" *War on the Rocks*, November 20, 2014, https://warontherocks.com/2014/11/the-cold-war-offset-strategy-assault-breaker-and-the-beginning-of-the-rsta-revolution/.

[29] Phil Haun, "Peacetime Innovation through Inter-service Cooperation: The Unique Case of the U.S. Air Force and Battlefield Air Interdiction" *Journal of Strategic Studies* 43:5 (2020), 13.

[30] Haun, "Peacetime Military Innovation through Inter-service Cooperation," 13–14.

terminal guidance against mobile targets. Eventually, the Air Force developed such a weapon with the CBU-97 sensor fuzed submunition (BLU-108), which incorporated laser and infrared sensors to detect and fire on enemy tanks.[31] In recent years DARPA has created a program known as Assault Breaker II to address the challenges of the real-time targeting of multiple Chinese ships and Russian tanks.[32]

Assault Breaker reimagined would likely include multi-domain land, airborne, surface, and subsurface unmanned ISR platforms, sensors, and processors to locate, identify, and track mobile land and maritime forces. The United States could use a combination of ISR platforms across multiple domains to overcome the enemy's local air superiority advantage. The targeting information generated from the ISR sensors could then generate air-, land-, or sea-based long-range strikes, with weapon systems employing semi-autonomous tracking against mobile targets. A current example of such an advanced weapon is the AGM-158C Long-Range Anti-Ship Missile (LRASM). The LRASM has a stealth-shaped body, a 1,000-pound conventional warhead, and a seeker that utilizes data-linked inflight updates and onboard sensors for terminal guidance. Multiple platforms can launch the LRASM, including F-18s, F-35s, B-1s, P-8s, and surface vessels with a mounted vertical launch system.[33]

One concern for such an Assault Breaker approach is that Russia and China could perceive these long-range capabilities as threatening their early warning, command and control, and nuclear forces, thereby inadvertently risking escalation.[34] The United States must be clear with diplomatic and military communication, exercises, and doctrine that its military capabilities in theater target only enemy fielded forces.

The right combination of investment in new technologies, doctrine, and training may provide a partial solution to extend deterrence. Still, US allies must also be willing to provide for their defense by investing in land and coastal forces capable of defending their territory. Capable surface forces must be able to fire, maneuver, and survive. Crucially, they must also be able to coordinate actions with US forces, as the Army of the Republic of

[31] CBU-97 Sensor Fuzed Weapon, www.globalsecurity.org/military/systems/munitions/cbu-97.htm.

[32] David Axe, "Pentagon Scientists Mull a Big Problem – How to Destroy a Whole Lot of Chinese Ships and Russian Tanks, and Fast" *Forbes*, March 9, 2021, www.forbes.com/sites/davidaxe/2021/03/09/pentagon-scientists-mull-a-big-problem-how-to-destroy-a-whole-lot-of-chinese-ships-and-russian-tanks/?sh=66f635a276d5.

[33] www.lockheedmartin.com/en-us/products/long-range-anti-ship-missile.html.

[34] Barry Posen, *Inadvertent Escalation: Conventional War and Nuclear Risks* (Ithaca, NY: Cornell University Press, 1992), 2; Forrest Morgan et al., "The Nature of Escalation" Chapter 2 in *Dangerous Thresholds: Managing Escalation in the Twenty-First Century* (Washington, DC: RAND, 2008), 24, www.jstor.org/stable/10.7249/mg614af.9?seq=1.

Vietnam coordinated with US air forces during the Easter Offensive. Allied development of organic capabilities is a challenge, even with additional investment. It is even more difficult politically for small nations to make the tough fiscal decision to invest in relatively modest military capabilities when there is an incentive to freeride and rely instead solely on the extended deterrence provided by US military might. However, recommendation five from those listed earlier highlights that air power is more effective when coordinated with a capable army. A viable ground force is essential for air power success. No independent US strategy can substitute for an ally willing and able to defend its homeland. US military and diplomatic engagement with allies should emphasize that the United States cannot extend deterrence alone. Any security guarantees should be contingent on partners maintaining credible organic military capabilities.

Final Thoughts

The problems facing the United States in the emerging era are considerable. The first is the shift in the international system away from unipolarity and the potential instability this could entail. In the Cold War, the primary focus for the United States and the Soviet Union was Europe. The United States must now contend with China in the Asian Pacific, Russia in Europe, regional actors in Iran and North Korea, and the threat from insurgent and terrorist groups.[35] As discussed, the types of aircraft required to address these different security challenges vary significantly.

Paradoxically, the biggest threat to the United States during this shift in the international system may come from within. For the past three decades, during its age of primacy, leaders grew accustomed to being able to intervene whenever and wherever they wanted. Unencumbered wars of choice in Iraq, Bosnia, Kosovo, Afghanistan, Iraq, and Libya ended in 2015 with Russian intervention in Syria. The United States must now recognize the shift in power dynamics. Demands that it could routinely level against weaker states, ranging from changes to domestic humanitarian policies to regime change, may now be untenable. The United States must understand the constraints imposed by China's rising power and Russia's reemergence.

The second challenge is the limitation of resources. While US defense spending remains more than double that of Russia and China combined, so long as the United States retains the role of enforcer of the global

[35] White House, "National Security Strategy," October 12, 2022, 11–12, www.whitehouse.gov/wp-content/uploads/2022/10/Biden-Harris-Administrations-National-Security-Strategy-10.2022.pdf.

system it will face a spectrum of security challenges, as recent aggression by Russia in Ukraine highlights.[36] During the Cold War, US military spending fluctuated between 5 and 10 percent of the gross domestic product, but this ratio has declined to 3–5 percent over time.[37] Long-term commitments to domestic programs, ever-growing debt payments, and inflation make it unlikely any real increase in defense spending will be forthcoming. Since 70 percent of the Department of Defense budget goes toward the enduring costs of operations, maintenance, and personnel, this leaves little space for the research and procurement required to maintain US competitiveness.[38]

Increased military requirements for near-peer competition, and with no foreseeable rise in defense spending, will, for the first time in decades, force the United States to make hard choices affecting its national security. Civilian and military leaders must be willing to set priorities and assume risk to a degree their predecessors did not. After two decades and $2 trillion, the decision to leave Afghanistan is an example of the type of hard choices the United States will continue to have to make.[39] The long-term competition facing the United States differs fundamentally from the periodic crises of the recent past. The United States no longer has the luxury of interventions of choice. Instead, it should adopt the foreign policy advocated, though not always practiced, by President Barak Obama of "do not do stupid shit."[40] Instead of expensive military operations, the United States must be willing to rely more upon diplomacy and burden-sharing. Supposed coalitions of the willing, such as the 2003 invasion of Iraq, to cover US unilateral action with the veneer of international support, must give way to enduring partnerships with nations prepared to make serious investments in their national defense.

[36] Peterson Foundation, "U.S. Defense Spending Compared to Other Countries," July 9, 2021, www.pgpf.org/chart-archive/0053_defense-comparison.

[37] Michael O'Hanlan, "Is US Defense Spending Too High, Too Low, or Just Right?," October 15, 2019, www.brookings.edu/policy2020/votervital/is-us-defense-spending-too-high-too-low-or-just-right/; Trading Economics, "United States Military Expenditure (% of GDP)," https://tradingeconomics.com/united-states/military-expenditure-percent-of-gdp-wb-data.html.

[38] Congressional Budget Office, "Long-Term Implications of the 2021 Future Years Defense Program," September 2020, www.cbo.gov/publication/56554; Peterson Foundation, "Budget Basics National Defense: DoD Spent $600 Billion on a Broad Range of Military Activities," August 2, 2021, www.pgpf.org/budget-basics/budget-explainer-national-defense.

[39] Watson Institute International & Public Affairs, "US Costs to Date of War in Afghanistan in $Billions FY2001–22" Costs of War, https://watson.brown.edu/costsofwar/figures/2021/human-and-budgetary-costs-date-us-war-afghanistan-2001-2022.

[40] David Rothkopf, "Obama's 'Do Not Do Stupid Shit' Foreign Policy" *Foreign Policy*, June 4, 2014, https://foreignpolicy.com/2014/06/04/obamas-dont-do-stupid-shit-foreign-policy/.

The United States must also be willing to curtail security guarantees to those nations that will not make hard choices to increase their defense spending and provide the ground and coastal forces required for the extended deterrence by denial strategies previously discussed.

A third challenge is that of general deterrence. In the Cold War, the superpowers could sustain a relatively stable system marked by few crises that risked nuclear warfare. However, the United States and Soviet Union could not avoid a spiraling arms race that resulted in a combined 70,000 warheads.[41] Today neither the United States, nor Russia, nor China, nor the rest of the world would benefit from another proliferation of nuclear weapons. Chinese nuclear forces, which had remained stable for years, are now forecast to triple.[42] This risk comes when the United States already faces the high costs of reconstituting its aging nuclear weapons and delivery systems. These expenditures, if fully funded, would consume over a quarter of all Department of Defense research and procurement spending.[43] Left unchecked, the spiraling costs to sustain a credible nuclear force posture could absorb the available funding to maintain the ability to fight modern wars, conduct irregular warfare, and develop new military capabilities to extend deterrence, as discussed next.

To control the costs of its nuclear arsenal, the United States should refrain from investing in destabilizing first-strike capabilities, such as plans to replace the Minuteman III intercontinental ballistic missiles (ICBM) with the new Sentinel ICBM, the ground-based strategic deterrent.[44] In addition, the United States should support arms-control talks to reduce the risks of nuclear arms races. The prospects of productive discussions do not appear encouraging now; the United States does not have strong bipartisan support for such negotiations as it did in the 1980s. China also has not indicated an interest in an arms-control regime that includes verification protocols. Even so, when there are opportunities, the United States should engage diplomatically with China and Russia and seek to initiate talks to create conditions for a stable nuclear deterrent that avoids a costly arms race.[45]

41 Federation of American Scientists, "Status of World Nuclear Forces" 2021, https://fas.org/issues/nuclear-weapons/status-world-nuclear-forces/.

42 Shannon Bugos, "Pentagon Sees Faster Chinese Nuclear Expansion" *Arms Control Association* (December 2021), www.armscontrol.org/act/2021-12/news/pentagon-sees-faster-chinese-nuclear-expansion.

43 CBO projections of $60 billion a year through 2030, against a $703.7 billion 2021 budget. Congressional Budget Office, "Projected Costs of U.S. Nuclear Forces 2021–2030" (May 2021), www.cbo.gov/publication/57240.

44 Federation of American Scientists, "ICBM Information Project," https://fas.org/issues/icbm-information-project/.

45 David Cooper, *Arms Control for the Third Nuclear Age: Between Disarmament and Armageddon* (Washington, DC: Georgetown University Press, 2021).

A fourth challenge is extending deterrence to US allies. The previously described multi-domain ISR and long-range strike capabilities differ fundamentally from the military force structure the United States has relied upon for the past six decades to fight modern wars. In the 1980s, AirLand Battle justified the next generation of weapon systems used not only to deter the Soviet Union in central Europe but afterward to fight the series of regional wars described in Appendix B. A key reason for the success of AirLand Battle was that it justified the new fighters and tanks the Air Force and Army already wanted. AirLand Battle's conventional force requirements fit the services' cultural preferences for air superiority and maneuver warfare. Unfortunately, this symmetry between extended deterrence force requirements and service culture no longer holds. A primary reason for the recent failure of AirSea Battle was that it highlighted the vulnerability of short-range land and carrier-based tacair when facing Chinese SAMs and A2/AD systems. Unlike AirLand Battle, which supported Air Force and Army procurement programs, AirSea Battle undermined the Air Force and Navy's top acquisition priorities. AirLand Battle generated a force structure that could extend deterrence against a peer competitor while being the preferred force for fighting regional modern wars, but AirSea Battle did not.[46] It remains a challenge to motivate the services to shift investment into a new force structure that differs from how they have historically fought and which may not be effective for the modern wars they are more likely to be called upon to fight in the future.

These four challenges contribute to a fifth problem of maintaining a sufficient conventional air force to remain effective in modern air warfare. Given the low priority such regional conflicts currently have within the Pentagon, securing the resources to maintain a sufficient conventional force structure will be challenging. How can US air forces retain adequate air superiority capabilities, primarily focusing on SEAD, along with an air-to-ground capacity to be lethal against enemy fielded forces? Further, how can US and allied surface forces maintain the ability to coordinate with air forces while retaining their organic capacity to threaten enemy surface forces?

Besides efforts described in allied burden-sharing and measures to avoid another costly nuclear arms race, the United States should continue to prioritize joint operations. Expensive investments in short-range air-to-air capabilities should be limited, and priority shifted toward maintaining SEAD capabilities and self-protection measures for combat aircraft. Investment should continue in new ISR capabilities against enemy fielded forces, advanced targeting pods and other sensors on strike aircraft, and

46 Haun, "Peacetime Military Innovation through Inter-service Cooperation."

more effective and efficient air-to-ground weaponry. The existing conventional air fleet should also be husbanded. One current challenge is maintaining the existing force structure when deployed air units are under the control of theater combatant commanders who have little incentive to conserve these scarce resources for future conflicts.

In addition to changing acquisition priorities and resource-conserving measures, the investment must continue to maintain expertise within the services for the direct attack of fielded forces. This investment means retaining small cadres of experts tasked with preserving and improving the tactics required to conduct effective air-to-ground operations and coordinate air and surface forces. The vital tactical air control system, with its air support operation center, air liaisons, and joint tactical air controllers, requires resources, personnel, and training in peacetime to perform its vital role in wartime. It requires the Air Force, Navy, Marine Corps, and Army to all invest in these force integrators. Also important are allied capabilities. US special forces should maintain their special operations air–ground system and engage with partner nations to train allies in effective air–ground coordination. Special forces should focus less on direct action, as they have for the past two decades, and return to their roots by assisting allies in developing organic capabilities and integrating these forces with US air forces.

These five challenges are formidable but not insurmountable if the United States comes to terms with the shifting international security environment and the constraints and risks such a system imposes on US action and interests. Wars of choice, common in the age of primacy, now threaten to hollow out core security capabilities and should be avoided wherever possible. These voluntary wars include not only independent strategic bombing campaigns but also enduring counterinsurgency and counterterrorism operations. Instead, diplomatic efforts should continue to reform alliances, with burden-sharing a prerequisite to any security guarantees. So too, should long-term diplomatic engagement with Russia and China continue by acknowledging their status as reemergent and rising powers and with US efforts prioritized toward mitigating conflicts and avoiding costly arms races. Under this emerging security environment, regional conflicts will likely have a lower priority than in recent years. However, maintaining the critical components for the effective direct attack of fielded forces will be vital when unavoidable conflicts arise. Tactical air power (TAP) theory provides insight into US success in modern air wars and generates recommendations (as previously listed) for the measures required to succeed today and into the future.

Appendix A Air Power Theory

The advent of the airplane introduced the question of how best to employ this new technology in warfare.[1] Military theorists have since been divided over whether air power should be viewed as a complement to or substitute for surface forces. Unsurprisingly, soldiers and sailors viewed aircraft as new weapons to enhance the tactical effectiveness of land and sea power. Commanders in World War I quickly grasped the advantage of having aviators observe and attack enemy positions. Aerial missions soon emerged for reconnaissance and observation, artillery spotting, close air support (CAS), interdiction, and air superiority. Meanwhile, some airmen began considering how to avoid enemy positions and directly target the enemy's heartland. Before the war, the German Navy had procured Count Zeppelin's rigid dirigibles for long-range naval patrol. They could overfly the North Sea and elude the Royal Navy to bomb English ports and cities. As the war progressed, airplanes replaced the Zeppelins, but the war ended before either side could adequately put strategic bombing to the test.

During the interwar period, three broad air doctrines emerged. On the Continent, military officers in Germany and the Soviet Union struggled to understand how to employ air power against enemy armies. Later in combat, they evolved the combined arms concepts known as Blitzkrieg and Deep Battle.[2] Tactical air power played a crucial role in supporting mechanized ground forces to breach and rapidly penetrate the frontlines and then paralyze the enemy by interdicting its lines of communication (LOC).

[1] H. G. Wells, *War in the Air* (London: George Bell & Sons, 1908).

[2] As discussed in Chapter 2, the Luftwaffe's doctrine of air–ground coordination evolved with its combat experience in the Spanish Civil War and the early campaigns of World War II. James Corum, *Luftwaffe* (Lawrence: University Press of Kansas, 1997), 271; Richard Simpkin, *Deep Battle: The Brainchild of Marshal Tukhachevsky* (London: Brassey's Defence, 1987).

On the periphery of Europe, on the Italian peninsula and the British Isles, airmen instead looked to project power over long distances. They believed the invention of the aircraft provided an independent means for waging war. The airplane was a strategic weapon that could avoid the attritional battles of World War I by passing over the trenches and directly attacking the enemy's true center of gravity, its population. Meanwhile, a third school was being formed across the Atlantic as American airmen created a doctrine for high-altitude daylight precision bombing reliant on new technologies to surgically strike the critical nodes of an enemy's economy.

World War II witnessed the widespread bombing of populations and economies throughout Europe and Asia. The results were mixed, but the advent of the atomic bomb and, soon thereafter, thermonuclear devices appeared to validate the premature claims made by the Italian General Giulio Douhet. Nuclear-armed air forces had now changed the very nature of war. Fortunately, the United States and the Soviet Union never launched the immense arsenals they assembled during the Cold War. Instead, the devastation expected from a nuclear Armageddon deterred a third world war that no one would win.

At the end of the Cold War, a fourth air power theory appeared to take advantage of the maturation of stealth aircraft and precision-guided weapon technologies. US airmen argued that they could now target an enemy nation's leadership and disrupt the regime's command and control over its military and population.

These four broad air power theories, which target the enemy's military, population, economy, and leadership, make different assumptions about the character of warfare and offer alternative theories of victory for how air forces can win or deter war. They also lead to diverse recommendations on organizing an air force, the types and quantity of aircraft to procure, the doctrines to adopt, and the required training. The three strategic bombing theories targeting populations, economies, and leadership have tended to be more aspirational, emphasizing how airmen prefer to employ their forces independently. By contrast, conventional tactical air doctrine has focused on efficient mechanisms to support surface forces. While there emerged an air power strategy for indirectly attacking an enemy army's LOC, conspicuously absent until now has been a tactical air power (TAP) theory for the direct attack of an enemy's fielded forces.

This appendix provides an introduction for those unfamiliar with air power theory by introducing a typology for four schools of thought delineated by target prioritization. Targeting provides the critical link between military operations and outcomes.

Air Power Theory

Air power is the ability to project force through the air to control and influence an opponent.[3] In warfare, air power has two aspects. The first is its ability to gain control of the air domain, use it, and deny its use to the enemy. Such an advantage is called air superiority. Air superiority can be localized to a specific area and timeframe or be more general and sustained. Permanent air superiority is known as air supremacy, or what Giulio Douhet called command of the air.

Air superiority may be obtained through sequential action, such as rolling back an enemy integrated air defense system (IADS), or by attrition, gradually weakening an enemy's air forces. Either way, air superiority is obtained through air-to-air, surface-to-air, or air-to-ground combat. Air superiority can, by itself, be a deterrent against enemy aggression. The victory of the Royal Air Force (RAF) over the Luftwaffe in the Battle of Britain denied Hitler's designs for invading England. However, air superiority over the Channel did not end the war. It would take another five years and the invasion of the Continent before Britain achieved victory. Air superiority alone may avoid defeat, but it usually does not win wars by itself. Instead, air superiority is a prerequisite for successful offensive operations.

The second component of air power is the ability to control or influence the land and sea. With air superiority secured, how will air forces be employed to achieve the desired military and political objectives? Air power theory provides the "theory of victory" for how an air force employs or threatens to employ violence to affect the decision-making and actions of an opponent to deter or win wars.[4] In practice, the essence of air power theory is providing the priority for what to target.[5]

In *On War*, Clausewitz explained:

> [Theory] is used to analyze the constituent elements of war, to distinguish precisely what at first seems fused, to explain in full the properties of the means employed and to show their probable effects, to define clearly the nature of the ends in view,

[3] This definition refers to the employment of air forces to deter, coerce, or defeat an enemy during times of peace or war. Air power is a component of military power, which, along with a nation's other instruments of power, are employed to achieve political objectives. Joint Chiefs of Staff, *Doctrine for the Armed Forces of the United States: Joint Publication 1* (Washington, DC: Department of Defense, March 25, 2013), I-1.

[4] In his study of maritime power, Julian Corbett points out that wars are decided where men live, on the land. Julian Corbett, *Some Principles of Maritime Strategy*, originally published 1911 (Annapolis, MD: Naval Institute Press, 1988), 16.

[5] Giulio Douhet, *Command of the Air*, originally published 1922 and 1926 (Washington, DC: Air Force History and Museums Program, 1998), 50.

and to illuminate all phases of warfare in a thorough critical inquiry ... Theory exists so one does not need to start afresh each time sorting out the material and plowing through it, but will find it at hand and in good order.[6]

At the organizational level, air power theory offers a blueprint for developing and maintaining an air force in peacetime and war. At the operational level, it provides the critical assumptions about the degree of air superiority required and, subsequently, the enemy center(s) of gravity to target. Air power theory assists a commander in answering crucial questions when developing a strategy: What is the desired political aim or end state? What is the causal logic (theory of victory) by which the application of air power will achieve or contribute to attaining the desired political end state? What targeting prioritization will most effectively lead to this political outcome?

What Is the Desired Political End State?

Air power strategy must begin with the end in mind.[7] What is the desired political objective? Are these aims great or small?[8] The most ambitious goal is regime change. For example, in the invasion of Iraq in 2003, the United States had the overthrow of Saddam Hussein as its objective. Because unlimited aims place the very survival of the enemy at stake, a coercive air power strategy alone is not likely to compel an adversary to make such dire concessions.[9] Obtaining such a significant objective usually requires instead a brute force strategy of invasion and occupation, where air power partners with ground forces.[10]

Limited objectives, by definition, are aims short of regime change. These may include demands that an opponent does not change the status quo. For example, in the Vietnam War, before the Tet Offensive, the United States' primary objective was to deter North Vietnam from supporting the insurgency in South Vietnam. After Tet, demands eventually

6 Carl Von Clausewitz, *On War* (Princeton, NJ: Princeton University Press, 1975), 141.

7 Clausewitz, *On War*, 579.

8 Limited versus unlimited aims has to do with the type of objective. It does not indicate the importance of the political objective or the level of military means employed.

9 Alexander Downes, "Step Aside or Face the Consequences: Explaining the Success and Failure of Compellent Threats to Remove Foreign Leaders" in Kelly Greenhill and Peter Krause, eds., *Coercion: The Power to Hurt in International Politics* (Oxford: Oxford University Press, 2018). He argues that coercing regime change is possible under certain unique conditions when brute force victory is assured.

10 Overthrowing the government may achieve a nation's political objectives and not end the conflict as the occupied may continue to fight.

were further reduced to letting Americans withdraw from Vietnam – a "peace with honor."[11]

Limited objectives are easier to obtain and occasionally may be achieved with air power alone. For example, the Linebacker II strategic bombing campaign against Hanoi brought the North Vietnamese back to Paris to sign a peace deal. But the concessions were minimal as the agreement was to the North's advantage. The US primary demand was for Hanoi to allow the Americans to withdraw from Vietnam. It was also a peace deal the North Vietnamese had previously accepted after their defeat in the Easter Offensive (see Chapter 7). In most cases, air power alone does not win wars, though, as previously mentioned, nuclear-armed air forces continue to deter a third world war. To sum up, the potential success of any air power strategy depends upon the nature of the desired political objective.

What Is the Air Power Strategy?

Air power theory provides the assumptions and causal logic for developing a strategy, whether for general deterrence in peacetime or a tailored brute force or coercive response during a crisis or war. An air power strategy links the means (air forces) to the ends (the desired military and political aims). How will the employment of air power cause the opponent to relinquish or forsake its objective? For example, in the fall of 1965, US combined air and ground operations in the Central Highlands caused the North Vietnamese Army (NVA) to suspend its military strategy of dividing South Vietnam (see Chapter 3). Here the allies utilized air and ground forces to deny the North Vietnamese their offensive objective.

Air power strategies can be distinguished by their causal mechanism. Air forces can defeat the enemy by brute force or coerce them into concessions. Clausewitz recognized that brute force was not the only way to employ a military. He observed that "the aim of *disarming the enemy* ... is not always encountered in reality, and need not be fully achieved as a condition of peace."[12] Instead, the "inability to carry on the struggle can, in practice, be replaced by two other grounds for making peace: the first is the improbability of victory; the second is its unacceptable cost."[13] Here Clausewitz identifies the two coercive

[11] US Presidential candidate Richard Nixon in his nomination acceptance speech at the Republican National Convention in Miami, Florida on August 8, 1968, pledged "an honorable end to the war in Vietnam," www.4president.org/speeches/nixon1968acceptance.htm.

[12] Clausewitz, *On War*, 91.

[13] Clausewitz, *On War*, 91.

mechanisms causing an opponent to accept otherwise unfavorable terms: denying the enemy its preferred strategy or imposing intolerable suffering.[14] Air power strategies can be categorized by whether they achieve their objectives by brute force, coercion/deterrence by denial, or coercion/deterrence by punishment. The choice of strategy then informs the critical operational question of what to target.

Targeting Priority

Since air forces are expensive, and resources for national defense scarce, a critical judgment for a nation is the type of air force to develop and maintain. In the interwar period, the United States debated whether the airplane should be considered a substitute for or complement to its army and navy.[15] This choice between an independent or a joint air force, in turn, depends upon how air power will be employed and what it will target. Targeting prioritization involves two steps: first identifying what is most vital or valuable to the enemy, and second determining which of these potential centers of gravity are most vulnerable to air attack.[16] Targeting is the critical link between means and ends by prescribing how to employ air power in brute force, coercive, or deterrent strategies.

Once the targeting priority has been decided, then by backward induction, the size and type of air force can be determined. For example, in the leadup to World War II, the US Air War Plans Division used its list of German targets as the baseline for calculating the total bomber force required.[17] Target type also informs decisions on whether to construct long-range bombers to conduct deep strikes against an enemy's population, economy, or leaders or acquire short-range combat aircraft to strike

[14] Sun Tzu also recognizes attacking an enemy's strategy as a preferred strategy. Sun Tzu, *The Art of War*, trans. Samual Griffith (Oxford: Oxford University Press, 1963), 77. Thomas Schelling identifies a third risk strategy. Here one side chooses a strategy of brinkmanship that risks escalation and high costs imposed on both parties should the conflict get out of hand: Thomas Schelling, *Arms and Influence* (New Haven, CT: Yale University Press, 1966). Brinkmanship is closely linked to the Cold War and the risk of escalation to nuclear warfare. The power willing to accept the risk of "rocking the boat" can coerce an opponent ready to make concessions rather than endure such danger. Phil Haun and Michael O'Hara, "The Brinkmanship Game: Bargaining under the Mutual Risk of Escalation" *Journal of Political Science Education* 18:3 (2022), 379–389.

[15] The most prominent in this debate was the US Army Air Corps Brigadier General Billy Mitchell. His court-martial brought national attention to the question as to the role of air power. William Mitchell, *Winged Defense: The Development and Possibilities of Modern Air Power Economic and Military* (New York: Putnam, 1925).

[16] Phil Haun, *Lectures of the Air Corps Tactical School* (Lexington: University Press of Kentucky, 2019), 140.

[17] Haun, *Lectures of the Air Corps Tactical School*, 198–203.

an enemy's fielded force. Historically, targeting an enemy's population, economy, and leadership has been called strategic, while attacking the enemy's military has been considered tactical.[18]

Targeting Populations, Economies, Leaders, and Militaries

Early air power theorists claimed the airplane had changed the very nature of war. Strategic bombing advocates believed the true center of gravity was not the enemy's fielded forces but their heartland, which the airplane could now reach. The priority on what to target differentiates air power theories.

Targeting the Population

The first and most controversial air power theorist was the Italian General Giulio Douhet. He believed the quickest way to win a war was by bombing cities with explosives, incendiaries, and chemicals. Paradoxically, he also viewed this as the most ethical approach to warfare. He believed terrorizing the population would bring a quick surrender with less suffering than that endured over four years of World War I.[19]

Douhet urged the targeting of civilians in his 1921 treatise *Command of the Air.*[20] He correctly anticipated that the next major war would require the total mobilization of industrial nations. He argued that there was no moral or legal distinction between the soldiers who fought at the front and the workers who made the weapons and provisions for war.[21] Douhet believed the population to be the vital center of a nation, vulnerable to air attack. Because of the vastness of the sky, an air force, unlike an army or navy, could avoid the enemy's defenses and immediately

[18] Evidence of this division is in the names given to USAF organizational structure. The USAF divided its combat forces into Strategic Air Command and Tactical Air Command through the Cold War. History of US Strategic Command, www.stratcom.mil/About/History/#:~:text=SAC%20was%20created%20in%20March,the%20Joint%20Chiefs%20of%20Staff.

[19] Douhet, *Command of the Air*, 5, 10, 25, 58, 60, 98, 128, 196.

[20] Douhet, *Command of the Air.* Douhet began his career as an artillery officer, where he first saw the potential for air power in 1911 in Libya in operations against the Ottoman Empire. He later commanded an aviation battalion in World War I but was court-martialed for criticizing the ineptness of the Italian Army. Incarcerated for a year, he was vindicated and reinstated in 1917. By 1918, he was directing the Italian Central Aeronautic Bureau and, in 1921, articulated his theory of strategic bombing in *Command of the Air.*

[21] Douhet, *Command of the Air*, 5, 10.

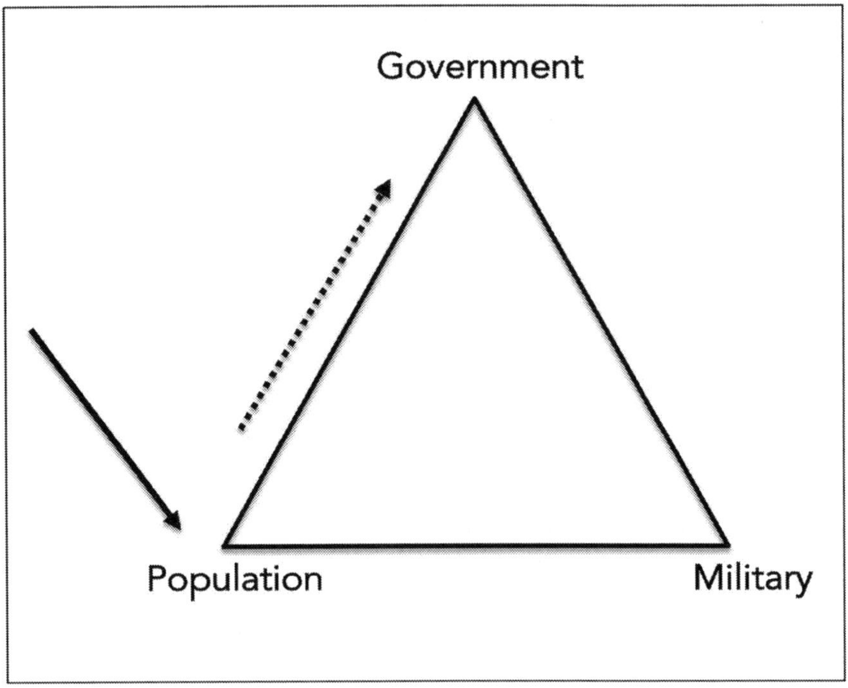

Figure A.1 Clausewitz's triangle: targeting the population

attack their population. By contrast, surface forces had first to defeat the enemy's land and sea forces before they could apply pressure against the population through occupation or blockade.

Douhet maintained the airplane to be an inherently offensive weapon. At the outset of a war, a nation should attack the enemy's air force on the ground to seize command of the air quickly and permanently. Once obtained, the large bomber formations he envisioned would then bomb enemy cities into submission. The causal mechanism for Douhetian strategic bombing was coercion by punishment, imposing such intense suffering upon the populations that they would compel their government to seek peace on any terms. To illustrate Douhet's causal logic, consider Clausewitz's triangular model for the state, which consists of the government, military, and population (Figure A.1).[22]

[22] For further discussion on how the Clausewitzian Triangle differs from the Clausewitzian Trinity's passions, chance, and reason see Clausewitz, *On War*, 89; Thomas Waldman, *War, Clausewitz and the Trinity* (Milton Park: Routledge, 2016).

Conventional military strategy first required enemy forces to be defeated in battle before pressure could be placed on the enemy's government to capitulate. But Douhet rejected the notion that the enemy's army or navy was a nation's center of gravity. The only military forces that required attack were the enemy's air forces, so they could not launch strikes against one's homeland. He believed command of the air could be gained and maintained easily. With command of the air secured, an air force could quickly achieve victory by targeting the enemy's true center of gravity, its population.

Douhet was not specific about how the population would force its leaders to accept an unfavorable peace. The options available were to overthrow or threaten to overthrow the government. Alternatively, even if the population did not revolt, a "benevolent" leader might concede out of concern over the people's suffering, as Emperor Hirohito claimed as his justification for Japan's surrender in World War II.[23]

Douhet advocated for an independent air force with a fleet of aircraft procured and maintained in peacetime. Only such an air force would be prepared for and dedicated to gaining command of the air at the outset of war. Air forces under the control of the army and navy would be dispersed and distracted by requirements to support surface forces. For an air force to be victorious, it had to be ready to seize the initiative, taking advantage of the surprise and flexibility inherent in air power. Going on the offensive further allowed the aggressor to concentrate and attack where it chose. By contrast, the defender had to disperse its forces to protect its military and territory, thus tendering the advantage to the attacker.

Under the direction of Air Marshal Arthur "Bomber" Harris, RAF Bomber Command came close to implementing Douhet's strategy with its nighttime bombing of German cities in World War II. So too, in the Pacific, US Army Air Force Major General Curtis LeMay targeted industries in urban areas, implicitly following Douhet's dictate when American B-29 bombers firebombed Japan.[24]

As it turned out, gaining command of the air in World War II was not as easy as Douhet had anticipated. The advent of radar and IADS allowed enemy fighters to concentrate against bomber formations.[25]

[23] Emperor Hirohito, "Imperial Rescript on Surrender (August 15, 1945)," https://en.wikisource.org/wiki/Imperial_Rescript_on_Surrender. Leaders could also decide to concede in anticipation that the population would later punish and/or remove it from power.

[24] Conrad Crane, *American Airpower Strategy in World War II: Bombs, Cities, Civilians, and Oil* (Lawrence: University of Kansas Press, 2016), 176–179.

[25] Haun, *Lectures of the Air Corps Tactical School.*

Even when obtaining air superiority, targeting civilians was criticized as ineffective, inefficient, and immoral. The bombing of German and Japanese cities did not lead to a quick end to war as Douhet had predicted but instead killed and injured millions and left tens of millions homeless.[26]

How the war ended in the Pacific, with the dramatic surrender of Japan in the days following the twin atomic bombings of Hiroshima and Nagasaki, provided the evidence needed by air power advocates to lobby successfully for an independent US Air Force.[27] In the Cold War that followed, Douhet's emphasis on punishing civilians appeared even more relevant with the advent of thermonuclear devices. Once married to intercontinental ballistic missiles, these weapons could be delivered worldwide in minutes. Douhet's terror bombing was reimagined as the critical ingredient for deterrence by punishment known as mutually assured destruction (MAD).[28] Thankfully, the unimaginable human suffering inflicted by a general nuclear war have thus far deterred crises from escalating across the nuclear threshold.

The punishment strategies targeting civilians in World War II inflicted intense suffering but did not end the war quickly or painlessly as Douhet promised. An alternative approach advocated by the US Air Corps Tactical School (ACTS) instead targeted the enemy's economy.

Targeting the Economy

Instead of bombing civilians, a strategic bombing campaign could target a nation's infrastructure. In the 1930s, the US Air Corps Tactical School developed a uniquely American concept of high-altitude daylight precision bombing (HADPB) to paralyze the enemy by targeting the nodes of its economic network.[29]

[26] For critiques on World War II and the bombing of civilians see Richard Overy, *The Bomber and the Bombed: The Allied Air War over Europe 1940–1945* (New York: Penguin, 2014); and Michael Sherry, *The Rise of American Air Power* (New Haven, CT: Yale University Press, 1987).

[27] The cause of the Japanese surrender continues to be contended by scholars. Still, the point is not whether the Japanese surrendered because of the atomic attacks but that the USAF successfully used strategic bombing of Japan as the justification for an independent air force.

[28] Bernard Brodie, *Strategy in the Missile Age* (Princeton, NJ: Princeton University Press, 1959), 402.

[29] The Air Corps Tactical School was the US Air Corps tactical air warfare school for its officers. The Air Force faculty lectured on the independent use of air power and developed over the 1930s a uniquely American theory of strategic bombing. See Haun, *Lectures of the Air Corps Tactical School.*

Like Douhet, ACTS faculty believed in the peacetime procurement of an independent air force consisting of large formations of self-defending bombers. Such formations could gain air superiority by seizing the initiative and then striking the enemy's vital and vulnerable economic centers. To do so required aircraft that could precisely hit concentrated targets. Tight battle formations would ward off enemy fighters, while the bombers flew at high altitude above the effective range of anti-aircraft artillery (AAA). These missions had to be conducted during the day so bombardiers could visually acquire their targets. The arrival of the B-17 Flying Fortress in the early 1930s, combined with the Norden bombsight, made the Air Corps dream of HADPB a reality.[30] In the leadup to World War II, former ACTS faculty designed the US air strategy against Germany and Japan, making HADPB central to US air war plans.[31]

Unlike Douhet, ACTS faculty argued that bombing civilians was immoral and ineffective.[32] They instead believed the center of gravity of a modern industrial nation to be its economy. A modern nation's economic network was concentrated and vulnerable to air attack. Striking key nodes would disrupt production and distribution. The ACTS faculty argued that paralyzing the economy would have two effects. First, denying the enemy the ability to produce weapons and supplies would reduce the capability to wage war. Such a constriction in production would, in turn, reduce the enemy military's probability of victory. Second, since the population also relied upon industrial output, economic paralysis would cause civilian suffering contributing to a coercive punishment strategy.

Figure A.2 expands Clausewitz's triangle into an equilateral tetrahedron (three-sided pyramid) to incorporate a nation's economic/material dimension.[33] The theory of victory for targeting a country's war economy placed indirect pressure on the government by decreasing the enemy's military capability and increasing the population's suffering.

Unlike the ACTS faculty, who advocated for the precision bombing of specific economic nodes, Air Marshal Hugh Trenchard, the father of the Royal Air Force, championed the area bombing of industrial areas. According to Trenchard, the most significant impact on production was not physical destruction but decreased productivity caused by low worker morale. The threat of bombing would deter workers from

[30] Haun, *Lectures of the Air Corps Tactical School*, chapter 1.
[31] Haun, *Lectures of the Air Corps Tactical School*, 195.
[32] Haun, *Lectures of the Air Corps Tactical School*, 141–142.
[33] Clausewitz does not address the economic/material dimension of war. Michael Handel, *Masters of War: Classical Strategic Thought* (Milton Park: Routledge, 2000), 109.

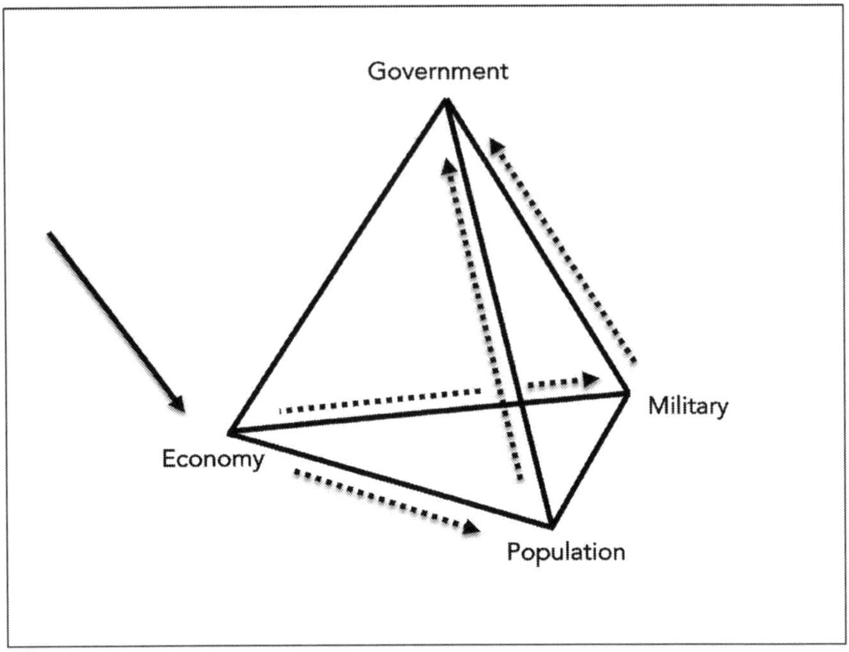

Figure A.2 Targeting the economy

returning to their factories.[34] In practice, Bomber Command's targeting of German industry in World War II differed little from the targeting of civilians advocated by Douhet.

The Combined Bomber Offensive by the British and Americans in World War II demonstrated the operational challenges of gaining air superiority and the subsequent difficulties of paralyzing an enemy's economy. The strategic bombing of the German and Japanese economies has further been criticized as inefficient, given the enormous resources dedicated by the allies.[35] Even when their national economies were paralyzed, this did not cause their leaders to surrender, as Germany and Japan remained defiant even after economic collapse.

The targeting of economies has rarely been decisive as modern economies proved resilient, and civilians remained either defiant or apathetic. The result has not been popular uprisings against the governments, as predicted by Douhet. The one possible exception was in 1999 when the

[34] Haun, *Lectures of the Air Corps Tactical School*, 7.
[35] Overy, *The Bomber and the Bombed*; Sherry, *The Rise of American Air Power.*

risk to a weakened Serbian economy, held hostage by the threat of North Atlantic Treaty Organization (NATO) airstrikes, eventually pressured President Slobodan Milosevic to concede Kosovo.[36]

Targeting the Leadership

At the end of the Cold War, US Air Force Colonel John Warden proposed a third strategic bombing theory, targeting a nation's leadership and its command and control.[37] Warden's five-ring model identified a nation's key elements, with the government's leadership being the most critical.[38] Targeting the innermost circle, Warden believed, would be the most effective means of achieving victory as a state's leaders controlled its military and population. Applying pressure directly to leadership and its command-and-control system would coerce the government to make concessions. Alternatively, attacking leaders could decapitate or paralyze the enemy so that its military and population could not offer organized resistance.[39] Figure A.3 illustrates how directly targeting the government's leadership and indirectly severing its command and control over its military and population could decapitate or paralyze the enemy.

As with the ACTS theory of attacking economies, the targeting of enemy leadership also required an independent air force able to penetrate a nation's IADS and then precisely strike designated targets. Stealth aircraft in Desert Storm, armed with precision-guided munitions, demonstrated the capability for conducting such surgical raids.[40] According to Warden, the air force required to attack a nation's leadership needed

36 Phil Haun, *Coercion, Survival, and War: Why Weak States Resist the United States* (Palo Alto, CA: Stanford University Press, 2015). There is still disagreement as to what exactly caused Milosevic to concede when he did. For examples see contrary assessments by two RAND reports: Stephen Hosmer, *The Kosovo Conflict: Why Milosevic Decided to Settle When He Did* (Santa Monica, CA: RAND Corporation, 2001); and Benjamin Lambeth, *NATO's Air War for Kosovo: Strategic and Operational Assessment* (Santa Monica, CA: RAND Corporation, 2001).

37 Warden developed the Instant Thunder air plan, the initial option for US air forces in the opening stages of the first Gulf War. Michael Gordon and Bernard Trainor, *The Generals War* (Boston, MA: Little Brown and Company, 1995), 75–101.

38 The next two rings represented essential energy production and economic infrastructure, respectively. The fourth ring represented the population, and the outer ring the military. John Warden "The Enemy as a System" *Air Power Journal* 9:1 (Spring 1995), 47.

39 Warden, "The Enemy as a System," 43.

40 The USAF called the F-117 a stealth fighter, but it had no air-to-air capability and was employed strictly as a bomber. It was called a "fighter" not because of its capabilities, but because pilots were recruited from the fighter community.

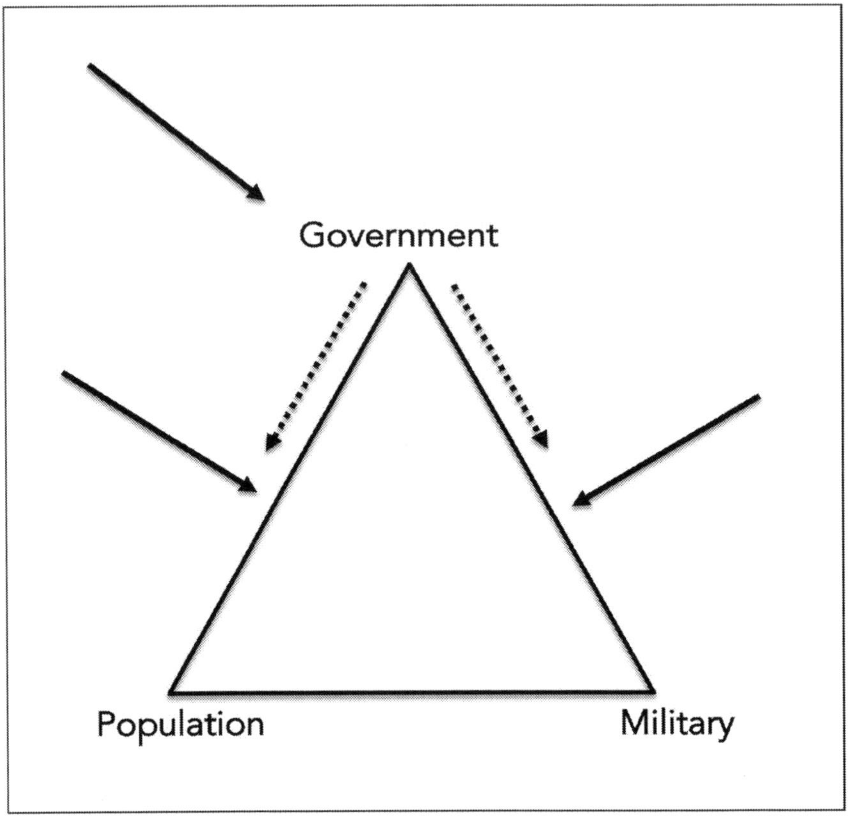

Figure A.3 Targeting the leadership

only a relatively small number of technologically sophisticated long-range stealth bombers.[41]

In practice, targeting a nation's leadership has been challenging as the granularity and timeliness of the intelligence required to conduct such strikes has proven elusive. In 1991, the US Air Force (USAF) bombed Iraqi President Saddam Hussein's palaces and searched for his Winnebagos in the Baghdad suburbs in vain. In 1999, the United States bombed Serbian President Slobodan Milosevic's empty bedroom. And in 2003, the United States accelerated the start time for the invasion

[41] Support aircraft for F-117 strikes included the ISR platforms required for target identification, threat assessment, battle damage assessment, the electronic jamming aircraft to disrupt enemy radars, and air refuelers.

of Iraq in a rushed stealth airstrike on an empty field outside Baghdad.[42] Leadership strikes, though appealing in theory, usually disappoint.

In addition to directly targeting a nation's leader, two alternative approaches have been attempted in recent wars. The first, crony attack, undermines a regime by attacking the elites who support it. Over Serbia, the United States inflicted economic losses on Milosevic's inner circle by targeting the factories they owned. Presumably, these elites would pressure Milosevic to seek peace. This strategy failed because Milosevic's cronies depended more on his support than he did on theirs.[43]

The second type of leadership targeting is aimed at non-state actors, such as insurgent or terrorist groups. The goal is to weaken and contain the group by killing or isolating its leaders. This attritional strategy, referred to derisively as "mowing the lawn," requires a different type of air force that prioritizes persistent intelligence surveillance and reconnaissance (ISR) combined with an on-call, surgical strike capability. The United States has conducted these counterterrorism operations through the widespread employment of armed drones. Remotely piloted aircraft (RPA) have targeted Al Qaeda and the Taliban in Afghanistan and Pakistan, and other groups throughout the Middle East and Africa.[44]

There are two primary challenges involved in targeting leadership. The first is the intelligence required to identify and track specific individuals. This detailed knowledge has proven nearly impossible to obtain against state leaders and is only possible against non-state actors when human intelligence sources can penetrate insurgent and terrorist networks. The second challenge for decapitating leadership is determining whether eliminating the leader will obtain the desired political outcome. Replacing a regime is fraught with the risk of a nation descending into chaos, as evidenced in Libya.[45]

Indirectly Targeting the Military

A fourth, non-strategic bombing, air power theory is to target the enemy's military indirectly. Robert Pape, in *Bombing to Win*, argues air

[42] Michael Gordon and Bernard Trainor, *Cobra II: The Inside Story of the Invasion and Occupation of Iraq* (New York: Vintage, 2007), 194.

[43] Stephen Hosmer, *Operations against Enemy Leaders* (Santa Monica, CA: RAND Corporation, 2001); Julien Tolbert, *Crony Attack: Strategic Attacks Silver Bullet?* (Maxwell AFB, AL: School of Advanced Air and Space Power Studies, 2006).

[44] Timothy Schultz, "Remote Warfare: A New Architecture for Air Power" in Phil Haun, Colin Jackson, and Timothy Schultz, eds., *Air Power in the Age of Primacy: Aerial Warfare since the Cold War* (Cambridge: Cambridge University Press, 2021).

[45] On leadership regime change see Alexander Downes, *Catastrophic Success: Why Foreign Imposed Regime Change Goes Wrong* (Ithaca, NY: Cornell University Press, 2021).

power strategies that attack enemy military capability are more likely to succeed than those striking the population, economy, or leadership.[46] He acknowledges that an air power theorist has never fully articulated the tactical application of air forces: "Coercive air strategies based on denying the enemy victory on the battlefield developed without the benefit of an air theorist to organize the ideas into a coherent set of principles, though John C. Slessor, a British who wrote in the 1930s came the closest."[47]

Slessor began *Air Power and Armies* with the disclaimer that the book was not about the strategic air campaign the RAF was preparing to fight, where "the decision will only be gained by direct action against the hostile vital centres." Instead, it was reserved for situations when an air force is required to support a land campaign.[48] Slessor believed the first objective of an air force was to win air superiority.[49] With air superiority secured, he prioritized targeting the enemy's wartime production and disrupting its supply lines. Only as a last resort should an air force directly attack the enemy's fielded forces.[50]

Slessor argued the airplane was not a battlefield weapon to be employed near troops, except on rare occasions such as the initial breakthrough of the enemy's defenses or to break up a counterattack.[51] Direct attack required specially designed low-altitude aircraft that would suffer significant losses.[52] Expending these air forces against targets within range of friendly artillery was also inefficient.[53] Despite these disclaimers, Slessor identified occasions when armies would be vulnerable to air attack; large columns on the march, troops traveling by rail, concentrated forces in reserve, and the army's command and control headquarters.[54] The critical impact of air power against such targets was to interfere "with *movement*, by striking at the communications, rail or road, serving the battle area."[55] Slessor concluded that "the primary task of the air striking force in a land battle must be to isolate the area attacked from reinforcement and supply."[56] He recognized the ability of air power to affect the movement of an enemy's forces but not how it could directly affect the massing and maneuvering of armies on the battlefield.

46 Robert Pape, *Bombing to Win* (Ithaca, NY: Cornell University Press, 1996).
47 Pape, *Bombing to Win*, 69.
48 J. C. Slessor, *Air Power and Armies* (London: Oxford University Press, 1936), 3.
49 Slessor, *Air Power and Armies*, 1–60.
50 Slessor, *Air Power and Armies*, 79–80.
51 Slessor, *Air Power and Armies*, 90; H. Smyth, "From Coningham to Project Coningham-Keyes: Did British Forces Relearn Historical Air-Land Cooperation Lessons during Operation 'Telic'?" *Defence Studies* 7:2 (2007), 260.
52 Slessor, *Air Power and Armies*, 100.
53 Slessor, *Air Power and Armies*, 91.
54 Slessor, *Air Power and Armies*, 92–97.
55 Slessor, *Air Power and Armies*, 123.
56 Slessor, *Air Power and Armies*, 212.

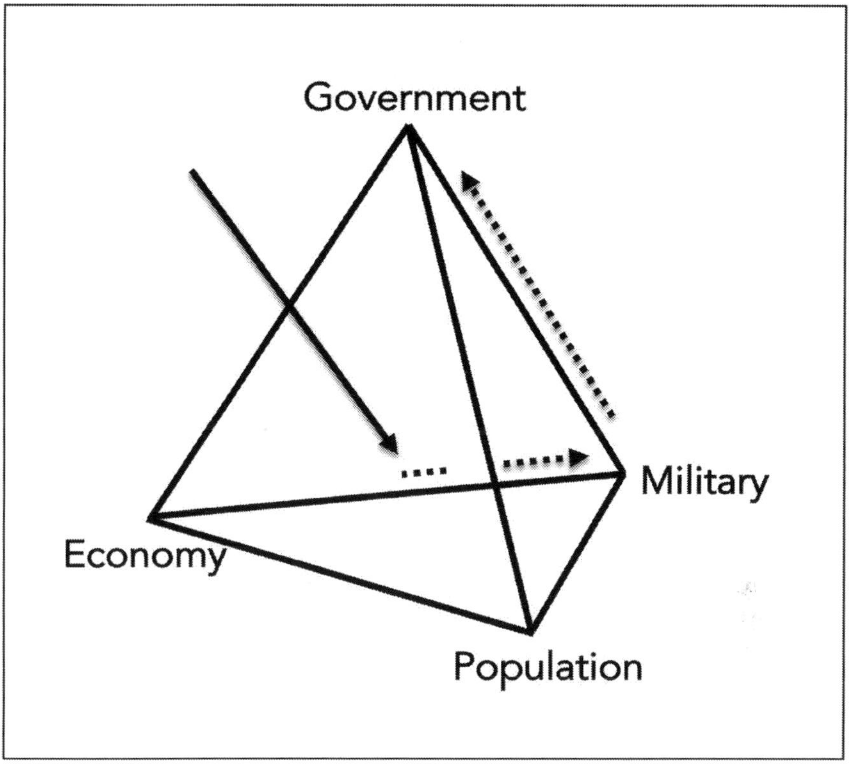

Figure A.4 Targeting military lines of communication

Pape concurred with Slessor on the two types of air power strategies that indirectly target the enemy's military capability.[57] The first is the strategic attack on an enemy's wartime production, espoused by the ACTS faculty. The second targets an enemy army's lines of communication (LOC) by air interdiction. Striking rail and road networks, fuel pipelines, and command and control facilities impedes or delays the deployment of forces, reserves, and the ammunition, fuel, and other supplies required for sustained conventional military operations. Figure A.4 illustrates the targeting of a military's LOC.

Pape claimed that indirectly targeting enemy LOC can be effective, but only against a conventional mechanized army dependent upon a massive resupply effort. Guerrilla forces, such as the Viet Cong in South

[57] Pape, *Bombing to Win*, 70–74.

Vietnam, were less reliant upon supply lines and therefore less susceptible to air interdiction.[58]

As demonstrated in Chapters 3–7, air interdiction of land LOC, while enticing in theory, underperformed in practice. Enemy forces anticipate interdiction efforts and stockpile or develop redundant and resilient supply lines. Independent air interdiction campaigns have not proven decisive in defeating enemy armies and coercing concessions.

Interdiction at sea, by contrast, has been more successful. In World War II, the allied interdiction of the German sea lines of communication (SLOC) across the Mediterranean in the North African campaign proved vital, as did the interdiction of Japanese supply lines in the South Pacific.[59] In the Vietnam War, the United States and South Vietnamese navies in Operation Market Time impeded the flow of NVA troops and supplies. Market Time effectively deterred the North from using the sea to support the Viet Cong. As a result, the North Vietnamese became more reliant on the Ho Chi Minh Trail.[60]

While air interdiction against enemy land LOC has not been decisive, such an air campaign can impose costs, requiring the enemy to invest resources and reduce the efficiency of its supply lines. At times, such delays can be critical. From 1968 through 1970, the Commando Hunt I and III air interdiction operations against the Ho Chi Minh Trail in southern Laos bought precious time for the South Vietnamese pacification and Vietnamization programs to take root (see Chapter 5). However, Commando Hunt I and III have been the exception, as most air interdiction campaigns against an enemy's land LOC have not achieved the desired military or political objectives (see Chapter 8).

This appendix has examined four existing air power theories that directly target the enemy's population, economy, and leadership or indirectly target their army's LOC. What has remained absent is a theory for directly attacking an enemy's fielded force. Clausewitz proclaimed in *On War* that "the grand objective of all military action is to overthrow the enemy – which means destroying his armed forces … battle is the one and only means that warfare can employ."[61] Until now, a theory

[58] Pape, *Bombing to Win*, 210.

[59] Thomas Hughes, *Overlord: General Pete Quesada and the Triumph of Tactical Air Power in World War II* (New York: Free Press, 1995), 93; Samuel Morison, *Sicily–Salerno–Anzio January 1943–June 1944, Volume IX of History of United States Naval Operations in World War II* (Edison, NJ: Castle Books, 2001), 38.

[60] Thomas Cutler, *Brown Water, Black Berets* (Annapolis, MD: Naval Institute Press, 1988).

[61] Clausewitz, *On War*, 577.

explaining how air power works in practice has been missing. To date, tactical air doctrine has focused instead on the organization, coordination, command and control, and supporting–supported command relationships rather than explaining why, how, and when air forces should attack armies. This book introduced tactical air power (TAP) theory to address these questions.

Appendix B Modern US Air Wars after Vietnam

This appendix provides overviews of the ten modern US air wars after Vietnam. Also included is the Afghanistan war of 2001. However, it is not counted as a modern air campaign because the Taliban did not have an integrated air defense system (IADS) to contest US air superiority. Still, the principles of tactical air power (TAP) theory apply in the Afghanistan case. These summaries provide the underlying justification for coding the nine operational and environmental factors from Table 8.3.

Desert Storm: 1991

The end of the Cold War provided a surplus of forces to respond when on August 2, 1990 Iraqi President Saddam Hussein ordered his Republican Army to invade Kuwait.[1] Six months later, on January 17, a US-led coalition of thirty-nine nations commenced a thirty-four-day-and-night air campaign. Desert Storm aimed to sever Iraqi command and control, destroy weapons of mass destruction (WMD), gain air superiority, and attrit Iraqi ground forces in preparation for a ground invasion to liberate Kuwait.[2]

A swift strategic bombing campaign named Instant Thunder, to contrast with the gradual escalation of Rolling Thunder, featured F-117 stealth bombers with high-tech sensors and precision-guided weaponry.[3] Their nighttime raids eliminated the highest priority targets in and around Baghdad, but after the dust settled, Saddam Hussein remained in power and in control of his military and population.[4] Evidence of his command over Iraqi forces can be found in four instances. First, two

[1] Thomas Keaney and Eliot Cohen, *Gulf War Air Power Survey Summary Report* (*GWAPS Summary*) (Washington, DC: US Government Printing Office, 1993), 29.

[2] Keaney and Cohen, *GWAPS Summary*, 2, 27, 50.

[3] Keaney and Cohen, *GWAPS Summary*, 36.

[4] Keaney and Cohen, *GWAPS Summary*, 69.

weeks after the start of the air war, he traveled to Basra to meet with his commanders. In a failed effort to jump-start the ground war, he ordered two mechanized divisions to cross the Kuwaiti border near the Saudi coastal town of Al Khafji.[5] Second, throughout the war, Saddam approved the daily targeting of Scud surface-to-surface missiles launched toward Israel and Saudi Arabia. Third, on February 26, as the coalition ground force breached Iraqi defenses, Saddam soon thereafter approved the general order for Iraqi troops to withdraw from Kuwait.[6] Finally, after the war he employed what remained of his Republican Guard to crush Shia and Kurdish uprisings. The inability of the US strategic bombing campaign to either decapitate Saddam's regime or to sever his command and control was obscured, however, by the operational acumen exhibited by the captivating videos demonstrating the technological marvel of precision weaponry.[7]

As with strategic bombing, US efforts at air interdiction also proved ineffective.[8] Airstrikes destroyed railways and bridges between Baghdad and Basra, but the Iraqis diverted traffic, utilized ferries, and built temporary bridges. Iraqi forces also had five months to stockpile supplies in the Kuwaiti Theater of Operation (KTO).[9] Though air interdiction reduced Iraqi transit capacity from 200,000 to 20,000 tons per day, fighting from static defenses, the Iraqi Army required only 10,000–15,000 tons.[10] The coalition's air commander, US Air Force (USAF) Lieutenant General Chuck Horner, summed up the challenges of air interdiction:

> Anybody that has a campaign against transportation [had] better beware! It looks deceivingly easy. It is a tough nut to crack. [The Iraqis] were very ingenious and industrious in repairing them [bridges] or bypassing them ... I have never seen so many pontoon bridges. [When] canals near Basra [were bombed], they just filled them in and drove across the dirt.[11]

[5] Only one battalion of Iraqi troops eventually made it to Al Khafji. Behind them, US airstrikes halted the follow-on column of armor short of the border. Keaney and Cohen, *GWAPS Summary*, 19; Thomas Keaney and Eliot Cohen, *Gulf War Air Power Survey Operations Report* (*Volume II*) (Washington, DC: US Government Printing Office, 1993), 273–275.

[6] Keaney and Cohen, *GWAPS Operations Volume II*, 307.

[7] Keaney and Cohen, *GWAPS Summary*, 92; Phil Haun, *Coercion, Survival, and War: Why Weak States Resist the United States* (Palo Alto, CA: Stanford University Press, 2015), 60–62.

[8] Keaney and Cohen, *GWAPS Summary*, 99.

[9] At the start of the war, the Iraqi Army had deployed an estimated 300,000 tons of ammunition, 30 million barrels of POL, and thirty days of food. Keaney and Cohen, *GWAPS Operations Volume II*, 173–184, 194.

[10] Keaney and Cohen, *GWAPS Operations Volume II*, 192.

[11] Keaney and Cohen, *GWAPS Summary*, 95.

Though the surgical, high-tech strategic bombing missions received press coverage, most airstrikes directly targeted the Iraqi Army in the KTO. The highest density of bombs fell on the regular Iraqi infantry divisions deployed along the Kuwaiti–Saudi border.[12] By the commencement of the ground invasion, 25–30 percent of the Iraqi Army had been attrited. Airstrikes destroyed approximately 10 percent of Iraqi armor and artillery, while the remainder resulted from desertions. Lacking food and water, demoralized soldiers abandoned their defensive positions as armed reconnaissance (recce) strikes disrupted the Iraqi fielded forces' supply distribution system.[13] When coalition ground forces breached the Kuwaiti border, none of the Iraqi frontline units mounted effective defenses. Instead, Iraqi soldiers surrendered by the thousands. Only one of the dozens of regular Iraqi divisions managed to mount a counterattack.[14]

Desertions did not weaken the Republican Guard divisions held in reserve along the Iraqi–Kuwait border.[15] Better trained, well-supplied, and loyal to Saddam Hussein, these troops also endured fewer airstrikes. The Republican Guard retained the ability to maneuver and concentrate, as demonstrated late on February 24 when the commander of the Tawakalna mechanized division received orders to form a blocking position in anticipation of the Iraqi withdrawal from Kuwait. Overnight, three mechanized brigades maneuvered over fifty kilometers to the west to face the US Army 7th Corps, where US armor quickly destroyed the Iraqis in what would be known as the Battle of 73 Eastings.[16]

US air power made its most significant contribution in Desert Storm by shaping the battlefield, eroding Iraqi strength and morale, and deterring most enemy forces from maneuvering from their dispersed static defensive positions. By contrast, air power played only a minor role during the 100-hour ground battle. Bad weather and poor visibility; the limited nighttime capability of tactical aircraft (tacair); the speed of the coalition ground force advance; the lack of visible terrain features to

[12] Keaney and Cohen, *GWAPS Operations Volume II*, 148.

[13] Keaney and Cohen, *GWAPS Summary*, 97, 107.

[14] The "Reveille Attack" against the right flank of the US Marine 2nd Division occurred in the early morning of February 25, which the Marines quickly neutralized. At daybreak the Marines Corps dispatched thirty-five Iraqi tanks. Frank Schubert and Theresa Kraus, eds., *The Whirlwind War: The United States Army in Operations Desert Shield and Desert Storm* (Washington, DC: Center for Military History United States Army, 1995), 187.

[15] Keaney and Cohen, *GWAPS Summary*, 10.

[16] Robert Scales, *Certain Victory: The US Army in the Gulf War* (Washington, DC: Office of the Chief of Staff US Army, 1993), 233–235; Schubert and Kraus, *The Whirlwind War*, 189, 192; Keaney and Cohen, *GWAPS Summary*, 116.

coordinate the fire support coordination line (FSCL); and several fratricide incidents combined to limit airstrikes in the KTO during the invasion.[17] As important, the coalition ground forces' superior combat power meant soldiers needed little close air support (CAS) as they chewed through the dispersed and static Iraqi defenses. As the ground war continued, coalition air forces attempted to cut off the hasty Iraqi retreat from Kuwait. However, anticipation over public and international outcry from images of 1,000 destroyed and abandoned vehicles strewn along the "highway of death" led US leaders to order a ceasefire prematurely and unilaterally before the Army's left hook had blocked the Iraqi exit route.[18]

As anticipated by TAP theory, during Desert Storm, the Iraqi Army dispersed and dug into the desert sands in reaction to the lethal air threat.[19] Al Khafji, the Reveille Attack, and the Battle of 73 Eastings proved exceptions. Most Iraqi units remained dispersed in static positions for the duration of the war until they either surrendered or retreated. As a result, coalition ground forces met little resistance and suffered far fewer casualties than expected.[20] Air interdiction and strategic bombing did demonstrate proficiency, with airmen precisely striking their targets with surgical skill. Still, these independent and indirect air attacks failed to achieve their military and political objectives. By contrast, the direct attack of Iraqi fielded forces before the ground invasion, while not independently decisive, played a primary role by shaping the battlefield for the successful liberation of Kuwait and the attrition of two-thirds of the Iraqi military.

Coding of Operational and Environmental Factors for Desert Storm

Instant Thunder and the air interdiction campaign are the only modern air operations where most operational and environmental factors favored air power, yet both failed. US air forces quickly seized air superiority over Kuwait and southern Iraq. The Iraqi IADS proved no match for US air-to-air interceptors and suppression of enemy air defense (SEAD) aircraft.[21] Iraqi fighters fled to Iran, and surface-to-air missile (SAM)

[17] Keaney and Cohen, *GWAPS Summary*, 24, 110–111.
[18] Keaney and Cohen, *GWAPS Summary*, 113.
[19] Keaney and Cohen, *GWAPS Summary*, 116, 137, 181; Keaney and Cohen, *GWAPS Operations Volume II*, 320.
[20] Keaney and Cohen, *GWAPS Summary*, 156.
[21] John Deur, *Wall of Eagles: Aerial Engagements and Victories in Operation Desert Storm* (Cleveland, OH: Intercept Publications, 1994).

operators learned to leave their radars on standby.[22] Iraqi SAMs downed eight coalition aircraft on the first three days of the air war but only five thereafter.[23] By contrast, coalition air losses to anti-aircraft artillery (AAA) were initially high for the first three days until Lieutenant General Chuck Horner, the theater air commander, imposed restrictions against flying at low altitude. This order limited the lethality of AAA but significantly reduced the effectiveness of US tacair tasked against Iraqi fielded forces.

As for air-to-ground capabilities, US air forces designed their tacair and trained aircrews to conduct low-altitude CAS and armed recce, which the USAF called battlefield air interdiction (BAI). These missions were designed to be flown under the low cloud ceilings of central Europe. From medium altitude, most tacair, without either targeting pods or precision weapons, proved ineffective in finding and striking Iraqi fielded forces.[24] However, there were exceptions as A-10 Warthogs employed thousands of precision-guided Maverick air-to-surface missiles, and F-111F and F-15E aircrew armed with infrared targeting pods and laser-guided bombs developed "tank-plinking" tactics against Iraqi armor.[25] B-52s also contributed to the effort, carpet bombing Iraqi divisions. However, unlike Arc Light missions over Vietnam, the USAF no longer had the Combat Skyspot surface-to-air radar units to control more precise strikes. Coalition air forces never reached the 50 percent attrition of Iraqi armor arbitrarily set by General Norman Schwarzkopf, the overall coalition military commander. He eventually became convinced, however, that coalition air power had sufficiently eroded Iraqi combat power to order the ground invasion.[26]

As for friendly and enemy ground force capabilities, the American and NATO armies had superior equipment, particularly advanced optical and infrared sights for their guns; these allowed them to outrange the Iraqi tanks, which proved no match. Even with their technological advantage and the joint combined arms doctrine of AirLand Battle, US air and ground force coordination proved deficient. Not allocating any BAI missions in the air tasking order (ATO) meant minimal interaction between air and ground leaders, resulting in significant tension and

[22] Keaney and Cohen, *GWAPS Summary*, 12–13.
[23] Keaney and Cohen, *GWAPS Operations Volume II*, 141; Keaney and Cohen, *GWAPS Summary*, 58–60; Robert Pape, *Bombing to Win* (Ithaca, NY: Cornell University Press, 1996), 228.
[24] Keaney and Cohen, *GWAPS Summary*, 16, 62.
[25] Keaney and Cohen, *GWAPS Summary*, 22; Keaney and Cohen, *GWAPS Operations Volume II*, 35; Pape, *Bombing to Win*, 244.
[26] Keaney and Cohen, *GWAPS Summary*, 15, 49.

friction once the ground campaign commenced.[27] Evidence of the lack of air and ground coordination includes the internal battle over where to set the FSCL. Ground commanders pushed the de-confliction line far out in advance for their Apache and ATACMS (Army TACtical Missile System) strikes, which restricted where uncontrolled airstrikes could continue.[28] The overmatch by coalition ground forces and the speed at which the war ended concealed weaknesses in the US tactical air control system and army air–ground system (TACS/AAGS).[29]

As for the five environmental factors, the dry climate of the Middle East was more conducive for air operations than the weather of either western Europe or Southeast Asia. Still, Kuwait's January and February poor weather conditions limited airstrikes at crucial times, including the first ten days of the air war and during the ground invasion.[30] The decision to fly at medium altitude amplified the impact of clouds that covered the skies 40 percent of the time. While weather would have only affected low-altitude operations 1–2 percent of the time, it negatively affected a third of medium-altitude missions.[31] Likewise, the Iraqis set fire to the Kuwaiti oil fields, producing smoke that limited visibility, further hampering CAS flown near friendly troops.[32]

Nighttime conditions also impacted airstrikes as most tacair had limited low light capability. The majority of aircrews did not yet have the night-vision goggles (NVGs) and infrared devices that allowed the US Army and Marines to fight through the night. AC-130s had additional night capability, but the threat level was too high in the KTO, as evidenced by the loss of an AC-130 in late January during the battle of Al Khafji.

As for geography and terrain, Kuwait's flat, open desert did not present line-of-sight problems, although the featureless landscape made target location on maps more challenging.[33] For air interdiction, the Iraqi roadways and rail lines crossing the Euphrates and Tigris rivers created choke points at key bridges, but overall the hard-packed soil allowed for the quick construction of bypasses.[34]

27 Keaney and Cohen, *GWAPS Summary*, 152–153; Thomas Keaney and Eliot Cohen, *Gulf War Air Power Survey Command and Control* (*Volume I*) (Washington, DC: US Government Printing Office, 1993), 314–315.
28 Keaney and Cohen, *GWAPS Summary*, 156–157.
29 Scales, *Certain Victory*, 174–175, 188.
30 Keaney and Cohen, *GWAPS Summary*, 171.
31 Keaney and Cohen, *GWAPS Operations Volume II*, 87, 260.
32 Keaney and Cohen, *GWAPS Summary*, 19; Keaney and Cohen, *GWAPS Operations Volume II*, 301.
33 Keaney and Cohen, *GWAPS Summary*, 170.
34 Keaney and Cohen, *GWAPS Summary*, 170.

As for civilians, they mainly affected the strategic bombing campaign, as evidenced by the collateral damage of the Al Firdos bunker bombing in mid-February that killed over 200 civilians. After this attack, US restrictions against airstrikes near Baghdad continued until the ground war commenced. By contrast, civilians had little impact on attacking Iraqi forces deployed in the desert.[35] Finally, while Baghdad provided concealment for Iraqi leadership, the desert did not offer as much protection for its armies. Even so, soldiers sought cover and concealment from their static defenses by digging berms, utilizing camouflage, and deploying decoys.

Iraq: 1991–1998

After the Cold War, the United States relied upon air power as the military instrument of choice in multiple crises in the Middle East and Balkans.[36] In March 1991, in the immediate aftermath of Desert Storm, Saddam Hussein employed his Republican Guard to quell internal uprisings. In response, the United States kept economic sanctions in place and imposed a southern no-fly zone and a northern safe area. While the southern restrictions applied only to Iraqi aircraft, the northern safe area also dictated no deployment of Iraqi ground forces.[37] In June 1993, the United States launched cruise missiles to destroy the Iraqi Intelligence Services headquarters in retaliation for a failed Iraqi plot in April to assassinate former President George H. W. Bush when he visited Kuwait.[38] Three years of sanctions finally compelled Saddam to cooperate with UN inspectors over its remaining WMD. Iraqi cooperation did not, however, result in the lifting of sanctions. By October 1994, with the depletion of Iraqi foreign reserves to purchase imports, a frustrated Saddam ordered elements of his Republican Guard to deploy again to the Kuwaiti border.[39] He withdrew the troops soon after the United

[35] Keaney and Cohen, *GWAPS Summary*, 179.

[36] For an overview of these crises, see Phil Haun, Colin Jackson, and Tim Schultz, eds., *Air Power in the Age of Primacy: Air Warfare since the Cold War* (Cambridge: Cambridge University Press, 2021).

[37] R. W. Apple, "U.S. Says Iraqi Generals Agree to Demands 'On All Matters'" *New York Times*, March 4, 1991; Michael Gordon and Bernard Trainor, *The Generals' War* (Boston, MA: Little Brown and Company, 1995), 444–447.

[38] David Von Drehle and R. Jeffrey Smith, "U.S. Strikes Iraq for Plot to Kill Bush" *Washington Post*, June 27, 1993, A1.

[39] Kenneth Bacon, "DoD News Briefing: Mr. Kenneth H. Bacon, ATSD PA," October 28, 1994; Phil Haun, "Air Power, Sanctions, and Containment: When Foreign Policy Objectives Collide" in Kelly Greenhill and Peter Krause, eds., *Coercion: The Power to Hurt in International Politics* (Oxford: Oxford University Press, 2018), 87–90.

States announced the deployment of additional combat aircraft, troops, and ships into the region.

A turning point in this long-term conflict occurred in May 1996 when Saddam finally agreed to the UN Security Council Oil-for-Food program, which began to provide relief from the sanctions. In September, Iraq tested the northern safe area by sending troops to Irbil to intervene in a Kurdish dispute. With a limited strike capability in northern Iraq, the United States could only respond with air and cruise missile strikes against Iraqi air defense systems in the southern no-fly zone. Saddam continued to test the resolve of the United States with "cheat and retreat" tactics by flying aircraft into the no-fly zone and harassing UN weapons inspectors. In October 1998, an exasperated Congress passed the Iraqi Liberation Act, signed into law by President Bill Clinton, which made Iraqi regime change official US foreign policy. In December, UN inspectors left Iraq for good. Immediately after their departure, the United States launched Desert Fox, with four days and nights of airstrikes to punish Iraqi intransigence and attrit its military and intelligence capabilities. Iraq absorbed the strikes, resulting in a stalemate that lasted four more years.

TAP theory partially explains air power's success in containing the Iraqi military from 1991 to 1998. Air power alone, however, could not restrain Iraqi ground forces in the southern no-fly zones and northern safe areas when Saddam decided to lash out. Nor did the combination of sanctions and the threat of airstrikes prevent Iraq from expelling UN inspectors. While overall successful in constraining Iraq, over time, frustration led US leaders to expand their political objectives from containment to regime change. Overall, air power and sanctions kept Iraqi forces in check, but they could not remove Saddam Hussein from power.[40]

Coding Operational and Environmental Factors Iraq: 1991–1998

Five of the nine factors favored air power. Of the four operational factors only air superiority favored US air forces. Air-to-ground capability against the Iraqi ground forces proved to be limited by the inability, without friendly troops on the ground, to target Iraqi fielded forces. Instead, the United States attacked what it could find, which proved to be Iraqi air defense systems in Desert Strike and military installations in

[40] Haun, "Airpower, Economic Sanctions, Coercion and Containment."

Desert Fox.[41] The only friendly ground force capability in Iraq was a limited number of peacekeeping troops enforcing the northern safe area, but these forces could not engage Iraqi forces or coordinate airstrikes. Finally, Iraqi ground forces had the freedom to maneuver, as demonstrated in 1993 when they deployed to the Kuwaiti border and again in 1996 when they deployed to Irbil.

As for environmental factors, all but concealment and cover favored the employment of air power. The desert climate, improved night capability by tacair utilizing NVGs and infrared sensing targeting pods, flat open terrain, and limited collateral damage concerns outside Baghdad favored US air operations.

Bosnia: 1995

While the conflict with Iraq continued, a series of crises, fomented by the breakup of Yugoslavia, erupted in the Balkans when Slovenia and Croatia declared independence in June 1991. While Slovenia's divorce was relatively peaceful, six months of fighting in Croatia led to UN Security Council intervention and the deployment of 15,000 peacekeepers.[42] The following year violence migrated to the southeast when Bosnian Serbs formed the Republika Srpska in anticipation of the Bosnian Croatians and Muslims announcing their independence.

Three years of bitter fighting left tens of thousands dead, two million as refugees, and the term ethnic cleansing entered the humanitarian lexicon to describe the violence. Overall, with Serbian support, the Bosnian Serbs had the military advantage, reflected by their soon controlling 70 percent of Bosnian territory. In response to the continued humanitarian crisis, the United States finally took the lead in international negotiations. By August 1994, under pressure from economic sanctions, Serbian President Slobodan Milosevic withheld his support from the Bosnian Serbs. By early 1995, the United States had also orchestrated an agreement to stop the infighting between Croats and Muslims, who formed the Bosnian Federation. In May, the ceasefire in neighboring Croatia ended as a Croatian offensive soon occupied the western half of Slavonia (the eastern region of Croatia). A Bosnian ceasefire brokered over the previous winter also buckled with the arrival of the summer fighting season. In July, Bosnian Serb forces massacred 7,000 Muslim men at Srebrenica in a supposed UN safe area. This event precipitated a

[41] David Knights, *Cradle of Conflict: Iraq and the Birth of Modern U.S. Military Power* (Annapolis, MD: Naval Institute Press, 2005), 200–210.

[42] Haun, *Coercion, Survival, and War*, 91–93.

more forceful US posture. The military balance shifted against the Bosnian Serbs, who, without the support of Milosevic, confronted a Bosnian Federation ground offensive supported indirectly by a US-led NATO air campaign targeting Bosnian Serb fielded forces. Most airstrikes were by Americans employing precision, laser-guided attacks to limit civilian casualties. On August 4, 1995, another Croatian offensive into eastern Slavonia generated 200,000 Croatian Serb refugees, many migrating into the Republika Srpska. The Croatian offensive along the northern Bosnia border loosened the Bosnian Serb stranglehold over Bihac, a western UN safe area. The previously encircled Bosnian Muslim forces joined the Croats in attacking the Bosnian Serb's western flank.

Meanwhile, NATO airstrikes, which commenced on August 30, pressured Bosnian Serb forces east of Sarajevo. As Federation forces moved toward the Bosnian Serb capital of Banja Luka, the two desperate and bickering Republika Srpska leaders, President Radovan Karadzic and General Ratko Mladic, traveled to Belgrade where they relinquished negotiating power to Milosevic. On September 15, NATO paused strikes after Milosevic, Karadzic, and Mladic agreed to a 51/49 partition of Bosnia.[43] However, the ground war continued until early October, halting only after the Federation controlled half of Bosnia. In November, negotiations at Dayton codified this new ground reality.

While US air power had some success targeting Bosnian Serb forces, it did not prevent the Serbs from maneuvering brigade-sized combat units across Bosnia.[44] Even while strategic bombing advocates trumpeted the success of air power alone, the military victory was the combination of NATO air power and the Federation ground offensive, which delivered a lasting peace to a fractured Bosnia.[45]

Coding of Operational and Environmental Factors for Bosnia

Of the nine factors, five favored air power. Three of the four operational factors privileged NATO air forces. NATO enjoyed air superiority over Bosnia and an air-to-ground capability that dropped two-thirds of its ordnance by precision delivery. While air–ground coordination between

[43] Under the agreement, 51 percent went to the Croat-Muslim Federation and 49 percent to the Republika Srpska.

[44] Central Intelligence Agency, *Balkan Battlegrounds: A Military History of the Yugoslav Conflict, 1990–1995 Volume I* (Washington, DC: Office of Russian and European Analysis, 2002), 395.

[45] Benjamin Lambeth, *The Transformation of American Air Power* (Ithaca, NY: Cornell University Press, 2000), 177.

NATO and Federation ground forces was lacking, the Federation could threaten the Bosnian Serb western flank. Even though they could not reposition large numbers of their mechanized forces to the west, the Bosnian Serbs did demonstrate the ability to survive and operate locally under the threat of NATO airstrikes.

Only two of the five environmental factors favored air power. Predominantly clear skies marked the Balkan summer, much-improved weather for air operations. However, at night NATO air forces had limited ability as most aircrew did not yet fly with NVGs and those with infrared sensing targeting pods had trouble identifying Bosnian Serb forces. Geography also favored air power. Though the rugged terrain made target identification challenging, the mountains created choke points for concentrating mechanized forces. In addition, the narrow Brcko corridor, which connected eastern and western Republika Srpska, made it more difficult for Mladic to reposition his troops. Concern over civilian casualties favored the Bosnian Serbs as NATO air forces, micro-managed by USAF Lieutenant General Michael Ryan, severely restricted strikes to avoid collateral damage that might split a fragile NATO effort. Finally, the forested Balkans provided sufficient concealment for the dispersed and camouflaged Bosnian Serb forces to avoid detection from above.[46]

Kosovo: 1999

While the Dayton Accords brought peace to Bosnia, ethnic tensions remained in the southern Serbian province of Kosovo. In early 1998, an ethnically Muslim Kosovar Albanian rebel group known as the Kosovo Liberation Army (KLA) gained popularity. By May, the KLA controlled 40 percent of the countryside. Serbian forces responded in July by driving hundreds of thousands from their homes. The United States reacted to this refugee crisis by dispatching to Belgrade Richard Holbrooke, the diplomat who had negotiated the Dayton Accords. Holbrooke threatened NATO airstrikes in October to convince Milosevic to withdraw his forces. The Holbrooke agreement allowed refugees to return to their homes before winter, but the peace proved short-lived as the KLA emerged from the shadows to take over the road checkpoints from the departing Serbian soldiers. Recognizing that the agreement abrogated territorial control over Kosovo, Milosevic reversed and ordered his troops back to their posts. In January 1999, Serb forces

[46] Haun, *Coercion, Survival, and War*, 88–106; Thomas Hughes, "Deliberate Force: Ambivalent Success" in Haun et al., eds., *Air Power in the Age of Primacy*, 54–75.

retaliated against the KLA slaying of three police officers by killing forty-five Kosovar Albanians in the village of Račak. The Račak massacre triggered international condemnation and a call for negotiations which began in February at Rambouillet, France. Milosevic would not make further concessions, however, and by mid-March the talks stalled. To coerce Milosevic, on March 24 NATO air forces, the majority of which were American tacair, commenced Operation Allied Force (OAF).[47]

Imagined initially as only three nights of airstrikes, OAF targeted fifty, primarily military, Serbian fixed positions. When Milosevic remained unmoved, OAF extended to an open-ended air campaign. Serbian forces reacted to the NATO bombings with an ethnic cleansing operation, expelling hundreds of thousands from their homes in winter. In response, NATO expanded its targeting to include Serbian fielded forces. Poor weather, rugged terrain, medium-altitude flight restrictions, a lack of a capable, friendly ground force, and an adept Serbian Army combined to negate the direct attack of fielded forces.[48]

Unlike other successful modern US air wars, instead of direct attack, airstrikes against Serbian infrastructure proved decisive. The combination of strategic bombing and economic sanctions strained the war-torn Serbian economy. As spring turned to summer, domestic political backing for Milosevic eroded. The tipping point came when Russia withdrew its support. Diplomatic pressure was key to Milosevic conceding when he did. Still, Russian intervention would have meant little without the continuous threat of NATO airstrikes, which held the Serbian economy hostage.[49]

Kosovo is unique in the annals of modern US air warfare as it is the sole case where strategic bombing proved effective when direct attack did not. Six of nine operational and environmental factors favored the strategic bombing of Serbia compared to only three of nine for the direct attack of Serbian forces. In the only other successful strategic bombing campaign, Linebacker II, the bombing of Hanoi did convince the North Vietnamese to return to Paris. Still, it was only to accept the peace deal they had already agreed in October 1972 following the NVA defeat in the Easter Offensive. In the case of Kosovo, however, without deploying a capable, friendly ground force, the direct attack of fielded forces failed. Instead, the impact of strategic bombing on the Serbian economy and the

[47] Haun, *Coercion, Survival, and War*, 112–119.

[48] Daniel Lake, "The Limits of Coercive Airpower: NATO's 'Victory' in Kosovo Revisited" *International Security* 34:1 (Summer 2009), 83–112; Haun, *Coercion, Survival, and War*, 120–121.

[49] Haun, *Coercion, Survival, and War*, 121–126.

anticipated political ramifications for Milosevic was what most likely caused him to concede Kosovo.[50]

Coding Operational and Environmental Factors for Kosovo

As for the four operational factors, air superiority was obtained quickly and maintained by NATO forces with a combination of US fighters patrolling the skies and stealth bombers attacking Serbian airfields. In addition, Serbian SAMs chose survival over lethality. They did not actively engage enemy aircraft unless there was no SEAD support on station, as happened with the downing of an F-117 outside Belgrade.[51]

As for air-to-ground capability, US air forces were well prepared for both strategic bombing and direct attack missions. By contrast, for a friendly ground force, the KLA proved incapable of either threatening Serbian forces or coordinating airstrikes. In addition, relatively well-trained Serbian troops could operate under the threat of airstrikes; without a ground threat, they traded their tanks for automobiles to continue their ethnic cleansing operations.

As for the five environmental factors, weather played havoc on operations over Kosovo until May, when the clouds cleared. By contrast, US air forces began to rely upon a new platform, the B-2 stealth bomber with its GPS-guided bombs, allowing all-weather bombing against fixed targets. Nighttime improved air operations over Serbia as it protected F-117s and B-2s. By contrast, Serb forces could mask their operations in Kosovo at night as US tacair did not yet have the next generation of advanced infrared sensors that could distinguish military from civilian vehicles. Geography and terrain had little impact on air operations near Belgrade, but the rugged terrain of Kosovo made target identification difficult, requiring airborne forward air controllers (AFACs) to circle overhead. Civilian populations had little impact on air operations in Kosovo but did affect strategic bombing in Belgrade, with the bombing of the Chinese Embassy, which killed three Chinese nationals, setting back negotiations by two weeks. Finally, for strategic bombing, there was little cover or concealment provided for Serbian infrastructure targets. In

[50] There is still disagreement as to what exactly caused Milosevic to concede when he did. For examples see contrary assessments by two RAND reports: Stephen Hosmer, *The Kosovo Conflict: Why Milosevic Decided to Settle When He Did* (Santa Monica, CA: RAND Corporation, 2001); and Benjamin Lambeth, *NATO's Air War for Kosovo: Strategic and Operational Assessment* (Santa Monica, CA: RAND Corporation, 2001).

[51] Phil Haun, "The First Night CSAR" in Christopher Haave and Phil Haun, eds., *A-10s over Kosovo* (Maxwell AFB, AL: Air University Press, 2003).

Kosovo, by contrast, the Serbian forces utilized buildings, camouflage, forests, and decoys to hide and distract NATO airstrikes.

Afghanistan: 2001

The war in Afghanistan, the United States' response to Al Qaeda's September 11 attacks on the World Trade Center and Pentagon, does not qualify as a modern air war as defined in this book. The Taliban did not field an IADS as US air forces assumed air superiority in the first hour of the war.[52] Without fighting for air superiority, the United States could immediately apply air power as part of a combined arms operation with the Northern Alliance to defeat the Taliban. Strategic bombing and air interdiction missions did not topple the Taliban, decapitate their leadership, or paralyze their command and control. Instead, the direct targeting of the Taliban's fielded forces by CAS proved decisive. Airstrikes coordinated by special forces joint tactical air controllers (JTACs) embedded in the Northern Alliance shifted the balance of military power. The unique, combined arms approach integrated precision-guided strikes and horse-mounted cavalry charges to overrun Taliban positions. The result was a speedy advance to take Kabul.[53]

In Afghanistan, conventional warfighting was brief, and the subsequent decades-long conflict featured counterinsurgency and counterterrorism operations. Counterinsurgency meant dispersing ground forces across large swathes of territory. Under such conditions, soldiers often did not have sufficient organic fire support. Allied armies depended on air power, from both manned and unmanned systems, to provide intelligence surveillance and reconnaissance (ISR), command and control, resupply, combat search and rescue, emergency evacuation, and emergency CAS for troops in contact situations. The mere presence of an A-10 overhead a friendly convoy was usually sufficient to deter an enemy attack.[54]

In addition to counterinsurgencies, special operations forces and intelligence agencies conducted counterterrorism operations in Afghanistan,

[52] Nicholas Blanchette, "Operation Enduring Freedom" in Haun et al., eds., *Air Power in the Age of Primacy*, 107.

[53] An excellent air analyses of Operation Enduring Freedom is in Anthony Schinella's *Bombs without Boots: The Limits of Airpower* (Washington, DC: Brookings Institute Press, 2019), 99–161.

[54] The author commanded an A-10 squadron deployed to Afghanistan from March to October 2004. During that period, the squadron flew hundreds of missions supporting US Army convoys, not one of which was engaged directly by insurgents while A-10s were observable overhead. On the occasions when A-10s responded, the insurgents quickly dispersed.

Pakistan, and other areas of the Middle East and Africa. They relied on aircrews operating remotely piloted MQ-1 Predators and later MQ-9 Reapers to provide persistent ISR and precision strike capability. In addition, special operations aircraft such as AC-130s supported the Joint Special Operations Task Force in nightly raids to systematically uncover and weaken Al Qaeda's network.[55]

This book has focused on modern air wars where the enemy contests the air domain and the United States confronts conventional enemy armies. However, since September 11, 2001, most air operations have been dedicated to counterinsurgency and counterterrorism operations. In these cases, air power has been more effective by providing CAS and not by armed recce, interdiction, or strategic bombing.

Invasion of Iraq: 2003

After the invasion of Afghanistan, President George W. Bush turned his attention to Iraq and the removal of Saddam Hussein. In June 2002, nine months before a ground invasion, US air forces commenced a clandestine air superiority campaign to roll back Iraqi air defenses.[56] By adjusting the rules of engagement for self-defense, aircrew responded systematically when Iraqi radars illuminated their fighters. They attacked not just those specific sites but the entire Iraqi IADS. By the beginning of the ground invasion in March 2003, the United States had long achieved air superiority. In anticipation of an air-only campaign, Saddam had ordered his armies to disperse rather than concentrate to defend strategic chokepoints.[57] As a result, US and allied ground forces met little resistance in an offensive that quickly turned into a race to Baghdad. By deterring the Iraqi Army from massing and maneuvering, air power had made its most significant contribution to the invasion's success before the first pair of American boots had touched Iraqi soil.

The threat of direct attack deterred Iraqi forces from concentrating and maneuvering as expected by TAP theory, while a strategic bombing

[55] See Timothy Schultz, "Remote Warfare: A New Architecture of Air Power" and Colin Jackson "Retrospect and Prospect" in Haun et al., eds., *Airpower in the Age of Primacy.*

[56] Benjamin Lambeth, *The Unseen War: Allied Air Power and the Takedown of Saddam Hussein* (Annapolis, MD: Naval Institute Press, 2013), 61–70.

[57] Joel Rayburn and Frank Sobchak, eds., *The U.S. Army in the Iraq War Volume I: Invasion, Insurgency, and Civil War 2003–2006* (Carlisle, PA: US Army War College Press, 2019), 73.

campaign to remove Saddam Hussein failed.[58] No concerted effort at air interdiction was even made.

Coding Operational and Environmental Factors Iraq Invasion

Overall, six of nine factors favored directed attack compared to four of nine for strategic bombing. The United States achieved air superiority over Iraq. While strategic bombing and direct attack had capable air-to-ground weapons, strategic bombing lacked the intelligence required to target an individual leader. Saddam Hussein took measures to ensure his personal security. In addition, though eventually the United States would deploy a capable army, where armed recce and strategic bombing strikes took place there were no friendly ground forces to threaten Iraqi troops. As for enemy forces, the Iraqi Army was capable of dispersing against the air threat.

Environmental factors of weather, night, and terrain favored all air operations. At the same time, civilians, particularly those near Baghdad, and adequate urban concealment made it challenging for strategic bombing missions to identify and strike targets with minimal risk of collateral damage.

Libya: 2011

While the United States struggled with dual insurgencies in Afghanistan and Iraq, the Arab World was shaken in 2010 by political unrest in Tunisia. Protests spread to Libya, Egypt, Yemen, Syria, and Bahrain.[59] In February 2011, the heavy-handed suppression of demonstrations in Benghazi by Libyan forces loyal to Muammar Qaddafi resulted in a countrywide uprising, with a loose coalition of rebel groups forming the National Transition Council (NTC).[60] Qaddafi responded violently, sending his troops and mercenaries to suppress the rebels. This aggression led to the UN Security Council passing resolutions in late February

[58] David Martin, "Ex-CIA officer on the strike that could have averted the Iraq War" *CBS News*, March 19, 2013, www.cbsnews.com/news/ex-cia-officer-on-the-strike-that-could-have-averted-iraq-war/.

[59] Lin Noueihed, "Peddler's Martyrdom Launched Tunisia's Revolution" *Reuters*, January 19, 2011, www.reuters.com/article/uk-tunisia-protests-bouaziziidUKTRE70I7TV20110119?edition-redirect=uk.

[60] Paul Salem and Amanda Kalec, "Libya's Troubled Transition" *The Carnegie Papers* (Washington, DC: Carnegie Endowment for International Peace, 2012), https://carnegieendowment.org/files/libya_transition.pdf, 3.

and March imposing an arms embargo, freezing Libyan assets, and establishing a no-fly zone over Libya.[61]

A multilateral force led by the United States, United Kingdom, and France commenced Operation Odyssey Dawn by striking Libya's IADS to achieve air superiority. However, the no-fly zone quickly expanded to strikes against Qaddafi's mobile ground forces.[62] By the end of March, the United States handed command and control over to NATO in Operation Unified Protector. Allied air forces initially had difficulty due to poor weather and a lack of actionable intelligence. In addition, they were required to cover a vast desert the size of Alaska. Limited NATO sortie availability, the inability to coordinate with rebel forces, and Qaddafi's forces adapting to blend in with civilians all contributed to NATO aircrew frustration.[63] Over time, however, the military balance slowly shifted as NATO air forces overhead inhibited the maneuvering of Libyan ground units. This change, along with the internal fracturing of Qaddafi's support along tribal lines, allowed the rebels to expand their territorial control. Qaddafi's forces, which stood at 76,000 before the war, had been reduced to 15,000 by June.[64] Over the summer, rebels, indirectly supported by NATO air forces, continued to make gains against the loyalists. NTC forces reached Tripoli in late August; after a week of street fighting, Qaddafi fled the capital to his hometown of Sirte. The struggle for Sirte continued until October 20, when a remotely piloted Predator identified a vehicle convoy. The Predator, joined by a pair of French Rafale fighters, attacked the convoy, and rebels later discovered and summarily executed Qaddafi.

TAP theory explains the outcome of Libya as air power deterred Qaddafi's forces from being able to concentrate and maneuver against the outnumbered, poorly organized, and weakly armed rebels.

Coding Operational and Environmental Factors for Libya

Two-thirds of the operational and environmental factors favored air power, with only a weak friendly ground force, the vastness of Libya's desert terrain, and concern over civilian casualties inhibiting air power in targeting enemy ground forces.

[61] On February 26, 2011, UNSC Resolution 1970 imposed an arms embargo, restricted travel, and froze assets. See www.un.org/securitycouncil/s/res/1970-%282011%29. On March 17, 2011 UNSC Resolution 1973 further established a no-fly zone in Libya to protect civilians: https://undocs.org/en/S/RES/1973%20(2011).

[62] Jahara Matisak, "Libya 2011: Hollow Victory in Low-Cost Air War" in Haun et al., eds., *Air Power in the Age of Primacy*, 182, 190.

[63] Matisak, "Libya 2011," 184. [64] Matisak, "Libya 2011," 184–186.

Index

1st Air Cavalry Division (USA), 67, 69, 73, 75
1st Infantry Division (USA), 67, 75

22nd Division (ARVN), 180
23rd Division (ARVN), 180, 181
25th Infantry Division (USA), 75
26th Marine Regiment (USMC), 95, 101

304th Division (NVA), 94, 98, 168
320th Division (NVA), 94, 179
324th Division (NVA), 94
325th Division (NVA), 94
3rd Division (ARVN), 94, 168, 169, 170, 171, 172

559 Military Transportation Group (NVA), 113
5th Division (ARVN), 172, 175
5th Division (VC), 174

73 Eastings, Battle of, 272, 273
7th Air Force (USA), 116, 125, 128, 147, 154, 156
7th Corps (USA), 272
7th Division (NVA), 174

9th Division (VC), 177

A-1 Skyraider, 4, 38, 39, 46, 48, 100, 183
A-10 Warthog, 4, 26, 31, 48, 206, 216, 224, 237, 274, 283
A-4 Skyhawk, 38, 39, 41, 48, 64, 65, 71, 121, 204
A-6 Intruder, 65, 71, 72, 84, 85, 122
AA-2 Atoll, 61, 86
Abrams, Creighton, 111, 118, 123, 130, 134, 135, 156, 162, 166, 172, 175, 177, 183, 197, 204
AC-119 gunship, 123, 175
AC-130 Spectre, 122, 123, 124, 130, 131, 132, 143, 147, 152, 154, 155, 161, 167, 169, 175, 185, 192, 211, 215, 216, 223, 237, 275, 284
AC-47 gunship, 72, 106, 122
Acheson, Dean, 82
Afghanistan, 2, 3, 4, 26, 74, 206, 207, 213, 215, 216, 225, 237, 246, 247, 265, 270, 283, 284, 285
Agent Orange, 70, 122
AGM-158C, 245
AIM-7, 63, 152
AIM-9, 62, 153, 191
Air Corps Tactical School (ACTS), 256, 260, 261, 263, 267
air interdiction, 3, 4, 5, 6, 7, 9, 10, 13, 14, 24, 25, 27, 32, 34, 38, 43, 47, 51, 54, 56, 58, 66, 84, 107, 116, 128, 130, 137, 139, 141, 144, 148, 161, 163, 164, 167, 186, 187, 192, 193, 198, 199, 202, 205, 206, 212, 213, 216, 218, 221, 222, 223, 224, 225, 226, 227, 230, 231, 235, 244, 267, 268, 271, 273, 275, 283, 285
Air Liaison Officer, xiv, 11, 14, 21, 23, 27, 136, 137, 161, 171, 212, 230, 234, 250, 251, 253, 255
air mobility, 105
air power theory, 9, 12, 13, 252, 254, 265
air superiority, 1, 2, 3, 7, 9, 12, 14–16, 18, 20, 22–26, 30, 33, 52, 64, 66, 85, 96, 103, 105, 115, 130, 131, 141, 142, 146, 147, 150, 152, 154, 157, 160, 161, 167, 177, 202, 207–210, 213, 218, 222, 230, 231, 236, 238, 240, 243, 245, 249, 251, 253, 254, 260, 261, 262, 266, 270, 273, 277, 279, 282–286
air tasking order (ATO), 26, 116, 205, 274
airborne command and control center (ABCCC), 117, 123
airborne forward air controllers (AFAC), 5, 23, 147, 166, 206, 282
airborne warning and control system (AWACS), 209

air–ground operation system (AGOS), 24
AirLand Battle, 5, 26, 204, 205, 210, 242, 249, 274
AirSea Battle, 249
Al Firdos bunker, 224, 276
Al Khafji, 271, 273, 275
Al Qaeda, 265, 283, 284
ALQ-51, 65
An Khe Pass, 180
An Loc, 31, 164, 166–168, 172–178, 175, 176, 177, 178, 181, 182, 183, 184, 185, 186, 195, 196–199, 225
ANGLICO, 213
Annamite Mountain Range, 112, 140
anti-access/area denial (A2/AD), 243, 249
anti-aircraft artillery (AAA), 48, 49, 52, 64, 65, 87, 96, 115, 116, 118, 122, 124, 125, 131, 132, 143, 146, 147, 149, 152, 154, 155, 167, 168, 185, 188, 191, 192, 204, 208, 209, 215, 222, 239, 240, 261, 274
Apache, 275
APX-80 Combat Tree, 152, 191
Arc Light, 73, 84, 91, 98, 99, 101, 121, 131, 136, 147, 162, 167, 169, 176, 179, 181–184, 194, 215, 223, 274
armed recce (reconnaissance), 5, 24, 25, 26, 27, 38, 45, 46, 47, 48, 49, 51, 53, 54, 57, 58, 59, 75, 79, 84, 90, 91, 92, 100, 101, 167, 184, 186, 189, 199, 205, 206, 207, 208, 212, 222, 225, 226, 227, 230, 232, 235, 236, 272, 274, 284, 285
Army of the Republic of Vietnam (ARVN), 11, 51, 55, 67, 74, 75, 80, 81, 88, 91, 92, 95, 105, 109, 134–141, 144, 145–149, 157, 158, 160, 161, 164, 165, 166, 168–172, 174–182, 184, 186, 193, 194, 196, 197, 198, 199, 222, 224
Assault Breaker, 244, 245
AT-3 Sagger, 180
ATACMS (Army TACtical Missile System), 275
Attleboro, 75

B-52 Stratofortress, 2, 12, 43, 44, 51, 72, 73, 75, 79, 80, 84, 88, 90, 91, 96, 98–103, 114, 115, 120, 121, 125, 130, 131, 134, 136, 140–143, 147, 152, 155, 156, 161, 162, 166, 167, 169, 170, 174–185, 192, 194, 197, 200, 202, 215, 218, 223, 229, 274
B-57 Canberra, 38, 48, 49, 71, 72, 143
Baghdad, 1, 224, 264, 265, 270, 271, 276, 278, 284, 285
Balkans, 206, 276, 278, 280
Ban Karai mountain pass, 112, 131, 133, 155
Barrell Roll, 113
Basra, 271
battle damage assessment (BDA), 99, 102, 123, 132, 156, 210, 211, 226, 232
battlefield air interdiction (BAI), 5, 26, 27, 205, 225, 226, 274
battlefield interdiction, 5, 24, 25, 26, 91, 225
Belgrade, 224, 279, 280, 282
Benghazi, 285
beyond visual range (BVR), 152
BGM-71 TOW anti-tank missile, 181
Binh Dinh province, 180
Binh Long province, 174, 177, 178
Black Crow sensor, 147
blitzkrieg, 16, 194, 251
BLU-82 (Commando Vault), 136
bomb line, 5, 20, 24, 25, 27, 226
Bosnia, 7, 8, 206, 217, 220, 221, 223, 225, 246, 278, 279, 280
Brcko corridor, 280
Bugle Note, 103
Bundy, McGeorge, 79

C-123 airlift aircraft, 70
C-130 Hercules, 70, 71, 93, 117, 136, 148
Cambodia, 8, 10, 11, 35, 43, 70, 73, 77, 91, 107, 109, 110, 113, 115, 116, 129, 130, 133–137, 139, 141, 144, 146, 148, 150, 156, 157, 158, 159, 162, 165, 166, 172, 178, 186, 219, 222
Camp Carroll, 95
CAS, 4, 5, 16, 22, 23, 24, 25, 26, 27, 38, 48, 57, 67, 69, 70, 72, 90, 91, 99, 100, 101, 105, 106, 146, 148, 167, 175, 184, 185, 186, 199, 204, 206, 207, 208, 212, 222, 224, 225, 226, 230, 232, 235, 236, 251, 273, 274, 275, 283
casualties, 1, 50, 52, 55, 74, 81, 83, 87, 90, 111, 126, 127, 145, 146, 148, 149, 172, 179, 182, 196, 204, 205, 223, 241, 273, 279, 280, 286
Cedar Falls, 75, 80
Central Highlands, 50, 67, 69, 70, 73, 75, 81, 89, 92, 150, 157, 159, 165, 167, 178, 179, 182, 255
Central Intelligence Agency (CIA), 46, 59, 125, 128, 237
China, 4, 11, 35, 55, 56, 58, 76, 78, 81, 86, 110, 131, 149, 158, 164, 178, 186, 187, 193, 217, 229, 242, 244, 245, 246, 248, 250
Clausewitz, Carl Von, 2, 12, 13, 28, 30, 33, 209, 210, 253, 254, 255, 258, 261, 268

Clifford, Clark, 82
cluster bomb unit (CBU), 48, 102, 124, 143, 156, 211, 226, 228, 233, 245
Cobra attack helicopter, 174, 175, 265
coercion, 3, 10, 38, 47, 54, 77, 84, 221, 255, 256, 258
Cold War, 2, 6, 9, 48, 107, 203, 216, 229, 242, 244, 246, 248, 252, 256, 257, 260, 263, 270, 276
collateral damage, 26, 105, 188, 210, 214, 217, 223, 233, 236, 276, 278, 280, 285
COLOSSYS, 123
combat air patrol (CAP), 61, 188, 240
combined arms, 3, 4, 6, 7, 10, 13, 15, 18, 19, 21, 23–25, 27, 29, 32, 34, 35, 54, 56, 74, 75, 77, 89, 91, 104, 106, 109, 136, 137, 139, 144, 158, 159, 162–164, 166, 168, 176, 178, 186, 202, 203, 205, 212, 221, 222, 224, 225, 228, 230, 231, 234, 240, 242, 251, 274, 283
Combined Bomber Offensive, 262
command and control (C2), 14, 20, 67, 75, 100, 101, 114, 116, 117, 146, 158, 180, 184, 186, 199, 208, 209, 211, 232, 235, 239, 242, 244, 245, 252, 263, 266, 267, 269, 270, 271, 283, 286
Commando Bolt, 121
Commando Hunt I, 8, 108, 109, 114, 115, 116, 117, 118, 120, 121, 122, 125–128, 134, 137, 139, 143, 160, 161, 268
Commando Hunt III, 110, 115, 130, 131, 132, 134, 142, 155
Commando Hunt V, 8, 140, 141, 142, 143, 146, 147, 148, 199
Commando Hunt VII, 132, 141, 150, 154, 155, 156, 161, 162, 166
concealment, 12, 29, 30, 32, 34, 70, 112, 144, 162, 214, 217, 223, 241, 276, 278, 280, 282, 285
Cooper–Church amendment, 11, 140, 144
counterinsurgency, 3, 12, 25, 70, 75, 158, 166, 206, 207, 211, 225, 229, 233, 235, 236, 237, 250, 283, 284
counterterrorism, 3, 12, 207, 229, 232, 233, 235, 237, 250, 265, 283, 284
cover, 12, 29, 32, 34, 44, 45, 48, 51, 69, 70, 73, 84, 91, 93, 100, 106, 108, 112, 113, 144, 214, 215, 217, 221, 235, 236, 241, 247, 276, 278, 282, 286
Croatia, 278

Da Nang, 46, 59, 71, 75
Dak To, 89, 178, 180, 181, 182
Dayton Accords, 279, 280
Deep Battle, 251
deep or direct air support (DAS), 5, 23, 27, 90, 225
Defense Intelligence Agency (DIA), 128
demilitarized zone (DMZ), 10, 11, 37, 42, 43, 45, 48, 54, 56, 66, 67, 75, 77, 78, 81, 87, 88, 89, 91–94, 96, 100, 111, 113, 133, 141, 142, 146, 150, 152, 153, 156, 157, 159, 160, 165–170, 172, 184, 186, 187
denial strategy, 3, 204, 242, 243, 256
Desert Fox, 277, 278
Desert Storm, 4, 5, 8, 26, 205, 212, 216, 220, 221, 223, 224, 225, 232, 263, 270, 272, 273, 276
Diem, Ngo Dinh, 35, 36
Dien Bien Phu, 10, 35, 92, 94, 96, 176
direct air support center (DASC), 69, 70, 100, 147, 171, 180, 182, 184
direct attack, 2–11, 13, 14, 23–25, 28, 90, 106, 109, 167, 176, 181, 185, 193, 196, 197, 199, 201, 203, 210, 218, 221–227, 229, 230–236, 242, 243, 250, 252, 266, 273, 281, 282, 284, 285
doctrine, 4, 5, 12, 14, 15, 17, 19–27, 91, 101, 159, 203, 204, 208, 211–214, 225–227, 230, 232–235, 245, 252, 258, 261, 269, 274
Douhet, Giulio, 6, 252, 253, 257, 259, 260, 262

Easter Offensive, 1, 2, 4, 8, 11, 12, 31, 32, 51, 141, 150, 151, 158, 162, 163, 164, 166, 167, 169, 174, 182, 183, 185, 190, 193, 195, 196, 197, 198, 199, 201, 202, 204, 216, 219, 224, 228, 246, 255, 281
EC-121, 62, 117, 118, 152, 155
electronic countermeasure (ECM), 65, 209

F-100 Super Sabre, 38, 40, 48, 64, 71
F-105 Thunderchief, 38, 40, 48, 52, 61, 62, 65, 71, 84, 86, 118, 153, 188
F-15 Eagle, 204, 205, 243, 274
F-16 Fighting Falcon, 204, 205, 243
F-4 Phantom II, 38, 39, 41, 42, 48, 52, 61–65, 71, 75, 86, 87, 118, 89, 93, 120, 123, 152, 153, 156, 166, 184, 187, 188, 190, 191, 204
F-8 Crusader, 39, 61, 62, 63
Fansong SA-2 radar, 64, 65, 153, 191
fielded forces, 1, 5, 7, 11, 13, 14, 21, 23, 24, 25, 27–28, 32, 34, 55, 77, 90, 99, 103, 106, 109, 137, 163, 167, 181, 184, 193, 196, 197, 199, 201, 202, 203, 205, 206,

208, 211, 212, 218, 224–226, 227, 230, 232, 233, 235, 241, 242, 243, 245, 249, 250, 252, 257, 266, 272, 273, 274, 277, 279, 281, 283
fire support coordination center (FSCC), 100, 101, 194
fire support coordination line (FSCL), 5, 20, 27, 226, 273, 275
flak, 45, 48, 49, 64, 115, 131, 143
Flaming Dart, 37, 38, 42
FM 100-20, 22, 23
follow-on forces attack (FOFA), 204, 230, 239, 282
forward air controller (FAC), 5, 20, 23, 69, 90, 95, 102, 117, 119, 120, 123, 124, 125, 147, 166, 177, 182, 184, 206, 230, 234, 282
forward line of own troops (FLOT), 27
forward-looking infrared (FLIR), 143
fratricide, 4, 5, 20, 22, 26, 90, 105, 177, 185, 226, 273
Freedom Train, 187
Fulbright, William, 82

general offensive, 10, 11, 76, 77, 88, 92, 94, 141, 149, 150, 157–160, 163
geography, 12, 19, 20, 34, 44, 45, 69, 165, 216, 241, 275, 280, 282
Germany, 9, 14, 234, 251, 261, 262
Global Positioning System (GPS), 215, 221, 223, 232, 282
Great Britain, 9, 14
ground liaison officer (GLO), xv, 235
ground-based air defenses (GBAD), 209, 238
ground-controlled interception (GCI), 61, 86, 152, 153, 191
Guam, 43, 72, 79, 102, 183
guerrilla, 30, 50, 51, 55, 104, 109, 129, 139, 208, 213, 236, 267
Gulf of Tonkin, 37

Haiphong Harbor, 56, 57, 59, 61, 78–83, 186, 190, 200
Hanoi, 10–12, 35–38, 42, 46, 47, 49–51, 54, 56, 57, 59, 61, 64, 66, 70, 73, 76–79, 81–86, 88, 91, 92, 94, 104, 106, 108, 110, 111, 113, 115, 127, 129, 130, 134, 137, 140, 141, 149, 150, 152, 158, 159, 163, 164, 166, 186, 187, 189, 190, 191, 192, 193, 197–203, 221, 255, 281
high-altitude daylight precision bombing (HADPB), 260, 261
Ho Chi Minh Trail, 4, 10, 11, 32, 37, 43, 45, 50, 51, 53, 54, 56, 69, 87, 93, 94, 108, 109, 111–119, 122–134, 136, 137, 139–143, 145, 146, 152, 154–157, 159–162, 187, 210, 216, 268
Holbrooke, Richard, 280
Honolulu, 47, 75
Horner, Chuck, 26, 271, 274
Hue, 11, 75, 93, 104, 105, 170, 172, 194
human intellligence (HUMINT), 236, 237
Hussein, Saddam, 205, 207, 221, 254, 264, 270, 272, 276, 277, 284, 285

Ia Drang Valley, 67
identification friend or foe (IFF), 86, 152, 191
Igloo White, 117, 118, 121, 125, 155, 161, 210
Infiltration Surveillance Center (ISC), 116, 117, 118, 121, 125, 232
Instant Thunder, 8, 263, 270, 273
integrated air defense system (IADS), 2, 52, 56, 61, 64, 66, 85, 152, 202, 203, 206, 207, 208, 209, 218, 222, 239, 242, 253, 259, 263, 270, 273, 283, 284, 286
Intelligence Control Center (ICC), 101
intelligence surveillance and reconnaissance (ISR), 47–49, 72, 90, 99, 101, 105, 125, 208, 210, 211, 226, 227, 230, 232, 233, 235–237, 240, 243, 244, 245, 249, 264, 265, 283, 284
intercontinental ballistic missile (ICBM), 248
Iraq, 1, 3, 4, 7, 8, 32, 205–207, 215, 216, 220, 221, 223, 225, 231, 233, 246, 247, 254, 265, 273, 276, 277, 284, 285
Iraqi Army, 1, 205, 212, 271, 273, 284, 285
Irbil, 277, 278
Iron Triangle, 75, 80, 100, 217
Island Tree, 156

Johnson, Lyndon B., 36, 37, 45, 46, 47, 50–52, 54, 55, 56, 58, 59, 64, 66, 75–83, 92, 104, 106, 108, 110, 111, 114
Joint Chiefs of Staff (JCS), 36, 42, 51, 56, 58, 59, 66, 78, 79, 82, 192
Joint Surveillance Target Attack Radar System (JSTARS), 210, 211, 244
joint tactical air controller (JTAC), 4, 5, 230, 234, 236, 250, 283
Junction City, 80

Kabul, 283
Karadzic, Radovan, 279
Kennedy, John F., 36
Kennedy, Robert, 110

Khe Sanh, 1, 2, 4, 8, 10, 30, 32, 76–78, 92–99, 100–108, 110, 114, 116, 139, 140, 145, 148, 160, 163, 166, 201, 202, 203, 219, 224, 225, 228
Khmer Rouge, 133, 134
Kissinger, Henry, 130, 140, 149, 197, 200
Kontum, 31, 73, 164, 165–168, 176, 178–186, 195–199, 225
Kosovo, 4, 6, 8, 206, 213, 216, 220, 221, 223–225, 230, 246, 263, 280–283
Kosovo Liberation Army (KLA), 280–282
Kuwait, 205, 212, 215, 221, 225, 270–272, 273, 275, 276
Kuwaiti Theater of Operations (KTO), 271–273, 275
Ky, Nguyen Cao, 51, 59, 75, 150
Kyiv, 1, 12, 237, 238, 239, 240, 241

Lam Son 719, 8, 11, 138, 139, 140, 141, 144–149, 157, 158, 160, 161, 162, 164, 166, 204, 219, 222, 224
Lam Son, 72, 194, 195
Laos, 4, 10, 11, 35, 38, 43, 45, 51, 52, 56, 57, 66, 69, 70, 73, 77, 78, 82, 84, 89, 91, 92, 93, 100, 107, 108, 109, 111–116, 118–121, 125, 126, 128, 130, 131, 133–135, 138, 139, 140, 141, 142, 144, 145, 147, 148, 149, 150, 152, 153, 156, 157, 159, 160, 161, 162, 165, 166, 178, 186, 187, 216, 222, 224, 268
laser-guided bomb (LGB), 120, 124, 143, 183, 184, 187–188, 232
Lavelle, John, 154, 156
Le Duan, 35, 36, 76, 88, 91, 137, 141, 149, 150, 160, 164, 199, 201
Le Duc Tho, 197, 200
Libya, 7, 8, 207, 215, 220, 223, 225, 246, 257, 265, 285, 286
lighting, 12, 34, 214, 215, 216, 223, 241
Linebacker I, 4, 8, 11, 28, 163, 164, 167, 183, 186, 187, 188, 190, 191, 192, 193, 196, 198, 201, 203, 219
Linebacker II, 8, 12, 35, 164, 199–203, 219, 255, 281
lines of communication (LOC), 6, 11, 14, 28, 32, 50, 92, 94, 109, 111, 113, 127, 129, 131, 140, 144, 147, 161, 199, 202, 251, 252, 267, 268
lines of operation, 28, 31, 144, 166, 217
Loc Ninh, 172, 174, 175, 177
Lodge, Henry Cabot, 82
Loi Phang, 194
long-range navigation (LORAN), 117, 121, 123, 153, 162, 189
Luftwaffe, 14–21, 27, 30, 251, 253

M-72 LAW, 174, 181
man-portable air defense system (manpads), 168, 188, 209, 215, 222, 239
Market Time, 28, 113, 244, 268
Maverick air-to-surface missile, 31, 211, 216, 274
McCarthy, Eugene, 83, 106
McNamara, Robert, 46, 47, 55, 57, 59, 66, 78, 79, 81, 82, 113, 117
McNaughton, John, 42, 79
Mekong River Delta, 69, 116, 136–137, 150
MiG-15, 191
MiG-17, 62, 153
MiG-21, 61, 62, 86, 87, 131, 142, 152, 153, 191
Military Assistance Command Vietnam (MACV), 51, 59, 67, 79, 111, 133, 136, 137, 150, 156, 159, 162, 166, 172, 175, 193, 197
Military Region I, 75, 87, 89, 169, 171, 198
Military Region II, 179
Military Region III, 172, 174, 175
Milosevic, Slobodan, 6, 206, 263, 264, 265, 278–282
mini-Tet Offensive, 111, 139
Mitchell, Billy, 6, 256
Mladic, Ratko, 279, 280
modern air campaign, 7, 9, 206, 207, 270
modern air warfare, 2, 5, 7, 9, 12, 25, 201, 202, 206, 215, 225, 236, 249
Momyer, William, 116
Moratorium, 129
moving target indicator (MTI), 122, 211
MQ-1 Predator, 233, 284, 286
MQ-9 Reaper, 233, 237, 284
MSQ-77, 84, 95, 99, 102, 121
Mu Gai mountain pass, 112, 131
mutually assured destruction (MAD), 260

Nakhon Phanom (NKP), 116, 155, 156, 232
napalm, 48, 143, 183
Nape mountain pass, 112
National Transition Council (NTC), 285, 286
NATO, 4, 6, 26, 204, 206, 207, 213, 224, 240, 241, 242, 263, 274, 279, 280, 281, 282, 286
Nguyen Hue Offensive, 11, 178
Niagara, 101
night vision goggles (NVG), 216, 223, 275, 278, 280

Nixon, Richard, 10, 11, 12, 110, 111, 114, 128, 129, 130, 134, 135, 138, 140, 141, 149, 150, 154, 155, 164, 183, 186, 200, 201, 255
Northern Alliance, 283
Novikov, Alexander, 18
nuclear, 2, 7, 48, 72, 202, 204, 227, 229, 230, 242, 243, 245, 248, 249, 252, 255, 260

O-1 Birddog, 70, 71, 89, 118, 119, 171, 183
O-2 Skymaster, 119, 125
OP35, 125, 126
Operation Allied Force (OAF), 281
Operation Odyssey Dawn, 286
OV-10 Bronco, 119, 120
OV-1C, 72

Pacific Air Force Headquarters (PACAF), 190, 192
pacification, 11, 76, 108, 109, 111, 114, 128, 129, 130, 133, 135, 137, 139, 158, 160, 161, 163, 165, 166, 268
Paris, 12, 106, 110, 114, 129, 149, 150, 164, 165, 199–201, 255, 281
Pathet Tao, 113, 126, 128, 133, 134
Paul Doumer Bridge, 81, 187, 188
Pave Knife, 184, 187, 188
Pave Nail, 120
Paveway, 124
petroleum oil lubricants (POL), 58, 59, 66, 124, 159, 192, 271
Phnom Penh, 134
Plei Me, 67, 73
Pleiku, 37, 73, 178, 180
post-Tet offensive, 111, 127, 129, 139
Prairie Fire, 125
prisoner of war (POW), 140
Proud Deep Alpha, 153
PT-76, 97, 174

Qaddafi, Muammar, 207, 285, 286
QRC-160, 65, 86
QRC-248, 86
Quang Tri, 11, 35, 93, 94, 147, 159, 164, 166, 167, 168, 170, 172, 176, 177, 178, 180, 183, 184, 185, 186, 192, 193, 194, 195, 196, 197, 198, 199, 212

Račak, 281
Rambouillet, France, 281
Raven FAC, 118, 119
RB-57, 38, 72
Red Army, 16, 17, 18, 19, 204, 205
Red River, 81, 187
remotely piloted aircraft (RPA), 232, 233, 237, 240, 265
Republic of Vietnam Air Force (RVNAF), 37, 38, 42, 45, 46, 51, 52, 60, 70, 136, 157, 158, 170, 171, 175, 182, 185, 198
Republic of Vietnam Military Forces (RVNMF), 108, 109, 111, 114, 135, 139, 157, 163
Republican Guard, 205, 271, 272, 276
Reveille Attack, 272, 273
Rock Pile, 95
Rocket Ridge, 178, 180
Rockeye, 211
Rolling Thunder, 3, 8, 10, 35, 38, 42, 59, 61, 66, 67, 72, 77–82, 84, 85, 87, 89, 90, 92, 106, 108, 109, 110, 111, 114, 116, 118, 126, 131, 137, 152, 163, 187, 190, 199, 203, 219, 223, 270
Rostow, Walt, 79
Route Package I (RP I), 59, 184, 186
Route Package II (RP II), 60, 184
Route Packages, 59, 60
Royal Air Force (RAF), 14, 19, 21, 22, 27, 253, 259, 266
RQ-4 Global Hawk, 233
rules of engagement (ROE), 64, 152, 190, 193, 223, 284
Russian Air or Aerospace Force (VKS), 12, 190, 193, 223, 229, 231, 238–241
Ryan, Michael, 154, 280

SA-2 Guideline, 52, 53, 64, 65, 85, 86, 96, 115, 131, 142, 149, 153, 167–169, 185, 188, 192, 194, 243
SA-7 manpad, 168, 185
Saigon, 35, 36, 50, 55, 59, 66, 67, 75, 79, 80, 89, 92, 100, 101, 104, 110, 127, 129, 135–137, 140, 150, 159, 160, 164, 165, 166, 167, 171, 172, 174, 178, 200, 218
Schwarzkopf, Norman, 274
sea lines of communication (SLOC), 113, 244, 268
Serbia, 7, 8, 206, 223, 224, 263–265, 278, 280, 282, 283
Sharp, Ulysses S., 52, 58, 78, 79
Shau Valley, 93, 172
Shrike, 65
Sihanouk Trail, 109, 137, 141, 143, 144, 159, 160, 166
Skyspot, 84, 96, 102, 117, 121, 147, 223, 274
Slessor, J. C., 6, 19, 20, 266, 267
Soviet Air Force (VVS), 14, 16–19, 21, 27

Soviet Union, 2, 4, 7, 9, 11, 14, 16, 17, 19, 35, 55, 56, 76, 78, 95, 149, 158, 164, 202, 204, 238, 239, 242, 246, 248, 249, 251, 252
Steel Tiger, 113
Stennis, John, 81
strategic attack, 14, 15, 19, 225, 226, 267
strategic bombing, 2, 3, 6, 7, 9, 10, 12, 13, 16, 19, 25, 28, 34, 36, 38, 53, 56, 66, 72, 77, 79, 83–85, 92, 164, 202, 203, 205, 206, 210, 212, 218, 221–225, 229, 230, 231, 242, 250–252, 255, 257, 258, 260, 262, 263, 265, 270, 271, 273, 276, 279, 281–285
Su-30 Flanker, 238, 240
Su-34 Fullback, 238, 239, 241
Su-35 Flanker, 238, 240
suppression of enemy air defenses (SEAD), 64, 66, 87, 142, 188, 191, 199, 208, 209, 230, 231, 240, 249, 273, 282
Surprise Package, 132, 143
Sycamore, 116, 117, 121, 123
Syria, 215, 240, 241, 246, 285

Tac Canh/Dak To, 178, 180, 181
tactical air control center (TACC), 116, 171
tactical air control party (TACP), 24, 70, 171, 174, 175, 194, 226
tactical air control system (TACS), 9, 69, 70, 75, 100, 148, 169, 170, 171, 174, 184, 197, 198, 212, 230, 275
tactical air doctrine, 14, 15, 19, 21–23, 27, 252, 269
tactical reconnaissance (tac recce), 48, 69, 101, 148
tactics techniques and procedures (TTP), 27, 226
Taliban, 206, 265, 270, 283
Tan Son Nhut, 101
TAP theory, 2, 9, 10, 12, 14, 28, 33, 35, 49, 73, 74, 76, 77, 91, 98, 103, 104, 106–109, 126, 127, 128, 130, 134, 136, 137, 139, 141, 148, 157, 161, 162, 163, 167, 176, 185, 194, 197, 201, 202, 207, 212, 224, 227, 228, 229, 237, 241, 250, 252, 269, 270, 273, 277, 284, 286
targeting pod, 187, 211, 216, 223, 232, 249, 274, 278, 280
Task Force Alpha, 156
Tawakalna mechanized division, 272
Tay Ninh Province, 172, 174
Tchepone, 115, 140, 141, 144, 145, 149
Teaball, 191
Tedder, Arthur, 20, 22
terrain, 12, 18, 34, 45, 69, 70, 91, 100, 103, 108, 112, 113, 121, 144, 147, 153, 162, 168, 216, 217, 221, 223, 235, 236, 241, 272, 275, 278, 280, 281, 282, 285, 286
terrorist attacks, 109, 111, 129, 137, 139, 144, 206
Tet Offensive, 10, 58, 76–78, 91, 92, 102, 104, 105–110, 114, 127, 135, 139, 150, 159, 164, 223, 254
Thanh Hoa, 42, 45, 47, 50, 187, 189
theory of victory, 3, 28, 253, 254, 261
thermonuclear, 2, 7, 252, 260
Thieu, Nguyen Van, 11, 51, 59, 75, 111, 137, 140, 145, 150, 157, 163, 165, 166, 172, 197, 200, 201
third Tet Offensive, 139
TPQ-10 radar, 95, 96, 99
Trenchard, Hugh, 6, 19, 261
troops in contact (TIC), 4, 185, 236, 283
Truong, Ngo Quang, 172, 176, 193, 194, 195, 198

U Tapao, 91, 102
Ubon, Thailand, 188
Ukraine, 2, 229, 237, 238, 239, 241, 247
Ukrainian Air Force (UKAF), 238, 239
US Air Force (USAF), 24–27, 38, 45, 46, 47, 48, 51, 52, 60–62, 64, 65, 69, 70–73, 85, 87, 89, 90, 95, 99, 114, 115, 116, 121, 122, 136, 152, 169, 171, 180, 183, 184, 189–192, 199, 200, 203, 210, 215, 217, 225, 226, 229, 231–233, 237, 257, 260, 263, 264, 271, 274, 280
US Marine Corps (USMC), 5, 23–25, 27, 37, 39, 46, 48, 60, 62, 67, 69, 71, 81, 87, 89, 91, 100, 120, 122, 131, 143, 146, 148, 183, 185, 203, 206, 213, 227, 230, 235, 250
US Navy (USN), 1, 23–25, 28, 37–39, 46–48, 50, 52, 57, 59–65, 67, 71, 72, 78, 84, 87, 90, 92, 99–103, 113, 117, 118, 122, 124, 131, 143, 148, 153, 155, 166, 169, 183, 185, 187, 189, 190, 191, 192, 196, 203, 204, 206, 213, 217, 230, 231, 243, 249, 250, 251

Vann, John Paul, 178, 183
Viet Cong (VC), 10, 11, 25, 35–38, 42, 51, 55, 57, 67, 70, 72, 75–77, 80, 81, 87, 88, 91, 92, 104–106, 109, 111, 113, 127, 128, 130, 133, 134, 136, 137, 141–143, 158–160, 163–165, 172, 174, 175, 180, 185, 217, 267
Vietnam People's Air Force (VPAF), 61, 86, 87, 115, 130, 152, 153, 167, 191

Vietnamization, 11, 108, 109, 111, 114, 129, 134, 135, 137, 139, 140, 141, 142, 145, 149, 158, 160, 161, 163, 165, 169–171, 268

Warden, John, 6, 263
weapons of mass destruction (WMD), 8, 205, 206, 270, 276
Westmoreland, William, 51, 55, 56, 66, 67, 72, 73, 75, 76, 79–81, 83, 87, 89, 95, 100, 101, 103, 104, 106, 111, 166
Wild Weasel, 65, 86, 153, 184, 188
Wise Men, 82, 106

Yankee Station, 60, 89

Printed in Dunstable, United Kingdom

74620986R00176